AMERICA'S SECRET ARISTOCRACY

BOOKS BY STEPHEN BIRMINGHAM

Young Mr. Keefe
Barbara Greer
The Towers of Love
Those Harper Women
Fast Start, Fast Finish
"Our Crowd"
The Right People
Heart Troubles
The Grandees
The Late John Marquand
The Right Places
Real Lace
Certain People
The Golden Dream
Jacqueline Bouvier Kennedy Onassis
Life at the Dakota
California Rich
Duchess
The Grandes Dames
The Auerbach Will
"The Rest of Us"
The LeBaron Secret
America's Secret Aristocracy

AMERICA'S
Secret Aristocracy

STEPHEN BIRMINGHAM

LITTLE, BROWN AND COMPANY
Boston Toronto

FIRST EDITION

Library of Congress Cataloging-in-Publication Data

Birmingham, Stephen.
America's secret aristocracy.

Bibliography: p. 323
Includes index.
1. United States — Social life and customs.
2. United States — Biography. 3. Upper classes — United States — History. I. Title.
E161.B52 1987 305.5'2'0973 87-4229
ISBN 0-316-09650-4

RRD VA

Designed by Patricia Dunbar

Published simultaneously in Canada
by Little, Brown & Company (Canada) Limited

PRINTED IN THE UNITED STATES OF AMERICA

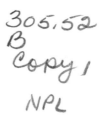

For Carol Brandt Pavenstedt
in memory

CONTENTS

PART ONE

First Peers of the Realm

1

Telling Them Apart

Whenever you hear an American speak of a *terrace* rather than a *patio,* of a *house* rather than a *home* or an *apartment,* of a *sofa* rather than a *davenport* or *couch,* of *curtains* rather than *drapes,* of *guests for dinner* rather than *company,* of a *long dress* rather than a *formal,* of a *dinner jacket* rather than a *tuxedo,* and of *underwear* rather than *lingerie,* chances are you are in the presence of a member of the American upper class. Upper-class Americans use the toilet, not the lavatory or the commode or the facilities or the loo or the little boys' room. Upper-class Americans go to boarding schools, not prep schools, where they earn grades, not marks. Upper-class Americans are either rich (not wealthy) or poor (not less well-off), and the prices they pay for things are either high (not expensive) or cheap (not inexpensive). Upper-class Americans say "Hello," not "Pleased to meet you," and "What?" not "Pardon me?" Upper-class American women do not have bosoms. They have breasts, or even tits when they are among their own kind, when other vulgarisms frequently emerge. The familiar four-letter word for sexual intercourse is a perfectly acceptable upper-class expression.

Brevity, simplicity, and the avoidance of euphemism are the chief hallmarks of the upper-class American vocabulary. When an upper-class American feels sick, he says just that, and never "I feel ill" or "I feel nauseous." Cuteness is anathema. Thus in an upper-class

American house you would never find a den or a rumpus room or a family room, though you might find a library or a playroom. Upper-class Americans do not own bedroom suites or dining room suites or any other kind of suites, or "suits." They own furniture, and if it is particularly good furniture, it is often simply called wood. Pretentiousness is similarly shunned. Thus to an upper-class American a tomato is a tom*ay*to, not a tom*ah*to. Upper-class Americans write "R.S.V.P." on the corners of their invitations, never "The favor of a reply is requested." Upper-class Americans give and go to parties, never to affairs, and if the affair being talked about is of the romantic variety, it is always, specifically, a love affair.

But, most important, the American upper class never talks about the upper class, or about any other sort of class, for that matter. Partly this is a question of delicacy and taste. It is simply not upper class to talk about class. Also, in a constitutionally classless society where an upper class has managed to emerge anyway, there is a feeling among members of the upper class that they are a somewhat illicit entity, a possibly endangered species. If one were to go about boasting of being upper class, who knows what sort of angry mob from below might rise up and challenge the precious barricades? So you will never hear a member of the upper class talk of "the right people," or "nice people," or even "the people we know." Instead it will be "our friends," or, more often, "our family and friends." This way, the polite illusion is created that the American aristocracy is a private, even secret, club, whose members all know each other and whose rules are observed without ever having to be written down or otherwise made public. Most frequently, when the American aristocracy speaks of itself in a general sense, it is in terms of "people," as in, "What will people say?" And if a member of the upper class behaves — as can happen — in a non-upper-class way, the reaction is "People just don't *do* that!"

In an upwardly mobile society, in which nearly everybody dreams of elevating himself to a higher social or economic stratum, there are some rules of upper-class behavior that are easy to learn. For example, when upper-class women swim, they do the Australian crawl, never the breaststroke or backstroke. It is easy to remember that the finger bowl has no function whatsoever — certainly not to dabble one's fingers in — and is to be removed, with the doily, and set at the upper left of one's plate, after which the dessert spoon and fork are to be removed from the service plate and placed on either side of it. It is easy to remember that it is acceptable to eat asparagus with one's fingers (if no tongs have been provided), while it is not acceptable to pick up the chop or the chicken leg in the same manner, unless one is dining *en famille*. It is never proper to squeeze the juice from a grapefruit half into a spoon.

But there are other more subtle, arcane codes by which members of the American aristocracy recognize each other and send signals to each other and that are more difficult to learn — which, it might be added, is the whole unwritten point of there being such codes. In addition to language and vocabulary, recognition is by name and by the association of name with place. Thus one should be able to remember that Ingersolls and Cadwaladers and Chews and *some* Morrises are from Philadelphia, while other Morrises are from New York and New Jersey, and so when meeting a Morris it is important to find out which family he or she represents. Livingstons, Jays, Bownes, Lawrences, Schieffelins, Iselins, Schuylers, and Fishes are from New York, while Otises, Saltonstalls, and Gardners are from Boston. Gardiners are from New York. Hoppins and Browns are from Providence, Pringles and Pinckneys are from Charleston, Des Loges are from St. Louis, Stumpfs are pre-oil Texas, and Chandlers are Los Angeles.

Over the past generation, America's upper-class boarding schools and colleges have become thoroughly democratized, but members of the upper class can still send signals to one another by the way they designate their schools. An upper-class Yale alumnus, for example, would never say that he had graduated "from Yale." He would say that he had studied "at New Haven." Following is a list of other upper-class schools and colleges, with their special upper-class designations:

Actual Name	*Upper-class Designation*
The Taft School	Watertown
The Hotchkiss School	Lakeville
St. Mark's School	Southborough
St. Paul's School	Concord
Miss Porter's School	Farmington
The Foxcroft School	Virginia
The Ethel Walker School	Simsbury
Choate–Rosemary Hall School	Wallingford

Smith College	Northampton
Vassar College	Poughkeepsie

But even more important and difficult than remembering names and their ancient associations with cities is mastering the American upper-class accent. Just as in England, where class is defined by accent, the American aristocracy has developed an accent peculiar to itself. It is a curious hybrid derived, in part, from the flat vowel sounds of New England, as well as from the New York accent that is sometimes described as "Brooklynese," with random borrowings from the drawl of the antebellum South. From the South comes a tendency to drop final consonants — as in "somethin' " or "anythin' " — or to elide initial letters in words such as "them," which makes a statement such as "I can't think of anything to give them" sound very much like "I cahnt think o' anythin' to give 'em." Final *r*'s are also dropped, whereby *paper* comes out "papuh," and *rear* is "reah." Interior *r*'s are elided as well, so that *apart* becomes "apaht," and *church* becomes "chuhch." Final *s*'s are almost, but not quite, lisped, so that the word *birds* is pronounced something like "budzh." Perhaps most difficult to master are the vowel sounds in simple words like *were,* where the audible vowel sound of the *e* almost sounds like the *i* in *prism.* On top of this, particularly among men, there has long been something called the boarding school stammer, a speech pattern whose origins are unclear but which may descend from the British public school stammer: "I — uh — oh, I say — wha-what would you say to — uh —," et cetera.

In perfecting an American upper-class accent, one rule to remember is the upper-class injunction to keep a stiff upper lip. The upper lip moves very little in American upper-class speech. But of course members of the American upper class do not have to be taught how to speak this way. They learn it from the cradle.

A comparison of the aristocracies of America and Great Britain is useful, for the American uppermost class has always looked to the British class system as its most satisfactory model. Even at the time of the American Revolution this was true, and many of the American "heroes" whose signatures grace the Declaration of Independence signed this document with great misgivings, distrusting the Revolutionary movement and not at all agreeing with Thomas Jefferson's notion that "all men are created equal." A number of American families have aristocratic forebears who managed to be conveniently "out of town" or otherwise unavailable when that document was being signed, and as we shall see, there are American families today who are just as proud of ancestors who failed, or refused, to sign as are those with ancestors who were Signers. Particularly in New York, Pennsylvania, and Maryland, enthusiasm for the Revolution was lukewarm at best, while in Boston, the Revolutionary cradle, it was intense. Even today, these philosophical differences between Boston and the rest of the East Coast more than two hundred years ago are expressed in a certain antipathy between the upper classes of New York, Philadelphia, and Baltimore and the upper class of the Bay Colony.

Like the British, many members of the American aristocracy are exceedingly rich while, like some British, some are not, though all manage to live in considerable style. How this is accomplished is sometimes unclear. But it has a lot to do with a creed that one ought to live only "on the income from one's income," that one should sell property only under the most desperate circumstances, and the belief that, every generation or so, there is nothing wrong with obtaining a fresh infusion of money through a well-orchestrated marriage.

At the same time, like the members of the Royal House of Windsor since Victoria's time, American aristocrats in their private lives often convey the impression of being rather ordinary people, neither particularly intellectual nor witty, committed to their friends and to lives that are comfortable and familiar, people who are not remarkable for being anything other than what they are and were born to be — and who are remarkable only for not having to demonstrate, or prove, who they are.

Like the queen of England, women of the American aristocracy rarely change their hairstyles. Nor do they show much real interest in fashion. When they go out-of-doors — which they like to do — they bundle up and will choose a down-filled coat over a mink if the former is warmer. The American aristocracy, like the British, is generally sports-minded. From England, the American aristocracy brought golf and tennis to this country. From Edward VIII's example, the American upper crust took up skiing. Now these sports have become too popular to still be classified as upper class, though the upper class still enjoys them. The great American sports — baseball, football, hockey, basketball — have never been popular with the upper class, though baseball, the most gentlemanly of these sports, has always found a few adherents. Such English sports as rugby and soccer — and even cricket and beagling — have long been enjoyed by pockets of the American upper class.

Like the English queen and her family, the American aristocracy has a passion for certain quadrupeds: dogs and horses. Since ancient times, the horse has been a mythic symbol of leadership. For centuries, kings and generals and emperors and caesars have had their portraits painted, and their images carved in bronze and marble, astride a horse. This of course is not to say that all members of the American aristocracy are superb equestrians, but it would be safe to assume that nearly all, at some point in their lives, have been taught to sit a horse properly in an English saddle. Fox hunting, the steeplechase, the point-to-point, polo — all popular with England's landed gentry, where they began centuries ago — remain popular with the American equivalent, who still buy their boots and riding attire in London.

And, just as the queen of England looks happiest surrounded by a pack of yelping corgis, so do the American aristocrats love their dogs. They love dogs, furthermore, in numbers. In an informal survey in New York not long ago, at a gathering where a number of America's oldest families were assembled, the guests were asked what they were giving their spouses for Christmas. A surprising number said that the gift was going to be a new dog for the family collection — if not for a husband or wife, then for the children or for some other close family member. From this, the conversation turned to books about dogs. *Everyone's* favorite dog author, it so happened, was Albert Payson Terhune.

This affection for certain domestic animals does not, however, extend to all forms of wildlife. Hunting, as it is in England, is a pastime enjoyed by the American aristocracy. But aristocrats of neither the English nor American variety would consider hunting squirrels, possum, or rabbits, or even killing the fox in the hunt. Birds, on the other hand, are a different matter — game birds: quail, pheasant, partridge, and grouse. Deer are hunted only when there is a specific ecological reason to do so. Mr. Robert David Lion Gardiner, for example, sixteenth lord of the manor of Gardiner's Island, which he owns, periodically takes small groups of friends on deer-hunting forays to his island in order to keep the deer population — which would starve if the island became defoliated by its numbers — under control. "It isn't a pleasant chore," he says, "but it simply must be done."

Like the British, the members of the American upper class are not really prejudiced against Jews and Catholics. For one thing, it is not upper class to express religious prejudice, though most members of the upper class would confess that they do not really "understand" Judaism or Catholicism. These religions are, after all, more demanding of their adherents and require the mastery of arcane languages, Hebrew and Latin. Over the years, a number of American upper-class families have intermarried with Jews and Catholics, but it was usually with the understanding that the outsider would convert to the prevailing Protestant mode — just to keep things simpler for future generations. In fact, most American upper-class families are proud of their long record of religious tolerance and of the fact that their aristocratic ancestors saw to it that an article guaranteeing religious freedom was written into the Constitution. When the Dutch colony of Nieuw Amsterdam became the British colony of New York, the old Dutch families did not suddenly become social pariahs. Of course, this is an additional reason why other upper-class Americans look on upper-class Bostonians as a somewhat special, peculiar breed. Puritan New Englanders hated — and tortured and hanged — people who rejected the tenets of their tiny sect.

In the early days of the Republic, the American aristocracy simply assumed that its members would run the new country — as presidents, governors, senators, cabinet members, ambassadors — just as the British aristocracy ran England. It was not until America's seventh president, the log cabin–born Andrew Jackson, that a man entered the White House who was neither a member of the old Virginia landed gentry nor an Adams from Boston. The aristocratic John Quincy Adams went so far as to call Jackson a "barbarian who could not write a sentence of grammar and hardly could spell his own name." (When Adams's alma mater, Harvard College, announced its intention years later of conferring on Jackson an honorary Doctorate of Laws degree, Adams was outraged by this breach of the class system and did everything in his power, unsuccessfully, to prevent it.)

In the years since Jackson, Americans continued to elect occasional members of the aristocracy to the presidency — up to and including Franklin D. Roosevelt — but the aristocracy itself had already become sorely disillusioned about the notion of American rulership and about running for high political office. For one thing, they had noted with dismay how fickle the American public could be about its political leaders. When things were going well, the country's officials were given all the credit. When things went poorly, the politicians were vilified and given all the blame. John Jay, hailed as a national patriot at the time of the Revolution, would have the sorry experience of learning that he had been burned in effigy by an angry mob a few years later. For another, political leadership — in the early days, at least — could be a financially ruinous experience. George Washington complained that the presidency was costing him so much money that he was in danger of going broke, and he very nearly did. He entered the White House as a very rich man and left it with hardly enough to patch up Mount Vernon, which had crumbled during his eight-year absence. Alexander Hamilton, a rich banker and the first secretary of the treasury, died leaving nothing but debts. So did Thomas Jefferson. It began to seem as though the only way politics could be made to pay in America was through corruption, and of course no aristocrat would stoop to that. Gradually, it became merely prudent for the American aristocracy to turn to other less visible — and vulnerable — forms of public service. Today, the American upper class shuns politics, and whether that is the country's gain or loss can only be a subject for speculation.

Like its British counterpart, the American aristocracy has always tried, at least, to honor the stern concepts of duty and morality. To these might be added a third: patriotism of the kind that has always inspired British gentlemen to lay down their lives for "King [or Queen] and Country." Patriotism, of course, involves heroism, and heroism involves bravery, and most members of the American aristocracy are proudly able to recite the names of ancestors or other relatives who fought or fell in war. In their houses are often displayed, in glass cases, the fading uniforms of such ancestors, along with appropriate medals, decorations, orders, and citations. As has been said of the British aristocracy, "They die well." "How he conducts himself in war is perhaps the truest test of a gentleman," says Mr. Goodhue Livingston of New York, who, as a second lieutenant in the field artillery in World War I, fought at Château-Thierry and was wounded at Soissons. Mr. Livingston is proud not only of that but also of his son-in-law, Moorhead Kennedy, who was taken hostage during one of the recent Iranian crises — a crisis being a way a gentleman can show his mettle.

But it would be wrong to dismiss the members of the American aristocracy as mere ancestor worshippers, though the time orientation of the upper class — in Britain and America — has always been toward the past, and knowing "where we come from." The majority of Americans focus on the future, on getting ahead, on rising economically and socially, on climbing, as it were. As a nation of social climbers, we are often eager to forget, or even deny, the past. The majority of Americans, after all, descend from humble immigrant beginnings, and to them the past seems to have almost nothing to say. The yellowing photograph of Grandma in her poke bonnet, plucking a chicken on the porch of her little farmhouse in Indiana, seems at best quaint and at worst embarrassing. What does it tell us other than that Grandma could pluck a chicken, shell peas, or candle an egg? How could Grandma even address herself to what her descendants have become: lawyers, doctors, college professors, corporate executives, media stars, owners of condominiums in Florida, and members of the country club? More important than Grandma's photograph is tomorrow's promotion, tomorrow's contract, tomorrow's party, next winter's Caribbean cruise.

But the American aristocracy feels just the opposite. Ancestry as well as kinship maintains upper-class cohesion. Distinguished family members of the past, moreover, are intended to inspire each new generation to lead a family into new arenas of distinction. Ancestors are cautionary figures, teachers, exemplars. They warn the children: "Do not let the family down." Timothy F. Beard of New York, who is president of the Order of Colonial Lords of Manors in America — the leading genealogical society in the country — recalls the words of an elderly cousin of his grandfather's, who warned him, "Don't lose the past. Most people don't even know the meaning of it. But don't be like the potato, with the best of you underground." The elderly cousin bore the imposing name of Mrs. Philadelphia Anna Stewart-Monteith Vines, and her mother-in-law was also a Stewart-Monteith, who could trace her descent from Henry VII.

Both the British and the American aristocracies detest publicity, which they see as a double-edged sword, even though publicity is what most of American "society" today is based on: items in the gossip columns, photographs in *Vogue, Harper's Bazaar,* and *Town*

& Country. But here the parallels between the British and the American aristocracies come to an end. In England, the aristocracy has become, in a real sense, the property of the British public, which theoretically could vote it out of existence tomorrow. As a result, everything that the aristocracy does, for good or ill, becomes the property of the public media. Even the queen of England can do nothing to prevent the vagaries of her children and other relatives from being reported in the press when they occur. Often the press office at Buckingham Palace takes on the aspect of an armed camp as staffers try to hold off the press, deny the rumors, and put the best possible face on things.

In the United States, the aristocracy no longer has this problem. It has been allowed to retire into the privacy, even secrecy, that it much prefers, and it is even grateful for the new breed of society, which thrives on publicity and cannot seem to exist without it, for having drawn the attention of the media away.

Who, then, are these people? Over the years, numerous attempts to codify, sort out, and list the members of the American aristocracy have been made, but nearly always without success. Americans, it seems, love to study lists, and thousands of volumes of *Who's Who,* the *Social Register,* and the *List of Society* have been published, with none of them approaching the fixity and accuracy of a *Burke's Peerage.* The most famous list of all was probably Ward McAllister's of the top Four Hundred, who were invited to Mrs. William Astor's ball in February of 1892. The list, when it was finally published, was something of a disappointment. For one thing, barely more than three hundred names were on it. For another, though a smattering of Old Knickerbocker names were included, Mrs. Astor's guest list seemed quite top-heavy with self-made railroad tycoons and their wives and other robber barons who had made questionable "Civil War Money." The old American aristocracy that had been in place for two hundred years before Mrs. Astor's ball seemed to have been able to resist even that notoriously bullheaded hostess's invitations.

In 1937, Ferdinand Lundberg published a controversial book called *America's 60 Families* in which he argued, cogently enough, that the most important American institutions — from schools and colleges, through the news and entertainment media, to Wall Street and the White House — were firmly in the grip of a handful of interrelated entrepreneurial families, from the Astors to the Vanderbilts and Wideners. What Lundberg was talking about, of course, was a plutocracy, a hidden government by the moneyed, and he made a well-documented point. But he was not talking about "society," or those who set the social tone as, in an aristocracy, the elite class does.

A dozen or so years earlier, in 1924, Mrs. John King Van Rensselaer had addressed that question in *The Social Ladder.* "Prominent today in published accounts of New York social events," Mrs. Van Rensselaer wrote, "are the Vanderbilts, the Astors, the Morgans, the Davidsons, the Belmonts, the Vanderlips, the Villards, the Goulds." And yet, she pointed out, only one of these families had "enjoyed social recognition as far back as Civil War times." That single exception was the Astors, and Mrs. Van Rensselaer dismissed the Astors rather loftily, commenting that "the first John Jacob Astor, born in Walldorf, Germany, came to New York . . . as a piano merchant." She added that not one of the above "socially prominent families" traced its lineage in America back to the Revolutionary era, much less to an era prior to that.

Today, a list of society's elite might include the Rockefellers, the Fords, the Mellons, even the Annenbergs and Estée Lauder. These names, of course, represent even newer money. But for all the Rockefellers' wealth, there are those today who can recall a time when Rockefellers were considered uncouth parvenus. Robert David Lion Gardiner remembers his grandmother forbidding him to play with the Rockefeller children. "No Gardiner will ever play," she announced, "with the grandchildren of a gangster." And the novelist Louis Auchincloss, whose own New York roots are deep, if not as deep as the Gardiners', once commented, "We put the Rockefellers in the same category as the Vanderbilts. It was hard to take them seriously. Now, of course, that I'm married to a Vanderbilt, we take the Vanderbilts somewhat *more* seriously." (Mr. Auchincloss's wife's mother is a Vanderbilt cousin.)

Despite all this, it is clear that in order to claim membership in American society today there are essentially only two rather loose requirements: money, the more the better, and the ability to advertise oneself. And these requirements are linked, because publicity today has a price tag. It can be bought. In other words, society today has wandered almost as far from the concept of aristocracy as it is possible to stray — because, from its beginnings, America's aristocracy has had almost nothing to do with money at all.

"Society," needless to say, is a tricky concept that has taken on different meanings to different generations. In its American colonial beginnings, it meant, first of all, *family*. And the only demarcation lines within it were those of the prevailing churches. Indeed, members of the clergy — a profession in which one does not customarily grow rich — stood very close to the top of the social scale. Society was also a matter of *breeding,* which had less to do with ancestry than with integrity, probity, civic duty, respectability, kindness, and good manners, as well as of deportment, speech, and what is today called body language, through which members of society communicated with one another: the way one entered a room or rose from a chair or bowed or curtsied or blew a kiss. All these are components of that hard-to-define quality of any aristocracy known as *noblesse oblige*. Finally, society stood for *culture* and refinement, and an appreciation of art, music, and literature. In other words, America's earliest aristocracy, like England's, was based on family notions of self-worth and self-esteem.

The founders of society in America were nearly all members of families who predated the arrival of the British fleet that turned Nieuw Amsterdam into New York. In her book, Mrs. Van Rensselaer offered a sampling of their names. She cited the Morrises, the Kings, the Gerards, the Houghs, the Hoyts, the Iselins, the Millers, the Wickershams, the Wyatts, the Fishes, the Whites, and the Magees. Modestly, she omitted her own name from this list. To it, she might have added the Livingstons, the Bownes, the Lawrences, the Schieffelins, the Burrs, the Schuylers, the Jays, the Ingersolls of Philadelphia, the Adamses of Boston, the Randolphs of Virginia, the Carrolls of Carrollton, Maryland, and many more.

Certain old American families seem almost inextricably entwined with their cities of origin. The Adamses and Saltonstalls and Winthrops, for example, are both *from* and *of* Boston, while the Pinckneys are *from* and *of* Charleston, South Carolina. They belong to their cities just as persistently as, in their minds, their cities belong to them. Other families, by contrast, seem to transcend the places they originally came from, such as the intricately interrelated Livingston-Jay-Beekman-Astor family, who all descend from a common ancestor, the first Robert Livingston, who settled in New York's Hudson River valley. Today, Livingstons are scattered across the face of the continent, from Florida to California. Others live in England, and some live as far away as Hong Kong. They are doctors, lawyers, bankers, congressmen (from states other than New York), diplomats, and interior designers. But wherever they are, and whatever they do, they are always, indelibly, *Livingstons.*

The old families have never believed that either money or publicity was the open sesame to social success or acceptance. Its members did not believe that then, nor do they now. For these founding families of America's aristocracy did not, as might be supposed, die out. Nor did they, through intermarriage with one another, become "watered down" to impotence and incompetence. In cities such as New York, Philadelphia, Boston, Charleston, and Savannah, their descendants still exist, leading quiet and for the most part productive lives, doing useful and often important work. Ten, twelve, or more generations later, they still cling to the cities that first nourished them, being none the worse Americans for the fact that they boast an ancient heritage and lineage, nor for the fact that their lives and activities are no longer considered spectacular enough to qualify for the society pages and the gossip columns. These families, in other words, are not like a breed of dinosaurs that enjoy one great era and then become extinct.

Nor do they sit in Brahmin-like seclusion in their quiet city houses on quiet city streets, contemplating their past or their family trees. The earliest Dutch and English settlers were people of stamina and grit who did not take easily to idleness or boredom; their descendants still do not. They are not, in the common sense, exclusive, nor do they form a fixed set that has erected impenetrable barriers behind which outsiders are never permitted to glimpse. On the contrary, they are for the most part open and friendly and perfectly willing to accept new acquaintances into their circle of friends, the only qualification being that the new friends should be willing to accept their standards of politeness and propriety, and behave as ladies and gentlemen.

Members of the American aristocracy have long distrusted lists. One's name on a list is an invasion of privacy, a threat to collective secrecy, an invitation to unwanted publicity or even notoriety. With their eyes on what the past has taught them, they can recall that it was bad publicity — really nothing else — that destroyed the brilliant political career of the aristocratic Aaron Burr in the early 1800s. Besides, they do not need a scorecard to tell them who their players are. In 1921, Maury Paul, the "Cholly Knickerbocker" gossip columnist for the old *New York World,* playfully drew up a set of lists in which he tried to separate two elements of society: the Old Guard and Cafe Society. On his Old Guard list, he included the name of Mrs. C. Oliver Iselin. No one would really have questioned whether Mrs. Iselin's name belonged on that list. It did, but Mrs. Iselin was not amused. She wrote to the editor of the newspaper, whom she knew, and politely asked, "Please see to it that my name is removed from this list."

Even more important, the members of America's aristocracy have an uncanny ability — through a kind of ESP or personal radar — to recognize each other. Antennae go out, and the signals are picked up. During the course of his military service in France, for instance, Goodhue Livingston found himself having lunch in the dining room of the L'Univers Hôtel in Tours. During the course of it, he happened to notice another gentleman dining on the opposite side of the room. "I recognized the man as an American, of course," he recalls today, "but I also knew I had never met him. And yet there was something very familiar about him, though it wasn't even a 'family look.' After lunch, I stopped over to his table and introduced myself. 'My name is Montgomery Livingston,' the fellow said."

Even in such newly settled places as Texas, fledgling aristocracies are forming and developing secret signals by which they recognize each other. The Wynne family of Dallas now numbers more than 150 members and publishes its own private genealogical volume, *Who's Whose Wynne*. At age twenty-one, each Wynne family member is presented with a distinctive family ring consisting of a trio of intertwined gold serpents of the Nile. Once a year, over Memorial Day weekend, the entire Wynne clan gathers for three days of festivities. These include feasting, all-night poker games, a Sunday worship service, and — the highlight of the reunion — the induction of new in-laws into the family. In Wynne family terminology, in-laws are called Mongooses, while blood members are known as Snakes — an allusion to the family ring and to the fact that, in nature, only a mongoose is a match for a cobra.

But our story does not begin in Texas. It begins on the older-established East Coast and with the union of two linchpin American families, the Jays of Westchester County and the Livingstons of New York.

2

A Royal Wedding

If there had been any national media to ballyhoo it at the time, it might have been called the Wedding of the Century. But the century was the eighteenth, and news in the American colonies traveled slowly and erratically, so that the announcement of the wedding that took place on April 28, 1774, did not appear in the *New York Gazette* until May 9. The announcement was appropriately subdued, in genteel keeping with the times, and merely noted the marriage of Mr. John Jay, "an eminent barrister," to "the beautiful Sarah Livingston" at her parents' country estate, Liberty Hall, in Elizabethtown, New Jersey. That was all.

In a more outspoken era, it might have been noted that John Jay was something of an upstart in New York society, whereas the Livingstons were by then *the* principal family in New York — if not the principal family in all America. It was not a case of a pauper marrying a princess, exactly, and the phrase "social climber" had not yet been invented, but a more lurid press might have made more of the difference in status between the Jays and the Livingstons and of the fact that on the day John and Sarah Jay exchanged marriage vows, the eminent barrister had allied himself with the richest and most powerful family in the New World. In an age more rapaciously concerned with gossip and spicy trivia, the discrepancy between the bride's and bridegroom's ages might also have drawn comment. John Jay was twenty-eight. His bride was barely seventeen.

Had there been a Suzy Knickerbocker or a Liz Smith around in those days, an edifying story might have been written about how cleverly John Jay had insinuated himself into the perfumed, private circle of the Livingston family and how carefully he had orchestrated his courtship — over her father's initial objections — of the William Livingstons' youngest, prettiest, and favorite daughter. There was even a minor scandal, involving an incident during the bridegroom's college days (to say nothing of other scandals that lurked in the upper branches of the Livingston family tree), to be unearthed. But, as it was, in this more innocent and polite of times, when members of the upper classes were treated with deference and discretion as a matter of course, the Jay-Livingston nuptials were announced with the terse precision of an item in the London Court Circular.

It had all started at New York's King's College — the predecessor of Columbia University — where young John Jay made the acquaintance of a fellow undergraduate named Robert R. Livingston, Jr., a cousin of Sarah Livingston's father. Soon the young men were the best of friends. After graduation, both men studied law and, that done with, Jay proposed to Robert Livingston that they form a law partnership together. Livingston enthusiastically agreed to the idea.

The next step up the social ladder occurred when Jay was invited to join The Moot, an elite men's club of New York lawyers that met on the first Friday of every month to discuss, over glasses of Madeira, disputed — or moot — points of law. The Moot had been founded in 1770 by Sarah Livingston's father, himself a barrister of considerable eminence. The Moot's membership consisted of a number of men who would later distinguish themselves in various ways. These included, in addition to Jay's partner, Robert Livingston, Egbert Benson, who in due time would become judge of the New York Supreme Court; James Duane, married to a Livingston, the first mayor of New York after the Revolution; and William Smith, also married to a Livingston, who would become chief justice of Canada. The club's founder, William Livingston, would go on to become the first governor of the state of New Jersey.

John Jay was one of the club's youngest members, but soon he had made himself an expert on Madeira and was given the job of selecting the wine. Politics was a taboo subject at meetings of The

Moot, and afterward the young men enjoyed lively bachelor evenings along Broadway. Thus it was not long before Jay was invited to visit the William Livingstons at Liberty Hall, where he was introduced to the delicious Sarah, who was then not quite sixteen.

Their courtship was decorous and seemly, though much too brief to suit her father, who considered her too young to have a serious suitor. On Jay and Sarah's outings together, they were always carefully chaperoned by one of Sarah's older brothers. And, though the social life of the day had a decidedly countrified, outdoorsy quality, there was plenty of it. There were popcorn parties and taffy pulls, amateur theatricals, charades and dances. The Social Club assembled on Saturday evenings at the tavern belonging to Sam Fraunces or at the summer clubhouse across the East River at Kip's Bay. There were dancing assemblies and twice-weekly turtle roasts on the riverbank, where fat green sea turtles were caught and netted, and cooked over open fires. There were games of quoits and *roque,* an aristocratic form of croquet played on a hard-surfaced field. There were hunting parties and horseback outings and hayrides. Indoors, there were whist parties and backgammon games and games of *crokinole,* and piano and harpsichord recitals. In winter, there were sleigh rides and skating and tobogganing parties. More serious matters were left to the Debating Club, which met every Thursday evening at six.

Still, one would never have known that a great war was coming, and when news reached New York in 1773 that a group of prominent Bostonians, dressed up as Mohawk Indians, had boarded East India Company ships at Griffin's Wharf and thrown 342 chests of tea from the London firm of Davison & Newman valued at £10,000 into Boston Harbor, it was treated by New Yorkers as a great joke. It was labeled, derisively, the Boston Tea Party. After all, who cared about tea? New Yorkers were not tea drinkers and much preferred hot chocolate or spiced cider, or a tot of Madeira.

Of much more importance were the more conventional variety of parties. Even the Lord's Day, which was such a sober occasion in Puritan New England, was a festive event in the New York colony, when everyone dressed in their grandest finery and trooped off to church, with services followed by the most elaborate and dressiest dinner of the week. In his courtship of Sarah Livingston, John Jay regularly accompanied her family on its Sunday trips to the Presbyterian Church in Elizabethtown.

Almost equally important as a social rite was "visiting." Because the mails were slow, it was customary for most visitors — who of course were always either family members or closest friends — to arrive both uninvited and unannounced, catching their hosts and hostesses by complete surprise. But this was part of the fun of visiting and having visitors. Since travel was by horse and carriage, over mainly unpaved roads, most visitors didn't just drop by for the afternoon. They came to stay for days or even weeks, bringing their servants with them, prepared to be entertained at parties and picnics and parlor games. Needless to say, one of the most frequent visitors at the William Livingstons' Liberty Hall that courting winter of 1773–1774 was John Jay.

Meanwhile, very much at the center of all this entertaining and socializing was a dashing and extraordinarily handsome young man named Alexander Hamilton. Alexander Hamilton was the era's most popular host and most sought-after guest. His appeal had to do with his looks and charm and obvious intelligence and not his family connections, because there were some people who muttered that Alexander Hamilton was actually a little common. And there were others who said that "common" was not the word for him, because he was something even worse than that. Where, for instance, had he learned those exotic — and even a little erotic — West Indian dances that he performed so well? Though still in his teens, he was mature and sophisticated well beyond his years and was included at every skating party and turtle roast that winter when John Jay was courting Sarah Livingston. Indeed, there were those who had supposed Sarah would eventually marry Hamilton, since he was also an admirer and was closer to her in age.

Alexander Hamilton was an eighteenth-century reminder that, if one is attractive and amusing enough, one doesn't need to be rich or of exalted family lineage to rise rapidly in high society. Has anything changed that much, more than two hundred years later?

John Jay was not handsome or amusing. He was slightly built and pencil-thin, with a Frenchman's figure, which was not surprising, since part of his ancestry was French. At twenty-eight, his thin hair — which, in the fashion of the times, he kept powdered and tied at the back of his neck in a ponytail — had already begun to recede from across his broad forehead. But his deep-set eyes, his long, hooked nose, and firm jawline gave him a decidedly patrician look — the look of a young Caesar. His friend and sometime rival Hamilton was a fashion plate. Jay, by contrast, nearly always dressed in black.

The commonest contemporary adjective used to describe his appearance was "sedate."

He seems also to have suffered from something of an inferiority complex. In writing to his friend Robert Livingston of what he saw as their personality differences — and to explain why they might work to balance each other as law partners — Jay said,

> It appeared to me that you have more vivacity. Bashfulness and pride rendered me more staid. Both equally ambitious but pursuing it in different roads. You flexible, I pertinaceous. Both equally sensible of indignities, you less prone to sudden resentments. Both possessed of warm passions, but you of more self-possession. You formed for a citizen of the world, I for a College or a Village. You fond of large acquaintance, I careless of all but a few. You could forbid your countenance to tell tales, mine was a babbler. You understood men and *women* early, I knew them not. You had talents and inclination for intrigue, I had neither. Your mind (and body) received pleasure from a variety of objects, mine from few. You were naturally easy of access, and in advances, I in neither. . . .

There is irony here. For it would be John Jay who would go on to become "a citizen of the world," while Robert R. Livingston, Jr., would go on to live a life at home in comparative obscurity.

The *Gazette* had been right, however, in describing Jay's bride as beautiful. Contemporary portraits show a young woman with gently curling, golden-brown hair, wide blue eyes beneath arched brows, full, humorous lips and a perfectly shaped nose, and the skin of a Dresden porcelain figurine. John Jay and Alexander Hamilton were not the only men of the period who were taken with Sarah Van Brugh Livingston. Both Aaron Burr and John Adams were smitten by her. And even the famously unsentimental George Washington snipped off and mailed to her a lock of his hair.

In the weeks before her wedding, Sarah and her mother worked at collecting the clothing and linens, the silver and pewter and china and glassware that she would need for her new house in New York. While her mother gave the bride-to-be lessons in running a household, dressmakers worked on Sarah's wedding dress and traveling costume, and servants prepared Liberty Hall for a wedding.

The main house, approached at the end of a gravel drive lined with maples, was a sprawling two-story Georgian affair built of brick and local stone. At one side of the entrance was a large double parlor, with a fireplace at either end. Across the hall was the dining room, and behind this was a cozy library. Upstairs were seven principal bedrooms, including a huge master bedroom, and there were fireplaces in every room, plus one tall enough to stand in, in the kitchen, where all the cooking was done. In a gabled attic at the top of the house were unheated cells — the servants' rooms.

But Liberty Hall was really a working farm and was very nearly self-sufficient. Outside were barns for the cattle, a dairy, stables for the horses, coops for the chickens, and folds for the sheep. There were vegetable gardens and cornfields, an herb garden, and an orchard of apple, cherry, and pear trees. Two ponds were stocked with trout and perch, and all around were pasturelands where the livestock could graze. Across one hillside stood several acres of original climax forest, which provided lumber for the farm and firewood for the house. A small regiment of barnyard cats kept the rodent population under control, and a troop of family collies — with names like Hannibal, Old Brutus, and Xerxes (to be memorialized as they entered the pet cemetery) — protected the sheep from predators. And of course no household was complete without its kitchen dog, whose duty was to lick the plates clean before they were washed by the scullery girl.

The wedding was to be only for family and close friends, but in the hundred years since the first Livingston had come to America, the family had gone forth and multiplied in quite dramatic fashion. The first Jay, who had arrived only a few years later, had done very nearly as well in producing offspring, and so family alone meant nearly three hundred people. Also invited were Verplancks and Brevoorts and Beekmans, Boudinots, Kissams, Alexanders, DeLanceys, and Schuylers, many of whom were already connected to the Livingstons or the Jays through marriage, along with the Van Cortlandts, De Peysters, Morrises, and Philipses — most of the reigning landed gentry of the colony.

On the day of the wedding, the carpets in the double parlor had been rolled back and tucked against the walls for dancing, the furniture had been sheeted and removed and stored in a barn, and fires burned in every fireplace, because it had been an unseasonably chilly spring. But bulbs had come up in the gardens, and Liberty Hall was filled with vases of jonquils and tulips and daffodils, and tall tallow tapers guttered from heavy silver candelabra. The guests arrived, both the men's and women's hair properly powdered, the women under huge hats swagged with tulle and feathers, carrying parasols, because the most disgraceful badge of shame a woman could display in those days was a freckle, which marked her instantly as *déclassé*. The men wore their pigtails, their cutaways, their ruffled jabots, their long doeskin vests, their tight-fitting knee breeches, calf-length hose, and patent-leather slippers with silver buckles. In terms of fashion, wealthy colonists had abandoned the hausfrau-ish look that had prevailed under Dutch rule and were openly dressing in the modes of the royal courts of London and Paris.

The bride looked radiant. She wore a cream-colored dress of silk brocade, embroidered with silver-gilt thread and appliquéd with vines and rosebuds of colored silks. Its sleeves were the fashionable elbow-length, adorned with tiered layers of white lace, while more white lace cascaded from her throat and across her bosom. She carried a white prayer book marked with a single white silk rose.

It was a wonderful day for the Livingstons. It would seem even more wonderful a few months later, when John Jay began to emerge as one of the most important and powerful men in the colonies. It was an even more wonderful day for the Jays, for the family into which they were marrying was the closest thing to American royalty.

The Livingstons were colonial manor lords.

Marriage — that was what propelled a dynasty, a family empire, just as it does today, as prominent family joined prominent family at the altar in mergers of both romance and power, weaving a web of privacy and privilege over the years that would be almost impenetrable to outsiders, a network that in time would seem almost incestuous, confounding genealogists.

Livingstons, for example, either already had married or soon would marry Beekmans, Van Rensselaers, Astors, Jays, Bayards, and other Livingstons. Jays married Bayards, who married Stuyvesants, who also married Bayards, who married Van Cortlandts, Van Rensselaers, Schuylers, and Philipses. Alexander Hamilton would marry a Schuyler, and Hamiltons would marry Fishes and Stuyvesants. Alsops would marry Robinsons and Roosevelts, and Roosevelts would marry Lispenards and Halls and other Roosevelts. Lispenards would marry Schieffelins, and Schieffelins would marry Jays and Trevors and Vanderbilts, while Jays would marry Iselins and Chapmans until nearly everybody was related to everybody else in some way or another, and until everybody could trace a tenuous relationship to either Charlemagne or Mary, Queen of Scots, or both. Royalty.

Of course this is not to say that all these marriages would be happy ones, that there would be no internecine family feuds, no faithless wives, no cuckolded husbands. There would be all of this and more. There would be scandals. There would be drunkenness and mental illness. There would be adulterous relationships, illegitimate children, divorces, bitter battles over money and inheritances, even a murder or two. All the things that can happen "even in the best of families" would happen within the American aristocracy, just as they have happened in every aristocracy from the beginning of time. And just as they happen today.

But the point is that the drama of America's interwoven aristocratic families has been played out — horror stories and all — against the tapestried background of American history. Their lives have managed to touch nearly every important event in some way or another, but often in ways that might surprise the average history student because, for the most part, American aristocrats have been able to keep their personal ordeals very private.

Only once in a while did chinks in the armored facade of the American aristocracy appear, providing a public glimpse of private agonies. By 1774, the year of the dynastic Jay-Livingston marriage, this had already happened to the Livingstons at least once. Runaway wives were no more a novelty in the eighteenth century than they are in the 1980s, but in the case of another Sarah Livingston, the allegation that she intended to sell her children into indentured servitude added a lurid fillip. This adventurous lady was the subject of the following public notice posted in the *Virginia Gazette* on April 6, 1769:

> Whereas my wife Sarah Livingston under the pretense of visiting her father and mother who live in Worcester County Maryland has eloped from me and taken her children with her, whom I am informed she intends to bind out as she gets over the bay; this is to forewarn all persons from receiving indentures of her for the said

children, and from crediting her on my account from the date hereof.

George Livingston

Otherwise, a concerted effort has been made to keep disturbing family secrets under careful wraps and family skeletons securely locked in family closets. For example, it is a well-known historical fact that Robert R. Livingston, Jr., who was John Jay's classmate and best friend, in later years (when that friendship had soured considerably, as we shall see) was the principal sponsor of Robert Fulton's experiments with steam propulsion. In gratitude, Fulton named his first steamship the *Clermont,* after his sponsor's Hudson Valley estate. Less well known are some of the more sordid details surrounding that relationship.

Fulton, perhaps to secure himself with his benefactors in the Livingston clan, married one of Robert Livingston's numerous cousins, Harriet Livingston. Theirs was a far from happy union. Soon Harriet was complaining to her Livingston relatives of her husband's infidelities, and presently she had even more serious charges. He was stealing, she claimed, her Steamboat Company stock and secretly selling it. Robert Fulton, his wife wrote, "is involved in the horrible sin against a defenseless woman, I must appeal to you for justice."

But her relatives elected not to involve themselves in Harriet's marital problems, and justice was not forthcoming. But when Robert Fulton died, Harriet had her revenge. She married a man of whom no one in her family approved, an Englishman named Dale.

"That Englishman Dale!" — as he is referred to today in the family that prefers not to remember, or has made it a point to forget, this villainous fellow's Christian name — took Harriet off to England with him, where he quickly spent what was left of Harriet's considerable Livingston fortune.

When Harriet died, her last request was that her body be returned to America for burial. The Englishman Dale complied and shipped Harriet Livingston Fulton Dale in her coffin back to the Livingstons — collect.

Not even an aristocracy is spared the vicissitudes of anguish and humiliation.

3

Manor Lords

Mr. Henry H. Livingston of New York City is a securities analyst specializing in transportation issues (after all, an ancestor financed the first steamship) with the aristocratic, Boston-based firm of Kidder, Peabody & Company. In his middle sixties, Henry Livingston is a tall, trim, ruggedly good-looking man, impeccably tailored and wonderfully well spoken, as befits a Livingston and an alumnus of the Hotchkiss School and Yale University ('40). His are a particularly *American* sort of good looks — weather-beaten, tanned, his face lined in all the right places — the looks of a proper country gentleman, which he is at least part-time. He is a member of either the ninth or the eleventh (depending on how one counts in this large and complicated family) generation of American Livingstons, and he has the prominent Livingston nose. Or perhaps, since the blood of Livingstons became commingled with the Jays' long ago, it should be properly called the Jay nose (both the earliest Jays and Livingstons had Roman noses). Thus, whether the nose today is a Jay nose or a Livingston nose is as debatable a point as any taken up by the pre-Revolutionary Moot club.

Henry and Maria Livingston keep an apartment on Manhattan's fashionable East Side, and their country place — Oak Hill, on the Hudson River — sits on two hundred acres of the vast demesne that in the seventeenth century became known as Livingston Manor, the largest and the first of the great manorships created in America by the English king. Oak Hill itself was built in 1795 by Henry Livingston's great-great-great-grandfather John Livingston and has been handed down through the family since then. A cousin, Honoria Livingston McVitty, owns a ninety-acre parcel of the old manorship nearby, and still other cousins own smaller lots of this scenic and historic land.

Oak Hill was the first house in the region built with large windows, seven feet tall and three feet wide, to command a river view. Built of brick that was baked on the premises, the walls of the house are two feet thick. Large, formal rooms — the smallest twenty-six by twenty-four feet — extend off a wide central hallway, and these are filled with Livingston family heirlooms and artifacts, eighteenth-century dining room chairs, and fine old family portraits.

"Yes," Henry Livingston says, "I was brought up always reminded that I was a Livingston, and that I was expected to conduct myself as one. The family was always very proper on manners. And we grew up surrounded by family portraits, and so it was hard not to get the impression that these people, who had died two hundred years ago, were a part of us, part of the family, and that we were a living part of their past. And yes, of course there are upper-class values that show up in people, that are born into people, and that tend to come out in a more affluent class — elements of taste, discretion, and morality which help to create people who know how to handle themselves, and who know how to accept responsibilities. It isn't something that was taught from my father's or grandfather's knee, exactly. It's something that, in a family like ours, comes through almost by osmosis — the knowledge that, as Livingstons, we were expected to rise to occasions."

By rising to occasions, Henry Livingston does not refer just to the grand occasions when numbers of his ancestors gallantly marched off to wars, to be decorated for bravery or to die on the field of honor, though he admits that this is part of it. There were also the small occasions, such as the time Mrs. Peter Van Brugh Livingston caught fire. She had appeared at a New York reception wearing a fashionable headdress of the day, a tall, nodding affair composed of blue ostrich plumes. The party was illuminated by glass lusterware candelabra, and at one point in the evening she became so engrossed in conversation that she stepped under one of these and nodded her plumes directly into the flames. The fire was quickly extinguished by other guests, and Mrs. Livingston was unhurt, although her headdress was ruined. But rather than make a fuss, she apologized to her hostess for the trouble she had caused and later told the story as a joke on herself.

Henry Livingston has four grown children, two sons and two daughters, but only one of his eight grandchildren so far — little John Henry Livingston — has the family name. "We intend to keep Oak Hill in the family if we possibly can," he says. "My children have always loved the place. There's a way you can set up a trusteeship so it's permanent. Also, since it's a landmark, there's a possibility we might get a special tax break if the house were opened to the public at certain times."

He can't help but grow a little wistful thinking about the old days of the colonial manor lords. "The manors were run like early corporations," he says. "Livingston Manor was run like an early version of IBM, and the point of the manorial system was to encourage the growth potential of the country. The manor lord was given the rights to hold courts, collect taxes, maintain roads, and to maintain his own militia, but the point was to develop the land and make it productive. The first lord sensed that there was lead and iron ore here, and Livingston Manor provided ninety-nine percent of the iron used in the Revolution. Settlers were encouraged to come as tenants, to provide a labor force. A tenant was given tools, food, seed, and the wood to build himself a house within a year. Then it was his to live in for his lifetime, plus one generation. Some manors had disgruntled tenants. Not us. The manor system was very carefully structured, and out of it the lords gained a perception of government, and a perception of what the land and the surrounding environment could yield. For instance, all the trade up and down the Hudson River was developed and managed by the Livingston manor lords. Breaking up the manors resulted in the same sort of mess that's come from the breakup of AT&T. You can't just keep dividing up land, and then dividing it again, every time someone dies. I'm not a Royalist, but the manorial system was a system that *worked*."

Needless to say, Henry Livingston is a member in good standing of the Order of Colonial Lords of Manors in America, a patriotic society of proven descendants of manor lords.

Looking back from a distance of all those generations, Henry Livingston can perhaps be forgiven for looking at the manorial system somewhat romantically. In fact, it was neither as pretty nor as simple as he describes it in the 1980s.

In the early seventeenth century, when the New York and New Jersey colonies were under Dutch rule, the Dutch West India Company had created a system of patroonships — *patroon* translates as "patron" or "master" — under which the company's more important officers were rewarded with large tracts of land to do with as they wished. The first of these was Rensselaerwyck, purchased in 1630 for Kiliaen Van Rensselaer, an Amsterdam-based director of the company, and Rensselaerwyck set the tone of the other land grants that followed. It consisted of more than seven hundred thousand acres on the west bank of the Hudson (including the town of Albany) and was purchased from the Indians for "certain quantities of duffels, axes, knives, and wampum," making it, along with the purchase of Manhattan Island, one of the better bargains in the history of real estate. Kiliaen Van Rensselaer never bothered to visit his property, but his descendants did, including, eight generations later, Stephen Van Rensselaer, who inherited the estate at the age of five and went on to found America's first scientific college, Rensselaer Polytechnic Institute, in 1824 at Troy, New York, just across the river from his family's property.

During the British colonial period, the British monarch continued the Dutch policy, granting manorships to important colonists who had proven useful, in one way or another, to the British cause or to British trade with the colonies. Among these manors were Pelham Manor, granted to Thomas Pell; Philipsborough, to Frederick Philipse; Morrisania, to Lewis Morris; and Cortlandt Manor, to Stephanus Van Cortlandt; these properties were always in choice locations, either in the Hudson River valley or along the Atlantic coast or Long Island Sound. But the very first of these British manorships, along with the title of lord of the manor that went with it, had been ceded to Robert Livingston in 1686 by James II. Thus, just as in the British House of Lords a premier peer is one bearing the oldest title of his degree, the Livingstons could consider themselves the premier American family.

On the other hand, if the Livingstons today tend to create the impression that they were granted their great manorial lands as the result of some noble and meritorious service to the king, this is incorrect. They earned their original land in quite a different way. They married it.

The first American Livingston — known as Robert the First or the first lord by his descendants, and who was Sarah Van Brugh Livingston Jay's great-grandfather — was born in Scotland of poor but genteel parents. His father, John Livingston, was a Presbyterian clergyman, a man of stern and uncompromising principles. When Charles II (who, it was rumored, had Papist sympathies) ascended to the throne of England in 1660, John Livingston refused to sign an oath of allegiance to the new king. As punishment, he and his family were ordered into permanent exile. The Livingstons fled to Rotterdam, where Robert Livingston spent his boyhood years.

Perhaps because he had seen what refusal to compromise or bow to the wishes of higher-ups had done for his father, young Robert Livingston appears to have decided two things as a youth: He would adapt to situations with chameleonlike ease, and he would cultivate friends in high places. As a young teenager, Robert had gone to work in the Dutch shipping trade, and by the time his father died, when Robert was eighteen, he had put aside sufficient savings for his next big step: America and the booming — and very lucrative — fur trade.

Tall, muscular, and rugged of countenance, as are many of his male descendants today, Robert Livingston was, essentially, an adventurer. In today's parlance, Robert would probably be called a hustler, a high roller, a social and entrepreneurial Alpinist, a seventeenth-century Donald Trump. In Europe, American beaver was in great demand and commanded high prices. Beaver muffs and tippets adorned the most fashionable European ladies, and beaver trimmed or lined the coats and headgear of kings and courtiers. In America, beaver pelts could be bought from the Indians for wampum, and wampum was easily counterfeited. Indeed, the manufacture of counterfeit wampum had become something of a cottage industry in Holland. A number of New England fortunes had already been made from the hides of the little dam-building mammal, but by the mid-1670s the New England fur trade was in trouble. In fact, when Robert Livingston arrived in the Massachusetts Bay Colony in 1674, the odds against his achieving success in the fur trade seemed formidable, even for an ambitious young man of twenty.

For one thing, the ponds and streams and swamps of New England had been hunted nearly clean of beaver, and the animal was close to extinction in the region. The only fresh supply of beaver lay west of the Hudson River, beyond the small trading settlement of Albany, New York. But, although New York had become a British colony ten years earlier, Albany remained a staunchly Dutch settlement, firmly under the sway of the Dutch Reform Church, and anything English was anathema. New Englanders in particular were distrusted. Furthermore, the beaver-rich lands west of the Hudson were controlled by the Five Iroquois Nations, and the Iroquois refused to trade with either the English or New Englanders, dealing only with the Dutch. This stood to give the Dutch traders of Albany something of a monopoly on the fur business. If the New England traders were to stay in business, Albany somehow had to be penetrated. Robert Livingston saw himself as the man uniquely suited to do this. He might be a Scots Presbyterian, but he spoke Dutch fluently. He could go to Albany and pass himself off as a Dutchman.

In Massachusetts, Robert had some tenuous but important connections: the powerful Winthrop family, a member of which had been an acquaintance of Robert's father. In Massachusetts, the Winthrops were very much the right people to know, and once the personable young man had presented himself to them, he waited for them to introduce him to the person he was looking for — ideally, someone in the fur trade who was interested in hiring a bright young man to be his agent in Albany, thus advancing Robert Livingston up to the next rung of his ascent. It wasn't long before just such a person appeared. His name was John Hull, and he had been frustrated in his attempts to deal with either the Iroquois or the New York Dutch. To Hull, Livingston pointed out that he was already bilingual and foresaw no difficulty in learning the Iroquois language. He had also foresightedly brought with him a freshly minted supply of Dutch wampum. Hull, who had nothing to lose, agreed to let the young man give the venture a try, and Robert Livingston promptly set off across the Berkshire and Taconic mountains.

Fortuitously, another very important person had just arrived in Albany. Or perhaps it was not so fortuitous, and Robert, who kept an ear to the ground in the shipping business, may have been well aware that Nicholas Van Rensselaer was heading for the Dutch settlement and would be arriving just a few weeks before Robert did; the timing seems too close to have been pure coincidence. Nicholas Van Rensselaer, son of Kiliaen Van Rensselaer, had been dispatched by his family in Holland to assume command of Rensselaerwyck, if "command" is not too strong a word, considering Nicholas's limited abilities.

Nicholas Van Rensselaer was an altogether curious man. He was given to periodic spurts of extravagant spending, and his family may have sent him to Albany — where there was nothing to buy except furs — to keep him out of the luxurious jewelry shops of Brussels, Amsterdam, and London, where he enjoyed purchasing emeralds, diamonds, sapphires, rubies, and pearls. He also occasionally went into spiritual trances, in which he heard voices and had prophetic visions. In one of these, he had seen Charles II sitting on the throne of England, and when he relayed this news to Charles — then still a prince and in exile in Belgium — Charles liked what he heard. When, a year or so later, Charles did ascend to the throne, the new king decided that Nicholas might have something, and Nicholas found himself named the official chaplain to the Dutch ambassador in London. Nicholas arrived in Albany bearing royal documents appointing him pastor and spiritual leader of the settlement, though how he obtained his ordination has never been quite clear.

To the residents of Albany, the arrival of Nicholas Van Rensselaer was probably not a welcome event. A patroonship without a resident patroon had been a much more easygoing place. And the fact that Nicholas was also the personal pet of the new British monarch can have done little to endear him to the Dutch settlers. But there was very little they could do about it. Nicholas had the king's blessing, and he owned the place — the town and all the countryside for miles around, as far as the eye could see or the imagination wander, the biggest patroonship of them all.

But it was clear from the outset that he had no idea how to run such a place. Having been handed Rensselaerwyck, he seemed to want to have nothing to do with it and rarely spoke to his neighbors and tenants — who were also officially his diocesal flock — though he was often observed in the streets of Albany sermonizing excitedly to himself. His first move was a frivolous one. It was to marry Alida Schuyler, the young daughter of the almost as rich and powerful Dutch Schuylers. Nicholas was his new wife's senior by a full twenty years.

Nicholas Van Rensselaer was as odd-looking as he was -acting. Though only thirty-eight, he looked much older. Thin and stooped, with peering, myopic eyes, he was nearly bald and, with the exception of a skimpy, sandy moustache, he appeared beardless, with a sallow, waxy complexion and a thin, blue-veined nose. By contrast, his eighteen-year-old wife was a handsome, buxom, pink-cheeked Dutch girl who was so outgoing that she seemed positively bouncy.

Still, since she was an aristocratic Schuyler and he was an aristocratic Van Rensselaer, they were Albany's *only* important couple, and when Robert Livingston arrived in Albany, Nicholas and Alida were the only right people to get to know. In an outpost the size of Albany, this was not difficult to do.

Sizing up the situation, and recognizing Nicholas's inability to run Rensselaerwyck, Robert Livingston quickly offered to give the Van Rensselaers a helping hand, and this was just as quickly accepted. To give Nicholas credit, he seems to have known that he was quite out of his depth with the estate. And so, with the title of secretary of Rensselaerwyck, Robert Livingston became what amounted to Nicholas Van Rensselaer's chief executive officer, leaving Nicholas happily with his visions and his voices. Soon Nicholas conferred another title on the fast-rising Robert: secretary of the city of Albany. And soon after that he was given a third and even more important post: secretary to the Board of Indian Commissioners, because by then, as he had promised, he had become one of the few white men to learn the Iroquois tongue. Now Robert Livingston wore four hats, because he was still the Albany representative of John Hull, fur trader of Boston. And if being on the Board of Indian Commissioners while simultaneously trading with the Indians represented a conflict of interest, no one bothered to mention it at the time.

As Nicholas Van Rensselaer's secretary, handling all his personal and business affairs while Nicholas was lost in the confusion of his mystical reveries, Robert Livingston may have noticed that Nicholas and Alida's marriage was a loveless one. It was certainly a childless one, and it may have been a sexless one. Alida was a beautiful young woman in her early twenties. Robert was a lusty young man just two years older. Nicholas was only in his early forties, but he seemed to be aging rapidly. Suddenly, in the autumn of 1678, after Nicholas and Alida had been married not quite four years, Nicholas Van Rensselaer became desperately ill, and his illness defied diagnosis and treatment as he worsened daily. According to a family story, Nicholas Van Rensselaer lifted himself from his deathbed that November and cried out for his secretary to take down his will. Robert Livingston rushed in, pen in hand, to take down the patroon's last wishes. But if such a will was ever dictated, it was never found, and Nicholas Van Rensselaer died intestate at age forty-two.

If you believe a Van Rensselaer rumor, still circulated to this day, Nicholas was poisoned. But by whom? Alida? Robert? Robert and

Alida conspiring together? Whatever the dark facts may have been, Robert Livingston and Alida Schuyler Van Rensselaer were married less than eight months later, and nine months after that — almost to the day — the new Mrs. Robert Livingston presented her husband with their first child, a son named Johannes, a nod both to Robert's father, John, and to Alida's Dutch antecedents.

Thus with Robert and Alida's marriage had begun the inexorable transformation of the vast patroonship of Rensselaerwyck into the even vaster Livingston Manor, with Robert as its first lord. Much more would have to happen, of course. There would be long legal battles over Nicholas Van Rensselaer's estate. Loyalties would have to be tested, relationships strained. Fires would be set, and blood would be shed. More land would be acquired, by fair means and foul, and from Indians only too willing to trade their lands for European goods and guns, until Livingston Manor would grow to a million acres.

4

Ancient Wealth

"Aristocracy," states a Chinese proverb, "is ancient wealth."

In America, of course, no wealth is really very ancient. But it is still a rule of thumb that the longer a family has had its fortune, the loftier is its degree. In America's unwritten class system, as little as ten years' added tenure can mark the difference between an "established" family and parvenus. By the time of John Jay's marriage, the Jays in America were already quite rich and well connected. But the difference in status between the Livingstons and the Jays was based on the fact that in 1679, when Robert Livingston took Nicholas Van Rensselaer's rich widow to the altar, securing her properties for his heirs, the first American Jay was still an impoverished youth in Europe, drifting from country to country, looking for his own main chance.

This was John Jay's grandfather Augustus Jay, a descendant of a once prominent French Huguenot family that traced its lineage in France back to the early sixteenth century. Augustus's father, Pierre, had been described as "an active and opulent merchant" in the city of La Rochelle, and at the age of twelve Augustus (or Auguste, as he was then named) had been sent to England to be educated. It is said in the family that the original name was *J'ai* — "I have it." But by 1685 they no longer had it. The position of Protestants in Catholic

France had always been shaky, and when the Edict of Nantes was revoked that year, all the family's property was confiscated. Augustus, then twenty, decided to seek his fortune elsewhere: first in Holland, then England, and finally in America, where he arrived in 1686. This was, coincidentally, the same year that Livingston Manor was ceded to the first Robert Livingston, with Robert as its first lord.

In New York, Augustus Jay found a pleasant and well-to-do Huguenot community of French escapees like himself, which worshipped at L'Église des Réfugiés, the "French Church." And soon Augustus Jay was also prospering as an importer and merchant. From England he imported homespuns and woolens and mohair, hats, gloves, and beer. In the West Indies he traded cargos of flour, bread, and pork in return for shipments of sugar and rum. Augustus Jay's merchant trading ships even journeyed to such remote ports as present-day Suriname, on the northeast coast of South America.

Like Robert Livingston, Augustus Jay was able to make a socially and financially auspicious marriage. In 1697, he married Anna Maria Bayard, a granddaughter of Govert Loockermans, who, when he died in 1670, was the richest man in the colony. On her mother's side Anna Bayard counted members of most of the great manorial families of New York — the Van Cortlandts, the Van Rensselaers, the Schuylers, and the Philipses — as her cousins. Anna Bayard's father, furthermore, was a nephew of Governor Peter Stuyvesant, and the Stuyvesants and Bayards were even more intricately related. Peter Stuyvesant's wife had been the former Julia Bayard, and Peter Stuyvesant's sister had married his wife's brother. Thus there had been a Mrs. Stuyvesant née Bayard and a Mrs. Bayard née Stuyvesant. In one quick marital maneuver, Augustus Jay had succeeded in collecting nearly the entire catalogue of Old Knickerbocker names as his in-laws.

This would mean that John Jay and his bride, Sarah Livingston, were cousins by marriage in a complicated sort of way through "the Schuyler Connection"; Sarah's great-grandmother had been a Schuyler.

Augustus and Anna Jay's union produced four children, three daughters and one son, Peter, John Jay's father. Peter Jay had been trained to follow in his father's international mercantile footsteps from an early age. At eighteen, he had been sent to Europe, where he transacted business in London, Bristol, Paris, and Amsterdam for the family firm. Returning to New York, he continued to follow his father's example by making a dynastic marriage. Peter Jay's bride was his mother's young second cousin, Mary Anna Van Cortlandt of Cortlandt Manor, the daughter of Jacobus and Eve Philipse Van Cortlandt and a granddaughter of the first lord of the manor of Philipsburg, Frederick Philipse (pronounced "Philip-see"). Thus it is possible to see why their son John, by the time he reached King's College, could consider himself very much to the manner, if not to the manorship, born.

John Jay cannot have had a particularly happy childhood. Of the ten children born to Peter and Mary Jay, in those days of high infant mortality, only seven lived to adulthood, and four of these suffered from mental or physical handicaps. An older sister, Eve, was emotionally disturbed from the time she was a little girl, and an older brother, Augustus, was mentally retarded and could never learn to read or write, despite the family's continued efforts with private tutors. Another older brother, Peter, Jr., and sister, Anna, had been completely blinded by smallpox in the epidemic of 1739. Despite their children's afflictions, Peter and Mary Jay had tried to raise their family in Manhattan until a few months after John Jay's birth in December 1745. Then, as Peter Jay wrote, "considering the helpless condition of part of my family," he decided to move to the country. The Jays settled in a large, rambling house in Rye, New York, overlooking Long Island Sound, where "the little blind ones" would be protected from "the dangers and confusions of the city life."

John Jay's education was somewhat eccentric, though aristocratically Spartan. As a child he had been taught "the rudiments of English, and the Latin grammar" at home by his mother, and by age seven he was deemed ready to enter grammar school. The school chosen was a church-run affair in nearby New Rochelle, which, as the name suggests, had been settled mainly by French refugees, from the provinces of Aunis and Saintonge. The school was run by the curmudgeonly Reverend Peter Stoope, a French Swiss who had been pastor of the French Huguenot Church, which had recently joined New Rochelle's Episcopal Communion. Dr. Stoope spent most of his days pondering arcane mathematical theorems and seemed unaware that his parsonage, in which his school was kept, was collapsing into near-ruin. John Jay would later recall that, in order to keep the snow off his bed in winter, he would have to stuff the broken windowpanes with chips of wood. Dr. Stoope's wife was in charge of the school's domestic arrangements and was "as penurious as he was careless." If there was anything at all served at a meal beyond a cup of thin soup, it might be a small piece of boiled potato or a bit of stale bread. Jay would also later tell of how, to avoid what to a teenage boy seemed like imminent starvation, he and his classmates would take to the woods in search of nuts and berries, which they would bring back concealed in their stockings, lest they be confiscated by Mme. Stoope. Dr. Stoope's school offered one advantage — the classes were taught in French, which would stand Jay in good stead later on when he was named a colonial emissary to Paris. John Jay endured three years of Dr. Stoope's school and its rigors before being brought home to Rye to be prepared for college by a private tutor.

At the time, the entrance requirements for King's College were that a boy be able to translate "the first three of Tully's orations and the six first books of Virgil's Aeneid into English, and the first ten chapters of St. John's Gospel into Latin"; to have a mastery of Latin grammar, and to be "expert in Arithmetick as far as Reduction." All this he was able to master, and when he was admitted to college he was just fourteen.

Politically, the man who would be hailed as a great Revolutionary patriot was already beginning to emerge, but it would be wrong to see him as a budding socialistic firebrand or militant anti-Royalist. On the contrary, the Jays and their friends were political conservatives. Like other well-to-do New Yorkers of the period, the Jays worried that a revolution would lead to government by the proletariat, a most unsettling thought.

The Livingstons, by contrast, were outspokenly Whigs. The literary circle of the era regularly met at the home of William Livingston, and at one of these gatherings John Jay's future father-in-law had rather shocked his guests by reading some ballads he had composed that appeared to mock the king and the monarchy. The Revolutionary movement, of course, was still only a matter of whispered speculation, something that was only vaguely in the air, and since the Livingston ballads might be considered seditious, it was decided that they should be burned, for safety's sake, by the public hangman.

The Jays, however, were merchants and resented any sort of outside government interference. John Jay's father had often spoken of how intolerable the situation had become, that a continent as large and as prosperous as America had grown should be ruled by a tiny island three thousand miles away. Independence was a much more recurrent theme in family conversations than revolution, and if independence from Great Britain could be achieved without the untidiness of war, that was what wealthy colonists like the Jays would have much preferred. Families such as the Jays felt they owed Britain nothing for their success in America. They had succeeded despite the burdens of British taxation. The fact that none of John Jay's eight great-grandparents had been English was important to him; three had been French, and five had been Dutch. Therefore, he was one of the few men of the Revolution who could say, as he did in 1796, "Not being of British descent, I cannot be influenced by that tendency towards their national character, nor that partiality for it, which might otherwise be supposed to be not unnatural."

The Jays and other early New York families like them were also, in a genteel way, opposed to slavery, and John Jay himself would later help organize the New York Society for Promoting the Manumission of Slaves. Though New York families such as the Jays kept slaves themselves, most had adopted the practice of paying their slaves small wages that were designed, in time, to permit slaves to purchase their freedom. On the other hand, these New Yorkers were willing to admit that theirs was a somewhat special situation. In New York, slaves were used primarily as household servants. In the South, slaves ran the vast factory-plantations and were considered indispensable to the southern economy. An antislavery stance was easy in the North. As one of John Jay's relatives once commented, "Freedom . . . greatly helps their morale and from a selfish point of view it makes a staff much easier to deal with."

John Jay's attitude would be a cautious one of wait and see. "Even if we could free all slaves now," he once said, "I do not think it would be wise. But we should prepare now for eventual abolition of slavery by educating our Negroes and giving them opportunities to learn a trade and earn their independence." As an independent merchant's son, he tended to equate freedom with free enterprise.

At college, John Jay had decided upon a career in law. An older brother, James, had already joined the family import-export business and was more or less running it while Peter Jay, now semiretired, busied himself managing his big farm and country estate in Rye.

John Jay's decision to become a lawyer had made his father a little nervous. The law had become the most snobbish of professions in New York and, through such institutions as The Moot club, had become an elite fraternity that welcomed no outsiders. A few years earlier, an association of New York lawyers had adopted a resolution designed to keep the profession, and the business, to themselves. It was a perfect catch-22 rule: No one could become a lawyer who had not apprenticed as a clerk, while, on the other hand, no clerk "who proposed to enter the profession" could be hired. But this stricture had proven to be impossible to enforce, and it had been loosened a bit. Clerks, the legal profession had conceded, could in fact train to be lawyers and even be licensed as such, but "under such restrictions as will greatly impede the lower class of the people from creeping in." Would his son be deemed a gentleman enough to be a lawyer, or would he be labeled a lower-class creeper? This worried Peter Jay.

Then, in the spring of 1763, when John Jay was in his last year at King's College, an incident occurred that could have ruined his career forever.

It seemed that, as a lark, a group of high-spirited young students had decided to set upon and smash a certain table that sat in a corner of College Hall. The sounds of splintering furniture attracted several professors to the scene, who proceeded to summon Dr. Myles Cooper, the college president, who was not amused. He lined the errant students up in military fashion and asked each young man, in turn, two questions: "Did you break the table?" and "Do you know who did?" To both questions, the young men answered "No" as Dr. Cooper moved down the line. Near the end of the line, the president approached Jay. "Mr. Jay, did you break the table?" Dr. Cooper asked. "No," was the reply. "Do you know who did?" "Yes," replied John Jay.

Dr. Cooper then demanded to know the names of those responsible for the nefarious deed, to which John Jay responded with a lawyerly argument in which he pointed out that nowhere in the college's regulations was there a rule that required a man to inform on his fellow students. Dr. Cooper was unimpressed, and John Jay was given a one-year suspension from King's College over the affair. Returning the following year, however, Jay completed his studies with honors and, in front of His Majesty's Council, General Thomas

Gage, and other colonial worthies, he delivered an impressive dissertation on the blessings of peace and was given his bachelor's degree in 1764.

Two weeks later, in return for the sum of two hundred dollars, he was admitted as a clerk-apprentice in the offices of Mr. Benjamin Kissam, a barrister "eminent in the profession," to serve for five years. He completed his training in four years, was admitted to the New York bar in 1768, and was ready for the next step upward — the dynastic marriage.

John Jay may have seen himself as a man more suited to the contemplative life of "a College or a Village," but his lively and ambitious young wife saw herself as someone cut out for far more than that. Sarah Livingston Jay was a woman who seemed to be designed for grand entrances, for great, theatrical descents down marble staircases, for red carpets and gilded ballroom chairs, for royal courts and courtiers and thrones where turbaned Nubians waved peacock-feathered fans. She seems to have been born with presence, with an ability, wherever she went, to take the center of the stage and hold the spotlight, and whatever her new marriage consisted of, she was determined that she and her husband were going to be in the thick of things — important things, national things, international things. She had brought into the marriage her Livingston dowry and her Livingston name, which could only help further her ambitions. For herself and her husband, she set her sights on the top. A favorite gesture was to touch her adoring husband's dark coat sleeve and whisper gently but urgently, *"Come, John!"*

Only a few months after the Jays' wedding, in 1774, Sarah's father, the steadfast Whig, was appointed to the First Continental Congress in Philadelphia and, at Sarah's urging, her husband was also invited to join this gathering of colonial notables who were convening to explore ways and means to settle their disputes with the Crown. It was a classic case of the ancient maxim that the son-in-law also rises.

Jay had remained reluctant to support the growing tide of opinion that advocated America's separation from the British Empire even if it meant violence. But Sarah Jay urged him that it was his patriotic duty, his historic calling, his God-given obligation to serve the country of his birth in its time of need.

At twenty-eight, he was one of the Congress's youngest members, and even to have joined this anti-Royalist body called for no small amount of courage. In the Congress, his father-in-law saw to it that he was given the important task of drawing up an address to the people of Great Britain listing the colonies' grievances against George III. At that delicate stage of British-American negotiations, any expression of opposition to the king could have meant an invitation to the gallows, but Jay brought it off and returned from Philadelphia to find himself a colonial hero.

At the Second Continental Congress, a year later, Jay addressed similar statements of grievances to the governments of Canada, Jamaica, and Ireland. In preparing these documents, it was clear that Jay had become a master of a kind of eloquent, drumrolling political rhetoric that was designed to stir men's souls. "Though vilified as wanting spirit," he wrote, "we are determined to behave like men; though insulted and abused, we wish for reconciliation; though defamed as seditious, we are ready to obey the laws, and though charged with rebellion, will cheerfully bleed in defense of our sovereign in a righteous cause."

Jay was in Philadelphia when the news of the events in Lexington and Concord swept through the colonies. The great war had begun. In the summer of 1776, Jay was attending the provincial congress of New York and therefore missed the opportunity to affix his signature to the Declaration of Independence. But he was chairman of the committee that drafted the New York State Constitution and shortly afterward was named the first chief justice of the state. In 1778, he returned to the Continental Congress and, in December of that year, was elected its president. Sarah was delighted.

Seventeen seventy-nine was a year of ferocious fighting, and Spain had entered the fray, loaning the colonists 219 bronze cannon, 200 gun carriages, 30,000 muskets, 55,000 rounds of ammunition, 12,000 bombs, 4,000 tents, and 30,000 uniforms, and would supply the revolutionaries with more than five million dollars in aid before the war was over. Britain had reacted angrily, and George III had offered the Spanish king the territories of Florida and Gibraltar, as well as cod-fishing rights off Newfoundland, if Spain would withdraw her support of the Americans. With Spanish sympathies hanging in the balance, it was decided that an emissary must immediately be sent to Spain to secure Carlos III's continued help in the Revolutionary cause. The man chosen for this high diplomatic mission was John Jay.

Sarah Jay, who had never crossed the Atlantic or set foot outside the American continent, was ecstatic. She would be curtsying before the Spanish monarch, and he would be kissing her hand. Was there any wealth more ancient than that of the Bourbon kings? There was never any doubt about whether Sarah Jay wanted to accompany her husband on his mission to Madrid. The only question was whether anyone could stop her.

5

A Gentleman's War

William W. Reese is a New York banker in his middle forties who is a member of the firm of J. P. Morgan & Company. He and his beautiful artist wife live in an attractive apartment on Park Avenue and keep a winter condominium in Palm Beach; all very ordinary upper-crust New York stuff, you might say. And yet William Reese is one of a number of quietly successful young Americans who take their descendancy from the early aristocratic families very seriously and who consider themselves aristocratically superior to what passes for New York "society" today — though they would never say so except in the company of close friends and others whom they recognize as their own sort. An aristocrat, by definition, never boasts of being one.

Bill Reese confesses to gaining a quiet pleasure walking about New York and feeling a sense of belonging to a place his ancestors helped build. "I can pass a building and think, That's the corner where my great-grandfather's house stood. That old building was where my great-uncles went to school. That little park used to be part of one of my ancestors' apple orchard, and that statue is of a relative of mine. My ancestors helped build that hospital, that museum. This was where the reservoir used to be until some of my ancestors, the Astors, gave the money to build the public library. . . ."

On his father's side, Bill Reese is descended from Livingstons, who, of course, are by now connected to everybody else, including the Astors, and on his mother's side the connections are to the Otises of Boston, about whom there are many family legends, many of which may be apocryphal. According to one, Mrs. Harrison Gray Otis, whenever she introduced herself, always quickly added, "And we are not in elevators. We were elevated when there were just stairs."

To maintain a sense of connection with his family's long American past, William Reese belongs to at least twenty patriotic, genealogical, and social organizations, including the Union Club, the Knickerbocker Club, the Rockaway Hunting Club, the Racquet & Tennis Club, the Down Town Club, the Church Club, the Badminton Club, the University Club, the Metropolitan Opera Club, the Society of Colonial Wars, the Military Order of Foreign Wars, the New England Society, the Order of Colonial Lords of Manors in America, the Society of the War of 1812, the St. Nicholas Society, the Sons of the Revolution, the Huguenot Society, the Sons of the American Revolution, the Mayflower Descendants, and the American Society of the Most Venerable Order of the Hospital of St. John of Jerusalem. As can be deduced, many of Mr. Reese's ancestors have fought in wars. "One has a special affection," he says, "for ancestors who have died fighting in wars for their country."

William Reese often lunches at the University Club, that marvel of McKim, Mead & White architecture at the corner of Fifth Avenue and Fifty-fourth Street in Manhattan, and the University Club also honors its war dead. On one wall of the club's entrance lobby, a bronze plaque commemorates club members who fell in World War I. On the opposite wall, a similar plaque memorializes those members who died in World War II. Mr. Reese, who is too young to have fought in either of these wars, often studies these two plaques. "I want you to notice something," he says. "The World War One plaque lists twenty University Club members who were killed in that war, which America was in only for a very short period of time. The World War Two plaque lists only eight members killed, or less than half, even though we were involved in that war for a much longer time. I like to think it is because World War One was the last war that was fought by gentlemen."

Other explanations for this discrepancy come to mind — more modern medical techniques, for example. Or the fact that World War II came at the end of the Great Depression, during which many gentlemen gave up their club memberships as a matter of economic necessity. But Mr. Reese's explanation is the aristocratic one, the nostalgic one, the romantic one, the proud one from a descendant of proud old families, and it has a certain piquancy and charm. Aristocracy, after all, is also a frame of mind.

In retrospect, the American Revolution often seems like a gentlemanly sort of war. Henry H. Livingston, for example, notes that "at least eight known members of the family fought in the Battle of Saratoga, and only one of these was an enlisted man. The others were all officers." Looking back, that war — during much of which John and Sarah Jay were out of the country on one sensitive mission or another — also seems like the last war in the history of the world in which everyone managed to conduct himself gloriously. Nothing about it seemed entirely real. If a man didn't feel like fighting in it, and could afford to do so, he could hire someone else to fight — and die — for him and still be counted as a patriot. In New York, in particular, which had always been a stronghold of Toryism, it was hard to take the whole thing seriously, at the war's outset, at least. New Yorkers hadn't really wanted a revolution anyway, and so when war began, wealthy families simply moved to their country places to be out of the line of fire. The Revolution was simply something to have done with, to get through, a probably unnecessary nuisance. Of course it was all quite different in Boston, where Revolutionary passions burned.

From a distance, in the beginning, the war seemed as quaintly exciting as a good game of chess, the red-coated British soldiers no more than toys made of tin. There was no question that the patriots would win in the end, and in the meantime — in New York, at least — nobody harbored any really hard feelings against the poor British or poor old George III. But the war had a certain glamour. It was a war fought dashingly on horseback, a war of flintlocks and rapiers and snuffboxes and muskets and whiskey and coonskin caps.

It was not long, however, before the harsh realities of the war became clear, and the American Revolution became a six-and-a-half-year period of terrible suffering and deprivation, during which thousands of young men would die or be mutilated, and the ordinary staples of life — sugar, salt, corn, and milk — would become so scarce as to be nonexistent, and children would die of starvation. At the war's end, women and children who had fled the cities to be out of the path of the fighting would return to their city mansions to find their homes looted or gutted by the British and precious family heirlooms stolen or destroyed. Out of the war would come tales of bravery and heroism, of luck against all adversity, as well as tales of brutality and betrayal.

Mrs. John King Van Rensselaer tells a tale that she admits may be a legend, though it has passed down through her family with specific names attached to the participants and so may be true. William Alexander, the sixth earl of Stirling, who had renounced his estates overseas to serve the Revolutionary cause, had sent his wife and children to his country house, The Sycamores, in Basking Ridge, New Jersey, to wait out the war. And soon, as other women were doing, Lady Stirling (who was Sarah Jay's aunt) had turned the house into a hospital to care for wounded soldiers and other refugees from New York. At one point, according to the story, the material comforts of life were at such a low point that there was only a single darning needle in the entire community. This precious commodity was passed from neighbor to neighbor, to sew bandages and mend and patch hospital blankets and clothing. One day Lady Stirling needed to borrow the needle and dispatched a little boy, Quincey Morton — the son of the Revolutionary general and signer of the Declaration of Independence John Morton — to fetch it from the last woman who had used it.

Quincey Morton obtained the needle, but somewhere along the route back to The Sycamores he stopped to play with some children his age, and when he reached Lady Stirling's house the needle was nowhere to be found. The loss of the darning needle galvanized the entire town. Young Quincey was grilled until he broke down in tears, but he had no idea where or how he had lost the needle. Then the whole town turned out to search for the needle, not in a proverbial haystack but across a considerable stretch of rural countryside. The search went on for hours, and every possible route Quincey might have taken was traced and retraced. Finally, a sharp-eyed member of the search party spotted a tiny silvery object speared in the trunk of a tree. It was the needle. When Quincey had stopped to play, it seemed, he had absentmindedly stuck the needle there and forgotten all about it.

Other Revolutionary tales have come down from more than word of mouth and have less happy endings. Helping Lady Stirling at her impromptu hospital was a young woman named Nannie Brown, an orphaned niece of the Brockholst family, who traced their lineage back to the first English lieutenant governor of New York and who, it may be redundant to report, were also related by marriage to the Livingstons (Sarah Livingston Jay's brother was named Brockholst Livingston). And during the Battle of Trenton a young lieutenant from the Virginia infantry named James Monroe was carried, wounded, to The Sycamores. While Nannie Brown helped to nurse him back to health, the two fell in love. When he recovered, he asked her to marry him, and she accepted his proposal.

Her Brockholst relatives disapproved, and so did Lady Stirling. Monroe, they insisted, was not good enough for Nannie Brown. His background was obscure; he was from a tiny settlement called Monroe Creek. His lineage was undistinguished. He was tall, stoop-shouldered, not particularly handsome or particularly bright, a drop-out from the College of William and Mary. He only wanted to marry Nannie Brown, Lady Stirling warned, because of her family connections.

And here it is important to state a rule of the American aristocracy that applied then and continues to apply today. An aristocratic wife can make an aristocrat of her husband, but it does not work the other way around. We shall see it happen again and again as men of lower social standing, or of no social standing whatever, manage to elevate themselves through the proper choice of a wife. But when men marry beneath them, they inevitably sink to the lower social status of their wives. A contemporary example of this rule at work occurred when King Edward VIII of England decided he must marry Mrs. Wallis Simpson.

And so, when Nannie Brown and James Monroe protested that their love was true, Major General Lord Stirling promoted his wife's friend's fiancé and made him his aide-de-camp, demonstrating that even an engagement to a young woman of good family could advance a man in the world. Plans for the wedding proceeded, and it was to be as grand an affair as wartime shortages and austerity would allow. The Van Horne family had offered their elegant family homestead on the banks of the Raritan River near New Brunswick for the wedding and reception, and Monroe had presented his bride-to-be with a gold engagement band inscribed with the words "Your consent gives content" inside the circle. He had also given her a necklace with a pendant upon which his profile was embossed. Working together, Lady Stirling and Nannie Brown pieced together a wedding gown out of whatever scraps of old silk they could lay their hands upon. The day of the wedding arrived, the bride was dressed, and the guests had assembled on the Van Hornes' sweeping lawn. Military musicians, recruited by General Stirling, were poised to play the Wedding March. At that point a messenger arrived on horseback with a brief note from the bridegroom. He had changed his mind.

Nannie Brown did not die of a broken heart but lived on in dignified spinsterhood for many years. James Monroe married a stately lady named Elizabeth Kortright who was of a "good," if not distinguished, family, though she had more money than Nannie Brown. But New York society would never forgive Monroe for his caddish act.

Thirty years later, when Monroe had become the fifth president of the United States, he encountered Mrs. Alexander Hamilton at a reception in Washington and approached her, holding out his hand. "I believe you know me, Mrs. Hamilton," he said. "I'm President James Monroe."

Mrs. Hamilton refused his hand and turned her back on him. "I do not wish to know a James Monroe," she said. "I do not wish to know a president of the United States who jilted my friend Nannie Brown."

James Monroe might have fought and been wounded in a gentleman's war, but he would never be a gentleman.

And this might be a corollary rule of the American aristocracy: One seldom gets an invitation to join its ranks more than once.

6

Coronation in New York

When the American Livingstons became rich, they began the usual title search into their Scots past and came up with the fact that the powerful earls of Callendar and Linlithgow were also Livingstons. This was sufficient for the American line to claim these earls and countesses as cousins. The cousinship, however, is so remote as to be almost undetectable. Nonetheless, through this connection the Livingstons are able to claim not just one but two family mottos. The first is *Si je puis* — "if I can." The second is *Spero meliora* — "I hope for better things," and indeed, after marrying John Jay, Sarah Livingston had found better things than she could ever have wished or hoped for growing up on a farm in New Jersey.

In Madrid, where the American Revolutionary cause was very popular, the Jays were the toasts of society, and Sarah Jay had danced with the widowed Carlos III, who had even — or so she would later claim — attempted a "flirtation" with her. John Jay's mission with the Spanish government met with mixed success. He failed to get official recognition of the United States from Spain, but he succeeded in getting a grant for about $150,000. And Spain's reaction to Great Britain's protests over this Spanish aid to America had been an attack on the British stronghold of Gibraltar.

The Jays' next diplomatic posting was to London and Paris, where

Jay was to aid Benjamin Franklin, John Adams, and Thomas Jefferson at a conference to negotiate a peace treaty with Britain. In London, John Jay took time off to commission a portrait of himself by Gilbert Stuart, whom he would later introduce to George Washington. It was the first of a collection of portraits that Jay would assemble and that would include portraits of Washington, John Adams, Jefferson, James Madison, Stephen Van Rensselaer, and Egbert Benson, a New York State official and longtime friend of Jay's. It was as though John Jay had decided to gather, in his collection, a pantheon of American national heroes, among whom his own likeness now seemed to him to belong.

On his treaty mission, Jay had been under specific instructions to come to no agreement that did not also satisfy the French government, whose support had been invaluable in the war. But, acting on his own, Jay had decided to deal directly with the British ministers, had persuaded the French government to let him do this, and as a result won terms more favorable to America than anyone had dared hope for.

Looking back from a perspective of more than two hundred years, the Jays' four-and-a-half-year stay in Europe seems almost astonishing. Today, American corporations routinely send executives for two- or three-year tours of duty in foreign cities where these employees — and their wives and children — complain of culture shock, of boredom and anomie, of loneliness and homesickness, and of an inability to get to know their foreign neighbors. And yet in the case of the Jays, when Europe was much farther away than it is today (an average crossing took nine weeks), we have two young and relatively provincial people who had never left the American continent before and who came from a comparatively new and still very rawboned town (herds of wild pigs still ran in the streets of New York, and the long skirts of fashionable ladies dragged in the mud of unpaved sidewalks) sweeping into the ancient capitals of Madrid, Paris, and London, having a wonderful time and managing to meet practically everybody there was to know. Not even obstetric interludes seemed to daunt Sarah Jay. One of her five children was born in Madrid, and another in Passy, outside Paris.

They met the celebrated and the notorious alike. They met the social reformer François de La Rochefoucauld. They met the controversial metaphysicist Franz Anton Mesmer and discussed with him his mysterious theories of planetary influence, animal magnetism, and hypnotism. They met Lovoisier the chemist, Adrien Legendre the mathematician, and the sinister Alessandro di Cagliostro, who performed magical acts and curses through the use of amulets, philters, and talismans. What was the Jays' secret? Was it her beauty and charm and wonderful manners? Was it his untrained but intuitive diplomatic brilliance? All of these things of course had something to do with it. But, more than anything, it was that both spoke perfect French, which was then the official language of the major European courts. No wonder the French government gave John Jay carte blanche to deal directly with the British in drawing up his treaty. One only has to recall the success of another French-speaking American emissary, Jacqueline Kennedy, who actually caused the great stone face of Charles de Gaulle to break into an unprecedented smile, to realize how quickly the French surrender themselves to foreigners who can speak their beautiful language properly.

In Paris, the Jays were enthusiastically taken up by the French nobility, even though they had come as official representatives of a system in which nobility would be no more. At Versailles, Sarah was presented for the second time to a reigning monarch, and to his queen, Marie Antoinette, who was delighted to hear from Sarah that a little American town was being named in her honor: Marietta, Ohio. Sarah was particularly impressed by the queen, even though she felt a bit uneasy about admitting it. In a letter home to her friend Mrs. Robert Morris in New York, she gave her impressions of the queen and also of the kind of giddy social life Sarah herself was leading:

> She is so handsome, and her manners are so engaging, that, almost forgetful of Republican principles, I was ready, in her presence, to declare her born to be a queen. There are, however, many traits in her character worthy of imitation, even by Republicans; and I cannot but admire her resolution to superintend the education of Madame Royale, her daughter, to whom she has allotted chambers adjoining her own, and persists in refusing to name a governess for her. The Duchess of Polignac is named for that office to the Dauphin. I have just been interrupted by a visit from the Princess Mazarin, who informed me that the Count d'Artois was expected here in eight days hence, and the Prince, her husband, soon after; so that I conjecture the siege of Gibraltar is to be abandoned. . . .

Europe, meanwhile, was caught up in something that was far more exciting than politics or what was going on across the ocean in America. Two Frenchmen, Joseph Montgolfier and his brother Étienne, had sent up a balloon filled with hot air into the sky. Next it would be a manned flight, in a great balloon decorated with crimson scallops, signs of the zodiac, wreaths, gargoyles and griffons, portraits of Apollo, and golden fleurs-de-lis. It ascended, then bobbed and tossed over the rooftops of Paris. Sarah Jay wrote excitedly home to her family after witnessing her first balloon flight that "Mr. Jay and I might think of taking our passage back home to America next spring on the wings of the wind." More seriously, she added that balloons "certainly might be used for carrying mail."

Ballooning captured Europe's imagination far more than the American Revolution. Balloon motifs were suddenly being used to decorate crockery, fabrics, wallpapers. Women's hairdos went up in balloon shapes, and the balloon-shaped dress, with balloon-shaped sleeves, became the fashion.

Marie Antoinette had introduced Sarah to the French court's dressmakers and milliners, and Sarah immediately began ordering dresses, hats, gloves, and accessories in these fanciful new styles. When the packages containing her Paris purchases were shipped home, her relatives — who had been reduced by wartime shortages to dresses of homespun cloth and even of potato sacks pieced together — gasped in astonishment. Never had they seen such finery. One ball gown was of Chinese silk into which real peacock feathers had been woven. Another contained so many layers of handmade Alençon lace that it weighed nearly twenty pounds.

Indeed, so gloriously bedecked and regal in her bearing had Sarah Jay become, so successful in employing those traits of Marie Antoinette which she had found "worthy of imitation," that one evening, entering a theatre in Paris with the marquis and marquise de Lafayette, the entire audience rose to its feet at the sight of her. They had mistaken the twenty-six-year-old Sarah for their twenty-eight-year-old queen.

When John and Sarah Jay returned to New York in 1784, they were given a hero's welcome. Cornwallis had surrendered at Yorktown, the war was over, and Jay had negotiated a marvelous peace treaty. Sarah, in her Paris finery, was an international celebrity. The Jays had become the absolute leaders of New York society. The Jays' big new house at 8 Broadway became the scene of glittering entertainments, and Sarah's "Dinner and Supper List" was probably the first list of who was who in New York society in American history. When her list was published in 1787, it was read avidly. It contained, among others, an Alsop, Aaron Burr, a Cadwalader, a De Peyster, a Gerry, a Huger, a Pinckney, a Van Rensselaer, two Lees, five Van Hornes, and seven Livingstons.

Sarah's list also included Alexander Hamilton and his wife, Betsey, who was the daughter of General Philip Schuyler, making Hamilton another Livingston cousin by marriage. But with Alexander and Betsey Hamilton one had to exercise a certain amount of care. Alexander Hamilton and Aaron Burr had never liked each other, and now their animosity was quite open. Burr had also made an auspicious marriage, to Theodosia Prevost, the widow of a British officer, and the Burrs entertained grandly at Richmond Hill, their mansion outside the city. But it was Burr who kept the rumors circulating that Hamilton was "not a gentleman" and had secrets in his past too scurrilous to mention in polite company. Hamilton, meanwhile, had things that were just as nasty to say about Burr. It had become impossible to entertain both men under the same roof.

Of course everyone had heard the rumors that Hamilton had an eye for the ladies and that he supported mistresses of a decidedly lower-class sort. But if his wife was aware of the gossip, as she must have been, she chose the patrician mode and ignored it. And Hamilton remained as suave and charming as ever, so it was impossible not to like him. It was also at this point not very prudent to dislike him. In 1784, the year of the Jays' return, he had organized the new nation's first bank, the Bank of New York, and was working on a national currency system based on the U.S. dollar. Aaron Burr announced that he would rather put his money in a mattress than in Hamilton's bank. Others were not so sure.

Sarah Jay skirted the issue by inviting the Hamiltons and the Burrs to alternate parties.

Her house at 8 Broadway was certainly designed for opulent entertaining. There were two dining rooms — a large one for formal gatherings, and a smaller one for more intimate affairs. There was of course a ballroom, and there were also other rooms that had no particular purpose other than to impress the guests. There was a room hung with red and gold leather, there was a blue and gold room, and there was a large parlor at the back of the house and "the small parlor" in front. At the head of the stairs was a tapestry room; beyond lay yellow rooms and red rooms and chintz rooms and damask rooms. Everywhere tall mirrors caught the candlelight, and beneath them lay tables and sideboards and buffets set out with massive silver serving pieces. Damask window hangings and costly carpets and cut-velvet upholstery in wine and golden hues completed Sarah's plush-era decor.

In Europe, she had made herself knowledgeable about French cookery and had even brought back with her from Paris her own French chef — a theretofore unheard-of luxury. Soon her menus were the talk of the town, and she had also learned the rule that every successful American hostess who came after her would have to master: In order to please the gentlemen guests, the food should not only be good, but there should be a lot of it. After the long years of wartime shortages, Sarah Jay's meals were downright sumptuous. A typical menu contained not only fresh lobster and beef but also shrimp and mutton and lamb and veal, fowl with truffles, pies, puddings, custards, ice creams, jellies, and fresh fruits in season — melons, wild strawberries, raspberries, and blackberries. She even introduced such rarities as oranges, pineapples, and bananas. From the fashionable *bonbonneries* — Joseph Corre on Wall Street and Adam Pryor on Broadway — came pastries, éclairs, petits fours, pound cakes, crullers, and cinnamon comfits, as well as candies of all varieties.

The crusty and eccentric French minister, Count de Moustier, had such a low opinion of American cooking that whenever he was invited out, he sent his personal chef as an advance party to prepare his meals for him. But in the case of the Jays' parties, he paid them the signal honor of leaving his chef at home.

Naturally, a couple who lived and entertained as grandly and conspicuously as John and Sarah Jay became the object of a certain amount of envy, particularly among Sarah Jay's less well-off female contemporaries. John and Abigail Adamses' daughter, Nabby, who was married to Colonel W. S. Smith, could barely suppress a certain waspish tone when she wrote home to her Massachusetts-based mother about the Jays' New York entertainments. "Mrs. Jay gives a dinner almost every week," she wrote to her mother in 1788, "besides one to the *corps diplomatique* on Tuesday evening." A few weeks later she wrote,

> Yesterday we dined at Mrs. Jay's, in company with the whole *corps diplomatique*. Mr. Jay is a most pleasing man, plain in his manners, but kind, affectionate and attentive; benevolence is stamped on every feature. Mrs. Jay dresses *showily*, but is very pleasing on a first acquaintance. The dinner was *à la Française*, and exhibited more European taste than I expected to find.

Still, despite all the glamour, one is tempted to wonder: Was the Jays' a *happy* marriage? The answer is that it was probably as happy as that of any ambitious and successful couple who find themselves in the public spotlight and enjoying it. The only rule of marriage in the American eighteenth century was that a wife was to be absolutely obedient to her husband. To a young woman of the period who was about to be married, Dr. Benjamin Rush had laid out the terms of marriage without mincing any words:

> From the day you marry you must have no will of your own. The subordination of your sex to ours is enforced by nature, by reason, and by revelation. Of course it must produce the most happiness to both parties. Mr. B. [the intended husband], if he is like others of his sex, will often require unreasonable sacrifices of your will to his. If this should be the case, still honor and obey him. . . . The happiest marriages I have known have been those when the subordination I have recommended has been most complete.

Sarah Jay, being a woman of both independent nature and independent means, may well have resented these harsh strictures. If she did, she was clever enough not to let her resentment show.

It was an era, furthermore, when public demonstrations of affection between the sexes were frowned upon, particularly among members of the upper, or "respectable," middle class. Earlier in the century, European visitors had been startled by the open way young American men and women "sparked," and the marquis de Chastellux, observing a courting couple holding hands in a park, had commented on "the extreme liberty that prevails in this country between the two sexes, as long as they are not married. It is no crime for a girl to kiss a young man." What the marquis did not realize was that the couple he had witnessed could not have been members of the upper class. Among country folk and others of the lower classes, the courting ritual of "bundling" — in which a young man and woman climbed into bed together, with all their clothes on, and kissed and cuddled — was still considered a proper way for young people to learn about each other's anatomies. But it is safe to say that John and Sarah Jay had never bundled.

As the eighteenth century drew to a close, American upper-class attitudes toward courtship and marriage became even more prudish and inhibited. All that was permitted was *flirting*. If a young woman found a young man attractive, she could cast her eyes downward and flutter her eyelashes. But if he reached out to her arm, she would tap his wrist prettily with the corner of her fan. It was a mating dance of little invitations, and little rejections, that went on and on.

Sarah and John Jay's marriage was also very much a business partnership. His assignments called for him to be away from her side for long periods of time, and during his travels she often retreated to her parents' estate, Liberty Hall. Their only communication during these periods could be through letters, and Sarah's letters kept him up to date on the political gossip of the day: "Poor Jacob Morris looks quite disconsolate. King says he thinks Clinton as lawfully governor of Connecticut as of New York, but he knows of no redress." And Jay's letters to Sarah were usually little more than lists of instructions concerning duties he wished her to perform: "On the road I met Mr. Sodersheim. . . . He told me Mr. McComb was in gaol, and that certain others had ceased to be rich. . . . Mrs. McComb must be greatly distressed. Your friendly attention to her would be grateful and proper."

Only now and then did John Jay let down his patrician side enough to let a little glimmer of affection show through, such as when he wrote, "Tell me," referring to her eyes, which he had not looked into for months, "tell me, are they as bright as ever?" And in her letters to him she was fond of calling her communications "little messengers of love."

In 1788, the gossip in New York centered on other things besides Sarah Jay's parties. There was important social news from London to the effect that fashionable people were now serving dinner at five or even six o'clock, though the author Horace Walpole had written, "I am so antiquated as still to dine at four." New Yorkers would likewise advance the dinner hour, even though this would mean that society people who dined out would have the novel experience of driving home in their carriages after dark. From Paris, where revolutionary talk was reported among the masses, came the news that a doctor named Joseph Ignace Guillotin had endorsed a new beheading machine. "My victim," announced the good doctor, "will feel nothing but a slight sense of refreshing coolness on the neck." In a very short time Sarah Jay's mentor, Marie Antoinette, would be treated to this refreshing coolness.

New York, meanwhile, buzzed with talk about an extraordinary newcomer in town. He was a thoroughly unprepossessing and even loutish little man named John Jacob Astor, but he was becoming a force in the financial community. He had arrived from Germany just a few years before, had atrocious manners, and spoke with an all but unintelligible German accent. It was said that his wife was the daughter of his boardinghouse landlady (this was true). He had started out as a musical instrument salesman but had gone into the fur trade and made a fortune. Now he seemed in the process of making a second fortune in Manhattan real estate — "Buy by the acre, sell by the lot" was his motto. Certainly he seemed socially unfit for Sarah Jay's "Dinner and Supper List." But how was he to be treated? Just as the Livingstons had made themselves the principal landlords in the Hudson River valley, Mr. Astor seemed bent on becoming the principal landlord in New York City.

In any society, a man who is suddenly very rich cannot be ignored. Some sort of accommodation to new money has to be made. Even in a supposedly fixed and hereditary aristocracy such as England's, it is always possible for the wealthy upstart to purchase himself a peerage. Was this Mr. Astor's plan?

It was beginning to look that way.

But by 1789, all this talk and speculation gave way to pure American chauvinism as New York prepared to inaugurate George Washington as the new nation's first president. In advance of this April event, the city flung itself into such a celebratory orgy of party giving as it had never seen before and would rarely see again. The new president set off from Mount Vernon through great triumphal arches, with wreaths of roses scattered in his path. In Trenton, New Jersey, he passed through thirteen rose-draped arches — one for each colony — supported by rose-bedecked columns, at the bases of which stood thirteen maidens in long white robes, bearing a banner that read, "THE HERO WHO DEFENDED THE MOTHERS WILL PROTECT THE DAUGHTERS." When he reached Elizabeth, New Jersey, the president boarded an enormous canopied barge manned by thirteen sailing captains to carry him across the Hudson River and deposit him at the foot of Wall Street, where he mounted red-carpeted steps to what looked like a maharajah's howdah slung with more banners and bunting. White rose petals were scattered in front of his feet as he made his grand, processional entrance to the city.

New York made the most of the year it would have as the nation's capital, and the Jays were in the thick of things. There were parties nearly every night. There were stately and formal cotillions and allemandes that required a dance master to call out the complicated figures. There were also spirited, high-stepping rigadoons. When the president and Mrs. Washington entered the presidential box at the opera, the audience rose to its feet, European-fashion. The president, in his powdered wigs, ruffled lace jabots, and lustrous velvet redingotes, clearly relished all this pomp and circumstance. On Tuesday afternoons Washington formally received visitors, and on Thursday nights there were state dinners. The most coveted invitations, however, were to Martha Washington's formal receptions, held on Friday evenings, at which Mrs. Washington stood on a raised platform above her guests or else seated herself on what looked very much like a throne. At these grand gatherings, tiaras began to make an appearance, and bowing and curtsying seemed to be coming back into style. During the day, the president rode regally about the city in his cream-colored coach — custom-made in England and emblazoned with his coat of arms — drawn by four, or sometimes six, matched bay horses. In the meantime, the Senate debated on how the new chief executive should be addressed: His High Highness the President of the United States of America and Protector of Their Liberties, or perhaps more simply, as His Patriotic Majesty. Meanwhile, it had been definitely decided that the president's wife would be called Lady Washington.

His Patriotic Majesty had, by then, named John Jay as his first Chief Justice of the Supreme Court.

One of the more snobbish and pretentious of the patriotic organizations that had sprung up during the Revolutionary period called itself the Society of the Cincinnati. Washington was a member, and so were Lafayette, Alexander Hamilton, and Aaron Burr. Its members were given titles — Count of This, Baron of That, and so on. John Jay was approached and offered an honorary membership in the order but declined, saying that he had no interest in a society that existed mainly for the purpose "of conferring honors on themselves."

Of course, in the years since those perfumed and sacheted days of wigs and perukes and silver-buckled boots, we have seen how close Americans have continued to feel to the nation and the social system they rebelled against. But in 1790, it was all too much for Thomas Jefferson. Seeing what was going on in New York during that first year of republican democracy, he had deep misgivings. It seemed to him that, having overthrown a monarchy, America was simply establishing a new one, with new monarchic trappings more elaborate than those it had endured before. Having outlawed one hereditary aristocratic system, it was establishing a new one — more rigid and courtly and stratified than ever.

It seemed a case of: The king is dead! Long live the king!

7

The Great Silverware Robbery

Americans have always been blessed — or cursed, depending on how one looks at it — by a very short collective national memory. And Sarah Jay's "Dinner and Supper List" demonstrates how very quickly, once a long and hard and bitter war is over, Americans are able to forget past hostilities and get on with the more important business of moving onward and upward along life's ladder. Within four years of the Revolution's end, the hatchet between Great Britain and America had been buried, old grudges and political differences had been put aside, and mortal enemies had become dancing partners at the Jays' soirées.

In a sense, Sarah's list was the social equivalent of her husband's peace treaty. It was designed to forgive old injuries and to assuage old wounds. Though it drew from the upper echelons of New York society, it democratically bridged any factional lines that might have existed within this privileged group. It included members of the old Dutch as well as the old English families who, in earlier conflicts, had not cared for each other all that much. Her list crossed religious barriers and included Presbyterians, Episcopalians, Quakers, and members of the Dutch Reform Church. The Burr-Hamilton feud was personal and based on jealousy as much as anything else, which made it difficult to deal with. But otherwise Sarah's guest list included the widow of a British officer (Mrs. Burr) and at least one former

British officer himself, Jacob Schieffelin, who had spent a year in an American prison before escaping to rejoin His Majesty's forces and taking a pacifist, Quaker wife. Invited to the Jays' dinners and suppers were former Whigs as well as former Tories, patriots to the American cause and traitors to it. What one's stance had been during the war no longer mattered. What mattered was getting on Sarah's list.

Cases in point were the Alsops, who were on the very first Jay list. It mattered not at all that the heroic and patriotic Jays should be welcoming at their dinner table the unheroic and unpatriotic Alsops. John Alsop, for example, had been an uncompromising Tory and anti-Revolutionist who considered Thomas Jefferson a dangerous radical. For a while John Alsop had been a member of the New York delegation to the Continental Congress, but when the Declaration of Independence was presented to him for his signature, he refused to sign it. As he wrote in his letter of resignation, he felt that the Congress had rashly closed the door to "reconciliation with Great Britain on just and honorable terms." In the Alsop family, John Alsop would become known as "John, the non-signer."

During the war, furthermore, an Alsop relative of the distaff branch named Peter Corne kept a secret life-size portrait of King George III in his cellar. Every night throughout the war, and even after it, Mr. Corne would lead his large family down into the cellar by candlelight, where he would solemnly command them, "Bow down to thy master."

John Alsop's son, Joseph Wright Alsop I — the first of many Joseph Wright Alsops — had refused to be conscripted into George Washington's army and had paid another man to serve in his place.

In fact, when researching his family's history, the writer Stewart Johonnot Oliver Alsop was struck by the fact that no male member of his family had ever fought in a war until his own tour of duty as a World War II paratrooper. Another Joseph, Joseph Alsop III, had followed his ancestor's example in the Civil War and purchased a substitute to fight for him. During the same war, Theodore Roosevelt's father, who was Stewart Alsop's great-grandfather, had gotten himself appointed to something called the Sanitary Commission, "an elegant draft dodge," according to Stewart Alsop. In his researches, Alsop also noted that no ancestor had ever worked for a salary, and he drew a parallel between these two phenomena. "It was not so much that my ancestors were cowards, though no doubt some of them were," he wrote. "They just hated the idea of being in a subordinate or dependent position." Alsops disliked taking orders from anyone, unless it was a king.

At Sarah Jay's parties, John Alsop and his wife were still unreconstructed Royalists. The Alsops had only one complaint about the British. During the war, the British had made off with the Alsops' family silver. "It was done by enlisted men or Hessian mercenaries, of course," John Alsop would explain. "No British officer or gentleman would have tolerated such a thing."

The Alsop family had been early settlers of Middletown, Connecticut, which had become an important colonial river port and where John Alsop had made a considerable fortune in ice — though not, it should be added, as a peddler with a horse and wagon. It had been John Alsop's canny notion that ice, which was free for the taking and in plentiful supply in the winter lakes and ponds of New England, might have much more value in the tropics, where refrigeration was a luxury. The Alsop ice was therefore loaded in great blocks aboard ships, insulated with thick layers of sawdust (which was also free, at local sawmills), and transported to the West Indies, bringing a fine price. In the West Indies, John Alsop bought sugarcane, which he transported back to sell to refineries and rum makers in New England. Thus there were profits at both ends of his Caribbean journeys, and his growing fleet of merchant ships was always well ballasted in both directions.

John Alsop maintained a country place in Middletown and, a few years before the war, had built himself a palatial mansion in Manhattan at the corner of William Street and Maiden Lane. It was in the garden behind this house that, when the first Revolutionary shots were fired, John Alsop had unwisely buried all the Alsop silver and jewels before retreating with his family to the relative safety of Middletown. Unfortunately, a number of other New Yorkers had the same idea, and gardens became a favorite spot for invading soldiers to look for buried treasure.

Six and a half years later, when the family returned to New York, a shock awaited them. Their house had been used as a barracks for British troops, and the place had been completely ransacked. The garden had been spaded up, and all the jewelry and silverware were gone. This included what was then considered the finest Oriental pearl necklace in America at the time and great quantities of solid silver dinnerware — complete table settings for forty-eight, as many silver service plates, silver trays, tureens, compotes, chafing dishes, candlesticks, candelabra, wine goblets, and finger bowls, all of them embossed with the Alsop family crest: a parrot clutching a cherry in its claws. All of it, furthermore, was American coin silver, with a higher silver content than sterling. It was considered an irreplaceable loss.

George Washington's inaugural ball, meanwhile, was also the first official debutante party in the United States of America. At the English court, young women of good family were presented to the monarch at Buckingham Palace, and it was deemed appropriate that America should adopt this custom and invite young ladies to be presented to society while making deep curtsies to the president of the United States. It was an indication of the extent to which President Washington had forgiven the Alsops for their lack of Revolutionary zeal that among the first young women invited to participate in this honorary rite was John Alsop's pretty daughter, Mary, who, like all Alsops, had a pertly independent streak.

At the ball, furthermore, the new president personally introduced Mary Alsop to a young lawyer friend of his, the Harvard-graduated Rufus King, who fell in love with her. When Mary Alsop and Rufus King were married a few months later, President and Mrs. Washington attended the wedding and sent a gift of a Georgian tea service with a note saying they hoped that this would at least in part replace the family's loss of its heirloom silver.

In 1796, Washington further honored the Kings by naming Rufus King the American ambassador to the Court of St. James's, a sensitive and important position in this post-Revolutionary period and one that would set King on a long course of distinguished public service, culminating in an unsuccessful campaign for the presidency against James Monroe. Possibly Washington dispatched the Kings to London to give the Royalist Alsops a firsthand taste of what the British ruling class was really like. More likely, he considered sending Americans with known Royalist sympathies to be a suave and mollifying diplomatic move. In any case, he cannot have expected one of the outcomes of the appointment.

In London the Kings were politely, if somewhat frostily, entertained by members of the nobility, who still had not quite gotten used to the idea that Britain had lost a war. And one evening, dining at a noble house in Mayfair, Mary Alsop King suddenly became transfixed by the silverware she was using. Looking about at the heavy pieces that adorned the table, she realized they were all familiar.

All of them were emblazoned with a crest depicting a parrot holding a cherry in its claws.

"Are you interested in silver, Mrs. King?" her hostess asked.

"I am interested in this," she replied. "Has it been in your family long?"

"My husband brought it from America," the hostess said. "We are very fond of it."

"I don't blame you," the wife of the American ambassador said bluntly. "I used to be myself." She then told of the cache of family silver that had been buried in her father's garden.

There was a little silence, and the subject of the conversation changed. But the next morning a large crate of silver was delivered to the American embassy. No note accompanied it.

For years until her death in the summer of 1971, one of the reigning *grandes dames* of Hartford, Connecticut, was Mrs. Corinne Douglas Robinson Alsop Cole, the mother of the journalist Alsop brothers, Stewart and Joseph. Mrs. Cole — Francis W. Cole was her second husband — was one of the last women of her era who was never seen without a hat. She wore a hat even in her own house and carried a reticule slung across her arm as she moved from room to room. Because of her cousinship to Roosevelts, Mrs. Cole was an Alsop by inheritance as well as by marriage, and one genealogist had actually managed to demonstrate that Mrs. Cole was her own cousin, a finding that amused her.

"I think that what my ancestor did in London was absolutely right," she said not long before her death. "It was Alsop silver, it had been stolen, and Mary King was quite right to speak up and get it back. I still have some very nice pieces from that service. If you ask me, that's one of the differences between the British aristocracy and American ladies and gentlemen. The British are too stiff and pompous, and hate having to admit they're ever wrong. Americans are more open, forthright, honest and forgiving. Americans are more — accommodating to the whims and shortcomings of other people. They're more *gracious*.

"For example, when my cousin Eleanor came through Hartford she would usually stay with me. But Eleanor was always rushing about the countryside on some mission or other for Franklin, and there were times when she'd say to me, 'I have to catch a five o'clock train in the morning for Cleveland, and so I'm afraid I'm going to need my breakfast around three-thirty A.M. But don't you get up.

I'll fix myself something in the kitchen.' But I would say to myself, 'Well, if the first lady of the land is going to be up for breakfast at three-thirty in the morning, I shall be up to join her.' And I would be. Would that happen in England — even for the queen? Not likely, I say. They'd send a servant up with a tray and spend the rest of the night in the land of Nod.

"The British are always so *superior*. My husband and I would notice it when we traveled in England — even in the finest houses. A certain sense of *condescension,* as though we Americans had never quite learned to do things right. I think what Mary King did about the silver was not just a spunky thing. It was the sensible thing, the right thing. Goodness me, if a relative of mine had stolen someone else's silver, and I'd been caught with the goods, I'd have immediately apologized, and sent the stuff back, of course — but with a note. To me, not even writing so much as a note to Mary was the most inexcusable part of it. But so British. Not even to apologize. Not very classy, if you ask me."

8

From Camping Out with Indians ... to Dinner at the Jays'

If the inclusion of the Royalist Alsops seemed a little odd on Sarah Jay's dinner list of guests, the inclusion of Mr. and Mrs. Jacob Schieffelin III seemed even odder. Jacob Schieffelin had fought for the British during the war. But as New York society closed ranks under President and Lady Washington, it had to be admitted that the young Schieffelins had much in their favor. Both were attractive and obviously well bred. The Schieffelin family pedigree, in pre-Revolutionary America and in Germany even before that, was excellent. Jacob Schieffelin had been an *officer* in the British army, not an ordinary soldier, and this stamped him automatically as a gentleman. And Jacob Schieffelin, as so many young men of the day were doing, had "married up," into one of New York's proudest families.

The Schieffelin family traces itself back to the thirteenth century, to the town of Nördlingen, in Bavaria, where the family were German Protestants from the very beginning of the Reformation. There is a family portrait, painted in 1538, of Hans Leonard Schieffelin with his two sons, adoring the Paschal Lamb, the family crest (*Schieffelin* is a corruption of the German word for "little sheep"). This Hans Schieffelin became a pupil of Albrecht Dürer's and was a distinguished painter and printmaker. In 1735, the first Jacob Schieffelin, a ninth-generation descendant of Hans, immigrated to Philadelphia, bringing with him a Schieffelin family bible, printed in 1560, which is still in the family's possession. His son, Jacob, Jr., married a Philadelphia girl of German extraction named Regina Ritschaurin, and their son Jacob Schieffelin III, was born in Philadelphia in 1757.

Jacob had grown up very much a Tory and a loyalist to the British king. As a young man he had gone to Detroit, where he went into the trading business with the Indians and was employed in the Indian department of the provincial government as secretary to Governor Henry Hamilton. With the outbreak of the Revolution, Jacob volunteered and was commissioned a lieutenant in the Detroit Volunteers. Here he was attached to the staff of his former boss, who was now General *Sir* Henry Hamilton, "with the rank and pay of an officer of the British Army." In this capacity, he was a part of the expedition that attacked and captured Vincennes, Indiana.

But when the French-speaking townspeople of Vincennes learned that France had sided with the American rebels, many of them pledged support to the rebel cause. Thus, when an American force led by Colonel George Rogers Clark set out from Kaskaskia, Illinois, for Vincennes in 1779, Vincennes was recaptured after a brief battle, and both Sir Henry Hamilton and Lieutenant Schieffelin were among the British officers taken prisoner. Both were transported to Williamsburg, Virginia, and imprisoned there in the "Old Gaol."

Jacob Schieffelin was only twenty-two years old at the time and, from all reports, was an exceptionally good-looking fellow with, it seems, a way with women. Instead of concentrating on ways to escape his jailer, he focused his attentions on the jailer's daughter and, by April 19, 1780, after less than a year behind bars, he was able to persuade this young lady to smuggle him a key to his cell. Escaping, he made his way by foot across Virginia and into Maryland, traveling at night and hiding in haystacks by day, and finally to Chesapeake Bay, where he was able to board a British man-of-war bound for New York, which was still in British hands. Here he was appointed a lieutenant in the Queens Rangers by Sir Henry Clinton and assigned to quarters in the home of John Lawrence and his wife Ann.

The Lawrences were an aristocratic family descended from Sir Robert Lawrence of Ashton Hall, Lancashire, England, who had accompanied Richard Coeur de Lion on the Crusades and who had been the first to plant the banner of the Cross on the battlements at Ptotemars, for which he had been knighted by the king and received a grant of arms. The first American Lawrence, William, had been given the original royal patent for Flushing, Long Island. With these royal patents went not only vast tracts of real estate (including what is now the entire town of Lawrence) but also great political power. In America, the Lawrences acquired even more distinction through marriage to the Bownes, an American family that was important in New York even before the Livingstons. So it is an indication of Sir Henry Clinton's high opinion of young Jacob Schieffelin that he was billeted with a family as prominent as the Lawrences.

But neither Sir Henry nor the Lawrences could have predicted the outcome of this arrangement — no sooner had the handsome lieutenant moved in than he had fallen head over heels in love with the Lawrences' beautiful twenty-two-year-old daughter, Hannah, and she had quite obviously fallen in love with him. Theirs was a whirlwind and, necessarily, a secret courtship, because what would colonial society — much less Jacob Schieffelin's military commander — have said if it had become known that the British soldier was wooing the Lawrences' daughter right under the family's roof? Hannah Lawrence kept a remarkable diary of the love affair in which she disguised herself under the pseudonym of Matilda, and Jacob under the romantic code name of Altimonte — presumably in case her parents happened to stumble upon her impassioned jottings and discovered what was going on. A typically breathless entry, for July 27, 1780, reads,

> The last evening gave me the company of the Gentle Altimonte. How ardent were his professions; how amiable does he appear. Can such simplicity of manner conceal a treacherous soul? Can such warmth and apparent openness of expression cover a heart acquainted with guile? But, ah! The world is full of dissimulation, and shall she from whom her friends expect unvarying prudence fix her affections on a young stranger, and throwing herself foolishly in his power abandon every other dear connection? . . . Perhaps I may yield — but yet what then may be my fate? But should my heart plead in his favour — where will be reason, where discretion?

Hannah Lawrence's misgivings were based on the fact that the Lawrences were Quakers and conscientiously opposed to any form of war. Yet here was Hannah, toppling helplessly into love with an army officer. Her dilemma was doubly poignant because she herself was passionately anti-British and had expressed her feelings in a "notorious" piece of verse a year earlier. Hannah's poems had been published in various journals and periodicals of the day, and in 1779 she had become incensed at the attitudes and manners of the British soldiers occupying New York City. A favorite gathering place for the redcoats, it seemed, was on lower Broadway, in front of Trinity Church and its cemetery. And here it also seemed — in the habit of soldiers anywhere and of any day — the young men enjoyed making improper remarks and indecent suggestions to young colonial ladies as they passed by. Hannah's poem addressing this situation was titled "On the Purpose to Which the Avenue Adjoining Trinity Church Has of Late Been Dedicated" and began:

This is the scene of gay resort,
Here Vice and Folly hold their court.
Here all the martial band parade
To vanquish — some unguarded maid. . . .

The poem continued with such quatrains as:

Heavens! Shall a vain inglorious train
The mansions of our dead profane?
A horde of undistinguished things,
That shrink beneath the frown of Kings. . . .

It continued in this vein for some twenty more lines. Hannah had left the poem unsigned, but she had dropped it deliberately on the sidewalk in front of the church, where she hoped it would be picked up and read by the British troops. It was, and a great sword-rattling fuss ensued among General Clinton's officers. Though the words of the poem seem rather mild today, they were denounced as high treasonous sedition at the time. Dropping the poem in the street was a courageous thing to do, because if its authoress could have been found — she was not — she could have been hanged.

And now here was the authoress of those words herself, in love with a member of the vain inglorious train, one of those undistinguished things, a redcoat soldier.

But Hannah Lawrence did not linger over this crisis of her conscience long. Scarcely three weeks after the above-quoted entry in her diary was written — on August 16, 1780 — Hannah's heart had prevailed, and she had succumbed to her lover's entreaties and agreed to marry him. To avoid a family furor over a marriage of different religious persuasions, they eloped in the classic way, with the bridegroom-to-be propping a ladder against his intended's bedroom window at midnight. She had climbed down the ladder into his arms, and they were married by the chaplain of his garrison.

In this marital escapade, the couple had been enthusiastically encouraged and abetted by Hannah's best friend, Miss Buela Murray (Lavinia in Hannah's diary), the daughter of Mr. and Mrs. Robert Murray, after whom New York's Murray Hill is named. The Murrays, also a wealthy Quaker merchant family, seem to have thrived on conspiracy and intrigue. The Murray mansion was situated on the Middle Road, approximately where East Thirty-seventh Street intersects Park Avenue today, and the Murray cornfields occupied the acreage where Grand Central Station stands today.

In the Revolution, the Middle Road offered an important shortcut between the lower Post Road to the south and the King's Bridge section of Manhattan to the north. After the battle of Long Island, Mrs. Murray watched General Israel Putnam's disheveled troops pass by her house in full retreat from the British. Later, she noticed a far superior British force approaching her house from the same direction and saw a chance to have a bit of fun. Recognizing Lord Richard Howe in command, she suggested to His Lordship that he and his officers might enjoy pausing at her house for a bit of refreshment. It had been a long, hot march, and so Howe gladly accepted. He and his men were so charmingly entertained by the Murrays that, by the time his northward march was resumed, General Putnam and his men were safely entrenched at Harlem Heights, where he would regather his forces to face the enemy. Thus Mrs. Robert Murray entered American history, as a not insignificant footnote, apparently unconcerned that while she herself was aiding the Revolutionaries, her daughter was promoting the amorous intentions of a British officer.

Soon after Hannah and Jacob were married, Schieffelin was posted to Quebec to deliver dispatches to General Sir Fredrick Haldeman, and his bride gamely offered to accompany him. Part of the journey was by ship, but once the party entered the St. Lawrence River, they transferred to smaller boats and then to canoes, which had to be portaged around rapids while the party continued on foot. Overnight accommodations were at primitive forts, when they could find them, or, when they could not, in makeshift tents or beneath overturned canoes. At one point, seeing a fire burning in the wilderness, the

Schieffelins approached it to find a band of Indian warriors with their wives and children.

"I was a little surprised," Hannah wrote home to her parents in New York. But the Indians

> made room for me between them with the greatest civility and perceiving I was a little frightened, by the haste with which I seated myself, and knocked my head in the flurry, they desired me in their language to take courage. Their heads were shaved and painted, and their appearance altogether savage, but their manners not at all so — I was shocked to see a scalp dangling by the side of one of their ears — it was the size of a dollar, and fixed in a wooden ring, while a lock of beautiful hair hung on his shoulder. On my observing it, he pointed to his head and pronounced the word "Yankee."

Nonetheless, Hannah added, "We slept sound till morning in our own tent and then pursued our course."

At another juncture, Hannah was introduced to the famous Molly, the favorite Indian concubine (Hannah tastefully used the word "Sultana") of Sir William Johnson, whose services in bringing the Iroquois nation under British sway had been rewarded by a baronetcy, a gift of a huge tract of land in the Mohawk Valley, and a pension of four thousand pounds a year for Molly. "I had the *honor* to sup with her in Captain Butler's tent, on a haunch of venison," Hannah wrote. "She has a sensible countenance, and much whiter than the generality of Indians, but her father was white. She understands English, but speaks only the Mohawk. Which has something extremely soft and musical in it when spoken by a woman. . . . " This half-Indian lady, Hannah Schieffelin noted, occupied a fine house on the banks of the St. Lawrence, where she lived with several of her daughters and was attended by "a great number" of servants. In her letter home, Hannah could not help commenting on Molly's attire at their venison haunch dinner: "She was . . . in a traveling dress, a calico beaded gown, fastened with silver brooches and a worsted mantel."

In 1781, the American Revolution officially came to an end, even though the British would not evacuate Savannah until July of the following year and would not remove the last of their troops from New York until November of 1783. With his commission as a British officer now meaningless, Jacob Schieffelin returned with his wife to

Detroit to resume his Indian trading business that the war had interrupted; here the fact that he had fought on the British side stood him in good stead with his Indian customers. Presently, the chief of the Ottawa tribe made Jacob a grant of seven square miles fronting on the Detroit River, and soon he had expanded his trading activities to Montreal, to the Northwest Territories, and even to London, where he spent a year in 1789–1790 acquiring goods for trade.

By 1794, Jay's Treaty settled any outstanding disputes that remained between the United States and Britain. President Washington had sent Supreme Court Chief Justice John Jay again to London, and the British had agreed to evacuate their posts between the Great Lakes and the Ohio River, which would lead to a wave of new settlement in the area. From a business standpoint, an important modification of Jay's Treaty was the one that permitted U.S. ships to carry cocoa, coffee, cotton, molasses, sugar, rum, and spices from the British West Indies to any port in the world. Shrewdly, Jacob Schieffelin decided that this was the moment to enter the lucrative West Indies trade, and in 1794 he returned to the port city of New York, which would become the center of it, bringing his wife with him.

Two of Hannah Schieffelin's brothers, Effingham Lawrence and John B. Lawrence, had founded a drug business on New York's Pearl Street as early as 1781, and with his brothers-in-law, Jacob Schieffelin proceeded to put together Schieffelin & Company, an import-export firm that would concentrate on herbs and spices and pharmaceuticals from the West Indies. Schieffelin & Company, the "Oldest Drug House in America," is still in business to this day, two hundred years later, dealing primarily in imported wines and spirits.

The partnership was fruitful almost from the beginning. On a single shipping voyage, Jacob Schieffelin made a profit of twenty-five thousand dollars, a considerable fortune in those days, and he was still not yet forty. With this money he purchased a large tract of rural farmland in upper Manhattan and there created Rooka Hall. The grounds of Rooka Hall were bounded on the south by Harlem Cove, an inlet of the Hudson River that is now covered by West 125th Street; on the west by the Hudson, with a splendid view of the New Jersey Palisades; and on the north by Hamilton Grange, the home of Alexander Hamilton, to whom Jacob Schieffelin sold several acres of land. After Hamilton's death, the Schieffelins erected a monument to their famous neighbor and friend.

By the late 1790s, the Schieffelins had entered an era of affluence and ease that would last for generations to come. For their winter residence, Jacob and Hannah Schieffelin acquired the Beekman mansion on Pearl Street, a spacious town house fifty feet wide, with stables in the rear. And every summer they made the trek by stagecoach, from one end of Manhattan to the other, to Rooka Hall.

And it would not be long before the Schieffelins would ally themselves, through marriage, to other early and prominent New York families — including the Jays.

Rooka Hall is gone now, but Hamilton Grange still stands, restored, a national monument at 287 Convent Avenue in Manhattan. And members of the Schieffelin family still make an annual pilgrimage to the neighborhood in which their ancestor's house once stood, even though it is now a rather shabby part of West Harlem.

"Every Thanksgiving, we try to go up there to attend services at St. Mary's Church," says Mrs. Margaret Trevor Pardee, who is Jacob and Hannah Schieffelin's great-great-granddaughter. "You see, my great-great-grandfather built that church — the First Episcopal Church of America, it's called — think of that! You see, in those days, Harlem was a wilderness. There was no church remotely near Rooka Hall, and at first the family was visited by a Sunday circuit rider during the summer, and services were conducted in the Jacob Schieffelins' parlor — my great-great-grandmother had converted from Quakerism by then, to accommodate her husband. Jacob Schieffelin also did the *very* drastic thing, once he'd given the land and built St. Mary's, of abolishing pew rentals — so St. Mary's was the first free-pew church in New York City! Think of that! The incorporation of the first congregation was held on Thanksgiving Day, so that's why Thanksgiving is a special anniversary for us."

Mrs. Pardee today is a diminutive and animated widow and great-grandmother herself, in her nineties, living in the apartment she has kept on Manhattan's East Side for the past forty years. "I had to give up my lovely old house on Long Island last year," she says. "My children made me. The house had ten bedrooms, and six baths. My children said it was just too much for me to keep up all alone, and I suppose they were right. Still, giving it up was a wrench." The house on Long Island was in Lawrence, a town named for her pre-Revolutionary ancestors. Watching Mrs. Pardee move about her apartment and listening to her random memories fleshed out by family genealogies and old scrapbooks filled with fragile and fading newspaper cuttings, it is easy to see why, in her debutante year — 1912 — New York society editors christened her "that petite pocket Venus, Margaret Trevor."

"As a little girl," she says, "I'd go to visit my grandfather Schieffelin, and sit on his knee, and he'd show me *his* grandfather's red British military coat and sword that were displayed in a glass case. They're now at the Revolutionary Museum at Fort Ticonderoga. But the best Schieffelin family stuff is at St. Mary's, which is at 421 West 126th Street. The old bronze bell hanging in the chancel came from one of Jacob Schieffelin's ships, and was used to toll the changing of the watches. The original Schieffelin stained-glass window is still there, and there are several other windows that were given by later Schieffelins. On the Schieffelin window, there's the Lamb of God, our family crest, and the same crest is on the St. Mary's Church flag on the south side of the altar.

"We Schieffelins have always been given a kind of *droit du seigneur* at St. Mary's. The first pew on the right is always reserved for Schieffelins. The pew opposite has always been for the Hamiltons — and all sorts of Hamiltons have worshipped there. On our Thanksgiving visits, we always make it a point to visit the rectory, a lovely old white building next to the church, where there's a portrait of Jacob Schieffelin in his uniform as a British redcoat. And we always like to pause for a minute or two beside the paving stone at the entrance to the church. It's inscribed with the names of Jacob Schieffelin and Hannah Lawrence Schieffelin, who are buried in the crypt below. Outside, in West 126th Street, we also like to remind ourselves that the street was originally named Lawrence Street, after Hannah's family."

Continuity — a sense of history encapsulated in a place, of generations flourishing from one to the next, of old loyalties respected, of love and marriage and children and family feelings carried on — matters to old families like the Schieffelin-Lawrence-Trevor clan. One of the Livingstons calls it a sense of "Aristofamily," since the suffix "crat" implies rule and rulers. These families did not rule, though some might have liked to. But they had standards that they lived by, and they had loyalty and pride.

Alexander Hamilton's bank, for instance, was not only New York's first bank. In 1789, the Bank of New York also made the very first loan to the U.S. government. The Schieffelin family's accounts have been handled by "Mr. Hamilton's bank" from its founding to the present day. It is still considered one of the most personal and attentive of banks. Years ago, when lady customers complained that there were few places in the city where they could refresh themselves between rounds of shopping, the bank installed its famous ladies' lounge — much more than a restroom, it was an antique-filled drawing room, staffed by a secretary-attendant, with adjoining powder rooms and dressing rooms. This ladies' lounge is reproduced in every detail in the bank's present Fifth Avenue office. And, so long ago that nobody at the bank really remembers when, a woman customer explained that she didn't like to handle "used money." Ever since, it has been the bank's policy in cashing checks to hand out only crisp and freshly printed bills.

"I wouldn't dream of letting any other bank than Mr. Hamilton's handle my financial affairs," says Margaret Trevor Pardee. "Of course Mr. Hamilton was much maligned in some quarters in his day. But he was our family friend, and was a man of great integrity and breeding."

Breeding! What is it? How does one define it? Is it character? Is it soul? Is it the glue of generations, the olive branch of peace? Is it what lies at the very heart and core of civilization — even of immortality, perhaps?

"Oh, my, I wouldn't know how to define it," Margaret Pardee says. "It's not just *refinement,* good manners, and all that, though that's supposed to go along with it. Oh, and it's also poise, I suppose. Poise, and an ability to talk comfortably with people on all levels, in all walks of life. That's what poise is, isn't it — an ability to communicate with people in any situation? I also think of it in terms of bigger things — courage, honesty, responsibility, loyalty, love — greatness of spirit and generosity of heart, truth. I mean . . . put it this way. I'm *proud* to know that my great-great-grandmother Schieffelin was raised in a New York mansion, and yet could go off on foot with her husband into the Canadian wilderness, and spend the night in an Indian campground with braves in war paint with scalps hanging from their ears. *They* sensed that she meant no harm to them, and *she* knew that they meant no harm to her. How did she know? Breeding. And I'm proud that she could sit down to dinner with an Indian squaw, and find her language 'musical.' What taught her to hear the music in it? Breeding. It's all a part of it. It's *not* snobbish — it's the opposite. Oh, I've known people in my time who would say that so-and-so was 'common,' or 'vulgar.' But I was never brought up to think I was better than anyone else, much less say so, and that's a part. And then I remember when I was younger, going to pay a call on a friend of Mother's, Adeline Gracie, who was eighty years old and ill. The Gracies are another old New York family, you know. Their house is now the mayor's mansion. But I remember calling on old Mrs. Gracie, and she was sitting in bed, reading Homer's *Odyssey* in the original Greek — which she was teaching herself! I thought to myself, When I'm old I want to be just like her! It's breeding. It's the kind of example that you set for someone else."

9

Livingston Versus Livingston

It had taken the Livingstons three American-born generations of breeding to achieve the kind of social kingship and queenship of society that John and Sarah Livingston Jay represented. The Jays needed only two, but John and his father had both reaped the considerable benefits that come with marrying up.

But there is evidence that even Sarah Jay's great-grandfather, the first Robert Livingston, yearned for the kind of respectability that later generations of his family would achieve. In the beginning, of course, his reputation as first lord of Livingston Manor was of being not only an opportunist but also of being something of a roughneck. The original "manor" was hardly that. It was merely a collection of crude log huts in the wilderness, and a far cry from the array of stately Livingston homes that now lines the Hudson Valley, though in marrying Nicholas Van Rensselaer's widow in 1679 Robert did become the proprietor of a comfortable house in the Albany settlement. To make the properties of his manorship produce and pay, Robert needed tenant farmers, and it was not long before Robert Livingston became known as a harsh and despotic landlord; early accounts of his proprietorship do not make it sound at all like an early prototype of the IBM Corporation.

When his tenants became delinquent in their rents, Robert, with his own armed constabulary, descended upon them to extract the money forcibly, often at gunpoint. If he failed to obtain the rents, Robert would burn the settlers out and drive off their cattle and other livestock. From contemporary accounts, bloodshed and death were common in these encounters, and the little township of Ancram, New York, is still said to be haunted as a result by wailing ghosts of murdered settlers. They howl on winter nights and are called the Ancram Screechers.

To complicate things, the perimeters of Livingston Manor were somewhat loose and imprecise. Because of the size of the estate, it was not always exactly clear where Robert Livingston's proprietorship left off. Furthermore, it was not at all clear how much of Livingston Manor lay in the New York colony and how much belonged to Massachusetts. By then, Connecticut and Massachusetts — both of which had derived from the Massachusetts Bay Colony — had more or less agreed on where their boundary lay. But Puritan Massachusetts and Dutch New York still disputed theirs. In the seventeenth century, New York claimed territory far to the east of the present state line, as far as the Connecticut River. Massachusetts, meanwhile, claimed territory lying as far west as the Pacific Ocean. For years, border disputes continued between the colonies, often violently, and it was not until as recently as 1853 that the boundaries dividing the three states were permanently assigned and fixed. Until then, chaos reigned. And Robert Livingston thought nothing of trying to collect rents from tenants on land that might or might not have belonged to him. There may not have been seriously aggrieved Livingston tenants in the Albany area, but a little to the east, on and around the Taconic Range in the disputed territory, there was nothing but trouble.

Until the border disputes were settled, the region around the little hamlet of Boston Corners, now in New York (and so named because it was once the corner of Massachusetts, or the Boston state), became a kind of no-man's-land, which made it an attractive headquarters for all sorts of outlaws and lowlifes — murderers, counterfeiters, poachers, and cattle thieves, who played a game called "dodging the line," free from the jurisdiction of either Massachusetts or New York. In this impossible-to-police place, illegal gambling, prostitution, and bare-knuckle fighting matches also flourished. Robert

Livingston claimed the territory belonged to him. Massachusetts did not agree. But Robert Livingston did not care what Massachusetts thought.

Robert and Alida Schuyler Van Rensselaer Livingston had four sons: Johannes (or John); Philip; Robert, Jr.; and Gilbert. John Livingston died young, and the remaining three boys were raised in a manner that modern parents would find quite peculiar, though it was standard at the time. Each colonial family was set up very much like a military unit, with supreme high commandership belonging to the oldest male member and authority descending through the other male members based on seniority. Thus, with his older brother's death, Philip Livingston became his father's chief adjutant and second in command. Philip had the authority to issue orders and mete out punishments to the next eldest brother, Robert, and so on, though all assignments and decisions had to receive the final approval of the commander in chief, their father. It was not a system designed to create sibling love, or even friendship, among the brothers. On the contrary, competitiveness and rivalry among brothers were encouraged, on the theory that this made everybody work harder for the common family cause. Pitted against each other from the beginning, the Livingston boys, not surprisingly, grew up hating each other.

The first casualty of such a system was often the youngest son, whose authority in a family seldom exceeded that of a foot soldier and errand boy. Youngest sons — who, under the rules of primogeniture, would inherit nothing from their fathers — were usually left to fend for themselves, and those with any ability at all usually found that the most respectable occupation left open to them was that of a clergyman. Poor Gilbert Livingston, however, trained for nothing except subservience, would become the family's first black sheep and would be written off with no more than a shrug. Among Gilbert's several weaknesses was a fondness for gambling, and he became a familiar figure in the gaming establishments around Boston Corners. In due course, Gilbert would spend time in prison for his debts, with none of his family willing to lift a finger to help him. After prison, the rest of Gilbert's life was spent hiding from his creditors.

As for Robert, the middle son, he was dreamy and dilettantish. He studied law, and practiced it in a desultory sort of way, but was more interested in the finer things in life — art, music, furniture, and sumptuary affairs. The boys' father showed little interest in, or use for, Robert, which naturally delighted Philip.

Philip, his father's principal son and heir, was early assigned as his father's chief henchman, a job he seems thoroughly to have enjoyed. By all accounts Philip, who was Sarah Jay's grandfather, became an even more aggressive landlord and rent collector than his father. Expressing his total disdain for his tenants, he described them as "worse than northern savages" and wrote, "Our people are hoggish and brutish. They must be humbl'd."

Leaving the untidy business of collecting rents to Philip, the first lord was able to distance himself from the cash register a bit and devote himself to the more respectable pursuit of a gentleman farmer: developing his lands. Certainly the prospects seemed almost limitless. The last glacier had stripped most of the land of its topsoil, and so it was not particularly suited for agriculture. But there were forests of valuable timber, hills filled with lead and iron ore, and waterfalls that could be used to provide power for the forging and shaping of iron as well as the grinding of grain. There were fields that could be cleared for the raising of chickens, pigs, sheep, and cattle. And finally there was the mighty Hudson River itself — a stream that ran fresh down as far as Poughkeepsie, where it picked up tidal water from the Atlantic — that teemed seasonally with spawning shad, sturgeon, and bass and that provided a natural avenue of navigational trade between upstate New York and one of the greatest harbors in the world.

This male pecking order, with Robert, Sr., as the absolute boss, son Philip as his right-hand man who did the dirty work, and young Robert as the not very hardworking gentleman lawyer, might have remained permanent if a fortuitous event had not changed everything. All at once, young Robert became a family hero.

How this happened is the Livingston family's Indian-down-the-chimney story. One night at the manor house, when Robert's father was in New York on business and Robert was staying with his mother, he became suspicious of a group of Indians moving through the trees outside in what seemed like a pattern of stealth. Young Robert lowered his lamp and got into bed, but he kept his eyes open. First he heard a noise on the roof above, and presently a pair of bare brown legs appeared through the top of the fireplace. An Indian was lowering himself into the house through the chimney, and no sooner had the entire Indian emerged on the hearth than Robert sprang out of bed, seized his shotgun, and killed the intruder. It was a little rash, perhaps, but it was clear that the Indian was up to no good and was probably an advance man for others who intended to raid the house and massacre its occupants. Robert was hailed for having saved his mother's life, and as a reward, his father changed his will and left thirteen thousand acres of Livingston Manor to Robert.

Having his younger brother elevated to hero status and losing a sizable share of his patrimony as a result did not sit well with Philip. The enmity between the brothers deepened.

Meanwhile, the boys' father had embarked upon a venture designed not only to make the family even richer but also to add luster — even glory — to the Livingston family name in the first immigrant generation. This involved the first lord's friend and fellow Scotsman Captain William Kidd. Captain Kidd, it should be remembered, had started his career as a respectable merchant seaman, had gone on to invest in Manhattan real estate, and by the late 1600s lived in a splendid house and was regarded in every way as a proper, even prestigious, member of New York society. It was Robert Livingston's notion that Captain Kidd should put out to sea again for the purpose of catching and bringing down pirate ships in the Red Sea. Kidd liked the idea, and with Robert Livingston spearheading the venture, a syndicate of investors was put together to finance the enterprise. It all sounded very respectable, even patriotic, and the Crown itself approved, giving Kidd permission to capture not only illegal pirate booty but also to attack and raid any enemy — i.e., French — ships that he might encounter. Naturally, the Crown would accept a percentage of the loot. Captain Kidd set off on this mission in the *Adventure Galley* in 1696, as his backers rubbed their hands in glee at the prospect of dividing millions in pirate treasure.

What went wrong has never been entirely clear, but it began to seem that pirate ships were in short supply and that Kidd had decided on his own that rounding them up was not where the real money was. To the dismay of his investors in New York, the shocking news came back that Kidd himself had become a pirate. Even worse, he had had the poor judgment to attack and loot at least two legitimate foreign ships that were not French at all but were flying the flags of Great Britain's allies. The Crown was outraged and set out to capture Kidd and bring him to trial.

When this was finally accomplished, Kidd added treachery to his miscreancy by testifying against his former backers and financial partners. Piracy pure and simple, he swore, had been the point of the scheme all along, and the whole thing had been masterminded from the beginning by Robert Livingston, first lord of Livingston Manor.

Of course there will always be the possibility that Kidd was telling the truth. History does not tell us, because Robert Livingston was never formally charged with piracy or brought to trial. And fortunately for Robert Livingston, and unfortunately for Kidd, a document that could possibly have cleared Kidd was inconveniently "lost." The court did not believe him, and Kidd was hanged in London on May 23, 1701. But, even though Livingston hotly denied Kidd's charges and was, in a sense, exonerated of them, the embarrassment of the Kidd affair would continue to becloud Robert Livingston's career with suspicions and rumors for the rest of his life.

Another rumor would also die hard — that Livingston had managed to slip aboard Kidd's ship while it was hiding in Long Island Sound and make off with most of Kidd's stolen treasure, which Livingston had buried here and there about his manor grounds to keep it from his fellow investors. To this day, hopeful souls with metal detectors can be spotted roaming about Rensselaer and Columbia counties, looking for the buried gold of Captain Kidd. If any was buried there, it has never been found.

Whispers about piracy would prove useful to Robert Livingston's growing number of enemies. Because of these insinuations, it was not until many years later, when he was sixty-three, that Robert was rewarded with what nearly every Livingston since has thought of as his natural due: high public office. And even then the post was not as lofty a one as Robert may have thought he deserved. In 1718, he was elected speaker of the New York provincial assembly. But the Captain Kidd "scandal" would be just the first of many that would stain the Livingston family's reputation for years to come.

In the meantime, the battle of the Livingston brothers continued. At the heart of it were the unequal shares of land and money the brothers would divide when their father died, but the fight was fought on every conceivable level. And the fact that the boys were required to live in close proximity did not ease the bitter situation. Philip Livingston had married "properly," to the aristocratic Catrina Van Brugh, of whom his parents heartily approved. He then promptly asserted his masculinity by siring, in short order, six sons.

Robert, after a series of dilatory romances with young women, all of whom his parents found thoroughly unsuitable — and none of whom lasted long — finally made an even more unsuitable marriage in 1717, to one Mary Howardon, of no family at all. Furthermore, not long after marrying Mary, Robert more or less abandoned her, though their union did produce one child, a son named Robert R. Livingston. (In the family's habit of doubling names, Robert R.'s full name was Robert Robert Livingston, and it was his son, Robert R., Jr., who was John Jay's early law partner.) When the boys' father died in 1728, he must have left the world convinced that Philip's would be the strong line of Livingstons and Robert's would be the weak line.

However, once Robert had received the inheritance that his youthful heroic act had earned him, the tables began to turn. Robert quietly began acquiring more parcels of property, and presently he was building a stately mansion of his own on his land. The brothers continued to quarrel over the most petty issues. When Robert's mansion was finished — a huge red brick Georgian house on a bluff overlooking a great curve of the Hudson — he wanted to call the estate Callendar after the Scots earls from whom the Livingstons were now grandly claiming descent. Philip, as the new manor lord, refused to let him use this name, claiming it was too lofty for a mere second son. Next, Robert obligingly proposed Ancram, the name of the Scots village where their grandfather had once preached. Once more Philip said no. And so Robert turned from Scots sources to French, with which his bossy brother could find no fault, and named his new place Clermont. It was a name that would go down importantly in American history, and Clermont the place remains today. This Robert Livingston would from then on be known as Robert of Clermont.

In the meantime, while Robert of Clermont was patiently trying to find a name for his estate that would pass muster with his brother, Philip, second lord of Livingston Manor, had ambitiously embarked on a project of his own, which he hoped would make him enormously rich. This was to mine the iron ore his father knew was lying beneath the manor lands and to build a forge to shape it. More and more of Philip's time, energy, and money were going into his forge, and yet by 1743 Philip's profits had been minimal. (It would take the Revolutionary War to make the forge profitable.) Philip was running up huge debts, and his creditors were making impatient sounds. To add to his woes, settlers on his manor lands were not arriving in sufficient numbers to generate the rents he needed to keep the place going. And on top of everything else, the number of tenants who were delinquent in their rents was growing; setting fire to their houses or driving off their cattle did not seem to offer any immediate financial solution to the problem. How galling it must have been to Philip to watch his younger brother next door getting steadily richer, living a life of luxury and ease and hardly working at all while he, the furiously hardworking Philip, was growing poorer by the day! And how very pleased, and even a bit smug, Robert of Clermont must have felt from his side of the fence watching the same thing happen! Was it possible that Robert of Clermont's line would one day be known as the rich line of Livingstons and Philip's would become the poor line? It most certainly was.

Soon the brothers were battling again, over water rights from the stream that divided their two properties. When Philip's forge and foundry, and workers' houses surrounding them, were finally completed, he got even with Robert by naming the new little ironworks Ancram, a name that Robert had wanted for his house.

The Battle of the Livingston Brothers would not end. Instead, it gathered momentum — a momentum that would carry their bitter rivalry on into the next generation as each brother seemed to enter a competition to see who could produce the most successful and distinguished offspring. Philip, with six sons to Robert of Clermont's one, must have assumed that he handily had the lead. And it is true that at least three of Philip's sons had major careers in government and politics. Philip's son William, who was Sarah's father, of course represented New Jersey in the First and Second Continental Congresses, though he left Philadelphia abruptly in 1776 to avoid voting on the Declaration of Independence, about which he had some Tory misgivings. In 1778, however, he was elected the first governor of the new state of New Jersey and was so popular in that post that he was reelected governor continuously until his death in 1790.

His older brother, Peter Van Brugh Livingston, was a successful merchant and Whig leader in New York and one of the founders of the College of New Jersey, now Princeton University. William and Peter's middle brother, Philip Livingston, Jr., was a member of the Continental Congress from 1774 until his death and, with fewer doubts than his brother William, signed the Declaration of Independence, though without the confident flourish of John Hancock.

And yet it was Robert of Clermont's one son, Robert Robert, who was able to do more for the family than all of his cousins combined. He was, like his father, a lawyer, but unlike his father, he was a brilliant and ambitious one. In the family, this would lead to his designation as "Judge Livingston." But even better than that, he married the richest girl in America. What his old uncle Philip must have felt when he witnessed that event can only be imagined.

She was Margaret Beekman, the eighteen-year-old daughter of Colonel Henry Beekman and the sole heiress to the immense Beekman patent, a quarter-million-acre tract comprising most of what is now New York's Dutchess County. Margaret Beekman was already a Livingston in a complicated sort of way. Her father was her new husband's uncle Gilbert Livingston's brother-in-law. Also, her mother was a Livingston and an heiress as well, the daughter of one of the original Robert Livingston's nephews, another Robert, who had followed his successful uncle from Scotland. Thus the newlyweds were second cousins once removed, the bride's mother was the bridegroom's aunt, and a total of three great fortunes — two from Livingstons and one from the Beekmans — joined hands in holy matrimony in 1744.

The consanguinity between Henry Beekman's daughter and Robert of Clermont's son could have been even closer if love had been allowed to take its course. Originally, Mr. Beekman had wanted to marry Philip and Robert of Clermont's sister Joanna, but Joanna's parents had rejected his suit. And so Beekman had countered by marrying Joanna's cousin Janet and got into the Livingston family anyway, through the back door, as it were. It seems that Robert and Alida Livingston objected to Beekman not because he had no money; he was very rich. But they didn't care for his looks. Henry Beekman had a prominent birthmark on his face, and the Livingstons branded him "disfigured."

Still, galling though it must have been to the jealous Philip, there seemed no questioning the fact that if Judge Robert and Margaret Beekman Livingston had children, as indeed they would, the Robert of Clermont line of Livingston descent would be far richer than that of the poor manor lord.

But if Robert of Clermont allowed himself to gloat over having so far outdistanced his older brother, there is no record of it. In any case, Robert of Clermont was far too busy buying the Catskill Mountains.

The aristocratic George Washington and his aristocratic Cabinet (left to right): General Henry Knox, Alexander Hamilton, Thomas Jefferson, and Edmund Randolph. (The Bettmann Archive, Inc.)

John Adams of the Boston aristocracy, second president of the United States. (The Bettmann Archive, Inc.)

Lieutenant Jacob Schieffelin and his wife, the former Hannah Lawrence. Their marriage raised eyebrows, since he was a British officer and her family were Quakers. (Courtesy of The New-York Historical Society, New York City)

Sir Richard Saltonstall, first of the long line. (Courtesy Massachusetts Historical Society)

Governor and Mrs. Leverett Saltonstall waiting for election returns on November 7, 1944. (Courtesy Massachussetts Historical Society)

Gouverneur Morris and his New York manor, Morrisania. (Both courtesy of The New-York Historical Society, New York City)

John Jay, America's first Chief Justice, and his beautiful wife, the former Sarah Livingston. They tied the dynastic knot of money, power, and property. (John Jay, The Bettmann Archive, Inc.; Sarah Livingston Jay, The Queens of American Society *by Elizabeth Ellet [Philadelphia: Porter & Coates, 1867])*

Liberty Hall in New Jersey, childhood home of Sarah Livingston Jay. (Illustration by Doris Stolberg from Patriot's Lady *by Lois Hobart [New York: Thomas Y. Crowell, 1960]. Copyright © 1960 by Lois Hobart. Reprinted by permission of Harper & Row, Publishers, Inc.)*

Clermont in Tivoli-on-Hudson, New York, home of Robert R. Livingston. (Courtesy of The New-York Historical Society, New York City)

John Jacob Astor. Whenever old families needed an infusion of wealth, his fortune would come in handy. (The Bettmann Archive, Inc.)

The eccentric John Randolph of Roanoke, Virginia.

Three Philadelphia aristocrats: Nicholas Biddle, Robert Morris, and John Cadwalader. (The Historical Society of Pennsylvania)

Charleston's Mrs. St. Julien Ravenel. She betrayed her class by spilling the secrets of St. Cecilia. (South Carolina Historical Society)

Franklin and Eleanor Roosevelt and their children in their Washington home in 1916, when Roosevelt was assistant secretary of the navy. (The Bettmann Archive, Inc.)

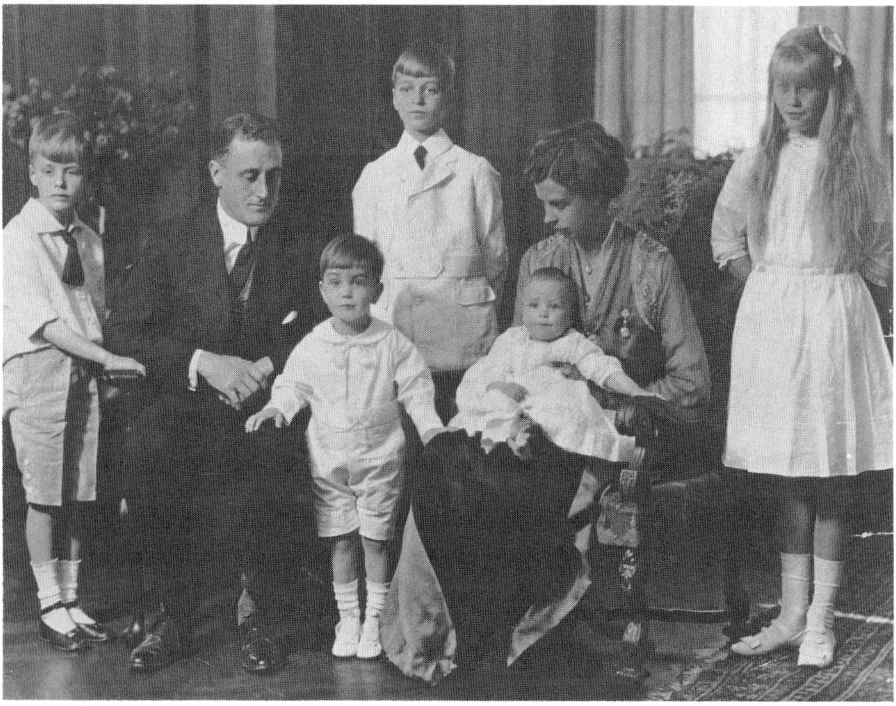

10

Weak Blood

Among all the first American families, those of Scots descent show a certain dominance — families begotten by big, robust, hard-driving men of the earth or of the sea who showed no shyness about their ability to impregnate their womenfolk with gonglike regularity and to produce, from these couplings, that essential commodity for carrying on their enterprises and their name: sons. One of the most notable of these men was the single progenitor of what was to become the leading family of colonial Virginia, the Randolphs. Like the descendants of Robert Livingston, the descendants of William Randolph today number in the thousands, thanks largely to the fact that William Randolph sired seven sons and two daughters, who gave him a total of thirty-seven grandchildren, a feat that was even more astonishing considering the 50 percent infant mortality rate in the seventeenth century.

But then we have a mystery. Why is it that, in some families, an ability has been maintained to produce at least one or two men or women of distinction in each succeeding generation, while in others the blood has begun to run so thin that talent — for business or public service or whatever — seems to have all but disappeared? In every family, of course, there is a different answer or cluster of answers, and yet the comparison between the Livingstons of New York and the Randolphs of Virginia is interesting. A Livingston has been mayor of New York City and later served as minister to France and secretary of state in Andrew Jackson's cabinet. Another Livingston also served as minister to France and had a hand in negotiating the Louisiana Purchase, even though, as we shall see, another Livingston scandal would somewhat taint that enterprise. New York City abounds in Livingston monuments, including B. Altman and Company, the St. Regis Hotel, the Hayden Planetarium, and the buildings that cover three of the four corners at Broad and Wall streets, all of which came from the drawing board of the architect Goodhue Livingston, who also designed the Mellon Bank in Pittsburgh, the Mitsui Bank in Tokyo, and the Palace Hotel in San Francisco. Robert Linlithgow Livingston, Jr., is a vigorous young congressman from Louisiana, while other distinguished Livingstons and Livingston relatives and relatives by marriage today include Carter Brown, director of the National Gallery of Art, S. Dillon Ripley, curator of the Smithsonian Institution, and John Jay Iselin, for many years the head of New York's Channel 13.

But the poor Randolphs, for all their numbers and for all their pride in being among the *first* of the first families of Virginia, have fared less well. Though the family started off with a great burst of procreational and entrepreneurial energy in the seventeenth century and continued strong well into the nineteenth century — through the fifth, sixth, and even seventh American generations — it is hard to think of a single twentieth-century Randolph who is distinguished for much more than a family heirloom or two and a great deal of family hubris. Perhaps this is because the Randolphs, as a family, did not encourage and abet such fierce competitiveness and rivalry among their male offspring as the Livingstons did. And perhaps that was because most of the early Randolphs had slaves to carry out their dirty work for them.

In many ways, the Randolphs and the Livingstons got off to quite similar starts. The first William Randolph arrived in Virginia in 1673, just a year before Robert Livingston's arrival in Massachusetts, and both men quickly demonstrated an ability to turn a confused local situation to their advantage. Since 1660, the Virginia colony had been governed by Sir William Berkeley, who had created what amounted to an oligarchy consisting of a few privileged families who had been given large plantations along the James River. One of these, called Bermuda Hundred, belonged to a planter named Henry Royall Isham, a descendant of Pocahontas and her English husband, John Rolfe.

Another planter was an English aristocrat named Nathaniel Bacon, whose estates composed much of what is now the city of Richmond. As in New York, a thriving fur trade with the Indians had been established, and with his Pocahontas connection Henry Royall Isham was one of the most successful of the Virginia fur merchants. At the same time, another lucrative product was being raised in Virginia — tobacco — and settlers were pressing westward into the fertile interior lowlands toward the borders of the colony to grow it.

The border colonists, however, found themselves frequently subjected to raids and massacres by the Indians, and these, they complained, were simply being ignored by Governor Berkeley, who was more interested in maintaining the Indian fur trade enjoyed by himself and his eastern shore friends than in assisting struggling tobacco farmers. In the years before William Randolph's arrival, a number of such Indian raids had occurred in the western part of the colony, resulting in the deaths of hundreds of white border farmers, and had gone unpunished by the governor. In 1676, a particularly bloody attack took place and, once again, Governor Berkeley made no attempt to come to the aid of his western colonists. This injustice was too much for Nathaniel Bacon, who, though he was betraying his class of plantation owners, organized an uprising — the famous Bacon's Rebellion — against the governor. In Bacon's Battle of Bloody Run, many Indians were killed.

It amounted to a small-scale Civil War, and before it was over Governor Berkeley had fled and Jamestown was burned. But then Nathaniel Bacon died of malaria and, with its leader gone, his cause fell into disarray. Berkeley took command of Jamestown again, and harsh reprisals were inflicted on all who had taken part in the revolt, including wholesale executions and confiscations of property. Among those properties confiscated, needless to say, were all those that had formerly belonged to Nathaniel Bacon.

But a confiscated estate needed someone to run it. Seeing a unique opportunity, William Randolph approached the governor and offered his services. Berkeley, who was eager to get his colony's affairs back to normal as quickly as possible, graciously accepted and awarded Randolph one of Bacon's former estates. Thus, almost overnight, William Randolph became a proprietor of a large Virginia plantation. At first, to be sure, his stewardship may have seemed a bit tenuous. Back in England, King Charles II had not been at all pleased with Governor Berkeley's handling of the rebellion and its aftermath, and had summoned Berkeley to London to deliver an accounting of it and possibly to reprimand him or even dismiss him. But, in a sudden death that may have changed the course of colonial history, Sir William Berkeley died shortly after reaching London and before his meeting with the king.

Meanwhile, William Randolph moved quickly to secure his place as a member of the Virginia landed gentry. And he did this in the classic way. He married the daughter of Henry Royall Isham, thereby consolidating the former Bacon estate with Isham's Bermuda Hundred. Once that had been accomplished, there was no way that any succeeding governor could ever dislodge the Randolphs or their heirs and assigns.

"William Randolph," writes H. J. Eckenrode, the otherwise affectionate family historian, "was essentially of the predatory type. . . . His great hawk nose indicated that he looked on mankind as his prey and knew how to make the most of his opportunities." This is putting it mildly. Before he was through, he had acquired more than ten thousand acres of land for himself and established a plantation for each of his seven sons.

The Randolph plantations were run rather like feudal duchies, and the seven Randolph sons were known by the lands they ruled. They were William II of Turkey Island, Thomas of Tuckahoe, Isham of Dungeness, Richard of Curles, Henry of Chatsworth, Sir John of Tazewell Hall, and Edward of Bremo. This generation soon established what would become something of a Randolph family tradition or habit — that of marrying close relatives, even first cousins. And so it would not be long before Randolph blood coursed through the veins of all the great Virginians, including John Marshall and Robert E. Lee. Thomas Jefferson himself was more than half Randolph. His father, Peter Jefferson, was a Randolph connection, and his mother, the former Jane Randolph, was the daughter of Isham Randolph of Dungeness. Jefferson's daughter Martha, furthermore, would marry her first cousin, Thomas Mann Randolph I, the governor of Virginia. The Randolphs would also display a family preference for taking very young wives. For example, John Marshall's bride (another Randolph connection) was only fourteen.

Of all the sons of the first William Randolph, it was perhaps Sir John Randolph of Tazewell Hall who had the most distinguished, albeit brief, career and who established the tradition that Randolphs should be given high political and diplomatic posts almost by virtue of being Randolphs. Educated at the College of William and Mary, he then went to England to study law at Gray's Inn, where his enrollment was recorded as "John Randolph, gent.," indicating that even in England a second-generation American could be elevated to the squirearchy. Later, he returned to England as the delegate chosen by the Virginia Assembly to present its grievances over tobacco to the king. It was a touchy mission, but the king so admired John Randolph's legal and diplomatic skills that he thanked his adversary by knighting him — an honor rarely bestowed on any colonial anywhere.

Though Sir John died young, his son, Peyton Randolph, carried on in his father's footsteps, and in the decade preceding the Revolution served as presiding officer in nearly every Revolutionary assemblage in the Virginia colony. Peyton married the daughter of Colonel Benjamin Harrison — whose brother would later become President William Henry Harrison and whose great-nephew would become President Benjamin Harrison — adding another to the litany of important American names that would decorate the Randolph family tree and extending the influence of the family into the territory of Ohio.

And yet in Peyton Randolph's generation, there were already signs that the fabric of Randolph family unity was beginning to weaken. Though Peyton Randolph was a devout patriot and Revolutionary, his younger brother — another John — was an ardent Tory, and the two brothers became bitter enemies. When the Revolution came, John Randolph sided with the king and eventually fled with his wife and daughters to England, where he remained loyal to the monarchy to the end. Even so, his dying wish was that his body be returned to Virginia for burial, which it was.

This John Randolph's son, Edmund Randolph, had strong Revolutionary sympathies and refused to accompany the rest of his family to England, thus creating another lasting rift, between father and son. Edmund was therefore raised by his patriot uncle Peyton and at age twenty-three became the youngest member of the Virginia Convention, which was the first of the states to adopt a constitution. Later, as governor of Virginia, Edmund Randolph played an important role in getting Virginia to ratify the U.S. Constitution and was rewarded by being made Washington's attorney general and, still later, secretary of state.

Edmund Randolph was unusual for a man of his social standing in the South in that he opposed slavery. He was also — because his Tory father had virtually disinherited him — one of the first poor Randolphs. When his uncle Peyton died, he was not rewarded with the comfortable inheritance he might have expected, but instead was saddled with all of his uncle Peyton's debts. These could have been settled by selling Uncle Peyton's slaves to another plantation owner. But this, as a matter of principle, Edmund refused to do. Instead, he kept his uncle's slaves on as his personal dependents, housing them, feeding them, and caring for them, even though this charitable course served only to plunge Edmund even more deeply into debt.

Then, in 1795, the first truly dark cloud fell across the Randolph landscape and a family belief that had developed, along with a certain hauteur and even arrogance, that Randolphs, being Randolphs, were beyond reproach. Edmund Randolph had by then been named secretary of state, succeeding his relative Thomas Jefferson. One of the most delicate diplomatic problems facing the new nation had become maintaining good relations with both the British and the French, who traditionally distrusted each other at almost every juncture. The French and English were always busily spying on each other, and thus it happened that a dispatch to Paris, sent by the French minister to the United States, Joseph Fauchet, was intercepted by a British man-of-war and sent back to the British minister in New York. In it, M. Fauchet accused Edmund Randolph of asking for money from France in return for trying to influence the American government against Great Britain. The Fauchet dispatch also hinted that Randolph was willing to sell American government secrets to France.

It was certainly a serious charge — blackmailing and espionage — and faced with it, Edmund Randolph immediately did the gentlemanly thing and resigned. Eventually, both charges were proven to be completely without foundation, and Edmund was able to secure a letter of apology and retraction from Fauchet. But the damage to Edmund's reputation had been done.

Then, as though this were not bad enough, his own government filed a claim against him saying that certain of his expenses while in office had been improper, and enclosed a large bill. This charge was never proven either, but Edmund, keeping the stiffest of possible upper lips, insisted on paying off every penny the government alleged he owed it. Needless to say, none of these allegations would have ever been made if it hadn't been common knowledge that Edmund Randolph needed money. And so, unfairly or not, the whispering continued that Edmund had been guilty of some sort of fiscal hanky-panky involving the government he had sworn to serve.

In his later years, he was able to redeem his tarnished reputation somewhat when he served as senior defense counsel for Aaron Burr in Burr's famous treason trial. Edmund's brilliance and erudition at the trial were credited for the "not proved" verdict, and the case is still studied in law schools as a masterpiece of legal defense. But Burr was not a popular defendant, and so this victory in his behalf did not restore Edmund to the eminence he might have hoped for.

In some ways, the Aaron Burr trial was a case of Randolph versus Randolph, since the foreman of the grand jury that handed down the indictment against Burr was Edmund Randolph's cousin John, known as John Randolph of Roanoke. John of Roanoke was the great-grandson of the first William Randolph, the grandson of Richard of Curles, the son of yet another John (not to be confused with John the Tory, Edmund's father), and the great-great-great-grandson of Pocahontas. As a politician, John of Roanoke served not only in the Virginia legislature but also in the U.S. Congress, where he quickly rose to be chairman of the House Ways and Means Committee and Republican House leader, and finally to the Senate. Though considered a brilliant statesman, John of Roanoke was an altogether peculiar individual. Thin, bent, emaciated, and often sickly, his behavior was nearly always eccentric and often downright demented.

He was very rich. He owned a vast Virginia plantation with a huge manor house and an enormous retinue of slaves, a splendid string of Thoroughbred horses, and a library of classics that was considered the finest in America. Yet, when he was in Roanoke, he lived hermitlike in two rude log cabins in the middle of a primeval forest. In the family, John of Roanoke was said to be one of "the weak strain" of Randolphs and to have "weak blood." He frequently collapsed in dead faints in which he seemed to have ceased breathing altogether. Yet he once rode his horse nonstop from Charleston to Savannah just to prove it could be done.

Politically, John of Roanoke vacillated wildly. At first, he was strenuously pro-Jefferson. Then he became virulently anti-Jefferson. At first he was outspokenly in favor of the French Revolution. Then, all at once, he denounced everything French and became even more outspokenly pro-English. In private, he claimed to loathe slavery. But in public utterances he defended it as God's gift to the South. (When he died, his will gave all his slaves their freedom.) He spoke often of his deep sympathies with the common man. Yet, in a speech, he once proclaimed, "I am an aristocrat. I love liberty. I hate equality." Quite often, in his public pronouncements, he seems to have enjoyed saying quite shocking things and making statements that started out seeming to take one side and ended up taking quite the opposite. When it was proposed, for example, that the salary of congressmen should be raised from $6 a year to $1,500 a year, John of Roanoke began by saying that he believed congressmen should be paid nothing at all, since they were "supposed to be gentlemen." But, he added, since congressmen were obviously not gentlemen, he was in favor of the raise, since that was about what a woodcutter earned, and a congressmen deserved no more than that.

He was a man of many hatreds and was famous for his acid tongue. He hated Patrick Henry, with whom he had a celebrated debate. He hated Henry Clay, with whom he had a famous duel (neither man was hurt). He hated Daniel Webster, and when the latter angrily accused him of being impotent, John of Roanoke replied, "I would not attempt to vie with the honorable gentleman from Massachusetts" — and he drew out the first syllable of "Massachusetts" so that the emphasis lay heavily on "ass" — "in a field where every nigger is his peer and every billy-goat his master." He hated Richard Rush and, when the latter was appointed secretary of the treasury, declared, "Never was ability so much below mediocrity so well rewarded — not even when Caligula's horse was made Consul." He hated Edward Livingston, who had been U.S. district attorney of the state of New York and mayor of New York City and who had drafted a new code of criminal law and procedure called the Livingston Code that had been acclaimed throughout the world. Edward Livingston had been dubbed the first legal genius of modern times, and no doubt John of Roanoke thought that this appellation should have been applied to him. Livingston, said John of Roanoke, "is a man of splendid abilities, but utterly corrupt. He shines and stinks like rotten mackerel by moonlight."

He was most famous, however, as an orator, and this in itself is odd. His voice was thin and fluty, and his manner was mincing and almost effeminate. He danced about the platform as he spoke, and yet he made many memorable observations, such as "The surest way to prevent war is not to fear it," which was later paraphrased by Henry Thoreau and even later by Franklin D. Roosevelt ("The only thing we have to fear is fear itself"). And he was most eloquent on his favorite theme, states' rights. "Asking one of the States to surrender part of her sovereignty," he once said, "is like asking a lady to surrender part of her chastity."

Though John of Roanoke had once been engaged to a young woman named Maria Ward — who later married Edmund Randolph's son instead — he never married, and so the weak strain of the family supposedly died with him. Among his last requests were that he not be buried in Washington, where he would lie among too many enemies, and that he not be buried conventionally, facing eastward, but facing westward, where he could "keep an eye on Henry Clay."

But the weak strain of the Randolph family was as nothing compared with what has been called the scandal strain. When John of Roanoke's father died, John's older brother Richard Randolph had inherited a plantation called Bizarre, which turned out to be aptly named. In the family tradition, Richard Randolph of Bizarre had been married when he was young — only twenty — and to his cousin Judith, the daughter of Thomas Mann Randolph, who was only sixteen. As was also something of a custom of the times, Judith's still younger and unmarried sister Nancy came to live with the newlyweds as her sister's companion and helpmeet in running the manor house. All seemed well at Bizarre until suddenly, horror of horrors, it was little Nancy who became pregnant, not Judith.

Desperate to keep the situation within the family — and out of the newspapers — the Randolphs tried to get Nancy married off to another of John and Richard's brothers, Theodoric, but Theodoric would have nothing to do with this scheme. Finally the tragedy was played out one night in October 1792 at a neighboring plantation called Glenlyvar, belonging to Cousin Randolph Harrison, where Nancy, Judith, and Richard paid a strange midnight visit. At Glenlyvar, Nancy either underwent a primitive abortion or gave birth to a child that died. The little corpse was found in a hastily improvised grave, and Richard and Nancy were charged with murder.

Never before in Virginia history had such a scandal rocked society as when Richard and his sister-in-law went on trial together. Never before had such highly placed dirty linen been aired before the public or had so many exalted names been linked in the lurid newspaper accounts of the affair — Lees, Marshalls, Harrisons, Randolphs, Jeffersons, all the names of high Virginia society that had Randolph connections, names that stretched into the highest reaches also of American politics and government. Nor did it reduce the magnitude of the sordid public spectacle when not one but two of the greatest lawyers of the day were hired to defend the pair: Patrick Henry and Cousin John Marshall.

The key defense witness, needless to say, was Richard's wife, Judith, who took the stand in her sister's behalf and comported herself, considering her tender years, with remarkable dignity and aplomb. With her chin held proudly high, she looked the prosecutor squarely in the eye and, in the clear and cultivated voice of a southern belle, swore under oath that nothing remarkable had occurred that fateful night except that her sister had had one of her "hysterical attacks." She had taken some laudanum for this, and then gone straight to bed. John of Roanoke also testified as to the fine character of his brother and young cousin.

In the end, Richard and Nancy were acquitted, but the ordeal of the trial and the scandal seemed to have broken Richard Randolph of Bizarre. He dropped from sight and died just four years later. His wife, Judith, lived on for many years but as a virtual recluse, dressed in widow's weeds. As for lively little Nancy, she seemed not to have been bruised by the affair at all. She bounced right back, and in 1812, still in her twenties, she married New York's Gouverneur Morris of Morrisania, whose family also owned most of New Jersey and who was then sixty. Because it linked the Randolphs and the Morrises, it was considered a brilliant marriage. Gouverneur Morris, among other things, had designed the American coinage system and suggested the terms "dollar" and "cent." He had served in the U.S. Senate, ran a powerful law firm, and was by then the chairman of the Erie Canal commissioners and was busily drawing up plans for the canal. And, of course, in time the Morrises would be linked in marriage to the Livingstons, who were linked to Schuylers, Jays, Van Rensselaers, Astors, Vanderbilts, Schieffelins, and practically everybody else, as dynasty joined dynasty to create the intimate network of an American aristocracy.

As for the most famous Randolph of them all, Thomas Jefferson, most American historians have tended to treat the third president's memory as sacrosanct. On the other hand, Jefferson was in some ways almost as strange a man as his cousin John of Roanoke. Tall and auburn-haired and handsome, Jefferson claimed to speak for the masses — the farmers, apprentices, and pioneers — and he claimed to despise what he called "the aristocracy of wealth." Yet no man of his day lived in a lordlier manner. He owned some two hundred slaves, a huge plantation, and the grandest house in Virginia. In the White House, his staff of fourteen servants included a French chef, and his dinner parties were frequent and lavish. At the same time, he cut down on the number of pompous, ceremonial occasions that George Washington had so enjoyed, was always willing to listen to all petitioners regardless of their social class, went about town like any other citizen, and often did his own grocery shopping.

It was his administration, furthermore, that dealt a fatal blow to primogeniture, the system of inheritance based on English law that permitted the owner of a manor or plantation to bequeath his property in its entirety to his eldest male heir, leaving all other male heirs (and all women) to fend for themselves. "The transmission of estates from generation to generation," Jefferson wrote, "to men who bore the same name, had the effect of raising up a distinct class of families, who, possessing by law the privilege of perpetuating their wealth, formed by these means a sort of patrician order, distinguished by the grandeur and luxury of their establishments." Yet Jefferson himself seemed to revel in that luxury and grandeur. Almost too much so — for he always managed to live far beyond his means.

Of course Thomas Jefferson was an extremely complex man. He was a musician, an architect, an inventor, philosopher, statesman, a brilliant lawyer, and a graceful writer. He was, by turns, a revolutionist, an idealist, and a professed believer in human rights. He was also, by many accounts, an ardent womanizer. That so many black American families have the name of Jefferson has long been a cause for comment. It was obvious that such a many-faceted personality would be seen by different people in different lights. To some, he was nearly a god. To others, such as his political foe Alexander Hamilton, he was "a concealed voluptuary . . . in the plain garb of Quaker simplicity."

But one thing is clear about the Great Democrat: He was an aristocrat to his fingertips. Consider this letter he wrote to his daughter Martha, when she was eleven and attending boarding school in Philadelphia, in which he outlined the aristocratic values of discipline, work, and the cultivation of high-minded things:

> With respect to the distribution of your time, the following is what I should approve: From 8 to 10, practise music. From 10 to 1, dance one day and draw another. From 1 to 2, draw on the day you dance and write a letter next day. From 3 to 4, read

> French. From 4 to 5, exercise yourself in music. From 5 till bedtime read English, write, &c. . . . Inform me what books you read, what tunes you learn, and inclose me your best copy of every lesson in drawing. . . . Take care that you never spell a word wrong. . . . It produces great praise to a lady to spell well.

The poor child was not even allowed time off for meals. This was the same daughter who would marry her cousin, become first lady of Virginia, and produce ten chidren, all of whom would engage in aristocratic endeavors. These ranged from the eldest, Thomas Jefferson Randolph, who tried without success to straighten out his famous grandfather's financial affairs when they became hopelessly entangled, to the youngest, George Wythe Randolph, who served as Jefferson Davis's secretary of war in the Confederacy.

All the great Randolph estates and plantations are gone now or have passed out of the family's hands. When Thomas Jefferson died in 1826, the years of lavish living as a *grand seigneur* had taken their toll, and he was virtually penniless. His dream house, Monticello, which he had designed and built himself, had to be sold off with all its furnishings and much of its land to pay his debts. For years it sat unoccupied and fell into near-ruin. Monticello probably would not be standing today if it had not been for an aristocratic Sephardic Jewish gentleman from Philadelphia named Uriah Phillips Levy — a great Jefferson admirer — who bought the place and carefully restored it to its former glory.

What, then, is the explanation for the decline of the Randolphs? How could a family that was able to rise so spectacularly in the eighteenth century manage to subside so ignominiously by the end of the nineteenth? Weak blood, of course, is one way to account for this. But it is also possible that William Randolph made his first mistake when he decided to create a huge plantation for each of his seven sons. Each son became an instant landed gentleman, and all were peers. The first Robert Livingston had a different philosophy, encouraging his sons to become rivals and competitors. It may not have made for a happy family, but it *did* make the boys work harder. In the South, the elegant Randolphs, cosseted and spoiled by slaves, could spend their days riding to the hounds, sipping whiskey, going to parties and balls, and doing really not much else at all. By the third and fourth Randolph generations, the whole idea of work seems to have become quite alien to them. When the Livingstons married their cousins and other close relatives, each new family became a kind of warring tribal unit, battling with each other for more money and more power. But when the Randolphs did the same thing, they simply settled more deeply into a life of affluence, indolence, and ease.

Unequal inheritances have always created bad blood within families. But perhaps equal inheritances can do even more damage to a family in the long run, and Robert Livingston seems to have had the notion that a blood feud or two was a good thing for the circulation and might make good blood pump harder.

11

Morrises and More Morrises

At least the Livingstons today have retained bits and pieces of what were once their great manorial lands. Considering the family feuds, and considering the ways the land might have been divided up among the many heirs, lost through folly, or sold off to pay debts, it is remarkable — even though a million and more acres have shrunk to only a few hundred acres scattered about the Hudson River valley — that there is still Livingston acreage more than three hundred years later. As a family, the Livingstons have shown a certain sagacity and shrewdness when it comes to real estate and hanging on to it, and real estate, after all, is what a landed gentry is all about.

The Morrises of Morrisania have been less fortunate than either the Livingstons or the Randolphs. Perhaps this is because the earliest American Morrises were not men of the land, like the Livingstons, but were men of the sea.

The first Lewis Morris, of the venerable New York and New Jersey Morris clan, was, in essence, a pirate, though there was a more polite name for it at the time. He was called a freebooter. He had been given a "letter of marque" from the British monarch, giving him the right to prey on any ships not flying the British flag. In return, of course, he was expected to split his booty with the Crown, and there is every evidence that he kept up his end of the bargain.

His nephew, another Lewis Morris, was in a somewhat more suitable trade. He acquired sugar plantations in Barbados and made a tidy fortune in rum. For this he was rewarded by being made first lord of the manor of Morrisania and was granted large tracts of lands on the mainland northeast of Manhattan and also along the coastal plains of New Jersey, where he became the colony's first governor under English rule. The Morris presence in New Jersey is today memorialized in the names of Morris County, as well as the towns of Morristown and Morris Plains, and in the Morrisania section of the East Bronx. Though the Morrises had been loyal Tories, they supported the Revolution, and Lewis Morris's grandson — yet another Lewis Morris, the third and last lord of Morrisania — was one of two Morrises to sign the Declaration of Independence, albeit somewhat reluctantly, knowing that it would lead to the eventual breakup of the manorial system and the end of the great manor house where he had been born. This Lewis Morris, known in the family as Morris the Signer, would also go on a special mission to the western frontier to win the Indians over from the British to the American side, and served in the Revolutionary Army as a brigadier general of militia. Later, he served two terms in the New York State Senate.

Yet none of the Morrises considered himself a man of the people, and most were outspokenly aristocratic in their views. "As New England, excepting some Families," the first lord once wrote, "was ye scum of ye old, so the greatest part of the English in the Province [New York] was ye scum of ye New." Even more aristocratic in outlook, if possible, was another of his grandsons, Gouverneur Morris, half brother of Morris the Signer.* Initially, Gouverneur Morris distrusted the whole idea of the Revolution, fearing that it represented an uprising of the proletariat and would result in the "domination of a riotous mob." But he greatly admired George Washington, whom he saw as a gentleman like himself, and served in the Continental Congress. In 1792, President Washington rewarded him by appointing him U.S. minister to France, and Gouverneur Morris became the only representative of a foreign country who would remain steadfastly at his post throughout the Reign of Terror. But Morris's distaste for the French Revolution was so ill concealed that he was not always a popular figure in Paris. At one point, during a revolutionary riot, his carriage was attacked by a howling mob with

*By then, the Morrises had become connected through marriage to the Gouverneurs, another colonial first family that had grown rich in the West Indian trade.

cries of "Aristocrat!" Morris, who was missing a leg, then thrust the stump of his leg out the carriage window and shouted back, "An aristocrat! Yes — who lost his limb in the cause of American liberty!" Thereupon, so it is said, he was roundly cheered by the crowd and allowed to drive on unharmed. He did not add that he had not lost his leg as a result of a battle injury but in a civilian carriage accident.

Finally, however, the hostility toward Morris in revolutionary France was so great that when Washington asked for the recall of the French Ambassador Edmond Genêt, Paris retaliated by asking for the recall of Morris. But, being a man of independent nature as well as independent means, Gouverneur Morris didn't just turn tail and go home. Instead, he spent the next four years touring the capitals of Europe and generally enjoying himself. He finally returned to New York in 1798, where he resumed his law practice and took up other matters. Among these were helping to design the Erie Canal system and marrying Nancy Randolph, the accused murderess and popular star of the Great Randolph Scandal.

Today, Mr. Benjamin P. Morris, Jr., a retired banker from Long Branch, New Jersey (whose father was mayor of that city for a number of years), recalls tales his grandfather Jacob Wolcott Morris used to tell about his elderly cousin Gouverneur in his later years. He enjoyed taking friends and family members on jaunts to Washington, where, mispronouncing his first name slightly, he would present himself as "Governor Morris." This provided instant entrée for the group to the highest levels of Washington society. Everybody assumed he was governor of some state or other and saved him from having to say he was a Morris of Morrisania and from explaining what that meant and what Morrisania had once been.

Actually, there have been three Morris families that have played important roles in American history, and as far as is known, none of these Morrises is remotely related to either of the other two. The second Morris family would include the descendants of Robert Morris, the other Morris who signed the Declaration of Independence, and who might be known as the Mystery Morris. Absolutely nothing is known about Robert Morris's background or parentage. He got his start when he was taken into the Philadelphia countinghouse owned by Thomas Willing, of the eminent Philadelphia Willing family, and was made a junior partner in 1757. Soon the firm was renamed Willing & Morris, and their bank has been called the economic father of the Revolution. Certainly Willing & Morris were the leading financiers of the Revolution, and Thomas Willing was rewarded for his patriotic efforts by being placed in charge of the nation's first financial system as president of the Bank of North America and later of the Bank of the United States. From 1781 to 1784, Robert Morris served as U.S. superintendent of finance, and none other than Gouverneur Morris served as his able assistant. During this same period, Robert Morris was also "agent of marine," meaning that he headed the Navy Department. He was offered, and declined, the position of secretary of the treasury in George Washington's cabinet.

Robert Morris lived grandly in two stately houses, one in Philadelphia and one in the country. He entertained lavishly, and among his most frequent guests were President Washington and the first lady. But by the late 1790s, Robert Morris seemed to have begun to believe in his myth as the man who footed the bill for the Revolution and in his reputation as a financial genius. He began to divest himself of his banking interests and to spend more and more time and money in western land speculations of the sort that would not begin to pay off for anyone until years later, after the Civil War. Presently, he was bankrupt, and for more than three of the last ten years of his life he was behind bars in debtors' prison. By the time he emerged in 1801, nearly everybody in Philadelphia had forgotten who he was, and those who remembered — to whom he still owed money — didn't want to be reminded. He died in Philadelphia in 1806. By then, two of his five sons had predeceased him, and the chance to found a great American family was past.

The third Morris family is also from Philadelphia, and these Morrises occasionally refer to themselves as "the *real* Philadelphia Morrises," leaving the impression that any descendants of Robert Morris are unreal, if not nonexistent. The real Philadelphia Morrises descend from Anthony Morris, who was born in London in 1654. Before coming to America in 1682, he had already converted to Quakerism, married, and fathered four children. Landing in Burlington, New Jersey, Anthony Morris purchased two hundred acres of land there, but within a few years he and his family moved on to Philadelphia, perhaps because another Morris family was already entrenched in New Jersey and Anthony Morris wanted to establish his dynasty elsewhere. This he certainly did. Anthony Morris had seven children by his first wife, who died in 1688. He then had three children by his second wife, who had had three previous husbands, and five more children by his third wife, who was the widow of Governor

William Coddington of Rhode Island. Subsequent generations have been almost as prolific.

Though the New York–New Jersey Morrises' fortune was based on sugar and rum, the Anthony Morris fortune was based on a more plebeian beverage — beer. On the other hand, when he established one of the city's first breweries, Morris may have been making a shrewd move, considering the number of German immigrants who would eventually settle in the city. These Philadelphia Morrises produced no Declaration of Independence signers, nor did they ever have a manor granted to them (manorships existed only in New York and Maryland), but they accounted for themselves very well. For nearly three hundred years, the descendants of Anthony Morris have produced business, civic, and social leaders in Philadelphia, active in the arts, professions, sciences, and education. "On the whole, I'd say our family has held up better than the New York Morrises, over the long haul," one of these Morrises commented not long ago. In a social sense, this is probably true. For generations, the Morris name has decorated the rosters of the most fashionable clubs and social institutions, and no board membership of a museum, symphony, opera, or charity ball is considered quite complete without a Morris on it. Morris men have been traditionally philanthropic, and Morris women have been some of the city's most energetic and popular hostesses. Among other things, the real Philadelphia Morrises are noted for that ineffable quality — charm.

But these Philadelphia Morrises are even prouder of another long family tradition, that of probity. In Philadelphia, it is important to remember, some things are more important than others. Even more significant than having ancestors who signed the Declaration of Independence is having ancestors who were on the board of directors of the Pennsylvania Railroad. From the very beginning, the Pennsylvania Railroad was run by Philadelphia's upper class. The Pennsy's presidents — Thomas A. Scott, George B. Roberts, Alexander J. Cassatt — were all picked out of the city's aristocracy. Furthermore, during its great heyday the Pennsy was the best-run and the best railroad in the United States. The great scandals and outrages committed by other railroad men of the time — William H. Vanderbilt ("The public be damned!"), E. H. Harriman (who brought strikers into line by hiring thugs armed with machine guns), James J. Hill, and Jay Gould, not to mention the notorious California big four, Collis P. Huntington, Leland Stanford, Charles Crocker, and Mark

Hopkins — that inevitably led to financial panics on Wall Street never touched the Pennsylvania. For years, the success of the Pennsy was proof that the upper class knew how to run things best.

Nor was the Pennsy's management ever stuffy or smug. On the contrary, the railroad was foresighted and ambitious. Until the presidency of A. J. Cassatt, for example, passengers from the West coming into New York had had to debark with their luggage on the Jersey shore and make the journey into Manhattan by ferry. Cassatt ordered two tunnels built under the Hudson River, four more under the East River, and the construction of that magnificent lost New York landmark, Pennsylvania Station. To be invited to join the Pennsy's board of directors was the most coveted honor in the city. Over the years, the board was composed of Biddles, Ingersolls, Cadwaladers, and Robertses — and nearly always several Morrises.

If the Philadelphia Morrises take a somewhat lofty view of their New York–New Jersey nonrelatives, the New York–New Jersey clan is perturbed not at all by this. "Our family was never interested in that city-society sort of thing," says the aforementioned Benjamin P. Morris, Jr. "My grandfather used to call it '*Sass*-iety.' We were country people. Grandfather Morris had a big farm in New Jersey, where I grew up. He also ran a gristmill and was a lay judge. For years, too, he had the title of wreck master, which meant he was in charge of salvaging all the shipwrecks along the Jersey coast. They even paid him for it." While the Philadelphia Morrises enjoy being featured prominently on corporate and philanthropic letterheads and in the society pages, the New York–New Jersey Morrises have tended to take up less flashy endeavors. Just as many of the early descendants of the first Lewis Morris were lawyers and country judges, so are many of the family lawyers today. Now an octogenarian, Benjamin P. Morris, Jr., is retired — unfashionably — in a small town near the Gulf Coast of Texas (these Morrises like to be near the sea) and in Iowa, where his son, Benjamin P. Morris III, is a lawyer. *His* son, Benjamin P. Morris IV, is in law school. And as far as is known, no New York–New Jersey Morris has ever married a Philadelphia Morris, real or unreal, or wanted to.

The Philadelphia Morrises, meanwhile, have proven to be a surprisingly cohesive family, and considering its size, there have been very few feuds. Alas, the same cannot be said for the New York–New Jersey clan, who, like the Livingstons, have been divided into two warring factions. It all happened more than a hundred years ago, and the issue, needless to say, was money. And it all started quite innocently with the death of Jacob Wolcott Morris's wife. Jacob Wolcott was Benjamin P. Morris's paternal grandfather, he of the big farm and gristmill and salvage contracts, and after his wife's death Jacob Wolcott decided to marry again. This was fine with his four children, particularly when Jacob announced that he was settling a large piece of his property on each existing child, while keeping, of course, a goodly piece for himself.

His new wife was the former Elizabeth Pearce, of a fine old Quaker family (the middle initial in all the Benjamins' names stands for Pearce.) But what no one expected was that Grandfather Jacob would then begin siring a whole new family of five more children. All would have been well if, by the time of Jacob Wolcott Morris's own death, the land he had kept for himself had not increased enormously in value as the whole of Monmouth County — much of which Jacob owned — had been turning into a suburb of New York City. Thus the children of his second family found themselves far richer than the children of his first. There were hard feelings all around between the half brothers and half sisters. Soon none of them were speaking to each other.

But then insult was added to injury, and irony was heaped upon irony by, of all things, Mother Nature. In the early 1900s, a series of severe Atlantic storms attacked the New Jersey coast, and much of what had been Jacob Morris's land was swept out to sea. Originally, he had owned a large tract of farmland to the east of Ocean Avenue in Long Branch. Today, there is nothing east of Ocean Avenue but beach. All Jacob's heirs suffered in that loss, but still the children of his second family came out better because their beachfront was still valuable. Now the Jersey Shore was becoming an increasingly popular summer resort, as it remains today.

A final blow to the family fortune was dealt in 1910 by human folly or, more accurately, greed. Into the Morris family came a man whose name the family has blessedly forgotten and who is referred to today simply as the Promoter. The Promoter had a get-rich-quick — or get-richer-quick — scheme. A seventeenth-century Dutchwoman, it seemed, named Anneka Jans had owned a large piece of property in Lower Manhattan. By 1910, this property included all of the Wall Street area, the Trinity Church and its burial ground, and all of New York City's Battery Park. But, said the Promoter, the title to this land was seriously clouded, and he believed that he could prove in court that the rightful owners of this real estate were the heirs of the first Lewis Morris. All the Promoter needed was money to press this case, and he was canvasing all the Morrises to chip in whatever they could to finance this legal claim. Obviously, the more each family member contributed to this cause, the larger would be his or her share of the valuable pie when it was finally cut up.

Everybody — her children, her grandchildren, her nieces and nephews — begged Jacob Wolcott Morris's widow not to get involved in this harebrained enterprise. But the temptation to end up owning a city park, a historic church with a landmark cemetery where Morris ancestors reposed in marble tombs of extravagant design, along with most of New York's financial district, including the Stock Exchange, was just too much for Granny Morris. She turned over everything she owned to the Promoter.

Does it need to be added that the case was thrown out of court and that the Promoter disappeared with every cent he had been able to collect, never to be heard from or seen again? Probably not.

Today nearly all the family lands in New Jersey have passed out of Morris hands, and Morrisania is nothing more than a dishearteningly depressed section of the East Bronx, a haven for drug dealers and criminals where no respectable citizen would dare to venture after dark. But the Morrises also have their mementos of former grandeur. And, as a family that started out as men of the sea, privateers, and sugar merchants, the Morris mementos are appropriately nautical. The oldest lighthouse still in service in America was built in 1763 at Sandy Hook, on the northernmost tip of the New Jersey peninsula, and Benjamin Pearce Morris of Iowa and Texas owns the original key to it. Not long ago, Mr. Morris's wife asked him, "Did your family own that lighthouse?" He gave her a look of aristocratic disbelief. "Hell's bells, woman," he replied. "We owned the whole damned state!"

12

Outsiders

By the beginning of the nineteenth century, there was common agreement among Americans of nearly every rank that the new republic *needed* an aristocracy. It *deserved* one. It was a part of the country's logical and manifest destiny. After all, the country had had a clearly defined aristocracy since the earliest colonial days, and no one seemed the worse for it. The American Constitution might, in a technical sense, appear to rule out an upper class. But the fact was that every nation of any importance in the world had let its cream rise to the top. The impregnability of the British social system and the sophistication of the French were firmly based on the concept of class. And a new nation destined for greatness demanded its own standard-bearers and arbiters of taste. To admit to the lack of such a leadership — or, worse, to an inability to establish one — was like confessing that America would always be second-rate, or so it seemed.

Furthermore, it seemed clear that the general populace not only wanted but also felt entitled to a class of people they could look up to, aspire to, gossip and speculate about, and try to copy in matters of fashion, speech, behavior, and interior decor. An upper class does not emerge by simply stepping forth and declaring itself such. It must have the support, admiration, respect — or at least interest — of all the classes beneath it in order to stay aloft. In America, the upper class seemed sturdily buttressed from beneath. Aristocracy seemed to have become democracy's cry, the people's choice as surely as if it had been settled at the ballot box.

The press both chronicled and endorsed the upper-class concept. At times, the newspapers of the day seemed to devote more space to the comings and goings and entertainments of the elite than to congressional decisions in Washington. And the fact that this sort of reporting sold papers was proof of the popularity of the theme. To be sure, there were a few spoilsports like Thomas Jefferson, who kept inveighing against the "aristocracy of wealth" and the "aristocracy of family." When, in a competition among architects for the design of the first White House, the prize was awarded to James Hoban, an Irishman, Jefferson was critical not only of the cost ($400,000) but also of the regal scale of the executive mansion. ("Big enough," Jefferson sniffed, "for two emperors, one Pope, and the Grand Lama.") Of course sour grapes could not be ruled out here; Jefferson had submitted his own White House design and came out in second place in the competition. Meanwhile, the general public seemed not to mind at all that Mr. Hoban's "design" was merely an abject copy of the duke of Leinster's palace in Dublin.

The women's fashion and self-help magazines of the period had become obsessed with propriety, with what was "proper" and "correct" and *comme il faut.* On the "model" country house ("which can be built for $2000 to $2500 anywhere in America"), one journal noted, "the second floor extends over the front porch, a thing, perhaps, undesirable if your house must face north, or if in a very cold section, but quite proper when well constructed, in moderate climates." On "The Art of Street Dressing," a fashion expert named Isabel A. Mallon wrote, "I think it may be said that the woman who walks may not wear a silk gown. It is quite proper for her in the depths of winter to have a velvet, velveteen, or corduroy frock trimmed with fur in which she may walk, but the silk frock is essentially dedicated to the carriage." Etiquette books, carefully delineating the differences in behavior between ladies and gentlemen and *hoi polloi,* abounded. When traveling alone, one of these texts cautioned, "ladies should avoid saying anything to women in showy attire, with painted faces, and white kid gloves . . . you will derive no pleasure from making acquaintance with females who are evidently coarse and vulgar, even if you know that they are rich." As for the opposite sex, one manual of the early 1800s observed, "It is not quite *comme il faut* for gentlemen to blow their noses with their fingers, especially in the street."

There were times when Americans' preoccupations with social propriety were misinterpreted, particularly by outsiders. Mrs. Douglas Cruger, for example, a New York Van Rensselaer, had brought home with her from Europe a number of statues of Greek and Roman gods and goddesses and installed them in her house on Fourteenth Street — a rather daring decorative touch for the nineteenth century, since the figures were either semidraped or not draped at all. When Mrs. Cruger announced her plans to have a dinner party to show off her new acquisitions, a friend wondered whether New York was ready for such displays of nudity. So, on the night of the party, Mrs. Cruger playfully covered her statuary, putting smocks on the female figures, aprons on the males. Bemused, a visiting Englishman turned to another guest, John Van Buren, and commented on how extraordinarily "modest" Americans seemed to be. "Oh, modesty isn't the word for it," replied Van Buren, a noted wit. "Why, we're so modest here that we tie curtains around the legs of our pianos." Later, in an interview with the British press on his American visit, the Briton reported the piano-legs quip as sober fact — it had come, after all, from none other than the son of the president of the United States.

The public, meanwhile, kept wanting to know *more.* It wanted to know who was who. It wanted the American aristocracy codified, listed; it wanted to have the families who were members of the aristocracy specifically sorted out from those who were not. Most of all it wanted the upper class ranked by *degree.* It wanted the equivalent of hereditary titles. But this, of course, was an impossible demand, since there were no fixed demarcations — an earl versus a duke or a viscount versus a baronet — to fall back on.

At first, the easiest thing for the press to fall back on seemed to be romance, and the lives of the elite were given the quality of a fairy tale or of a nineteenth-century operetta. It was not uncommon, for example, for an important social event to be written up in verse, as was the case after a grand ball given by Mrs. William Douglas in New York in 1816:

And, pray, who were there? is the question you'll ask,
To name the one-half would be no easy task.
There were Bayards and Clarksons, Van Horns and Le Roys,
All famous, you well know, for making a noise.

There were Livingstons, Lenoxes, Henrys and Hoffmans
And Crugers and Carys and Barnwells and Bronsons
Delanceys and Dyckmans and "little Devoe"
Gouverneurs and Goelets and M. Peccio. . . .

The doggerel continues in this vein for many, many more stanzas.

If this sort of reporting did not satisfy readers' curiosity about rank, a hint of mystery was injected. In New York, for example, much was written about the Upper Ten, but explaining who the Upper Ten actually were was quite another matter. Each reporter on the social scene had his or her favorite list of names, and so the actual composition of the Upper Ten remained glamorously elusive. At first, the criteria for membership seemed simple enough — family lineage, cultivation, tradition, manners. Money, it was pointed out, had nothing to do with it, because the Upper Ten certainly would have to include such families as the Brevoorts, who were Old New York, elegant, charming, cultivated — and totally impoverished. The notion that one could buy one's way into the upper class was considered laughable.

But soon these simple criteria for social acceptance would begin to crumble. The problem was that New York was simply growing too rapidly for the native-born to cling to their claims of social preeminence. Socially qualified — and moneyed — outsiders were arriving from everywhere: from Europe, from New England, from the South, from the Midwest and even the Far West. The social term for these outsiders was "bouncers"; they appeared to have bounced up from nowhere. One could chuckle about all these new-money bouncers, but it was impossible to ignore them. They were too conspicuous.

As a result of these outside pressures, the patrician Old New York families who felt, with certain justification, that they had founded and built their city and left their indelible stamp upon it began quite uncharacteristically to draw their wagons into a circle and to exhibit the first signs of exclusivity. Exclusivity, of course, meant keeping other people out, but the trouble with exclusivity was that it could be mistaken for snobbishness, and snobbishness was not a proper upper-class trait. Exclusivity could also lead to a kind of creeping obsolescence, and obsolescence could lead to obscurity. The Old New York families were not quite ready for that. And so, from the circle of their wagons, the Old New Yorkers peered cautiously out at the surrounding new tribe of prancing bouncers to see whether possibly one or two of these might be considered candidates for tentative admission.

A transition was taking place from an aristocracy of family to an aristocracy of family *and* wealth. The foresighted might have guessed that before too long an aristocracy would emerge based on money alone, but meanwhile, without anyone's realizing it, a delicate compromise was being worked out between old money and new. It was a kind of quid pro quo arrangement. The newcomers would provide fresh wherewithal with which to do things, and the Old Guard would show the newcomers what things to do and how to do them. The formal coming-to-terms between old and new money was almost like the relationship between an Old World schoolmaster and his frisky schoolboy charges — between Mr. Chips and his "boys." The youngsters might consider their schoolmaster ridiculously hidebound, stuffy, and quaint. But they nonetheless respected him for his wisdom, acknowledged his lofty standards, and loved him for his sweet and gentle ways.

Dealing with the wealthy parvenu has always been a problem in any society, whether in nineteenth-century Manhattan or in twentieth-century Scarsdale, where the new neighbor on the street is regarded with curiosity and suspicion. Put another way, the wealthier the parvenu, the more quickly the problem must be solved. In England, the rich upstart is often handed a knighthood, on the theory that if he is given a gentleman's title he will start behaving like one.

But a title would have done little to gentrify John Jacob Astor. In appearance, Mr. Astor was far from attractive. Short and pudgy, with small hands and feet and wispy, sand-colored hair that grew out of his head in all directions, he usually seemed to be falling out of his clothes. His round little stomach had a way of popping the buttons off his shirts and vests and trouser tops, and he often looked in need of a bath. He was slightly walleyed, so when he fixed his gaze on you with his left eye, his right eye appeared to be focused somewhere beyond your left ear. His thick and guttural Low German accent was almost impossible to understand. He chewed tobacco and used any handy receptacle — a flowerpot or an empty teacup — as a spittoon. His schooling had been minimal. He could read and do simple sums, but his spelling was atrocious and his handwriting an illegible scrawl. He was also, by 1800, probably New York's richest man.

His lineage was far from distinguished. His father had been a German butcher. For years, rumors would circulate in New York about an Astor "family secret," which was that the Astors were Jewish. This may very well have been true. Family historians have traced the name back to eighteenth-century Spain, when it was Astorga, and there is a possibility that the family were Marranos, or secret Jews, who merely pretended to convert to Christianity when the Spanish monarchs issued their expulsion edict in 1492. In any case, the family for some reason was forced to flee Spain in the 1700s and settled in Walldorf, near Heidelberg, Germany. Here John Jacob was born in 1763, and here the name became Ashdor. More than anything else, the Jewish rumors probably stemmed from John Jacob Astor's exceptional business shrewdness, a talent often attributed to Jews.

In any case, John Jacob had left home at age seventeen with only a few coins in his pocket and began making his way across the face of Europe, on foot, in the proverbial search of a fortune. Later, he would say that he had set down three rules for himself: to work hard, always to be honest, and never to gamble. Whether or not he actually kept the latter two of these resolutions is open to question, but he did keep the first one. For three years, he worked in London for an older brother, George, who sold musical instruments. Tiring of this, he headed for America and arrived in 1784 with the equivalent of twenty-five dollars in cash, and seven flutes to sell on consignment for his brother.

In New York, he found work with another older brother, Heinrich, who spelled the name Ashdoor and who, like their father, ran a smaller butcher shop, in the Bowery. But it was not long before the younger Astor grew restless with butchering, married Sarah Todd, the daughter of the woman who ran his boardinghouse (known simply as the Widow Todd), and then set off into the wilds west of the Hudson to enter the lucrative fur trade.

Actually, Sarah Todd was a prudent choice as a wife. She brought with her as her dowry three hundred dollars, John Jacob Astor's first working capital. She was also able to claim that she was related distantly — very distantly — to the Brevoort family, which gave Astor his first brush with respectability. Having made a quick fortune in the fur business — as anyone who was able to peddle counterfeit wampum to the Indians had no trouble doing — Astor returned to Manhattan to go into the real estate business.

Real estate was something nearly all the Old New York families thought they understood. Most of the early fortunes were based on land deals: acquiring land, attracting settlers, and collecting rents. It was a simple, and comparatively effortless, way to secure a steady income. Landlords, like English country squires, were considered gentlemen, and the title even had the ennobling word "lord" in it. But Mr. Astor's real estate deals were of a Byzantine complexity such as had never been seen before. There was nothing dishonest per se or — at the time — illegal about Mr. Astor's land transactions. But to ordinary lessor-lessee agreements he added clauses and fillips that were his own inventions. A tenant, for example, might find that he had leased a parcel of Astor land for a ninety-nine-year period for what he had thought was a fixed annual sum, only to discover, when he examined the small print, that the lease contained escalator clauses depending on how the land was used or how productive it became. Another tenant might learn that though, in his lease, he had the property through his lifetime and that of another generation, any buildings placed on the land belonged to Mr. Astor and his heirs and assigns forever. Or the reverse gimmick might be offered. The tenant might lease a building, but the land it sat upon would always belong to Astor.* It all smacked of sharp practice, but Astor was able to make his leases withstand the scrutiny of the courts — for a long time, at least. And it had to be admitted that, as a businessman, John Jacob Astor was innovative.

Soon Astor and his wife moved to a spacious residence at 221 Broadway (later the site of the first Waldorf-Astoria Hotel). Next door, at 223 Broadway, lived Aaron Burr, and the two men became friends and would eventually be partners in some interesting real estate transactions. But Astor had already made powerful enemies in high places, and none other than a former secretary of the treasury, Albert Gallatin, had declared that he would never handle John Jacob Astor's accounts. "He dined here last night," Gallatin wrote sneeringly, "and ate his ice cream and peas with a knife." This troubled Mr. Astor not at all. He was quite capable of handling his own accounts. He boasted that he knew his rent rolls by heart, and probably did.

The richer he got, furthermore, the more miserly and tightfisted he became. Every lady and every gentleman of the period had a

*When New York's first subway system was being planned, it was discovered that much of the earth through which the city planned to tunnel was the property of Astor heirs.

favorite charity or public service to which he or she either gave money or donated time. Astor had none. This was not designed to endear him to the Upper Ten, but the maddening thing about Astor was that he appeared not to care one whit. His only charity, he declared, was himself. Once, when a charity seeker reminded him that his son had given more to a certain cause than he had, Astor grinned crookedly and said, "My son can afford it. He has a rich father."

But it was the Astor manners, if one can even call them that, which were particularly offensive. In the middle of a business meeting, for example, a potential client was startled to see Mr. Astor remove his quid of chewing tobacco from his mouth and absently begin tracing a watery design with it on a windowpane. Indeed, one cannot help but wonder how much of Mr. Astor's coarseness was intentional, part of a carefully concocted persona designed to put people off. There were a number of times when businessmen confessed that they had perhaps agreed to Astor's terms more quickly than they should have, simply in order to get out of his unappetizing presence. He complained of digestive problems, and his hostesses, in turn, complained that Mr. Astor made "indescribable digestive noises" at their dinner tables. He was fond, furthermore, of describing in vivid detail the various medical solutions that doctors had prescribed for his misbehaving stomach. One doctor recommended that, to stimulate his digestive system for the day, Mr. Astor be tossed naked in a blanket by his servants every morning. Another doctor advised daily dosages of mother's milk, and a young wet nurse was hired to breast-feed the tycoon. Of such matters were Mr. Astor's dinner conversations.

Albert Gallatin's son, Albert Eugene Gallatin, found Mr. Astor's table manners even more deplorable than his father had, and wrote in 1820: "Really Mr. Astor is dreadful. . . . He came to *dejeuner* today; we were simply *en famille,* he was sitting next to Frances [Gallatin's sister]. He actually wiped his fingers on the sleeves of her fresh white spencer [jacket]."

Why, one wonders, did polite New Yorkers put up with such a ruffian? For one thing, by 1835 John Jacob Astor was the richest man in the New World, and his children, as they say, had great expectations. He and Sarah had eight of these. Three died young, and three were daughters. One of the girls ran off with Colonel Walter Langdon during the War of 1812 and was never heard from again. A second married, first, Adrian Bentzon, governor of the Virgin

Islands, and second, an Englishman, the Reverend John Bristed. Both these husbands deserted her. The third daughter made the country's first "titled" marriage, to a Swiss count, Vincent Rumpff, and then promptly died. The count, though he might have hoped to become one, was not an Astor heir. In a carefully prepared premarital agreement that his wife's father had gotten the count to sign, all her money went straight back into the Astor family coffers.

The elder of John Jacob's two sons, John Jacob Astor, Jr., had had a fall in childhood and was mentally incompetent for the rest of his life. This left only the younger son, William Backhouse Astor, named after a merchant friend of his father's, to carry on the family name.

It seemed a spindly sort of start for a great American family tree and for what John Jacob Astor insisted was to become the House of Astor. And yet that is exactly what it was destined to be. John Jacob Astor would not only amass the greatest real estate fortune in the world. He also founded a family that would make more money, and keep more money, and keep it for a longer period of time than any other family in American history.

To a man such as John Jacob Astor, even a family marriage was a business matter. In 1818, after several years as a high-living bachelor, John Jacob's son William Backhouse decided to settle down — and to take a Livingston as his bride. She was nineteen-year-old Margaret Rebecca Armstrong, the daughter of General John and Alida Livingston Armstrong. This union would definitely advance the social standing of the Astors, and it would add substantially to the Livingston family coffers. But there was a catch to it, as there usually was with an Astor lease (William Astor was, in a sense, leasing his bride for life). In a premarital agreement drawn up by the bridegroom's father, the bride was required — in return for a sum of money that seemed princely to the Livingstons but was nothing to Astor — to sign away her dower rights to the Astor fortune. This meant that, if her husband predeceased her or if the marriage ended in divorce, all Astor money would be returned to the Astor family. This agreement was to be a model used in Astor marriages for generations to come. It was also Astor's means of circumventing the laws against primogeniture.

A new rule was being laid down for the American aristocracy. Old money could refresh itself through marriage to new money, but there was usually a price to pay.

Meanwhile, things had been looking up for the Livingstons in other ways. By 1807, "Chancellor" Robert R. Livingston, Jr., had managed to live down the embarrassment of what is known in the family as his Louisiana Purchase caper.* Over, too, were his years of living in the shadow of his former friend and classmate John Jay and of having to bolster his ego with a second-rate New York State administrative title, which he had officially lost six years earlier.

Ever since meeting Robert Fulton during his Paris days, Livingston had been working closely with Fulton on his ideas for steam and submarine propulsion. In Paris, the two had demonstrated a submarine boat, the *Nautilus,* and in 1802 had conducted successful trials of a paddle-wheel steamboat on the Seine. But neither the French, British, nor U.S. governments had shown much interest in these inventions, and the whole idea of steam-driven vessels had been branded Fulton's Folly.

But the two had persisted, and the steamboat had become very much a Livingston family affair. Fulton married a Livingston cousin, and the men were soon joined by Robert Livingston's wife's brother, John Stevens. In 1802, Livingston had been able to obtain an absolute monopoly to operate steamboats — before there were such things — in all the waters within and surrounding New York State. In obtaining these exclusive rights, it certainly had not hurt that Livingston himself was a former New York State official and that his brother Edward was at the time mayor of New York City. With renewals, this monopoly would extend for the next thirty-five years.

On August 17, 1807, Fulton's Folly was ready for her maiden voyage up the Hudson River. She was christened the *North River Steam Boat* — later to be renamed the *Clermont* after Robert Livingston's estate — and she was certainly an ungainly-looking affair, 130 feet long and only 16 feet wide, with a 16-foot paddle wheel. It

*In 1801, President Jefferson had offered the chancellor the position of minister to France with the specific assignment of negotiating with Napoleon for the purchase of "Louisiana," which then meant the Florida Panhandle and the port of New Orleans. Two years later, however, Livingston's negotiations with France were still dragging on with no agreement in sight. To assist him, Jefferson then dispatched James Monroe and, just two days after Monroe's arrival, Napoleon startled the entire world by offering the United States not only the land it wanted but the entire Louisiana Territory — 825,000 square miles, an acquisition that would double the size of America. Then, most unwisely, Livingston had decided to claim full credit for the purchase, and to do so altered the dates in his calendar so that it appeared the French offer had been made *the day before* Monroe's arrival. He issued a self-serving statement to the press to that effect, which, needless to say, was immediately and indignantly denied by the White House. Livingston was summarily removed from his French post, and — humiliation piled on humiliation — was replaced by his brother-in-law John Armstrong. Livingston spent the next year and a half wandering about Europe, sulking and licking his wounds.

was hard for most people to see how such a long, skinny vessel managed to stay upright in the water without keeling over on its side. A large crowd of jolly onlookers turned up at the pier to see the *North River* off, and there was a great deal of joking. What the spectators had come to see, of course, once the craft had built up a full head of steam, was a huge midriver explosion. Instead, disappointed, they watched as the steamship slid smoothly out of her dock and moved upriver against the tide at a brisk pace. Twenty-four hours later, the *North River* made an intermediate stop at Robert Livingston's Clermont, and eight hours after that, she docked safely in Albany. Soon the boat was operating on a regular schedule between the two cities.

The success of Robert Fulton's steamboat, and of the Fulton-Livingston partnership, was not an unmixed blessing for the Livingston family. As mentioned earlier, Fulton's wife would claim that her husband was improperly appropriating and selling shares of steamboat company stock that were rightfully hers. Soon, rival steamboat companies would be challenging Livingston's monopoly to New York State waters with lawsuits that were costly to defend.

One of these upstarts was a rough-spoken giant of a man named Commodore Cornelius Vanderbilt. An ex–ferryboat captain, Vanderbilt was given command of a steamboat owned by a man named Gibbons and began operating it on the Hudson in opposition to Livingston's line and in defiance of the Livingston monopoly. Livingston promptly obtained a restraining order from the courts, which Vanderbilt also defied, but he failed to reckon on the power of the Livingston connections. As mayor of New York, Edward Livingston had appointed a former Revolutionary soldier named Jacob Hays to the police force and in 1802 had given him the resounding title of high constable of the city of New York. Jacob Hays was dispatched to serve the papers on Vanderbilt and to take the commodore into custody. "If you want to arrest me," the commodore told Hays angrily, "you'll have to carry me off my boat!" The high constable promptly jumped aboard, grabbed the huge commodore under the armpits, and threw him over the railing onto the dock.

Still, despite such attempted inroads and uprisings, it had to be admitted that Fulton and Livingston had revolutionized American transportation. The trip by sailboat from Manhattan to Albany had taken anywhere from a week to ten days, depending on the tides, the winds, and the weather. Now it could be done in just over twenty-four hours, and as refinements to Fulton's invention were developed, the length of the journey was cut to less than half of that. Soon there was overnight service, and a popular song was called "Why Do They All Take the Night Boat to Albany?"

The steamboat also had a profound effect on the environment of the Hudson River valley and of other peaceful river valleys across the United States. Gone were the sleek and stately Hudson River sloops that, with tall masts and broad sails, plied their silent way up and down the river. In their place were the noisy steamboats, blowing raucous whistles and belching steam. Soon, along the riverbanks, would come even noisier and dirtier railroad trains, and in the wake of the railroads would follow the superhighways, with the exhaust from internal combustion engines despoiling the air.

But the steamboat was the first mode of transportation to open up the city to the surrounding countryside. Steam-driven ferries and private yachts made Manhattan an easy commute from such outlying river communities as Tarrytown, Hastings-on-Hudson, and Dobbs Ferry.

John Jacob Astor may have helped invent high-powered Manhattan real estate deals. But Robert Livingston and Robert Fulton had helped invent suburbia.

13

Endangered Species

The American aristocracy wasn't very old before its members were complaining that things just weren't what they used to be. The basis of their lament was that "new money," such as Mr. Astor's, was forcing the concept of "old family" into the shadows and that precious standards of gentility and manners and probity and public service were disintegrating in the process. One of the first to sound the alarm was the New York diarist and gentleman George Templeton Strong, who started recording his impressions of a diminished social scene in 1835 and who bemoaned:

> How New York has fallen off during the last forty years! Its intellect and culture have been diluted and swamped by a great flood-tide of material wealth . . . men whose bank accounts are all they can rely on for social position and influence. As for their ladies, not a few of who were driven in the most sumptuous turnouts, with liveried servants, looked as if they might have been cooks or chambermaids a very few years ago.

A generation later, in 1867, Mrs. Elizabeth Ellet echoed the same sentiments in a book titled *The Queens of American Society,* in which she lovingly celebrated the lives of bygone ladies named Livingston, Jay, Morris, Roosevelt, Beekman, Van Rensselaer, Van Cortlandt,

Adams, and Otis — and rather pointedly omitted any mention of Astors or Vanderbilts. Of these families, who were Mrs. Ellet's contemporaries, she had nothing at all nice to say:

> These leaders of gayety flutter in the admiring gaze of the stupid and ignorant masses, but they are not worthy to be named in the same category with those who can boast better claims to distinction than merely the possession of money. It is not worth our while to treasure the names of ladies of this order, who have made themselves conspicuous entirely by the extravagance of their entertainments, the excessive costliness of their dress, or their disregard of all feminine discretion. It is very easy to create a sensation in New York, or any large city. Where there is a display of unbounded wealth, such old-fashioned articles as morality and good taste are often despised. . . . The wildest stories are extant in current gossip about these dames of the gay world. One, who is building a splendid house near Central Park, is said to get herself up with hasheesh for dissipation. Another, overturned in a pony drive, and almost swooning, faintly exclaimed, "Take me to my children!" — "She'll have to be introduced to them," observed a cynical bystander. To rise and reign among the money-worshiping idiots of this kind of fashion in New York . . . it is only necessary to possess millions and scatter money lavishly for show. No matter how the riches are obtained: dishonesty, cruelty, repudiation of debts, even fraud, provided it comes not under the ban of law, are lost in the brightness with which wealth covers its possessor. But such worse than vulgar parvenues dare not aspire even to admission to the society ruled by ladies such as are illustrated in this volume. . . .

Still, despite her obvious outrage, Mrs. Ellet was able to see a ray of hope in the situation. Cream, she believed, would always rise to the top. Of the vulgar parvenues, she wrote:

> The really excellent will never mingle with them. Their day to shine must be short, even among the golden-calf idolaters of New York. That city, as well as others, can boast her pure-blooded, pure-mannered aristocracy, deserving respect as well as admiration, and exercising a healthy influence over all grades.

Mrs. Ellet also defended the title of her book, and in a preface to the volume she noted that certain of her friends had commented that elevating her book's subjects to the status of royalty "seems out of place in the society of a republic." But, said Mrs. Ellet,

> We are all accustomed to hear of any leading lady that she is "a perfect queen," the "queen of society," a "reigning belle," the "queen of the occasion," &c. The phrase is in every one's mouth, and no one is misled by it. The sway of Beauty and Fashion, too, is essentially royal: there is nothing republican about it. Every belle, every leader of the *ton,* is despotic in proportion to her power; and the quality of imperial authority is absolutely inseparable from her state. I maintain, therefore, that no title is so just and appropriate to the women illustrated in this work as that of "queens."

Meanwhile, twenty years before those words were penned, another celebrated Manhattan diarist, Philip Hone, had interred New York's regal families in two short sentences. From an 1847 entry in Hone's *Diary:*

> Died yesterday, Mr. James Roosevelt, in the eighty-eighth year of his age; a highly respectable gentleman of the old school, son of Isaac Roosevelt, the first president of the first bank of New York,* at a time when the president and directors of a bank were other sort of people from those of the present. Proud and aristocratic, they were the only nobility we had — now we have none.

The American aristocracy would continue writing its obituary for the next 150 years. Perhaps this was because the concept itself seemed a collective oxymoron, a contradiction in terms, and that therefore, having been illicit from the start, it had always been an endangered species, doomed to extinction. And yet, as it would turn out, both Mr. Hone and Mrs. Ellet were wrong in their predictions. The aristocracy had not died out with the above-mentioned Mr. Roosevelt, nor would the "pure-blooded, pure-mannered aristocracy" be able to resist the social inroads of the parvenus for very long. After all, the aristocracy could not go on marrying its cousins or other close relatives forever. As this intramural marital pattern had already done in England, it began to produce some very odd people indeed in the United States.

*Hone was mistaken; Isaac Roosevelt was the second president of the Bank of New York. The first was Alexander Hamilton.

A case in point is the Roosevelt family, who showed a fondness for marrying Alsops, Livingstons, Robinsons, an occasional Astor (Franklin D. Roosevelt's half brother, James Roosevelt, married Helen Astor), and Delanos, but mostly other Roosevelts. The paternal great-great-great-great-grandfathers of both Franklin D. Roosevelt and his wife, Eleanor, for example, were brothers, and when Franklin D. was running for the presidency in 1931, *Fortune* magazine, attempting to unravel the Roosevelts, worked it out that his son James was "his own sixth cousin once removed." Meanwhile, Eleanor Roosevelt's father was Franklin D. Roosevelt's godfather.

All American Roosevelts descend from a common ancestor, a Dutch immigrant to Nieuw Amsterdam named Klaes Martensen Van Rosenvelt who arrived on these shores in 1644, some thirty years before the first Robert Livingston. The Roosevelts' rise, however, was not as rapid and spectacular as the Livingstons', and both Roosevelts who became U.S. presidents emphasized the populist point that their common ancestor was "very common" and could not even spell his name. For four generations, American Roosevelts busied themselves in trade, farming, and real estate management, and prospered modestly. It was not until the fifth generation that the family produced a really rich Roosevelt. He was James Roosevelt I, a wealthy hardware merchant. He was followed by his son Isaac, who in addition to becoming a bank president also built New York's first sugar refinery and became the first family politician as a member of the New York State Senate. After Isaac, it became something of a Roosevelt family tradition to enter public service. In all, there have been five Roosevelts who have held the post of assistant secretary of the navy. These have been Henry Livingston Roosevelt, Theodore Roosevelt, Franklin D. Roosevelt, Theodore Roosevelt, Jr., and Theodore Douglas Robinson.

In the nineteenth century, the Roosevelt name acquired additional luster — and money — through James Henry Roosevelt, who, like his collateral descendant Franklin, was stricken with polio in the prime of his life and who, like Franklin, refused to let his illness defeat him. A brilliant lawyer, he continued to practice law from his sickbed and, when he died, was the first Roosevelt multimillionaire. Since he had never married, most of his fortune was left to found New York's Roosevelt Hospital, to the distress of his many nieces and nephews.

But, at the same time, some peculiarities were beginning to show up in the Roosevelt family tree. There was the case of the battling Roosevelt brothers, for instance. These were the two sons of Robert Barnwell Roosevelt: Robert Barnwell, Jr., and John Ellis Roosevelt, whose rivalry erupted into a nineteenth-century tabloid scandal. Both brothers had built large places adjacent to each other on Long Island, but in order to protect their respective domains from each other both erected tall and ugly spite fences — topped with jagged pieces of broken glass and barbed wire — around their houses. Both brothers married twice, and both of their two marriages ended in divorce. By his first wife John Ellis had two daughters, one of whom married her second cousin, Philip Roosevelt, and the other of whom married a man named Fairman Dick, who was killed in a hunting accident. For his second wife, John Ellis chose the daughter of a Navy paymaster who was twenty-five years his junior and also the sister of his brother's second wife. This marriage was soon in the divorce courts, and the case reached the newspaper headlines when Robert Barnwell Roosevelt, Jr., took the witness stand to testify against his older brother, describing the "unprintable" language of a stevedore that he had heard John Ellis use to verbally abuse his young wife in drunken rages.

Drink was becoming something of a family curse, particularly in the Roosevelt line that was also graced by Livingstons. Philip ("The Signer") Livingston's grandson, Edward Livingston, had a daughter, Elizabeth, who married Edward Ludlow. Their daughter, Mary Livingston Ludlow, married Valentine Hall, Jr., whose considerable inheritance came from a British land grant. Valentine Hall had been an alcoholic and had led a life of wild carousal and dissipation as a youth. But then he had reformed and, in the process, had found God. He hired a full-time preacher to live with his wife and family in his gloomy mansion on the Hudson, and to whomever would listen, he and his live-in clergyman would deliver sermons together on the evils of drink and the joys of joining hands with Jesus. His relatives dreaded the periodic visits that were required to this dour household and the hellfire-and-brimstone homilies that inevitably went with them.

Valentine Hall was an autocratic man who dominated his wife and demanded only that she be beautiful and bear him children. The latter she did six times, producing four daughters and two sons. The oldest of the girls, Anna, would become Eleanor Roosevelt's mother. All the Hall children were in one way or another peculiar.

The two boys, probably in rebellion against their sermonizing, teetotaling father, both became alcoholics and were members of the high-living nineteenth-century crowd that moved in the wake of Diamond Jim Brady. Both were guests at the notorious "Jack Horner Pie" dinner that was tossed in Brady's honor by James L. Breeze in the 1890s. A stag affair for twelve guests only, its highlight came when a huge pie was rolled in, out of which stepped a naked dancing girl who was presented to Brady. Lest the other guests be disappointed, she was soon joined by eleven other ladies, similarly unclad.

When Valentine Hall, Jr., perhaps mercifully, died in 1880 at the age of forty-six, his children really began to kick up their heels. Daughters Edith, Elizabeth, and Maude became hard drinkers and heavy gamblers, falling in and out of love with great rapidity and always with inappropriate men. Son Valentine Hall III was the heaviest drinker of all and lived reclusively in his bedroom in the family mansion, where all day long he sat at a window, drinking, with a shotgun across his knees. At any stranger or family member who appeared within his range he would fire a shot that was usually, thanks to his condition, well off-target. Still, it was a disconcerting habit that "Uncle Vallie" had and one that made visits to the house something of an ordeal. Fortunately, he was carried off by drink at an early age.

Anna seemed to be the only straight one of the Hall children, and for this she was considered the most peculiar of all. But she, too, would demonstrate certain eccentricities, and her life would also be cursed by alcohol. While still in her teens, she announced her engagement to a handsome neighbor, Elliott Roosevelt, who was then just twenty-one. It was thought to be a splendid match — because of who the Roosevelts were and because it united two prominent Hudson Valley families — and an engagement party for Anna was thrown by Miss Laura Delano, whose older sister Sara had married Elliott Roosevelt's cousin James and would become Franklin D. Roosevelt's mother. The Delanos, whose American ancestry went back to 1621, considered themselves even grander than the Roosevelts, and with an ancestral fortune made in the China trade, they were even richer.

The future seemed bright for young Anna Hall and Elliott Roosevelt. In a few years' time, his brother Teddy would be governor of New York and, a few years after that, president of the United States. But for all his good looks and charm, Elliott Roosevelt did not have his older brother's famous stamina and gumption. He suffered from something that at the time was diagnosed as epilepsy but may in fact have been a brain tumor. He was subject to sudden fits, dizzy spells, and violent headaches. To relieve his pain from these, he also resorted to the bottle. In addition, he felt no need, nor desire, to work, and despite a number of efforts on his family's part to find him jobs, he was never good at anything and preferred parties, polo, and riding to the hounds from the huge mansion he built for himself in Hempstead, Long Island. It wasn't long before Anna Hall Roosevelt realized that she had married a drunkard and a wastrel.

She herself, meanwhile, was turning out to be far from the perfect wife. She fancied herself, and was, beautiful, and she was extremely vain. When her daughter Eleanor was born, she complained that the child had inherited the overlong Livingston nose, and from the time Eleanor Roosevelt was a little girl, she was constantly reminded by her mother that she was plain. When, no doubt as a result, Eleanor grew to be a painfully shy, introverted, and solemn adolescent, her mother gave her the cruel nickname "Granny." At the same time, Anna Hall Roosevelt enjoyed rhapsodizing about her own good looks and liked to boast that Robert Burns had been so smitten by her that he had recited his poetry to her while she was having her portrait painted in Switzerland.* Anna was also fond of foreign travel and, perhaps to escape her alcoholic husband, was often on extended tours about the world, disporting herself while becoming a stranger to her children, who were left in the care of governesses and nurses. If Anna Hall Roosevelt was proving an imperfect wife, she was also an even more imperfect mother.

Anna and Elliott Roosevelt had three children — Eleanor; Elliott, Jr.; and Gracie Hall, the last a boy despite his name (in later life he would use the name Hall Roosevelt) — but with the birth of each child the parents' quarrels became more violent. The more Anna berated her husband over his drinking, the more he drank, and by the time she was twenty-five Anna had a new complaint: the ordeal of living with her husband was causing her to lose her looks. Elliott began to threaten to commit suicide, and he would disappear for months at a time while his cast-off family had no idea of his where-

*This, at least, is the unlikely family tale passed on by Anna's grandson, James Roosevelt, in his book, *My Parents*. Robert Burns died in 1796, and Anna Hall Roosevelt was not born until 1863. It was either a different poet, or Robert Burns was singing to her from his grave.

abouts. During one of these absences his son Elliott, Jr., died of smallpox at the age of four.

At the time, various European health spas were widely touted as providing cures for alcoholism, and when she could find him, Anna began escorting her husband to a series of these drying-out resorts. None of them worked. After her son Hall was born during the last one of these trips, Anna decided she had had enough of Elliott. She had discovered among other things that he had squandered all but $200,000 of his inheritance. In a panic, Anna had her husband committed to a hospital for the mentally ill in Paris. She then returned to America and immediately instituted a lawsuit to have him declared legally insane by the U.S. courts so that she could be given control of what was left of his money. Naturally, the case made tabloid headlines.

From Paris, Elliott Roosevelt countered with a claim that he had been kidnapped by his wife, that all she was after was his fortune, and that he was being victimized by his family. Pending settlement of the matter, he was released from the French mental hospital and promptly moved in with a Parisian lady of easy virtue, upon whom he began spending more money. He claimed that she gave him "love instead of lectures." To try to clear up the whole untidy business, Teddy Roosevelt was dispatched to Europe to reason with his brother. He found Elliott in terrible shape. But he succeeded in persuading Elliott to return to America, enter an alcoholism treatment center, and set up a trust to care for his wife and two surviving children. In return, Anna would agree to drop her lawsuit against him. But Elliott's stay at the American clinic lasted only a week or so before he was back at his old routine. When Anna refused to let him back into her house, he disappeared again. Eventually he turned up at a relative's farm in Virginia, and Anna and her children moved to a house in mid-Manhattan.

The family's troubles, however, were far from over. Within a few months of her husband's return from Europe, Anna Hall Roosevelt became ill with diphtheria and died in her New York house. Her looks gone, withered by illness, she looked much older than her twenty-nine years. Even on her deathbed, she refused to see her husband. Two years later, he too was dead from injuries suffered in a fall, presumably when drunk. Thus Eleanor Roosevelt was an orphan at ten with a baby brother to care for. Over the next years, the two children — sometimes separately, sometimes together — would be taken in by a long series of relatives and family friends, some of whom were more caring than others. During this period, also, Eleanor would watch her uncle Theodore become president of the United States and her cousin Alice, whom the press had dubbed The Princess (and who had been Eleanor's best, if not only, childhood friend), cavorting delightedly in the public spotlight.

Against this backdrop of family discord, financial and emotional chaos, neglect, and psychological abuse, it is perhaps astonishing that Eleanor Roosevelt would emerge as a woman who, in periodic polls of most admired women in the world, is still ranked near the very top of the list.

Or perhaps hers was a case of "class will tell."

Class, however, did not tell in the case of Eleanor's little brother Hall. Like his father, Hall Roosevelt was sent to Groton and Harvard, where he was a superior student and seemed destined for great things. But then something happened, as had happened to his father. He married, had a son, Danny, divorced, and began drinking heavily. One day at the family mansion at Hyde Park, in a drunken rage, he picked up his young son and hurled him to the ground, breaking his collarbone. Though drunk, Hall insisted on driving Danny to the hospital and, on the way, turned his car over in a ditch. The trip to the hospital was completed by a New York state trooper. For a while, the family's hopes centered on young Danny, but he was killed in an airplane crash while still young. Hall Roosevelt's drinking increased, and he enjoyed taking his young nieces and nephews — who thought it all marvelous fun — on barhopping and nightclubbing adventures in New York, unbeknownst to their parents. He died at age fifty, a failure and a disgrace, and the despair of his sister, who loved him dearly.

Perhaps, by the nineteenth century, the American aristocracy had begun to believe that it could behave exactly as it chose and that any aberrant carryings-on could be tolerated and brushed off as mere upper-crust "eccentricity," just the way titled eccentrics have long been tolerated and even encouraged in England. In Boston, for example, it has been said that if an Adams chose to stand on her head in the middle of Boston Common, her friends would merely comment, "By the way, I saw Abigail Adams today. She was standing on her head in the Common," and that would be that. Certainly many aristocratic American families tend to speak almost proudly of their eccentric relatives, and the Roosevelts are no exception.

In the James Roosevelt branch of the family — the so-called Hyde Park branch, as opposed to the Oyster Bay branch — the first James Roosevelt had a son named Isaac, the bank president, and Isaac had a son named James, whose passing was noted by Philip Hone and who had a son named Isaac, who had a son named James, and so it would go. (The practice of re-using first names in alternating generations was common among a number of old families; because the first John Jay had a son named William, William had a son named John, and Williams and Johns have taken generational turns in the Jay family's naming process right down to the present day.) The second Isaac Roosevelt was the first family eccentric. He was a doctor who refused to practice medicine because he couldn't stand the sight of blood.

His son James was more a rebel than an eccentric. He married twice. His first wife was Rebecca Howland, and this was considered a respectable union. Breaking the son-naming pattern and adding a new, Roosevelt fillip to it, their only son was named James Roosevelt Roosevelt, who came to be known as "Rosy" Roosevelt. When Rebecca Howland Roosevelt died in 1876, her widower made a second marriage that was considered less respectable, to Sara Delano. There was nothing wrong with the Delanos, of course, except that she was twenty-six and her husband was fifty-two, twice her age. Even that might have been acceptable if Sara had not been exactly the same age as her husband's son, Rosy. It was whispered that Sara was more interested in Rosy than she was in his father. In any case, James and Sara Roosevelt's son was Franklin Delano Roosevelt. Sara became passionately devoted to her only child and ignored her husband. Mother and son made long and frequent journeys to Europe, leaving James Roosevelt behind.

James Roosevelt's older son, Rosy, was also rebellious. Having married, quite properly, Helen Astor, he had a son, James IV, and then divorced his wife — the first divorce in the family — and proceeded to marry an English barmaid named Betty, which was a scandal because Betty was obviously a "commoner." Though many members of his family refused to accept Betty, Rosy and Betty's was a long and happy marriage.

Rosy's son James was less fortunate. He became involved with a young woman who, it was said with confidence, was no better than a streetwalker. When he insisted on marrying her, he was both disowned and disinherited by his father, and his marriage, unlike his father's, was not a success. Still, this James was not as unhappy as he might have been. His mother left him a nice share of her Astor millions in a trust fund that yielded him an income of sixty thousand dollars a year, though he ignored this windfall. After his streetwalker returned to the pavements, he became a recluse and lived in an abandoned garage in the Bronx. When his trust officers asked him how he intended to spend his income, he told them it was none of their business. Certain members of his family, knowing he was rich, tried to befriend him and lure him back into the Roosevelt fold, but he told them to leave him alone. When he died, just in case they might have been remembered in his will, his relatives gave him an expensive funeral, "as would befit a Roosevelt." But when his will was read, all his millions were left to the Salvation Army.

Aunt Laura Delano, Sara Delano Roosevelt's youngest sister, was also a little "different." Having been jilted by a lover who had left her to marry one of her other sisters — there were eleven Delano children in that generation — she had become a spinster, and invited a distant unmarried female cousin to live with her in spinsterhood. Theirs became a lifelong, passionate relationship. Though they quarreled frequently and bitterly, there were always tearful reconciliations. As Aunt Laura Delano grew older, her oddities grew more pronounced. She dyed her hair a bright purple and developed a fixation that the end of the world was at hand. One morning she awoke to find the skies unnaturally dark. Her maid explained that a solar eclipse was taking place. But later Aunt Laura appeared at the family breakfast table, dressed in her finest traveling costume, gloved and hatted and carrying her jewelry case. "Despite what they say," she announced, "this is clearly the end of the world. I have dressed for the occasion. I have my jewels and I am ready to go to heaven."

But of all the troubles that have seemed to plague the Roosevelt family, perhaps the most baffling is the long-standing enmity that existed between Franklin and Eleanor Roosevelt and their mutual cousin, the famously sharp-tongued Alice Roosevelt Longworth. As children, Alice and Eleanor — they were the same age — had been the closest of friends. Alice had been a bridesmaid at Eleanor's wedding (accepting the invitation, Alice had written, "It will be too much Fun!"). And yet, during FDR's White House years, Alice had only the most rude and caustic things to say about the couple residing at 1600 Pennsylvania Avenue. She enjoyed comparing her own father's robust physique with Franklin Roosevelt's physically handicapped one, and once declared that FDR was "dragging the whole country into the wheelchair with him." At parties, she performed hilarious, and cruelly accurate, imitations of Eleanor Roosevelt, mimicking Eleanor's fluty voice and somewhat lisping speech. Fluttering her hands helplessly about her, Alice would say, "Oh, dear me, we never did know what to do with these big flippers, did we!" Once, having heard of these performances, Eleanor Roosevelt asked Alice Longworth to demonstrate one for her. Wickedly, gleefully, Alice launched into one of her imitations. Whether Mrs. Roosevelt was hurt or amused by Alice's act she was too much a lady to let on.

Was it simply politics that caused Alice to act that way — the fact that most of the Hyde Park Roosevelts had been Democrats, while the Oyster Bay Roosevelts were for the most part Republicans? Was it the old rivalry between the two branches of the family, which was essentially based on the fact that the Hyde Park Roosevelts had more money? "Oh, my dear, you don't understand at *all,*" Mrs. Longworth said to the author not long before her death. "You see, when I was growing up, we were taught that we were *Roosevelts.* We were filled with family *hubris* up to *here,*" and she raised her hand high above her head. "And then, out of absolutely *nowhere,* sailing down the pike, came — *Franklin!*"

But this does not seem an entirely satisfactory explanation. Franklin D. Roosevelt did not come exactly out of nowhere. He came, splendidly, out of Groton and Harvard, and before his crippling illness had been a fine and handsome figure of a man. "His eyes were too close together," Mrs. Longworth snapped. Then she added, "Franklin was the sort of boy you invited to the dance, but not to the dinner."

Within the family, it had always been said that Alice had simply been envious of Eleanor and felt that, in terms of husbands, Eleanor had made the better catch — a catch that Alice would have dearly loved to make for herself. Alice Longworth's husband, Nicholas, after all, had risen no higher in public life than to become speaker of the House of Representatives. Alice had long enjoyed disparaging her Cincinnati in-laws (though the Longworths were very much of that city's aristocracy), describing her husband's family as "hopelessly provincial Midwest *boobs.*" Alice Longworth's husband had died leaving her a meager estate. Franklin Roosevelt had died leaving his wife a reasonably rich woman.

But Mrs. Longworth vociferously denied that envy had anything to do with her hard feelings. "I've heard that sort of thing over the years," she said, "and it's *simply not true* that I would have liked to have married Franklin. His eyes were too close together! I begged Eleanor not to marry him for just that reason! I've even made a tape recording, which can be played after I die, in which I state absolutely, once and for all, that I never *once* considered setting my cap for Franklin." Then she added, "As far as I'm concerned, my father is the only Roosevelt who really belonged in the White House."

And yet, in terms of the Franklin Roosevelts' marriage, Alice Longworth was known in the family to be a troublemaker. During the White House years, when Mrs. Roosevelt was traveling extensively for Franklin, serving as her husband's legs, Alice Longworth and her friends kept careful tabs on the president, noting when he stayed out late, whom he seemed to be paying special attention to at parties — and seeing to it that any news which would imply that the president was seeing other women got back to Eleanor. Could this unhelpful activity over fourteen years' time be based on nothing more than the proximity of a pair of presidential eyes?

Years earlier, at Franklin and Eleanor Roosevelt's wedding, where Alice had served as a bridesmaid, her father had come as a guest and as president of the United States. At the reception that followed, the press had been invited in and immediately descended on the president and his pretty, quick-witted daughter. While Alice preened and posed and the flashbulbs popped, the bride and groom found themselves standing all alone in a far corner of the room, a receiving line of two with no one to receive.

But later, with FDR in the White House, the tables had been turned on Alice. Now Eleanor was the first lady of the land and one of the most photographed women in the world. Eleanor had succeeded in making Alice feel she had been reduced in status to a second-rate Roosevelt, and it stung — just as plain, old-fashioned, ordinary envy always stings.

And yet perhaps it is comforting to know that even an old, aristocratic American family — one filled with *hubris* up to *here* — can be subject to the same woes and torments, the same base and petty emotions and motivations, as ordinary mortals are. This is part of the image that, for decades, the members of the British aristocracy, up to and including the royal family, have managed to project: that here is a group of reassuringly ordinary people going about the business of daily living and trying to cope with the problems of life as they arise. This stance of ordinariness may go a long way to account for the durability and longevity of the British class system. But the trick is to appear to be socially awe-inspiring at the same time. It's a difficult trick to pull off, and one that some families manage better than others.

PART TWO

Brahmins, Knights of the Chivalry, and California Grandees

14

Knowing One's Place

There are certain American cities whose distinct traditions have had sufficient weight to shape and define the attitudes of their leading citizens even to the present day. New York is not one of these special cities. Boston, on the other hand, is, and the emergence of the celebrated Boston Brahmins can be traced from the city's earliest beginnings. As the historian Thomas O'Connor noted in a history of the city prepared for the Boston Public Library in 1976, "Like the priestly Brahmin class of the ancient Hindus who performed the sacred rites and set the moral standards, the new leaders of Boston society emerged as the self-styled 'Brahmins' of a modern caste system in which they were clearly the superior force."

When one thinks of Boston Brahmins, one's thoughts fly immediately to such names as Adams, Saltonstall, Lodge, Gardner, and to Lowells, who speak only to Cabots, and to Cabots, who speak only to God. But there are other Boston families who are just as old, and in some cases older, and just as proud and even more public-spirited, than the Lowells or the haughty Cabots. Brahmin families would also include the Forbeses and the Codmans, the Coffins, Macys, Folgers, Wetmores, Starbucks, Winthrops, Derbys, Crowninshields, Perkinses, Parkmans, and Pickerings. The first Massachusetts Cabot did not set sail from the Isle of Jersey until 1700, missing the *May-*

flower by three generations, while such families as the Balches, Palfreys, Woodburys, and Conants were already prosperously settled in Salem when the first Endicott landed there in 1628.

Before they called themselves Brahmins, of course, they were known as Puritans. Puritan Boston was settled by hierarchical, aristocratic, generally intolerant, and yet education-driven people. When John Winthrop arrived on the Massachusetts coast in 1630 to colonize the Shawmut Peninsula, it was with the promise that his followers would be permitted to practice their religion as they, and not King Charles I, saw fit. But Winthrop, as governor, quickly made it quite clear that he felt some Puritans were born to govern. Others were born merely to worship, while others were not even fit to call themselves Puritans at all. It took considerable pressure from voters in and around the Massachusetts colony to get Governor Winthrop to go so far as to make public the charter he had brought with him from England. Only when Winthrop finally, and very begrudgingly, did so did seventeenth-century Bostonians discover that they had been entitled to hold gubernatorial elections on an annual basis — an item in the charter that the governor had chosen to keep to himself. Though the term would not come into use until at least two hundred years later, Winthrop was the first Boston Brahmin.

From the beginning, proper Puritans were expected to excel, both intellectually and financially. In 1647, legislation providing for a public school system was approved. For the elite, Harvard College had been established even before that, in 1636. Equal stress was placed on the importance of making money, and for the balance of the seventeenth century the Puritans prospered as tradesmen and artisans, providing, for a price, services for each new boatload of immigrants as it arrived. In so doing, Boston can be said to have invented the concept of the service industry in the United States. In the eighteenth century, Bostonians expanded the services they offered to the international scale, investing heavily in shipbuilding and overseas trade. Men named Hancock, Amory, and Faneuil made tidy fortunes from importing rum and spices from the West Indies, and even — though their descendants don't like to be reminded of it — such luxuries as opium from the Orient. More than likely, it was to help rationalize and atone for such dubious, if very profitable, activities that the Massachusetts Temperance Society was organized in the 1800s.

At the same time, and probably for the same reasons, a certain sobriety and lack of showiness in terms of dress and style of living were cultivated as hallmarks of proper Boston Brahminism. Thrift was an important Puritan concept, and out of this grew the Boston notion that the best way to conserve a family fortune was to live only on the income from one's income. In *The Proper Bostonians*, Cleveland Amory told the famous story of the Boston matriarch who was asked where she got her hat. "My hat?" she responded. "We *have* our hats." That anecdote is now forty years old, but the Boston attitude toward hats remains very much the same today, and the hat, ageless and shapeless, still seems designed to suit any number of Boston heads on a wide variety of occasions, indoors or out. (To dress the hat up a bit, one can affix to it a little pin.) Boston's late Mrs. Isabella Stewart Gardner — who, of course, was originally a New Yorker — shocked Boston by wearing diamonds in her hair, as well as, on occasion, a Boston Red Sox cap to the opera. Neither headdress was a proper Boston hat.

Examples of this hatted species of Boston woman can usually be found lunching at the Chilton Club on Dartmouth Street, where members are expected to be properly married or respectably widowed. Unmarried or divorced women are acceptable as guests only if accompanied by a married or widowed mother, grandmother, aunt, or other close female relative. The Chilton Club has an almost pathological dread of being publicized or of having its interiors photographed. Once, when visiting Boston in the 1930s, Eleanor Roosevelt was invited to stay at the Chilton. Though she was not a member, an exception was made for the wife of the president of the United States. Mrs. Roosevelt, however, had the poor judgment to call a press conference during her visit, and the prospect of having its rooms invaded by a horde of reporters and photographers with popping flashbulbs sent a tremor of dismay throughout the club's membership. In the end, Mrs. Roosevelt was required to hold her press conference on the club's front steps.

The nineteenth century was a difficult time for Brahmins, during which — despite their education — their tolerance of outsiders was severely tested and found seriously wanting. First, in the 1840s and 1850s, came the massive immigration of Irish from the Great Potato Famine, when the phrase "No Irish Need Apply" began to appear with increasing frequency in Boston's Help Wanted columns. During this period, at the entrances to saloons as well as the fancier restaurants, signs were also posted that advised, "No Dogs or Irish Admitted." This was the era, too, that saw the formation of many of the city's prominent men's social clubs — the Somerset, the Union, and the Tavern — which excluded Catholics, Jews, foreigners, and women. Even today, though the Somerset Club contains a special, if somewhat dowdy, basement dining room for women, women are required to enter the club through a special ladies' entrance. Upstairs, in decidedly more elegant, Victorian surroundings, Boston's Brahmin males have lunch or sip the Somerset's special creation: the sweet martini, made with sweet vermouth instead of dry, which no one who has not grown up in Boston seems to appreciate. Here, the masculine Brahmin sumptuary code may also be observed — three-piece suit, usually dark; regimental-striped Brooks Brothers tie; dark Oxford shoes of balmoral or blucher design. Like its distaff equivalent, the Chilton, the Somerset offers overnight accommodations to members. Several years ago, the late Mrs. Abigail Adams Homans found herself in a taxi that could not navigate Beacon Hill in a snowstorm. She asked her driver to pull over to the Somerset Club, where she got out and requested a room for the night. The club's steward demurred. It was club policy, he explained, that unaccompanied women could not be supplied with rooms. "Very well," said Mrs. Homans, "I'll go out and get my taxi driver to spend the night with me." She got her room.

Brahmins had long prided themselves on their tradition of public service and on their support of cultural and social welfare programs. But as antislavery sentiments and the abolitionist movement began to take hold in New England, the Brahmin response was to create the American Colonization Society. Under the auspices of this organization, wealthy Boston businessmen contributed large sums of money to be used to purchase the freedom of slaves from southern owners. The plan, however, was not to invite these newly manumitted blacks to come to live in, and enjoy, the socially conscious and liberated air of Boston; it was to pack them onto boats and ship them back to Africa.

While all this was going on, the Brahmins watched with increasing dismay as, by dint of their sheer numbers, the Irish began assuming political power in the city. Soon Irish names were appearing on the city's board of aldermen, and Harvard, of all places, went so far as to award an honorary doctorate to the Catholic bishop of Boston. Faced with such encroachment upon their formerly sacred territory, many Brahmins simply elected to move out of town. The still-Brahmin suburban enclaves of Dover, Marblehead, and Pride's

Crossing are a result of this emigration and date from this turbulent century.

Today, though some Brahmins have moved away and others have quietly gone underground, there are still others who are manfully struggling to regain their lost political leadership of the city, which they continue to see as their God-given right and destiny. One of these is fiftyish Mr. John Sears, a descendant of a long line of Brahmin Searses, who still believes he has a chance to become another in a long line of Boston Brahmin mayors of the city. To be sure, Sears was overwhelmingly defeated in 1982 by the Greek-descended Michael Dukakis. On the other hand, in an earlier election, Sears lost a mayoralty race against Kevin White by a mere eight hundred votes.

The Brahmin spirit lives on, and so does the shabby-genteel Brahmin style of living. Mr. Sears's digs on Acorn Street, in the eighteenth-century brick-and-cobblestone heart of Beacon Hill, are a small town house filled with aristocratic clutter and smelling faintly of dust and ancient book bindings. On one bookshelf are 220-year-old copies of Thomas Hutchinson's *History of the Colony of Massachusetts Bay*. In the kitchen, where Mr. Sears sees no reason he should not entertain a guest, ancient rum bottles are displayed, each emblazoned with the Sears family crest. The Sears walls are crowded with yellowing family photographs — including several of Richard Sears, who was America's first national tennis champion — and nineteenth-century oil portraits. There is also a rubbing from a sixteenth-century brass plaque that was discovered on a church in Colchester, England, depicting a 400-year-old Sears patriarch with his wife, three sons, and a daughter. "I've been able to trace the ancestries of everyone in this picture," Mr. Sears told a visitor not long ago, "except this one," pointing to the third figure from the right, who looked as though he might be the oldest son. "We just can't seem to figure out *what* happened to him." As he talked, Mr. Sears sipped a tot of rum — the family drink, and the source of the family fortune — out of a cracked, cream-colored jar that had originally contained English marmalade. His wife, it must be inferred, does not buy her hats. She *has* them.

In New York, meanwhile, the phenomenon of Brahminism simply could not have occurred. New York could not afford to indulge in the kind of xenophobia that characterized the Brahmins. Just as New Yorkers today come largely from somewhere else, so did New York's first families — from England, Scotland, France, Germany, Ireland,

and Holland. By the mid-seventeenth century, New York was also home to America's first Jewish population of any significance, families who had made their way out of Spain and Portugal, via Holland and South America, to the New World. Though Governor Peter Stuyvesant tried, briefly, to homogenize the city under the mantle of the Dutch Reform Church, it didn't work. The colony's population was already too diffuse, too many foreign languages were being spoken, and too many foreign currencies were in circulation. This helps explain why, when the Dutch surrendered Nieuw Amsterdam to British rule, the old Dutch families did not become second-class citizens. On the contrary, Van Rensselaers, Verplancks, and Van Cortlandts went right on marrying Jays, Livingstons, Morrises, and Schieffelins as they had been doing all along, creating a more tolerant, polyglot aristocracy.

In Philadelphia, on the other hand, barely a hundred miles away, it was all very different. Just as old Bostonians are very *Bostonian* in their outlook, Philadelphia is defined by *Philadelphians,* but there any similarity between the two cities ends. Boston was founded by Puritans, Philadelphia by Quakers. Philadelphia was shaped by a tolerant, democratic, anti-intellectual community that was open to all. Boston was based on intellectual excellence and business competitiveness. In Philadelphia, the city of brotherly love, it was considered evil to strive. And so Boston produced Ralph Waldo Emerson, Henry David Thoreau, Nathaniel Hawthorne, and Oliver Wendell Holmes, along with veritable legions of Adamses, Saltonstalls, and Lodges. But Philadelphia didn't. Instead, it produced genteel, well-mannered, and mild-spoken generations of Chews, Ingersolls, and Cadwaladers who were devoted, more than anything else, to what is called gracious living. Later, when Boston was fretting over an invasion of Irish peasantry, Philadelphia was preening itself over the fact that the roadbed of the Pennsylvania Railroad was regarded as the smoothest in the nation. The University of Pennsylvania, beloved by old Philadelphians, is not now, nor has it ever been, a Harvard, nor has it produced the caliber of graduates that Harvard has — the educators, the political and business leaders, the Nobel and Pulitzer Prize-winners. On the other hand, Philadelphians can boast, with justification, that Penn has by far the lovelier campus.

Given Philadelphia's anti-intellectual origins, it is not surprising that Philadelphia's upper crust should place more emphasis on form than on substance. A certain air of unreality also obtains. In Philadelphia, for instance, one grows accustomed to hearing — and leaving unchallenged — the assertion that "Philadelphia is the second-largest city in America," even though it isn't, if indeed it may have been, once upon a time. One hears other comments that New Yorkers, or even Bostonians, for that matter, would find incomprehensible, such as when Philadelphia's Mrs. George Brooke Roberts announced not long ago that "Philadelphia was the first city in America to omit the sherry with the soup course." She said this, furthermore, with as much pride and conviction as she would have if declaring that Philadelphia had been proclaimed the unequivocal national winner of the war on poverty, drugs, and crime. And, speaking of Boston — a city with which Philadelphia is often compared, to the displeasure of Philadelphians — the late Miss Anna Warren Ingersoll once made this mystifying observation: "In Boston, one never gets enough to eat."

On the other hand, when one thinks about it, one sees Miss Ingersoll's point. Compared with Boston's elite and its legendary fondness for scrod, cod, and baked beans, Philadelphia's aristocracy is proud of the sumptuous tables it sets, with menus featuring such delicacies as Maryland soft-shell crab, terrapin, and canvasback duck.

The Ingersolls, meanwhile, are an archetypal Old Guard Philadelphia family. Pre-Revolutionary, the Ingersolls predate in eminence the better-known Biddles. In fact, in Philadelphia there is a fond saying that, "When a Biddle is drunk, he thinks he's an Ingersoll." All Philadelphia Ingersolls descend from Jared Ingersoll, Jr., the son of His Majesty's agent in Connecticut, who, after graduating from Yale in 1765, came down to Philadelphia to read law under Joseph Reed. During the war, he was finishing his education in London at the Inner Temple. Upon returning to Philadelphia, he became the city's leading lawyer, numbering Robert Morris and Stephen Girard among his clients. According to Charles A. Beard, Jared Ingersoll's practice "was larger than any others . . . his opinions were taken on all important controversies, his services engaged in every litigation."

Since then, the Ingersolls have been almost relentlessly uncolorful, producing generation after generation of staid and worthy Philadelphia lawyers. In the woodsy "outburb" of Penllyn today there is what amounts to an Ingersoll family compound. Here, in a series of widely spaced brick and stone mansions, live, among other family members, Mrs. Charles E. Ingersoll, Mrs. George F. Ingersoll, Mrs.

John H. W. Ingersoll, Mrs. Robert S. Ingersoll, Jr., dowagers all, and, until her recent death at a venerable age, the clan's dowager spinster, Miss Anna. The Ingersoll widows' houses are connected by a series of long, graveled drives whose pebbles appear to be of identical size and color, and so much attention is paid to appearances here that two black gentlemen do nothing all day but rake the Ingersoll gravel back into place after a motor vehicle has passed, erasing the tire marks — something that would be considered an outrageous extravagance in Boston.

True *Philadelphians* — and the word is always stressed in such a way as to differentiate those who are "of Philadelphia" from those who are not — do not sip their drinks out of old marmalade jars. On the other hand, they can be equally disdainful of fuss over matters that might be regarded as mere politesse. Miss Anna Ingersoll mixed her martinis by adding a splash of vermouth to a partly filled gin bottle, shaking the mixture vigorously, and pouring the result into glasses at room temperature. At her dinner table, her antique silver service was arrayed at the sides of each plate with xylophone-like precision — silver of that creamy luster that can come only from daily polishing. And yet, at the center of the table, there was always a bottle of Heinz's catsup and a jar of French's ballpark mustard. And the napkins were paper.

Philadelphians, the eminent University of Pennsylvania sociologist and historian E. Digby Baltzell has suggested, can seem to outsiders so proper and beautifully mannered that they also appear insular and smug. Indeed, a number of leading American corporations, including IBM, Gulf & Western, and Exxon, have had trouble placing top executives in Philadelphia. Their wives find the social atmosphere too inbred and frosty and have trouble making friends. But Philadelphians would not have it any other way. To them, the people perfectly fit the place.

Another city where the place seems to characterize the aristocrats, rather than the other way around, is Charleston, South Carolina. "Charleston," as any visitor to this city will be told at least a dozen times before they leave, "is where the Ashley River and the Cooper River meet to form the Atlantic Ocean." The gentle humor of this local adage, along with the gentle sounds of the two rivers' names ("Flow gently, sweet Ashley . . ."), is in perfect keeping with the gentleness and softness of the city's mood — a city of gentlefolk. The saying also conveys the city's quiet pride in its conviction that if Charleston is not the center of the civilized universe, it somehow ought to be. This feeling persists here, even though, to most travelers along the Northeast Corridor, Charleston seems somewhat off the beaten track.

A lively discussion can be generated in Charleston these days on the subject of whether Charlestonians are or are not in imminent danger of losing their distinctive regional accent. If they are, the villain will be that ubiquitous medium, television, which seems bent — to Charlestonians, at least — on getting everybody to talk like Californians. Charlestonians treasure their accent almost as much as they treasure their city's reputation for gentility, and yet it, like so many other institutions nowadays, seems threatened by people who, as they say here, are from "off." The Charleston accent is hard to describe, and it is said that only native Charlestonians can recognize it when other natives speak it. Its vowel sounds are flattened, somewhat like those of New England, and there are certain elisions — "li'l" for "little," for example. And the "r" sound is never heard in the word "Charleston." But it is definitely not a southern drawl. One woman describes it as "like a Boston accent, but a little slower and softer," and that is as good a description of it as any. Are Charlestonians about to lose their accent? Here, of course, most people fervently hope not, and some say that, instead, Charlestonians are becoming fluent in two modes of speech. As one man says, "The minute I leave town, I lose the accent completely. But the minute I come back, I pick it right up again."

Charleston has been called the most aristocratic city in America, and it may well be. It is here, enshrined in a countinghouse on Broad Street, that the first cannonball fired on Fort Sumter from the Charleston Battery reposes under a plaque stating that this was the shot that started the "War of Northern Agression." It was here, also, that shots from the Union side at Fort Sumter came back, showing that the fort was still fighting, and what is also called the "War of the Chivalry" would end up memorialized on a tablet beneath the portico of St. Philip's Church, listing Charleston's Confederate dead. The list is very long, and it is studied very carefully, because these dead were all Charleston gentlemen. The triumphant and the tragic mingle bittersweetly in this city of old houses, painted in the pale pastel colors of the Caribbean, their long, distinctive side verandas stretching at the perpendicular away from the city's streets, the better to catch the ocean breezes in summertime.

Charleston is, if nothing else, a reminder of two pertinent facts about America's hidden aristocracy. The first is that an aristocracy is not *necessarily* snobbish, "exclusive," or unfriendly and aloof to outsiders; it can, on the contrary, in its gentility be warm and welcoming to strangers, almost to the point of naiveté. The second is that an aristocracy does not *necessarily* have to be rich, since most of Charleston's aristocrats are not.

The notion of "the chivalry" is taken very seriously here. So is the notion of honor, or honour. Under the unwritten chivalric code, borrowed straight from that of medieval knights, a man must be brave, truthful, dutiful, and manly. A man's word must be *better* than his bond, because his word cannot be insured. A promise, no matter how ill advised, must be kept. A woman's name must never pass a man's lips except in terms of respect, and a gentleman must be willing to fight for his country, his honor, or his lady. If he has wronged any other man, he must offer his life in expiation. It is belief in the chivalry that has kept Charleston proud and propped up through its "bright and bitter" days — the days when she ruled the South, and the days when she became the scapegoat of the nation, the city that had lost the war.

The great Charleston families who uphold this great tradition are the Hugers and the Legarés (pronounced "You-gees" and "Luh-grees"), the Prioleaus, the Izards, the Pinckneys and Pringles, Ravenels, Rutledges, Middletons, Manigaults, and Gaillards, to name just a few of the proudest and oldest names that are also emblazoned on the entablature outside St. Philip's, many of them struck down fighting for the Confederate nation while barely in their teens. Belief in the chivalry has stood Charleston in good stead through even more recent, more troubling times, such as when a young man named Gordon Langley Hall came to town in the 1950s.

Hall was dapper and attractive, appeared to have some money, and claimed to be an Englishman. "He had an English accent," says Jack Leland, a reporter for the *Charleston News & Courier* at the time, "and in this town an English accent is all you need to have everybody fall over you." Gordon Langley Hall called himself a writer and, indeed, had published a book of boys' fiction called *Peter Jumping Horse* about the adventures of an Indian youth. "He was also a great name-dropper," says Jack Leland. "In New York, he claimed to be a good friend of the Whitneys, Isobel Whitney I think he said it was. That impressed folks here." And so it was not long before Gordon Langley Hall was taken up by Charleston's literary set, and it was not long after that that the Pringles, in their gracious Charlestonian innocence, had a dinner party for him. His social future among the Charleston aristocracy seemed assured.

Hall also claimed to be "the adopted nephew" of Dame Margaret Rutherford, which managed to make him seem almost a titled personage. Typically of Charleston, none of these claims was checked. A man's word, after all, was his *word,* and it was unthinkable that a gentleman would lie. And so Gordon Langley Hall's social star continued to rise. He bought himself one of the "good" old Charleston houses on Society Street, entertained elegantly for the Pinckneys, Pringles, Manigaults, and others, and by 1953 he was perhaps the most popular young bachelor in Charleston.

To be sure, a few faintly disquieting facts had emerged. For one thing, it appeared that Mr. Hall might be the town's most popular bachelor, but he would not quite qualify as the town's most eligible one. He seemed to be a homosexual, with a particular fondness for young black boys. A local grocer had refused to send a delivery boy to Hall's house because of a certain incident. Still, Charleston aristocracy considered itself sophisticated enough and generous enough to overlook such a harmless peccadillo. What went on in Mr. Hall's bedroom behind closed doors was certainly of no concern to social Charleston people, who considered it unseemly to repeat such gossip, anyway.

Then, in 1953, a more serious incident occurred. In England, Princess Margaret had become romantically involved with Group Captain Peter Townsend, not only a man quite a few years her senior but also a man who had been divorced. News of the romance, and of the royal family's upset over it, had begun appearing in American newspapers. Gordon Langley Hall at this point presented himself to his friend and next-door neighbor Peter Manigault, the president and publisher of the *News & Courier,* with a proposal. He was, Hall said, a close personal friend of both Princess Margaret and Captain Townsend, and he would be delighted to write a series of intimate articles on the pair who were rocking the foundations of the Crown as it had not been rocked since the days of Wallis Warfield Simpson. Manigault, sensing a scoop of sorts, eagerly agreed, and Hall was given the assignment. When Hall's stories began appearing, they naturally came to the attention of the news syndicates, and it was not long before the aristocratic Peter Manigault had a telephone call from a friend with United Press International. Not only did Hall's stories appear to be fiction, Mr. Manigault was told, but Buckingham Palace had been contacted and an equerry of the princess had replied that Princess Margaret had never met a person named Gordon Langley Hall and, in fact, had never heard of him. Peter Manigault canceled the series of articles and sat back to lick his wounds. The chivalric code had been seriously violated.

This episode prompted Jack Leland, at the newspaper, to check on the Dame Margaret Rutherford story. Dame Margaret replied that, yes, she had met Gordon Langley Hall once or twice, but that he was certainly not her nephew, adopted or otherwise. Once more, Charleston wondered about Gordon Langley Hall, but once again the doubts were dismissed. He seemed such a nice young man. Perhaps such vagaries should be forgiven and forgotten. After all, everyone occasionally makes mistakes.

Hall's next move was even more bizarre. This was to announce to his social Charleston friends that he was going to have a sex-change operation. It was almost as though Hall were trying to test this most tolerant and indulgent group of people to see how much outrageous behavior he could get away with and still be included within their charmed circle. The answer seemed to be that he could get away with quite a bit. Of course, some people were privately appalled. But Charlestonians shock in a quiet and tasteful way, and the final consensus seemed to be that this development, again, should be treated as a personal matter, and that it was not up to Charleston's leaders to be judgmental about it. The Charlestonian code dictated that, once a man had been accepted as their friend, he would always be treated as a friend, even after he had decided to become a lady. Hall departed for Johns Hopkins University Hospital, where the operation or series of operations was performed, and when he returned to Charleston he was a she with a new name: Dawn Pepita Langley Hall. Social Charleston welcomed the new woman back into its fold with its customary hospitality.

In 1959, Dawn Langley Hall announced her engagement to one John Paul Simmons, described in the announcement as "a Charleston engineer." This was not quite true. John Paul Simmons was a mechanic at a local service station. Also, John Paul Simmons was black.

At last, the newly created Miss Hall had gone too far. Once a year, in the spring, Charlestonians who own historic houses open their homes and gardens for "house tour," in order that the general public and tourists can see how Charleston's gentry lives. It is deemed a great honor to have one's house placed on house tour. That year, the Hall house on Society Street was conspicuously absent from the list of houses to be toured. The curtain had finally fallen on Dawn/Gordon Langley Hall, and when the curtain falls in Charleston, it falls forever. With a collective sigh of relief, Charleston went about the business of trying to forget that such a person had ever existed.

Charleston's aristocracy does not go in much for vindictiveness. In fact, the worst punishment that social Charleston can mete out is so severe that, to anyone's knowledge, it has never been administered. This would be to be "dropped from St. Cecilia." (Since Charleston has never had a *Social Register,* no one can be dropped from that.) Charleston's St. Cecilia Society and the annual ball it presents represent one of the most rigidly erected social bastions in America. Like the Philadelphia Assembly and the Baltimore Cotillon — aristocratically spelled with but a single *i* — the St. Cecilia Ball is also one of the country's oldest social institutions. The society was first organized in 1737 as an amateur concert society and, little by little, became more interested in putting on balls than in presenting concerts until, in 1822, the concerts were given up altogether and the ball became the society's sole raison d'être.

Like the Philadelphia Assembly and the Baltimore Cotillon, the St. Cecilia Ball is important because it codifies the Charleston aristocracy. It carves, as it were, the names of who is who in Charleston in stone. One is either a member of St. Cecilia or one is not, leaving the society hopelessly beyond the reach of social climbers. Charleston may welcome, and take in, outsiders like Gordon Langley Hall, but St. Cecilia membership is another thing altogether. As is the case in England, for a duke to entertain a viscount at dinner is hardly uncommon. But for a viscount to *become* a duke is next to impossible. As is peculiarly the case in America, on the other hand, the St. Cecilia Society is shrouded in secrecy. The list of its membership is neither carved in stone nor made public anywhere else, though the plaque in front of St. Philip's Church is embossed with the family names that would most likely qualify as members. Only a St. Cecilia member would be able to tell you who the other members were, and this no member would ever do.

More than eighty years ago, a Charleston aristocrat named Mrs. St. Julien Ravenel published a volume called *Charleston: The Place and the People,* an affectionate portrait of the city, in which she came closer than anyone else to revealing how the society works. Though Mrs. Ravenel has long ago been gathered to her Charleston ancestors, there are Charlestonians today who feel that she was a traitor to her class for telling as much as she did and that her book should have been suppressed for this reason alone. Of St. Cecilia's membership, Mrs. Ravenel wrote:

> If a man's father or grandfather, or any of his immediate kindred, have belonged before him, there is little doubt that he will be chosen. Nevertheless blackballs (two suffice to exclude) have fallen, when the applicant was a notoriously unworthy scion of his family tree. If a new resident, or of a family recently brought into notice, there will be inquiry, perhaps hesitation, and a good backing will be desirable. But if he be of character and standing calculated to make his membership acceptable to the Society, he will be elected, — unless he has some adversary; then he may fail. The presenter of such a one will make careful examination into public feeling before subjecting his friend to mortification; and will withhold the letter if in doubt. When a man is elected, the names of the ladies of his household are at once put upon "the list" and remain there forever. Only death or removal from the city erases them, — change of fortune affects them not at all.

The St. Cecilia Society is a men's club in the sense that its board of governors is all male, but it is more than that. Its ball is also a coming-out party to the extent that certain of each season's debutantes are invited, but the majority of the female invitees are well beyond debutante years. What the ball is, most of all, is an exercise in nostalgia, a pleasant anachronism left over from antebellum times. It is an old-fashioned "card dance," where the dance card of every lady in attendance is completely filled out well in advance. Only waltzes and slow fox trots are played, plus an occasional Charleston, and no Latin American music — and certainly no rock — has ever been heard at a St. Cecilia Ball. Other rules abound. Although champagne is served with supper, no other alcoholic beverages are served in the ballroom. Gentlemen may, and do, repair to a separate room and partake of a glass of wine — and hip flasks of more potent liquids have been known to appear in the gentlemen's washroom — but ladies are not permitted to drink, not even wine, anywhere on the premises.

No actors or actresses may attend the ball, even when they are out-of-town guests of members. Neither may a divorced woman, even if she was deemed the injured party in the action. A divorced man, on the other hand, may attend, provided he has not remarried. As for a young woman whose father is a member of the society, she may of course attend, provided she has not had the poor taste to marry a man who is a nonmember. In that case, she may attend, but neither her husband nor her children may do so. A young woman from "off" may be able to attend as an out-of-town guest of a member, provided she passes the careful "family background" check of the invitation committee. But if she has lived in Charleston for a year or longer, she is considered a resident, and no longer from off, and cannot attend. Young women have been known to spend eleven months a year in Charleston and the twelfth month elsewhere just to be able to qualify for the St. Cecilia Ball as out-of-town guests.

The dance is held in a historic, if somewhat run-down, hall in downtown Charleston, and no photographers from newspapers or magazines have ever been permitted to photograph it, though many have tried. Everyone in town knows when the ball is to take place, but no mention of the event is ever made in the local newspaper. "They wouldn't dare," says one Charlestonian, but that isn't quite true. The Manigault family, who own the *News & Courier,* have long been St. Cecilia members, and silence on the matter is part of the chivalric code. In fact, so touchy is the whole subject that some Charlestonians have been known to sit at home in darkened houses on the night of the ball, so that their neighbors will think they have gone to it. Others make elaborate arrangements to be out of town, in order to be able to say that they are "going to have to miss St. Cecilia."

Meanwhile, the ball itself is a vivid reminder that money alone means nothing in Charleston. It is perfectly acceptable for a Charleston woman to own just one St. Cecilia ball gown, which she will wear to the party year after year and leave, for the remaining 364 days, packed away in tissue paper before passing it on to her daughter. And if a gentleman cannot afford white tie and tails, or even to rent a dinner jacket, a dark suit with a black bow tie is considered quite proper attire. For a gentleman to dress this way is even considered a part of the great chivalric tradition.

" 'To be dropped from the St. Cecilia,' " Mrs. St. Julien Ravenel wrote, "is an awful possibility sometimes hinted at, but which (as far as known) has never come to pass." Those words were penned in 1906. Eighty-one years later, it still has never come to pass, and the membership of St. Cecilia remains as fixed as the earth's orbit around the sun. Even Mrs. Ravenel's bit of tattling on the society did not get her family dropped.

Charleston has other little jokes that it likes to tell visitors about itself. A local fertilizer factory emits a distant odor in one part of town, and when visitors comment on it, Charlestonians like to wink and say, "What you're smelling is just the odor of our decaying aristocracy." But, just as it isn't quite true that the Ashley and Cooper rivers meet at Charleston to form the Atlantic Ocean, that quip isn't quite true, either. Charleston's aristocracy is not decaying. It's still going strong.

15

O Ancestors!

Of all the hundred-plus hereditary societies in the United States today — and which include such diverse organizations as the First Families of Ohio, the Piscataqua Pioneers, and the Swedish Colonial Society* — there are probably no two more prestigious, or more misunderstood, groups than the General Society of Mayflower Descendants and the Order of First Families of Virginia.

The Mayflower Descendants is the easier of the two societies to comprehend. It was organized in Plymouth, Massachusetts, on January 12, 1897, to celebrate the return to America from England that year of the history of Plymouth written by Governor William Bradford, titled *Of Plimoth Plantation.* Bradford's history had been uncovered at Fulham Palace in London, and after delicate negotiations with the Consistory Court of the Diocese of London — spearheaded by such American officials as U.S. Senator George F. Hoar — the document was finally on its way home. In genealogical circles, this was an event equivalent in importance to bringing the America's Cup back from Australia. Ever since, the Society of Mayflower Descendants has been busily gathering genealogical data on who, indeed, may qualify for membership in the society. As an indication of the

*Not composed of descendants of Minnesota pioneers but of colonists who settled the Colony of New Sweden on the Delaware River in 1638, in what is now the state of Pennsylvania.

enormity of the society's task, its first volume of researches did not appear until nearly a hundred years later, in 1973, and traced the descendants of only five actual *Mayflower* passengers. It traced these lineages, furthermore, from the 1620 arrival of the ship only up to the time of the Revolution, or for roughly five generations. At this rate, it may be centuries before the society's heroic work is finished.

The General Society of Mayflower Descendants has very strict requirements as to who may join its membership. All members must be able to prove descent from one or more of twenty-three male *Mayflower* passengers. These are:

John Alden
Isaac Allerton
John Billington
William Bradford
William Brewster
Peter Brown
James Chilton
Francis Cooke
Edward Doty
Francis Eaton
Edward Fuller
Samuel Fuller
Stephen Hopkins
John Howland
Richard More
Degory Priest
Thomas Rogers
Henry Samson
George Soule
Myles Standish
Richard Warren
William White
Edward Winslow

This, of course, is not the full roster of *Mayflower* passengers, which ran to a hundred-odd names. Nor is it even the full list of men who signed the famous compact in the *Mayflower*'s cabin, who were forty-one in number. But it is, the society implies, the list of the twenty-three "most important" men on the ship's passenger list.

It excludes, among others, women and children. It also excludes eighteen passengers who arrived under the designation "Family Servants and Young Cousins." It does include the eleven men who were permitted — or permitted themselves — to use the honorific title of Mr., and a few more who used the slightly grander designation of Master. But it should be noted that none of the male *Mayflower* passengers used the title Gent. after his name, the equivalent of Esq. and an indication that the man was a person of property or education, or both.

To be fair, on the other hand, the Society of Mayflower Descendants has never claimed that its forebears were in any sense members of an aristocracy, or even of a moneyed upper class. The society's interest is simply in American history and genealogy. At the same time, the society is not above pointing out that a number of prominent and distinguished citizens are proven descendants of *Mayflower* passengers. These include Boston's Adams family, and both Adams presidents, as well as Presidents Ulysses S. Grant, Zachary Taylor, both Roosevelt presidents, and William Howard Taft and all the Taft clan of Ohio. Thanks to John D. Rockefeller, Jr.'s, marriage to the former Abby Aldrich, all their children became *Mayflower* descendants, including the famous five brothers, John D. III, Nelson, Winthrop, Laurance, and David. Others with bona fide *Mayflower* antecedents include Henry Wadsworth Longfellow, Mrs. Ralph Waldo Emerson, the first Mrs. Jefferson Davis, and the bankers J. P. Morgan and George F. Baker. Grandma Moses was a *Mayflower* descendant, as are General Leonard Wood and Admiral Alan Shepard, the seventh man to walk on the moon and the first to use its surface for golf practice. Even Winston Churchill had an ancestor who was a *Mayflower* passenger.

But, without exception, the passengers themselves were a lowly lot, which even their descendants will usually acknowledge. In *The Fathers of New England,* Charles M. Andrews has stated the matter bluntly: "A group of English emigrants," he writes, "more socially insignificant could hardly be imagined. . . . Their intellectual and material poverty, lack of business enterprise, unfavorable situation and defenseless position in the eyes of the law, rendered them an almost negative factor in the life of New England." And the historian Bradford Smith, himself a descendant of the most notable of the Pilgrim Fathers, William Bradford, has said,

> They were all working men, tailors, merchants, wool combers, weavers, sawyers, hatters, carpenters. . . . The false notion that they were noblemen . . . is especially ironic in view of the fact that the chief distinction of the Pilgrims and their claim to our continual veneration is that they established a caste-free government of free men, making no attempt to duplicate the system of degree and station which existed in England and by which the leaders, if they had been smaller men, might well have hoped to advance in the new world.

The late social historian Dixon Wector agreed. "Almost without exception," he wrote, "the first permanent settlers in America — F.F.V.'s, *Mayflower* passengers, Knickerbockers and Quakers — were drawn from the middle and lower classes, from the aggressive, the dissenter, the ne'er-do-well, the underprivileged and the maladjusted. . . . As has often been said, 'Dukes don't emigrate.' "

And yet the very fact that out of this ragtag and bobtail group of Pilgrim Fathers came men and women who would become business, political, and social leaders may account for the continuing appeal of claiming *Mayflower* ancestry on the part of Americans. The *Mayflower* and its scruffy load seem to encapsulate the American dream of the self-made man in an alien land — the dream of every immigrant since — and to embody the moral of the Horatio Alger success story, that every Tattered Tom and Ragged Dick can go from rags to riches in America if he is diligent enough, resourceful enough, toils hard and honestly enough. Since its founding, the Society of Mayflower Descendants has continued to grow in numbers. Today, there are society chapters in all of the fifty states. By 1960, there were 11,000 S.M.D. members, by 1970 there were more than 14,000, and by the 1980s membership was pushing close to 20,000. It has been estimated by Walter Merriam Pratt of Massachusetts, a governor general of the society, that "some three or four *hundred* thousand could be members, but they just don't know it." Thus have the descendants of twenty-three humble and for the most part illiterate men become a significant part of the American population.

Most members of the Mayflower Society take it very seriously (William Howard Taft applied for membership when he became president). But, because of the organization's size and the general lowliness of the Pilgrim Fathers' family backgrounds, the society has also been the subject of some celebrated aristocratic put-downs. Boston's famous Mrs. Isabella Stewart Gardner, for example, wearying of a friend's recital of her *Mayflower* antecedents, commented, "Well, I understand the immigration laws are much stricter nowadays." And Mrs. Harrison Gray Otis, when asked whether her ancestors had arrived on the *Mayflower,* is said to have replied, "Oh, no. We sent our servants on that. We came over on the second boat." Actually, if this tale is true, Mrs. Otis had a point. The second boat to arrive at the Plymouth Colony, the *Arabella,* carried a more distinguished passenger list, including the first member of the American Whitney family and Sir Richard Saltonstall, a nephew of the lord mayor of London and the progenitor of the only American family to have produced eleven unbroken generations of Harvard men and no fewer than eight governors of Massachusetts. Yet no Society of Arabella Descendants exists, which is perfectly all right with the Mayflower Society. "The Mayflower Society," insists Walter Merriam Pratt, "is not interested in the wealth of its members, or their social standing, or their politics. The Pilgrims believed in the equality of all men."

As for the Order of First Families of Virginia, the story is a little different. Officially, membership in the F.F.V. is restricted to individuals who are "lineal descendants of an ancestor who aided in the establishment of the first permanent English Colony, Virginia 1607–1624." This means that, contrary to popular assumption, neither the Randolphs nor the Lees qualify as F.F.V.'s, since both families arrived later. (The Lees, meanwhile, have their own hereditary society — the only American family to do so — the Society of the Lees of Virginia, composed of descendants of Richard Lee and his wife, Anne Constable Lee, who came to Virginia in 1639.)

But, beyond this, the ancestral claims of the F.F.V.'s become somewhat murky. F.F.V. members like to point out that not only did their forebears arrive on American shores thirteen years earlier than the *Mayflower,* but also that these men were of a more patrician background. To prove it, they note that of the 105 men in the original Jamestown expedition of 1607, no fewer than 35 bore the all-important appellation of Gent. attached to their names, and that out of the 295 men who were actually counted as founders of Jamestown, 92 were listed as gentlemen on contemporary records. Furthermore, certain F.F.V.'s have attempted to fancify and romanticize some of their antecedents' occupations. For example, the earliest American ancestor of the Byrd family was listed as a "goldsmith." Not content with the fact that a goldsmith might have been socially a step or two above a blacksmith, the Byrds have argued that "goldsmith" was "an old expression for banker."

But serious historians have disputed all this. In *The First Gentlemen of Virginia,* Louis B. Wright has said,

> Of the background of most of the settlers who were careful to sign themselves "Gent." we know next to nothing. . . . The cold truth is that the English origins of nearly all of the colonists, even those who founded aristocratic families, are unknown. . . . Though the First Families of Virginia may have in their veins the bluest blood in all England, the proof of their descent will rarely stand in either a court of law or a council of scholars.

There are other problems with the F.F.V.'s involving arithmetic. Of the original 105 Jamestown colonists, for instance, not a single one appears to have left a descendant of any sort in Virginia. In the arduous years that followed, from 1607 to 1610, during which some 800 additional settlers arrived, came the so-called starving times. Despite the introduction of such crops as carrots, parsnips, and turnips, hundreds of colonists died of starvation and malnutrition, while others tried to sustain themselves on a diet of cattail roots, marsh marigolds, Jerusalem artichokes, and other wild plants. By 1609, having buried more than 500 of their men, women, and children, the Virginia colony had been reduced to just 67 souls, and by 1610 the colonists were prepared to abandon Virginia and try their luck in Newfoundland. Indeed, the survivors were headed down the James River when they encountered the *Virginia* coming upriver with 150 new settlers and new supplies. With this new blood, the colony's population rose to about 200. And yet, of these, only five are known to have left descendants in Virginia. And so the First Families of Virginia today are not properly the descendants of the first colonists, but the descendants of the first families who came to wealth and power — Lees, Randolphs, Fairfaxes, Peytons — after the colony, and its damp, malarial climate, had been conquered. Or, as James Truslow Adams put it, "There was not a gentleman of leisure in Virginia until well after 1700 — unless he were a jailbird or a redskin."*

The idea that personal identity and worth can be achieved through a continuity of ancestors seems as old as man himself, and the notion

*Of course Adams had a genealogical axe to grind as the chronicler of the *Mayflower*-descended Adams family of Massachusetts.

that traits could be absorbed from one generation by the next existed long before the science of genetics. It goes beyond atavism. There are even echoes of cannibalism here. In fact, many cannibal societies believed that by eating the flesh of their fiercest and bravest enemies, the fierceness and bravery of those enemies would enter their own bodies, and those of their children, and be perpetuated within the tribe forever. In the fifth century B.C., Herodotus wrote of certain Scythian tribesmen who ritually devoured their own parents. When the patriarch of a family grew old and venerable, he was sent up into a tree and made to hang from a limb by his hands. The tree was then shaken by his young sons and family members. If the father did not fall, he was judged not ripe enough to be eaten. But if he fell, he was avidly consumed by his descendants in order to acquire and preserve the richness of the patriarch's wisdom and experience for future generations. It was considered a great honor to be eaten.

In older American cities, particularly in the South, old families have kept track of themselves, and their forebears, though without the aid of formal genealogical societies. In some places, the idea of genealogical codification is almost repugnant. A secret aristocracy, after all, ought to be kept just that, a family secret as closely guarded as how much money one is worth. Cities such as Charleston, New Orleans, and Savannah, for example, have little use for *The Hereditary Register of the United States,* a heavy, six-hundred-plus-page volume, published annually, that lists American hereditary societies, their officers and bylaws, a "Revolutionary War Ancestors' Honor Roll," registered coats of arms, heraldic charges and symbolism, and other ephemera of family-treedom. Nor have these cities exhibited any interest in a *Social Register,* or any other kind of social list. In these cities, everybody knows who is socially acceptable and who is not. The family name is more than the symbol. It tells the whole story. Not long ago, the daughter-in-law of a Charleston Pinckney gave birth to her first son, having already had two daughters. "Just think of it," her mother-in-law exclaimed, "my first grandchild!" Affronted, her daughter-in-law asked her what she meant. "This one will carry on the *name,*" the baby's grandmother replied.

For many years, the city of Washington published a slim edition of the *Social Register*. It was held in low esteem because it attempted to do the impossible: collect the names of socially acceptable Washington and official Washington, which are not necessarily the same thing, all in one volume. To Old Guard Washington, it made no sense at all to see a member of the old-line Claggett family listed in the same book as the ambassador of Angola, with the implication that the two families were on an equal footing. The problem was solved in 1930 by Mrs. Helen Ray Hagner with the publication of *The Social List of Washington,* known affectionately as The Green Book for its green felt cover, and which drew a sharp distinction between social and official Washington. Furthermore, The Green Book — and its carefully anonymous board of governors — had no hesitancy about dropping high government officials from its pages if, it felt, they didn't comport themselves properly. Supreme Court Justice William O. Douglas was dropped when, at the age of sixty-seven, he took a twenty-three-year-old woman as his fourth wife. Major General Harry H. Vaughan, an official in the Truman administration, disappeared from the Green Book's pages because, so it was rumored, "of the way his socks slop sometimes over his shoes."

Mrs. Hagner devised a private set of symbols and notations that she used in her card file of potential listees. "BD," for example, indicated Bad Drunk, and the initials "OF" appeared on Mr. Justice Douglas's card just before his banishment from the book, denoting Old Fool. The Green Book is run by Mrs. Hagner's granddaughter today, Mrs. Jean Shaw Murray, and though the list is now computerized, similar notations are still fed into the computer. And the identity of the book's board of governors, whose decisions as to who is in and who is out are final, is still a closely guarded secret. "They have to be anonymous," Mrs. Murray says, only half-seriously. "Their lives would be in danger," so coveted are Green Book listings.

Old Guard Washingtonians, who can be said to form the social core of The Green Book, cheerfully refer to themselves as "the Cave Dwellers," a term indigenous to Washington and an indication that these are families which have retired to a private, unseen, almost troglodyte existence in the city among their relatives and friends, far removed from the comings and goings of the city's more visible, if transient, political society. A Cave Dweller defines a member of those families who have lived in the capital for generations, and whose bloodlines are thoroughly woven into the fabric of Washington's social and economic history. Today's Cave Dwellers have ancestors who were also Cave Dwellers. "Oh, yes, they used to call us that even when I was young," says Mrs. William S. Farr, a cheery woman in her eighties who has lived in Washington all her life and whose grandfather Francis Griffith Newlands founded what is still one of the city's most exclusive enclaves, the Chevy Chase Club.

Washington, as the nation's capital, is necessarily another of those special cities where a sense of place can seem to overpower, and delineate, the attitudes of its upper class. In New York, it is more significant for a Jay or a Livingston to be a *Jay* or a *Livingston* than to be a New Yorker. To the secret aristocracy of Washington, the key is to be *of Washington.* When Pierre L'Enfant began sketching his plans for the city in 1790, there was no particular reason for its being where it was. It was not a great seaport or the juncture of two major rivers. Congress had simply decided that there was where the capital would be. The early leaders of the city had to invent a reason and a meaning for it, and so they themselves became its raison d'être.

Washington's Old Guard has been accused of being peculiarly snobbish in contrast with the elite of other cities, and in a sense it is, due to the peculiar nature of the town. Like Hershey, Pennsylvania, Washington is a one-industry city, the industry being government. American government and politics being what they are, the people in positions of power are both transients and transplants from other places. They change from one election to the next, they are rarely interested in putting down roots, and they are too busy competing with one another to bother about catering to any establishment or trying to emulate its values. Just as transient and rootless as the political ins and outs are the families who run and staff the many foreign embassies and consulates in town, and the Cave Dwellers have come to regard all these people as social riffraff, not worth the trouble of befriending. In turn, the people whom political and diplomatic Washington talks about, reads about, or even cares about are not the Cave Dwellers. Ignored, the Cave Dwellers sound both snobbish and xenophobic when they talk about "those people," and they use their very anonymity as a badge of special superiority and prestige. It is a form of snobbery that would probably not be tolerated in any other city. But because it is Washington, the Cave Dwellers get away with it.

Such names as Claggett, Belin, Glover, Leiter, Beall, and Peter can all be found in history books about Washington and, in most cases, are in the Washington telephone book — as well as The Green Book — today. And these are just a sampling of the old families who can trace their lineage back to Robert Peter, the first mayor of

Georgetown; to Bishop Thomas John Claggett, the first chaplain of the U.S. Senate; and to the glamorous Leiter sisters, who set the fashion and social tone of Washington in the 1800s.

Once upon a time, the Cave Dwellers played an important role in official Washington, in a day when blue bloods were in the White House and when the only embassies that counted were the British, the French, and "perhaps" the Spanish and the Italian. But no longer, in a time when, according to people like Mrs. Farr, Washington is just "too much come and go." Today, Cave Dwellers may still be seen playing golf at the Chevy Chase Club, dining at the Metropolitan Club, and entertaining quietly — and assiduously without publicity — at their city mansions on and off Connecticut and Massachusetts avenues. But few Cave Dwellers will be spotted at power lunches, political cocktail parties, splashy charity balls, corporate fund-raisers, or diplomatic dinners. The Cave Dwellers leave that part of Washington life to others who have more recently arrived, who have come from distant places the Cave Dwellers would never consider visiting, and whose backgrounds are obscure. "We don't have the slightest interest in those who come and go," says Mrs. Fontaine Bradley, whose husband is a descendant of Robert Peter. "I'm not really interested in getting to know them," she says, "and I don't think they would be interested in getting to know us."

There is, of course, some understandable nostalgia for the old order. "I don't know very much about politics these days," says Mrs. Sidney Kent Legaré, who is called Minnie and who is not only old Washington but whose husband is even older Charleston. "You see, Washington used to be like a family. The minute you came back to town after being away for the summer, you left cards at the White House, and the Chief Justices received on Wednesday, the embassies received on Sunday, and the Patton sisters — they were very much up in politics — received every Sunday. But the whole world has changed. Washington has become part of the world." At least there is solace in the fact that, though the world may have changed, the Cave Dwellers remain, indestructible in their secret caves, and that all of them know exactly who the others are.

For a number of years, Minnie Legaré helped run the Dancing Class, which was not a dancing class at all but a series of exclusive white-tie dances held at Washington's Sulgrave Club. "It was a very small dance group that had nothing to do with politics," she says. "Just the people in Washington and *some* people from the diplomatic corps, the attractive ones. Everyone wore their best jewels and best dresses, but we closed it in 1968 because we wanted to keep it as it had always been, and people didn't want to bother with white tie anymore."

The people who don't want to bother with white tie are, of course, the new people. In the past twenty years, particularly, the diplomatic corps in the capital has expanded enormously, and the turnover in Congress has been noticeably heavy. In addition, there has been a new group of people — wealthy contractors, real estate developers, lawyers, doctors, and automobile dealers — that has come to Washington determined to rub shoulders, socially, with the city's political power brokers. This is easy to do, they have discovered. All one needs is a house on Foxhall Road, the name of a good caterer, and a willingness to give lots of parties. Starting with House members, who are notoriously invitation-prone, these hosts and hostesses can move on quickly to senators, cabinet members, Supreme Court justices, and important foreign ambassadors. Some of these social entrepreneurs have even made it into The Green Book ("the Yellow Pages," says one Cave Dweller disparagingly). All of this activity has served only to further isolate the Cave Dweller families from the well-publicized whirl around them.

A few members of old Washington families, to be sure, have tried to fight against this isolation and to adapt to the new order. One of these is thirty-four-year-old Martha Custis Peter, who is a direct descendant of Martha Custis Washington as well as of Robert Peter. Miss Peter works as a paralegal, is involved in political activities, and does volunteer work for Common Cause, though she admits that her mother cannot understand her. "My mother keeps asking, 'Why don't you do Junior League?' " she says. "This used to be such a small town. We would keep pretty much to our own circle and look at all the newcomers and sort of ask, 'Who *are* they?' But Washington has become such a cosmopolitan city. I don't think we can afford to be as snobby these days."

But Miss Peter is very much an exception to the Cave Dwellers' rule, and most are content with their isolation and with their "own sort." "This is now a town where, if you've got the money, the clothes, and the jewels, you can make it socially," says Mr. Clement E. Conger, the White House and State Department curator, who traces his own lineage back to William Ramsay, the founder of the town of Alexandria. "That didn't used to be so, but it is now." The

Congers do not choose to "make it" socially. Neither do Mr. and Mrs. Francis Girault Addison III. Mr. Addison, a banker, is a descendant of Colonel John Addison, who settled in Maryland in 1667. "We *choose* to be invisible," says Mrs. Addison. "I'm a member of such groups as the Colonial Dames and the Junior League, of course. But there are many people here who live very privately, and they are the backbone of Washington. They are the docents at the galleries, the hospital volunteers, and the supporters of the symphony. They just don't want any notoriety, they don't want their names used."

And so, invisible and impregnable, Washington's secret aristocracy sits back in its comfortably upholstered caves and watches — through a lorgnette, as it were — with bemusement as what passes for Washington "society" today comes and goes.

Other southern cities, such as Savannah, New Orleans, and Montgomery, also have their versions of Washington's Cave Dwellers, though their roots do not go quite as deep. Savannah, for example, was not settled until 1733, and Montgomery was not much more than an Indian trading post until 1817. New Orleans, on the other hand, can boast that its most famous drawing card, and still its principal preoccupation, Mardi Gras, was first organized in 1699. It also has a most unusual social history. In its early days, under French rule, the city suffered from an acute shortage of women. As a result, if many old New Orleanians probe deeply enough into their family trees, they are likely to find female antecedents who were native American Indians. In 1721, the king of France, to remedy this situation, dispatched eighty-eight young women to New Orleans from Paris. These ladies, however, were all former inmates of French houses of correction. For the next several years, the king continued to send "correction girls" to the colony until, in 1728, came the first "casket girls." The casket girls were of a better class, even though most of them came from French orphanages, and they earned their name because each girl carried with her a small "casket," or *cassette*, of clothing and personal effects. The correction girls had come with nothing but the clothes on their back.

The first respectable women to arrive in New Orleans were so besieged with suitors that duels were fought over the prettiest ones, and — with the cooperation of the Ursuline nuns who had accompanied them as chaperones — some were chosen by lots cast by eager bachelors, and a few were even sold, just like slaves, at auction to the highest bidder. In the generations that followed, of course, during which the city became a more seemly and class-conscious place, a sharp distinction would be drawn between descendants of correction girls and descendants of the *filles à la cassette*. To be a descendant of a *fille à la cassette* was soon the equivalent of having an ancestor on the *Mayflower*. In fact, by the mid-twentieth century, a mathematically minded New Orleanian was able to calculate that, if each claim to descent from a casket girl was correct, each girl would have had to have given birth to a hundred and sixty-two children.

Moving even farther south, to St. Augustine, Florida, one encounters another puzzle and anomaly. St. Augustine is the oldest city in the United States — founded in 1565, half a century before Jamestown or Plymouth and more than a hundred years before New York. And yet no hereditary society of the First Families of St. Augustine, or even the First Families of Florida, exists. If any descendants of the founding families of St. Augustine exist, they have all moved elsewhere, pulled up their roots, and forgotten where those roots were.

16

Beer and the Bourgeoisie

Naturally enough, the majority of the oldest of America's aristocratic families have their roots in our oldest cities, the seaports of the East Coast. This is not to say that the newer cities of the Midwest — opened up to trade and commerce by the nineteenth-century expansion of the railroads — do not have their Old Guard, or "first cabin" families, but just that they are not as long established. Two of the great "founding families" of Chicago, for example, the Fields and the McCormicks, were relative Johnny-come-latelies to the business of dynasty creating. Cyrus McCormick, with his reaper patent, did not arrive in Chicago until 1847, when the future Windy City was described as an insignificant lakeport. Marshall Field — though from a family that can trace its descent from Zachariah Field, who arrived in Dorchester, Massachusetts, about 1629 — was a poor farmer's son when he arrived in Chicago in the 1850s and did not acquire the famous store that bears his name until 1867.

Cincinnati has its still wealthy and prominent Tafts, and Cleveland has its Mathers and Cases and Boltons. But in these cities, as elsewhere, the first-cabin families have been somewhat eclipsed by newer wealth: railroad money, Civil War money, and money that is even newer than that. Just as in Boston the Hancocks and Otises and Quincys have been overshadowed by the later-arriving Cabots and

Lowells, and in Philadelphia the Ingersolls, Willings, and Chews have been outflanked by Biddles, Cadwaladers, Pews, and Campbell's Soup Dorrances, the old families of Detroit — Newberrys, Algers, and Joys, who used to boast that "a Ford could go anywhere except into society" — now feel quite overwhelmed, fiscally and socially, by the "internal combustion money" of the Fords and Dodges and Chryslers, as well as by "people nobody had even heard of ten years ago," such as Lee Iacocca. To the old families of the East Coast — to Livingstons, Jays, Schieffelins, and the like — anything west of the Allegheny Mountains tends to be dismissed as "new money." There were, after all, no Declaration of Independence signers from west of Pennsylvania. And so the corollary is that the Middle West lacks traditions and therefore breeding.

In St. Louis, on the other hand, one of the oldest Midwest cities, the situation is a little different. The city is justly famous for its publishing Pulitzers, its shoemaking Florsheims, its retailing Stixes, and its beer-brewing Busches and their Anheuser and Orthwein cousins. The Florsheims and Stixes have never made a secret of the fact that they are Jewish and arrived in America in the mid-nineteenth century with the first wave of German-Jewish immigration. The Pulitzers, on the other hand, have a problem in St. Louis, since it has long been rumored that the Pulitzers were "originally Jewish" but have preferred to conceal this fact. All that is known is that the family is "of Magyar descent," from Hungary, and that the first Joseph Pulitzer used to stress the point that his mother, at least, was a Roman Catholic. For some reason, the same rumor has also circulated about the Busch family, though there is absolutely no evidence to support it. But it has something to do with the fact that, a number of years ago, August A. Busch, Jr., "had to build his own country club" because, presumably, the St. Louis Country Club didn't want him. And a certain amount of local jealousy can't be ruled out — since the Busches have made a great deal of money from a very plebeian commodity and live like medieval Bavarian barons on their estate at Grant's Farm, where they are enthusiastic dispensers, as well as promoters, of their product.

But from the prominence of German and Central European names in St. Louis today, it should not be assumed that St. Louis's real roots are German as, say, they are a few hundred miles to the east in Cincinnati. St. Louis's true roots and real aristocracy are French, dating back to 1764, when the settlement was named after Louis XV.

Descendants of the French pioneer families today will point out that the street prosaically named Main Street was originally the Rue Royale. Walnut Street was the Rue Bonhomme, Market Street was the Rue de la Tour, Second Street was the Rue de l'Église, Third Street was the Rue de Granges, and so on.

As might be expected, the first colonists in St. Louis came up the Mississippi River from New Orleans. There, in 1763, Gilbert Antoine de St. Maxent and Pierre Laclède Liguest, New Orleans merchants, obtained from the French director-general of Louisiana the exclusive right to trade with the Missouri River Indians and with those west of the Mississippi above the Missouri. The following year, a party headed by Auguste Chouteau headed upriver to the selected site of their trading post near the juncture of the two rivers. The post was immediately successful, and packets of fur, wheat, and flour traded from the Indians were floated downriver to the New Orleans market. Hearing of the success of the St. Louis colony, French from the Illinois territory, unwilling to live under British rule, came downriver to St. Louis, and within a year some thirty French families were prosperously established there.

In 1765, when the British military took possession of the Illinois country east of the Mississippi, the French commander, Louis St. Ange de Bellerive, withdrew with his troops to St. Louis and assumed military command of the colony. Officially, the territory belonged to Spain, but Spain had not exercised her authority over it and permitted St. Ange de Bellerive to act in Madrid's behalf until 1770, when the first Spanish lieutenant governor took over. Thus, with the exception of a Spanish official and a handful of Spanish soldiers, the entire population of St. Louis was French and Roman Catholic. The French families proliferated and intermarried with one another to such an extent that, by the time the territory was transferred to the United States, it was estimated that two-thirds of the population of the city was in some way related to each other.

The great French families of St. Louis today include the Peugnets, Cabannes (some use an accent as Cabannés), Gareschés, and Chouteaus, and it was the two original Chouteau brothers, Auguste and Pierre, who made the biggest fortune, having worked out a monopoly to trade in furs with the Osage tribe. But the Gareschés and Desloges and Cabannes, to whom the Choteaus are marvelously interrelated, did not do badly, and all the old French families have patriotically persisted to this day in giving their children French first names: Eugénie, Pierre, René, Marie, and so on. Today's Auguste Chouteau represents the eighth generation in a direct line from the first Auguste Chouteau, who headed the first settlement party. Today's Desloges — whose family motto is only half-jokingly said to be *Après moi le Desloge* — own the St. Joseph Lead Company and a house with an underground ballroom filled with statues of other saints.

Since for years the principal marketplace for everything St. Louis produced was New Orleans, it was natural that the city should have adapted some of New Orleans's social customs. Here, St. Louis's restrained answer to Mardi Gras is the annual Veiled Prophet's Ball, held every October since 1878, and restrained because St. Louis has tried to avoid the atmosphere of carnival hoopla and tourist appeal that has come to characterize Mardi Gras, though there is a public parade. Here the identity of the annual Veiled Prophet Queen is revealed for the first time to her "subjects." The identity of the Veiled Prophet himself — he is indeed heavily veiled — is supposedly never revealed. But, since most people are not very good about keeping secrets, and since both the queen and the prophet are selected by a committee, the queen's identity is seldom a complete surprise, and the name of the gentleman behind the veils usually leaks out sooner or later. The ball itself, held the night before the parade, is a more exclusive, by-invitation-only affair where the enthroned prophet holds his Court of Love and Beauty, the season's selection of debutantes. The Veiled Prophet Ball committee tries to select its queen with as much care as Miss America judges, with points given for looks, talent, and poise, as well as for family background. The Veiled Prophet Queen is then required to promise that she will not become engaged or marry for a full year afterward, or until her debutante career is over. Several years ago, however, the queen was discovered to be not only married but four months pregnant.

The French have traditionally never gotten along well with either the British or the Germans, and so, while families like the Chouteaus and Desloges have frequently married each other, they have rarely married Anheusers or Busches or Orthweins, or any of the descendants of the German immigrants — Jewish and non-Jewish — who began arriving in St. Louis in the mid-nineteenth century. At the same time, the old French families of St. Louis, though intensely proud of their heritage, have never lived in the cocoon of aristocratic self-assurance that has characterized some of the old eastern families.

They have shown little tolerance for nonconformity, unconventionality, or eccentricity, and it is hard to say what St. Louis society would have made of as bizarre a creature as Gordon Langley Hall. Families such as the Chouteaus and the Desloges came to St. Louis as traders, and they have remained such: conventional businessmen and their families leading conventional lives. Desloges toil for such familiar causes as the Heart Fund, and serve as trustees and directors of the Missouri Historical Society, and try not to get their names in the paper for any untoward reasons. Living more as members of a *haute bourgeoisie* than as aristocrats, they have placed much emphasis on *politesse* and *comme il faut*. They might be said to form the historic backbone of the *Social Register* and such proper institutions as the sedate St. Louis Country Club — which, once upon a time, supposedly did not want August A. Busch, Jr., as a member.

And so, as they say here, "Gussie Busch built his own country club." But it wasn't exactly a country club. What he founded, and built, was the Bridlespur Hunt Club, devoted to horse shows, four-in-hand racing, and fox hunting. To be sure, it bore a certain resemblance to a traditional country club. Situated on twelve rolling acres in what is now a development called Huntleigh Village, its clubhouse called to mind a Virginia manor house, to which Mr. Busch added stables, kennels, a race course, a show ring, and a swimming pool. Busch and his fellow charter members, several of them his relatives, considered adding a golf course but decided against it. It was not horsey enough. Bridlespur held its first annual horse show in 1928, about which the *St. Louis Post-Dispatch* commented somewhat waspishly, "The competitors were the club's charter members, and the spectators ranged from those noted in the Social Register to those lucky to be listed in the telephone book." But, insists Mr. Busch, "what we all had in common was horses. We all loved horses and hounds and hunting, and we all had a helluva good time."

The upper classes, in America as well as England, have long had a passion for animals — horses and dogs in particular, as England's queen herself continues to demonstrate. And it was in the 1920s that many newly rich Americans started to take up horsey sports as a possible passport to instant aristocracy and instant old money.

Actually, as upper-crust — or at least expensive — sports go, fox hunting isn't very old. And not only is it a relative newcomer to the panoply of rich men's pastimes, but it was also not even introduced by the upper classes. Nor was it originally thought of as a sport.

Fox hunting dates only to the seventeenth century, when England was becoming overrun with foxes that were attacking flocks of chickens, geese, and other domestic fowl. The first fox hunts were organized by poor farmers, and out of sheer necessity, in an attempt to bring the marauding fox population under control. Even today, in the sheep-farming country of western Britain, the fox is a serious threat during the lambing season, and hunting the fox is a grim business, not undertaken for the fun of it at all. All the modern trappings of the fox hunt — the rigid dress code, which changes seasonally, the arcane vocabulary, the elaborate rules — represent even later developments.

In fact, some sports purists claim that fox hunting is not properly a sport at all, since there are no winners and no losers — not even the fox, which, in American hunts, is always spared. It is, they argue, merely an equine fashion show at which the hunters display their custom-made pink coats, their skin-fitting white breeches, and their three-thousand-dollar British-made boots; a pastime for social climbers. Games with a more aristocratic tradition are golf, tennis, and polo, which can be played on horseback or on bicycles, or even croquet or *roque,* a game so aristocratic that, in the seventeenth century, only members of the French royal family were permitted to play it. The origins of golf, meanwhile, are lost in the mists of prehistory, though a version of it was played by the ruling class in Roman times, and the Romans are credited with having introduced golf to England and Scotland. (The east window of Gloucester Cathedral, dating from the mid-fourteenth century, depicts a figure wielding a club who looks very much like a golfer, though why a golfer should appear in an ecclesiastical setting is a mystery.) Tennis is an equally ancient game and may have originated in either Egypt or Persia as early as 500 B.C. And polo is probably just as old, with its origins in pre-Christian Asia, though it was not taken up by the English-speaking world until its discovery in India in the middle of the nineteenth century by the British Raj, which formed the Calcutta Polo Club in 1860.

And so, with the creation of the Bridlespur Hunt, the battle lines were drawn between the members of the St. Louis Country Club, who preferred their traditional and genteel golf and tennis, and Mr. Busch's flashy new endeavor. Each group looked sniffily down its collective nose at the other. It was not that Mr. Busch was interfering with anybody. When his fox hunters incorporated the Huntleigh area in 1928, it enjoyed the distinction of having the most horses and the fewest people of any municipality in St. Louis County. Its 680 acres were inhabited by 53 horses, 24 foxhounds, and only 17 people. But it was Mr. August Anheuser Busch, Jr.'s, *style* — or some would say lack of it — that rubbed Old Guard St. Louis the wrong way.

For one thing, as far as the French families were concerned, here was the German-descended Mr. Busch trying to act like an Englishman. For another, there was the sheer, almost vulgar, vastness of Mr. Busch's wealth. His fortune has been estimated to be as much as $300 million, though he has periodically pooh-poohed that figure as being $200 million too high. August Busch has gone to none of the right schools. In fact, he has had very little formal education at all, which, he cheerfully admits, is because none of the right schools or even the wrong ones would take him. "Without a doubt," he says, "I was the world's lousiest student," though the University of St. Louis finally awarded him an honorary Doctorate of Laws degree in 1969. Then there have been his well-publicized marital adventures. He has been married four times — widowed once, divorced twice — and his third wife, whom he married when he was fifty-three, was the daughter of a Swiss restaurant manager and was only twenty-five. For this and other reasons the Busches have never been given the nod by the *Social Register*.

Meanwhile, August Busch enjoys living in a truly imperial style. His estate at Grant's Farm, a 281-acre tract encompassing the farm and log cabin where Ulysses S. Grant was raised, includes a thirty-four-room French Renaissance château, air-conditioned stables where he keeps his prize collection of Clydesdale horses, barns to contain a million-dollar collection of antique carriages, and a private zoo with chimpanzees (which are often dressed up in costumes), deer, buffalo, longhorn steer, and other animals that are allowed to roam freely in their natural habitat, as well as an elephant named Tessie. Not the least bit modest about his immodest surroundings, August Busch opens Grant's Farm to the public on a daily basis, and visitors can tour the place on miniature trains, all free of charge.

Busch's flair for self-promotion — and the promotion of his beer — has been prodigious, and he is famous for the huge parties he has tossed at the farm for wholesalers, retailers, and even saloon-keepers, who are exhorted to keep pushing his beers across their counters to customers. He is a man who clearly loves to be in the spotlight and to see his name in public places. Though he may regard himself as an aristocrat, he is hardly a secret one. When he bought the St. Louis Cardinals in 1953, the old Sportsman's Park was promptly renamed Busch Stadium. He claims to hate the nickname Gussie, but the newspapers persist in calling him that, which gives him a chance to deliver broadsides at the press, which get his name in the papers all over again. He is also famous for his hot temper, for loving to raise particular hell if things don't go his way at the brewery, and for his barnyard humor.

There was, for example, a scene at Bridlespur a number of years ago that Busch still roars over. "I remember once," he says, "the hounds found a fox over at Grey's farm, and they ran for an hour without check. One by one, the quitters dropped out, and finally there was no one left but Julius Van Ralde and myself. Van Ralde's horse hit the top rail of a fence and went down, and Van Ralde landed face first in a cow pie. He sat up and put his hand to his cheek and yelled, 'I'm bleeding!' I could see the son-of-a-bitch wasn't hurt. So I tossed him my handkerchief and left him to figure out the problem for himself!" Then there have been innovations at Bridlespur that would make members of older and more sedate hunt clubs in Virginia and Maryland blanch with horror. At Bridlespur's annual horse show, Busch introduced a "costume class" competition, and one year it was won by Andrew W. Johnson, the head of the International Shoe Company, who came as Lady Godiva, wearing a wig and a sheer flesh-colored body stocking, with his toenails and fingernails painted red, riding bareback on a white horse. August Busch roars at that one, too.

For several years, the rivalry between the Bridlespur set and the Country Club set merely simmered, amounting to little more than mutual disdain. But then, in 1932, things heated up considerably when it was learned that Prince Friedrich Wilhelm von Hohenzollern, the grandson of Germany's former kaiser, would be touring in America and that one of the cities the prince planned to visit would be St. Louis.

With bona fide royalty looming on the social horizon, the competition over which club would have the privilege of entertaining His Royal Highness became fierce. To the chagrin of the Country Club, and to the everlasting joy of Bridlespur, the prince responded that he would rather do some fox hunting than play golf. And even though the prince himself showed up for the hunt in shockingly improper attire — an ordinary business suit, a foulard tie, and a brown felt fedora — it was a resounding victory for Bridlespur and August Busch, and a humiliating defeat for the Old Guard.

Over the years, Bridlespur has made it a point to entertain distinguished horse people from out of town along with other visiting celebrities, and all this has resulted in fulsome coverage of Bridlespur — and Busch — in the local press. The club has never quite topped its historic coup with Prince Friedrich Wilhelm, but it has tried, and on at least one occasion it has been host to a bogus nobleman introduced to St. Louis as Lord Forkingham of Duncington.

Lord Forkingham was the sly creation of Bridlespur members James Busch Orthwein (August Busch's nephew) and Andrew Shinkle and was actually Mr. Russell Forgan, a stockbroker from New York who had agreed to go along with the prank. Forgan was able to muster a passable English accent, and as Lord Forkingham, he spent several days being wined and dined by *le gratin* of St. Louis, who never bothered to consult an atlas, where they would have found that there was no such place as Duncington. On the morning His Lordship (who St. Louis had decided should be addressed "Your Grace") was scheduled to join the hunt, Orthwein and Shinkle, knowing that Forgan had not sat on a horse in decades, supplied him with the most reliable and best-mannered mount in Shinkle's stable. In his borrowed pink coat and topper, His Grace set off after the hounds. He managed quite well until he reached his first fence, where horse and rider unceremoniously parted company. While the other members of the hunt gathered solicitously around, His Grace picked himself up, dusted himself off, and said, "Certainly the worst beast that I have had the misfortune to ride in twenty years!"

The result was that the joke backfired on Mr. Shinkle. "For weeks afterward," says James Orthwein, "everyone went around talking about that marvelously sporting Lord Forkingham and that lousy horse of Shinkle's. Shinkle was wild, but it was like the priest who shot a hole in one on Sunday. The joke had gone over so well that we were afraid to tell the truth. The others might have made trophies out of our backsides."

As St. Louis expanded after World War II, the Bridlespur Hunt was forced to look for further, less settled land beyond the city. This they found to the west, in the rural reaches of the town of New Melle, where the club purchased a hundred pristine new acres in 1954. At about this time, too, since a number of Bridlespur members — including August Busch — had comported themselves with distinction in wartime service, the two principal clubs in St. Louis decided that they might as well bury the hatchet. And so the mountain came to Mohammed: the St. Louis Country Club issued a gracious invitation to August A. Busch, Jr., to join its membership. Mr. Busch accepted with equal graciousness.

It was, they say in St. Louis, the only thing he really wanted in the first place. It was also proof that it is usually folly to try to impede the momentum of big money in America. And it was proof, as has been demonstrated again and again throughout America's history, that if old money is to survive with even a shred of dignity, it must, at some point, come to terms and make its peace with the new.

17
O Pioneers!

"Everyone knows," says Mr. Gorham Knowles of San Francisco, "that Jimmy Flood's grandfather was a bartender, and that his grandmother was a chambermaid. That doesn't matter here. What matters today is that the Floods are ladies and gentlemen."

In just three generations' time, the Floods of California have become an aristocracy — of sorts. Like moneyed families in Chicago, Denver, Dallas, and Oklahoma City, this California aristocracy is not very old, not very secret (indeed, quite conspicuous), and has decided to turn what might elsewhere be considered a minus into a plus. San Francisco's elite may, as they say here, all be "descended from prospectors and prostitutes." But they can also take pride in the fact that the aristocracy that has evolved from this is older than that of either Los Angeles or San Diego.

The Floods of San Francisco are one of the city's Irish Big Four families, otherwise known as the Silver Kings: James C. Flood, William S. O'Brien, James Graham Fair, and John William Mackay, four men who were not so much unscrupulous as plain lucky. Big Jim Flood, described by social historian Dixon Wector as a "poor gamin of the New York Streets," came to San Francisco with the gold rush and found work as a bartender at the Auction Lunch Rooms, so called because the gold exchange was right around the corner. In the kitchen of this establishment worked Will O'Brien, who earned local renown for his Irish fish chowder, which he made extra thick with potatoes. Out in front, Jim Flood was known for serving generous slugs of whiskey, and the Auction Lunch Rooms became a popular watering hole for prospectors coming in from the fields. Neither Flood nor O'Brien knew anything about prospecting for precious metals, but, as drinks flowed — and tongues were loosened — Jim Flood kept his ears open. It wasn't long before he had heard of a promising site in the Comstock area near Virginia City, Nevada. Recruiting two other Irishmen, John Mackay and Jim Fair, to provide additional financial backing for the trip, Flood and O'Brien set off for Virginia City to stake a claim.

The Comstock Lode was a unique event in mining history: a bonanza discovered by a prospector on his very first dig. What the boys unearthed was the biggest single pocket of silver ever found in the entire world, a long vein of shiny metal fully fifty feet wide. When it was discovered, the Comstock Lode was estimated to be worth $300 million. That estimate proved to be on the low side. From the time of its discovery in 1859 until the mine's depletion ten years later, the Comstock poured some $500 million worth of silver into the pockets of the four original investors.

San Francisco's other Big Four royalty, the so-called Railroad Kings of the Central Pacific, were Collis P. Huntington, Leland Stanford, Charles Crocker, and Mark Hopkins. They were a truly unsavory quadrumvirate without redeeming social value who fit into the robber baron category of the era comfortably. It was Huntington who, as the railroad's lobbyist in Washington, persuaded Congress to pay his company, out of taxpayers' money, $16,000 per mile for track laid over flatland and $32,000 per mile for track laid over foothills and mountains. It then occurred to Huntington to redraw the map of California, adding mountain ranges all over the place, on the gamble that nobody in Washington knew anything about the state's actual topography; his hunch was quite correct. It was Mark Hopkins, the bookkeeper of the foursome, who proposed that the Central Pacific pay its imported Chinese coolie labor force in cash, thus eliminating the need to keep any books. It was the huge, red-bearded Crocker who was the company's muscle man. He kept the railroad's workers in line by marching up and down their ranks with a pistol in one hand and a bullwhip in the other. The dignified-looking Leland Stanford was in charge of political matters in California. He was a useful front man because he at least *looked* honest. As governor of the state, he kept Sacramento out of his company's hair. Though it was hard to say, exactly, since no books were kept, it was estimated that the Central Pacific cost about $27 million to build. The railroad foursome was able to divide up about three times this sum without ever having to invest a penny of their own money.

These men may be said to have laid the groundwork, financially and socially, for modern California and its famous freewheeling style. From them, it seems only a short step to the land of freeways, oil wells, backyard pools, custom-built cars parked along South Rodeo Drive, and power lunches in the Polo Lounge. But there is also an older, much more grand, and much more gracious California that some California families remember. This was a world that came into existence nearly a hundred years before the gold rush and lasted until well after it was over: a world of vast tracts of land stretching for miles along the seacoast and for miles inland to the Sierra foothills, land covered with golden grass and wild mustard where huge herds of beef cattle grazed — twenty-five thousand to fifty thousand head was the size of the average herd — where Thoroughbred horses were corralled, and where jackrabbits the size of dogs leapt through the underbrush. It was a world of week-long family fiestas and *ferias,* of rodeos and roping contests and horse races. It was a world of vast adobe haciendas with ballrooms big enough to hold three hundred dancing couples, where string ensembles provided mood music at mealtimes, where desserts were frappéed with ice imported from Alaska, where women's gowns were fitted by *couturières* from Paris and where men's tweeds were ordered from Savile Row and Bond Street. We are talking, of course, of the century-long era of the true *Californios,* the first white settlers, the *rancheros* who brought with them in their veins the true *sangre azul* of the Catalan and Castilian grandees of seventeenth- and eighteenth-century Spain and who used the ennobling titles of Don and Doña. Many of their descendants still do, because, as elsewhere, the original aristocracy has not died out. It has just gone underground.

"Each of these families knows who the others are," says Mrs. Michel François Amestoy II of Los Angeles, a descendant of one of the first California families, "but you don't read about their doings, unless it's for charity. Many are certainly successful, but the brash competitiveness that sets the business tone in California is not their tradition." These are the families who brought their proud Spanish culture to California, who introduced agriculture to the region, who founded the major cities, and who forged the state constitution. And, though their domain, which once stretched from San Diego in the south to Monterey in the north, has shrunk considerably, it is not true, as is often assumed, that the old Spanish land grant families "lost all their land," though some did, and for a variety of reasons, as we shall see. Many were able to keep their land, and there are Spanish families in California today that are collectively richer than the Floods and Crockers.

The mellifluous old ancestral names are Avila, Alvarado, Carrillo, de la Guerra, Nieto, Ortega, Serrano, Sepulveda, Verdugo, Vallejo, Yorba, Cota y Asuna, Cordero, Dominguez, Osuna, and Amador. Many of these are descendants of the first party of white men who entered California overland from Mexico in 1769 with Father Junipero Serra and Gaspar de Portolá. Their mission was to discover the port of Monterey, about which fabulous reports had been heard, and to Christianize the Indians. One of the party's first encampments in "Alta California" was at the mouth of a creek that they christened Dos Pueblos — they found two Indian villages there — a few miles west of the present city of Santa Barbara. Of these original pioneers, fourteen men decided to remain and establish themselves, and their womenfolk were sent for. And of these first fourteen, at least nine have descendants scattered throughout California today.

One of these first fourteen was José Roberto Carrillo. Another was José Francisco de Ortega, who married Maria Antonia Victoria Carrillo, José Carrillo's niece, one of the first of many dynastic marriages between California's founding Spanish families. Ortega was a man of particular stature in the group. With the rank of sergeant, he commanded the advance guard and was chief scout and pathfinder for the company in its search for Monterey Bay. His duty was to scout ahead of the company, then retrace his steps, and collect his soldiers for the next day's march. This probably meant that he was a man of education and could read and write, for he was expected to keep careful records. It also meant that he was expected to deal with the native Indians. This proved fairly easy, since the Canaliño Indians of Southern California were a docile and submissive group who quickly accepted the Spaniards as their masters. For one thing, the Spaniards had firearms, and it did not take long to demonstrate to the Indians what a gun was capable of doing. The Indians were almost equally impressed with the Spaniards' horses, creatures the

Canaliños had never seen before. Still, José de Ortega was considered the linchpin of the group. Father Serra himself wrote of him, "His soldiers would be replaced, but Ortega never."

Meanwhile, the search for Monterey Bay proved frustrating. In 1542, the Portuguese navigator Juan Rodriguez Cabrillo had sailed up the California coast in search of the Northwest Passage, the legendary navigable saltwater canal that imaginative mapmakers had assumed must stretch across North America to link the Atlantic and Pacific oceans. Cabrillo had failed to find the alleged trans-American waterway, but he had reported glowingly of a magnificent bay and harbor he had entered, which he had named Monte Rey in honor of his king. But Cabrillo's navigational instruments had been primitive. And if the bay in question was where Cabrillo had said it was supposed to be, it was certainly a disappointment, not at all fitting Cabrillo's description when Ortega reached it. (Monterey Bay is more a roadstead, a gentle indentation in the shoreline, than a protected bay.)

Though there is no way of knowing, it is more than likely that the bay Cabrillo was describing was San Francisco Bay, nearly a hundred miles north of Monterey. Almost forty years after Cabrillo, in 1579, Sir Francis Drake had sailed right past the entrance to San Francisco Bay and never noticed it, probably because the Golden Gate strait was shrouded in one of its famous fogs. But when, nearly two hundred years later, José Francisco de Ortega was exploring the coastline northward on horseback, he arrived at the Golden Gate and could go no farther. Though he reported finding, inside the harbor entrance, "a bay big enough to hold the ships of all the navies in the world" and would be credited with having discovered the Golden Gate along with one of the world's greatest seaports, he believed that his expedition had been a failure. He had been blocked from venturing farther northward by an impassable arm of water. And San Francisco Bay still did not fit the description of the bay Cabrillo had named Monte Rey.

In 1784, King Carlos III of Spain, through his viceroy in Mexico City, began handing out grants of land to the first soldier-settlers and their families who had come up from Mexico to help establish Spain's historic claim to the California territory. In all, some twenty-three land grants were made between 1784 and 1821, and since California's land seemed limitless, the tracts bestowed on the pioneer families were truly princely in size. José Francisco de Ortega's grant, which he received in 1795, was — perhaps because of his failure to rediscover Cabrillo's bay — relatively small, a mere 26,000 acres. Others were considerably larger. Juan José Dominguez, one of the original fourteen, was given 76,000 acres, which he named Rancho San Pedro. It included thirty square miles of what is now Los Angeles County, most of Los Angeles Harbor and Terminal Island, Redondo Beach, the Palos Verdes Peninsula, part of what is now the city of Long Beach, and what are now the entire cities of Carson, Torrance, and Compton. There was a slight hitch to these royal grants of land, which no one paid much attention to at the time but which would become important later on: They were essentially just permission to graze livestock on the *ranchos*. Water rights and rights to minerals that might lurk underground were not included. Still, considering that this land today sells for as much as $100,000 an acre, the Spanish rancheros had been given some nice real estate, and even then, they were on their way to becoming very rich.

"Don José de la Guerra's house in Santa Barbara had forty rooms, all grand," says one of his descendants, the splendidly named Dr. Juan de la Guerra y Noriega Barrett, whose other, non-Spanish grandmother was a Randolph of Virginia. "Whatever culture or stability California has, you have to attribute to these Spanish families. They brought their silver and crystal. Their sons were sent to Europe to be educated. They lived on their ranchos in a style that, outside of the South, was little enjoyed in early America."

Actually, Dr. Barrett understates the situation. By 1850, when California became a state, its economy was based almost entirely on the raising of beef cattle, despite the gold rush. In fact, the gold rush only created a period of inflation, which caused the price of beef to rise, and besides, when a ranchero had forty thousand head of beef cattle grazing on permanent pasture, fluctuation in beef prices, upward or downward, meant little. Here is the way just one family, that of Don Nicolàs Den, and his wife, Doña Rosa Antonia Hill de Den, and their family lived on their Rancho Los Dos Pueblos, outside Santa Barbara, in that halcyon period between 1840 and 1860. It was quite typical.

Don Nicolàs was an educated, pre-Famine Irishman who had studied medicine at Trinity College, Dublin, and come to America in 1834 to seek his fortune in the Land of Golden Opportunity. In California, he had met and married Rosa Antonia Hill, the daughter of Don Daniel Hill and Rafaela Louisa Sabrina de Ortega de Hill, who was a granddaughter of the original José Francisco de Ortega. (By the nineteenth century, it was commonplace for the daughters of the older Spanish families to marry later-arriving Irishmen, who had a reputation for being good and pious Catholics; as a result, many California descendants from the distaff side of land-grant families have names like McGettigan, Brady, Donohue, Donohoe, and FitzGerald).

Doña Rosa and Don Nicolàs, like their peers and contemporaries, believed in large families and had produced ten healthy children out of eleven pregnancies. Despite all her childbearing, Doña Rosa had kept her trim, girlish figure, and since she had been married at sixteen, she was only in her early thirties when her last child was born. Doña Rosa was proud not only of her looks and figure but also of her reputation, throughout Southern California, as a hostess. In this career, her large family was absolutely no encumbrance to her. She had literally a legion of servants to attend to her every need.

Doña Rosa's personal household staff numbered fifty, and this of course did not include the *vaqueros* who did the range work — the rounding-up of cattle for branding or butchering, the breaking of horses, and the like — or the gardening staff. Her head cook was a California Indian named Jacobo, who was assisted by his half-breed wife Refugia and a crew of Chinese and Filipino kitchen assistants, all under the supervision of a Portuguese majordomo. Jacobo was locally famous for his culinary innovations. He invented potato chips long before George Crum of Saratoga Springs and was able to transform these paper-thin wafers of crisply fried potatoes into all manner of fanciful shapes — shamrocks, stars, crescents, rabbits, hearts — to amuse the children. He had a particularly magical way with roast fowl. A turkey, for example, might arrive at the table looking like a traditional Thanksgiving bird, plump and browned and basted. But when the carver cut into it, he would encounter not a single bone.

The *cocina,* or cookhouse, was in a separate building, to keep kitchen odors out of the main house, and so was the laundry, which, considering the size of the household at Dos Pueblos, was one of the busiest places on the ranch. This was run by Simosa, an ample Mexican woman, and a crew of local Indian helpers. Pure white Castile soap was manufactured on the premises out of tallow, rendered with wood-ash lye in a hundred-gallon iron kettle that had been salvaged from the wreck of a whaling ship.

This is not to say that imported goods were in short supply.

John Jay Chapman, the mad belletrist praised by Edmund Wilson. (The Bettmann Archive, Inc.)

St. Louis's ebullient and irascible August Anheuser Busch. (Missouri Historical Society, photographer: Strauss)

The Great Splurge era produced "cottages" like Rosecliff in Newport. (The Preservation Society of Newport County)

Wedding garments of Mr. and Mrs. Auguste Chouteau worn by their descendants, Miss Beatrice Chouteau Turner and Mr. Auguste Chouteau VI (c. 1910–20). (Missouri Historical Society, negative number: Objects 204)

Presentation of Lila Childress as queen of the Veiled Prophet's Ball, 1935. (Missouri Historical Society, photographer: Eugene Taylor, negative number: Events 152)

Boston's staid Somerset Club, on Beacon Hill. Ladies still must use a separate entrance. (Courtesy Massachusetts Historical Society)

The Hotchkiss School in Lakeville, Connecticut, and its longtime headmaster, George Van Santvoord. (The Hotchkiss School)

American royalty mixes well with British: J. Carter Brown, Jr., of Rhode Island and the Princess of Wales. (UPI/Bettmann Newsphotos)

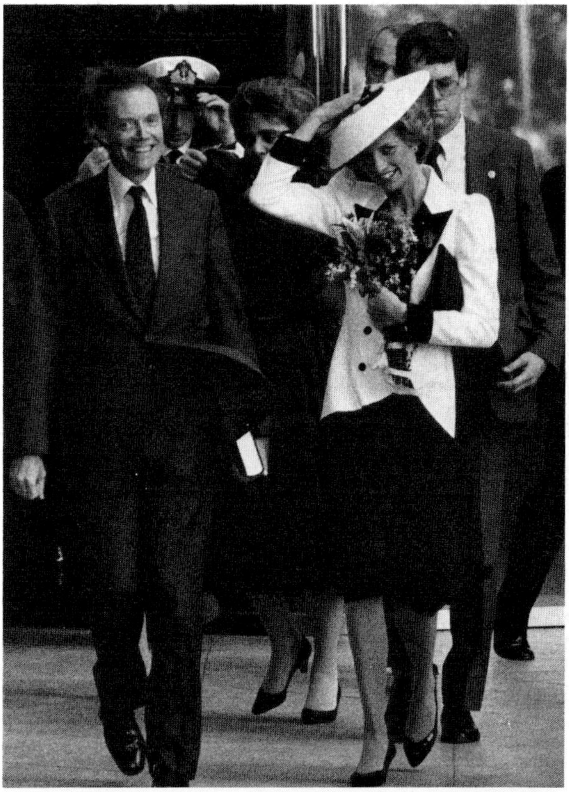

Newport's reigning couple, Mr. and Mrs. John Jermain Slocum, at left, with Mr. Stanley F. Reed at right.

Doña Francesca de Ortega de Brady of San Francisco and her son George T. Brady, Jr., in heirloom Spanish costumes (c. 1930). (Courtesy of George T. Brady, Jr.)

A membership certificate of California's most exclusive club, the Society of California Pioneers. Members must prove an ancestor arrived before midnight on December 31, 1849. (Courtesy of George T. Brady, Jr.)

Still the life of the party at over ninety, Mrs. Margaret Trevor Pardee, great-great-granddaughter of Jacob and Hannah Lawrence Schieffelin and kin of Roosevelts, Jays, Lispenards, and Livingstons. (Copyright © 1984 by Scott Areman)

New York's Henry H. Livingston and his family mansion, Oak Hill, on the Hudson River.

Periodically, Livingstons from all over the world — too many to crowd into a group photograph — assemble at Clermont on the Hudson River to celebrate almost three centuries of family continuity. (NYT PICTURES/Penny Coleman)

Jacobo's larder was supplied with curls of candied Chinese ginger, brought on ships from Cathay. Curry and chutneys came from India, and English traders brought rum-flavored coffees and Dutch bonbons filled with exotic liqueurs. There were *pâtés de foie gras* from France, smoked salmon from Sweden, kippered cod from Norway, peat-smoked O'Mara hams from Ireland, cashews from Brazil, pears in crème de menthe and peaches in brandy from England, and bars of maple sugar from Vermont. In the west wall of a canyon near the cookhouse, Don Nicolàs had ordered a deep cellar dug. Twice a year, freighters dropped anchor off Rancho Los Dos Pueblos to deliver huge cakes of ice that had been carved off living glaciers along the Alaskan coast. These were stored in the ice cellar, covered with sawdust and salt, and lasted even through the hottest summer months. Thus were Dos Pueblos and other ranchos like it provided with the ultimate luxury in Southern California at the time, refrigeration, as well as plenty of ice for mixed drinks. One of the lessons Doña Rosa taught her daughters was the technique by which a lady can avoid perspiring in hot weather: Hold an iced drink against the inner wrist and let the cooler blood circulate throughout the body.

The main house, or *casa grande,* at Dos Pueblos was a long, rambling, one-story affair of white stucco with red-tiled roofs, surrounded by wide verandas. The principal rooms were large and high-ceilinged to accommodate the massive pieces of Spanish furniture — the long sofas, the tall mahogany chests and armoires that were favored by the rancheros and their wives. The larger pieces had been shipped from Spain around the Horn, and the smaller pieces had made their way across the Isthmus by mule train. The floors of the hacienda were of tightly packed earth, but they were covered with thick rugs from Persia. In the main dining room, fifty people could be seated in richly upholstered high-backed chairs to admire Doña Rosa's table settings. Her silverware — the pistol-handled knives, the three-pronged forks — was of the heaviest available, and she was particularly proud of an Irish Georgian silver tea service, a family heirloom of her husband's that was polished daily by the bare, damp palms of her Indian servants. Doña Rosa's dinners were memorable for one special touch: Her china always matched the course being served. That is, if the course was pheasant, the dinner plates had a pheasant design; peaches would be served in bowls decorated with peaches, and so on. This seemingly endless collection of bone china had been custom-made for her in English kilns.

The hacienda at Dos Pueblos even had air-conditioning of sorts. To begin with, the adobe walls were more than two feet thick, and the terra-cotta roof tiles were designed to reflect, rather than absorb, the sun's heat. The encircling verandas of the house shaded the windows, and all around the house, tall stands of cypress, palms, and olive trees provided further shade. Finally, every room in the house contained an earthenware *olla,* or water jar, sitting on a japanned tray in one of the deeply recessed windows. These jars were filled every day with cold well water by the servants, and evaporation through the porous clay helped to cool the rooms.

One wing of the house was set aside for the Den children, and this was the domain of Nicholosa, the head of the nursery, and her retinue of Indian baby-sitters. Nicholosa, in turn, was under the supervision of Doña Rosa's personal maid, Maria de los Angeles.

Every Sunday morning, without fail, the entire family trooped off to mass, which was said either in the mission at Santa Barbara or in the family's private chapel at the ranch. Priests frequently visited Dos Pueblos, and even occasionally — a great honor — the *obispo* himself, Father Alemany, journeyed south to Dos Pueblos from faraway Monterey. Sunday afternoons were invariably given over to informal family fiestas, where a freshly killed bullock would be barbecued over a hardwood coal fire, the servants turning and basting the carcass on the huge spit as it roasted. And there would be games: horse races on the beach, roping calves against a time limit, bulldogging steers, and jousting with padded sticks. The cruel sports, such as bullfights and bear fights and cockfights, which the Anglos enjoyed, were never permitted.

Music was an important part of every Spanish don's family life, and after dinner Doña Rosa's family gathered around her concert grand piano while she played and sang. The rancho also employed its own musicians — guitarists, cellists, mandolinists — who played during all family meals, breakfasts, lunches, and dinners, seven days a week. Besides music, Doña Rosa's other great passion was her garden. Her favorite flower was the rose of Castile, after which she had been named, and these were planted in profusion outside the hacienda, along with hollyhocks, Matilija poppies, anise, and potted Italian cypresses. Her great-granddaughter, Katherine Den Cheney Hammond of Montecito, would recall Rosa as an old lady, moving slowly through her flower beds with Pedro, her Indian head gardener, in tow, pointing to a shrub that needed trimming here, a bud that should be nipped there, and to blossoms that should be picked for the flower arrangements in the house, which she mentally arranged as she moved along to be able to tell her maids precisely what she wanted done.

Dos Pueblos also contained a twelve-acre fruit orchard. The citrus fruits — limes, oranges, lemons, and grapefruit — were used primarily in the house for decoration. Only the peaches, apricots, pomegranates, pears, olives, figs, and apples made their way to the table.

If this style of life seems remote and dreamlike, even insular, it was really not. For one thing, it was more or less duplicated at every California rancho between Monterey and San Diego. For another, despite the seeming isolation of the ranchos, perched on the edge of the continent, before telephones, railroads, and even paved roads between the East Coast and the West, the rancheros were sophisticated people for their time. By 1860, the Dens' oldest son, Manuel, was at school in England, and in 1861 the Dens had just returned from a fourteen-month tour of Europe — and were planning a round-the-world tour — when the first cannon were fired over Fort Sumter, causing them to postpone any further travel.

Finally, the seemingly endless stream of visitors to ranchos like Dos Pueblos kept the rancheros from becoming out of touch. Because friends and relatives had to travel long distances on horseback to visit, when they came they stayed for weeks, even months. It was customary, furthermore, for a visitor — whose own horse was bound to be tired from the journey — to be presented with a new horse, as a gift, from the don. To give away a new Thoroughbred to a visitor was regarded as no more than a simple, welcoming expression of hospitality, a gesture no more important than a kiss or a handshake. The Spanish dons were notoriously indifferent to the value of money, as, indeed, they could afford to be. But the Spaniards literally treated money as though it were a plaything. Another commonplace at ranchos such as Dos Pueblos was for a visiting guest, after being shown to his apartment, to find on his dressing table a large box filled with gold and silver coins. The guest was expected to help himself to this money, to take as much or as little as he might need during his stay for expenses. It was a custom that one might wish were still practiced in hosts' homes today, but to a nineteenth-century Spanish doña, seeing that her guests' quarters were supplied with boxes of money was as routine as a modern hostess seeing to it that her guest bathroom contains fresh soap and clean guest towels. This largesse was available to commercial guests as well: the dressmakers who periodically came to the rancho from Paris to measure the ladies of the house for their gowns, or the tailors and bootmakers who traveled halfway around the world from Bond Street to fit Don Nicolàs for his bespoke suits, tweeds, riding breeches, and boots.

In 1850, when California joined the Union, the dollar became the unit of currency, and paper its principal medium. The dons, whose traditional faith had been in gold and silver, found it difficult to take the new paper currency seriously at all. Outsiders were sometimes shocked to see Spanish dons light their imported Cuban cigars with ten- and twenty-dollar bills, as Don Nicolàs occasionally did. It was assumed that this was their way of flaunting their great wealth. More accurately, it was their way of showing their disdain for the new paper stuff, which they regarded as worthless anyway.

The only time that money was taken even halfway seriously was when it came to gambling. The Spanish dons, almost without exception, were great gamblers. Gambling was in their blood; it was a sport. They would bet on anything. At their great *ferias,* rodeos, and horse races, huge sums of money changed hands between dons — won and lost with equal cheerfulness.

Though Don Nicolàs had married a major heiress, he was by no means an idler. He was a dedicated rancher, and since their marriage in 1836, he had increased the value of Rancho Los Dos Pueblos enormously, adding to its herds of cattle, improving the quality of its beef and the price it could command at the marketplace, and adding to its stable of Thoroughbreds until they numbered more than 200, while his cattle were virtually uncountable at more than 25,000 head. By the 1860s, he had acquired the 8,875-acre Cañada del Corral Rancho from an improvident Ortega cousin of his wife's, as well as part of the 8,919-acre Tequepis grant, and was leasing 35,499 acres of the College Ranch from the Catholic Church. All told, Don Nicolàs controlled 114,000 acres of the finest ranch land in California. He had also been active in a civic sense — campaigning for better roads in California, underwriting a project to build a graded road from San Buenaventura to San Luis Obispo across the Gaviota Pass, and laying the groundwork for the famous Concord stagecoach, which would carry mail between Santa Barbara and Lompoc and other northern towns.

It was a strange and ironic twist of history, then, that the years of the Civil War, which would spell an end to the glorious age of plantations and gracious living in the South and would leave the Old South a civilization gone with the wind, should also have marked the end of the era of the rancheros in the California Southwest. But in the case of California, the villain was not a tragic war between the states. Instead, it was the farmer's greatest and most inscrutable adversary, the weather. If it had not been for a meteorological fluke, California today might be owned entirely by perhaps thirty Spanish-American families.

Water had never created much of a problem for the rancheros. In fact, at times, there had been almost too much of it. In the winter of 1861–1862, there had been what historians still refer to as the deluge — five straight weeks of pouring rain that came flooding down through the canyons to the sea. The normally sleepy Dos Pueblos Creek became a raging avalanche of churning white water, carrying with it huge boulders and the trunks of uprooted trees; here and there a miner's cabin, lifted from its foundation in the hills, bobbed crazily along the surface. Landslides and mudslides cascaded through the canyons and into the sea, and the sea turned brown for miles offshore. In the downpour, a number of adobe houses simply melted away, but the buildings of Rancho Los Dos Pueblos were made of sterner stuff and, fortunately, had been built on high ground. When the great rain ended, the damage to the ranch was minor. About two hundred head of cattle had been drowned, but this was a small loss to a rancher who had more cattle than he could count. The surrounding landscape, meanwhile, had gained a whole new shape. Landslides had created new canyons, ravines, and gullies, and the great Goleta Estuary, and an island within it, had become so silted in that it was now nothing but a shallow swamp.

During the spring and summer of 1862, the hills around Dos Pueblos had never been greener. The rains had brought a new layer of rich and loamy topsoil into the valleys, and it was decided that the great deluge had been a blessing to the farmers.

But by January of 1863, the normal winter rains had not come, and the hills were brown again. As the month progressed, the many little streams that fed Dos Pueblos Creek began drying up, one by one, and waterfalls that had cascaded down the canyon walls disappeared. Soon Dos Pueblos Creek itself was nothing but a series of puddles, green with algae, and the estuary that had become a swamp was now a flatland of sun-baked mud strewn with the corpses of fish and waterfowl.

By May, there had still been no rain, and a kind of awesome hush began to settle over Southern California. The heat was merciless, and the hot, debilitating winds that Californians call the Santa Anas blew in from the Mojave Desert. There were dust storms now, whirling down from the parched hills, and a temperature inversion — of the same sort that causes Southern California's smog today — made the dust hang in the air for days, turning the sky yellow and the sun into an alien, dull-copper disk. The sunsets transformed the skies into strange, sickly colors of green and purple. The cattle moaned for food and water, and desperate ranchers went into the foothills to cut down oak trees to provide food for their starving animals. All through the summer no rains came.

Throughout Southern California, ranchers watched with dismay as one after another of their great beasts tottered forward, sank to its knees, then fell on its side and died. In the sun, their skins became dried husks of cowhide, stretched across the frameworks of their skeletons, and the dreadful stench of rotting flesh blew through the canyons on the dusty winds. Down from the mountains came the scavengers, the coyotes and the cougars and the grizzlies, and buzzards, which had never been sighted so close to the sea before. Soon the skeletons were picked clean, and the birds, too sated with carrion to fly, sat about their trophies like grim guardians of death. Next, late that summer, came an invasion of *chapules,* or grasshoppers, millions upon millions of insects eager to devour whatever traces of greenery were left. And the chapules were quickly followed by an epidemic of smallpox that surged through the entire state and particularly ravaged the Indian population. In Santa Barbara alone, the Indian population was reduced from twelve thousand to a mere forty. There were no more string quartets playing at mealtimes at Rancho Los Dos Pueblos now. Beyond the hacienda, Doña Rosa's flower gardens were reduced to rows of chewed and withered stalks. The fruit and olive trees died, and even the desert-hardy palms turned brown, uprooted themselves in the dusty soil, and toppled. And what was happening at Dos Pueblos was not an isolated disaster. It was happening to every ranchero in the state. As one ranchero, Pedro Carrillo, wrote to a friend in Los Angeles about conditions in Santa Barbara County:

> Everybody is broke, not a dollar to be seen, and God bless everyone if things do not change. Cattle can be bought at any price, Real Estate is not worth anything.
>
> The chapules have taken possession of Santa Barbara, they have eat all the Barley wheat, &c., there is not a thing left by them, they cleaned me entirely out of everything and I expect if I do not move out of this Town soon, they will eat me also. Dam the Chapules. . . .

In a panic to sell what remained of their cattle, ranchers dropped their price to as low as $12 a head. Then it was $8 a head. Then it was $3 a head, and then it was zero. No one wanted the sick and half-starved animals. And meanwhile, in faraway Washington, the country was too busy fighting a Civil War to pay much attention to the plight of supposedly wealthy Spanish-American ranchers in Southern California.

If the year 1863 was disastrous, 1864 was even worse. Again, no rains fell that winter, and the heat during the summer was even more severe than it had been the year before. At Dos Pueblos, the herd that had numbered as high as twenty-five thousand head in 1862 had been reduced to just forty animals by mid-1864, and it was decided at Dos Pueblos and the other big ranches that there was only one practical — and humane — recourse: wholesale slaughter of the remaining animals. Their hides could be tanned and sold. Their bones could be boiled, and the tallow extracted could be sold for glue. What remained of their flesh could be pressed into cakes called cracklings and sold for hog feed at a penny a pound. And so, with heavy hearts, this was what the ranchers set about doing, and what animals were left of their once mighty herds were systematically destroyed.

Some rains came in 1865, but it was far too late. The cattle business was dead, and never again would cattle form California's economic base. Without their cattle, of course, the rancheros had no livelihood and no source of income. With their aristocratic nonchalance about financial matters, few of them had any savings to speak of. All they had left was their land, but what was there to do with it? The experience of the Great Drought had left most Californians leery about any sort of agricultural endeavor in the southern part of the state. Even the land seemed worthless.

And now, into their midst descended another breed of scavenger. Down from San Francisco, the state's financial center, came the Anglo bankers. The Anglo bankers had a solution to the ranchers' problems. It was something that Spanish dons had never given much thought to, and it was called a mortgage. One by one, the dons began mortgaging their lands and, one by one, unable to meet their mortgage payments, they discovered that failure to pay meant foreclosure. Foreclosure, of course, could be put off by obtaining another mortgage on another land parcel. And so the inexorable process began by which the great landholdings of the Spanish families were steadily eroded and slipped out of Spanish hands into the hands of Anglos.

This, at least, is how the descendants of the old Spanish families prefer to explain the loss of their lands today — it was the doing of the villainous Anglo moneylenders. The early Spaniards, they point out, did not fully understand what the bankers were up to, since most of the Spaniards spoke no English. (Doña Rosa de Den, for one, had never learned English; by the time the Great Drought was over she was a widow, and, having led such a pampered life, she may not have had any comprehension of why her great fortune was suddenly disappearing.) The only flaw in this charge of victimization by Anglos is that one of the most notorious moneylending firms of the day was the Spanish company of Pioche & Bayerque, in San Francisco. Pioche & Bayerque charged an interest rate of 5 percent per month, compounded monthly, and this steep charge quickly became the going rate at all the other banks.

At the same time, independent speculators who had made money in the gold rush heard that Southern California land was selling at dirt-cheap prices and that for loaning a rancher a few hundred dollars one could, through foreclosure, end up owning several hundred acres. Thus these men began acquiring land for speculative purposes. The land-poor Spanish families just didn't have the wherewithal to compete in this process.

After the Civil War, too, there arrived another group that would change the demographic profile of California. Santa Barbarans today call this the Eastern Black Sheep Era. To have produced a black sheep in one's family isn't of much concern today, but in the Victorian age it was a serious matter indeed. Black sheep were given a certain amount of money and told to remove themselves as far away from home as possible, which meant California. Thus it was that branches of a number of prominent eastern and middle western families were established on the West Coast during the 1870s and 1880s. These include, in Santa Barbara, the Mortons (salt), Fleischmans (yeast and distilleries), Armours (meat), Hammonds (organs), and Firestones (tires), and Forbeses of Boston. Farther north, in the Carmel Valley, can be found a descendant of New York and Newport's colorful Mrs. Stuyvesant Fish on his Palo Corona Ranch. San Francisco's prosperous Folger family (coffee) descends from the early Folgers of Nantucket, presumably from a black sheep.

Meanwhile, though the Great Drought drastically undermined the fortunes of the founding Spanish families, their properties had been seriously under attack prior to 1864. When California became a state, the Spanish landholders had been assured that their rights to the lands granted by the Spanish king would be completely respected. In theory, at least, it was all very clear-cut. In fact, in the bureaucratic tangle of creating a new state, it turned out to be all very complicated. Part of the problem was that the early land grants were very loosely worded. A man's property, for instance, might be described as extending "from the side of the mountain" to "the willow grove," and thence to "the big oak," and from there to "the bank of the creek." These demarcations had been perfectly clear to the early settlers, but over the years these landmarks had altered and in many cases had disappeared. Furthermore, many of the land grants described acreages in numbers that were probably guesswork, with the notation "*mas o menos*" (more or less) at the end. The new American bureaucracy insisted on surveyorly precision, which was almost impossible. The early rancheros had let their cattle roam freely, unfenced, relying on their brand markings — and each other's honor — to distinguish one man's cattle from another's. The new bureaucracy felt that properties should be properly separated by fences. It wasn't enough for a rancher to say that he "knew" which tract of land belonged to him and which belonged to his neighbor. Now he had to prove it, which meant that a rancher had to take his claim to an Anglo court in order to defend it.

This in itself was a hardship. Not only did a rancher have to employ a lawyer, he in most cases also had to hire an interpreter, since most of the land-grant owners, like Doña Rosa, spoke only Spanish. In court disputes between English and non-English-speaking claimants, the issue frequently became racial. It was a matter of "Spaniards" versus "real Americans," "Mexicans" versus "Yankees," olive skin versus white skin. In a judicial system dominated by Anglos, the decisions handed down often went against the "ignorant Mexican."

To complicate things further, in his final days as California's last colonial governor, Pio Pico had handed out land grants indiscriminately in return for bribes, feathering his nest for retirement from public life. Some of these grants were deemed legitimate. But, at the same time, other less scrupulous types, seeing what Señor Pico was doing, did a lively business selling forged land grants over Pico's forged signature. Some of the forgeries were obvious, but others were less so, and once again it was up to California's courts of law to decide which were which. The courts became clogged with land-grant cases, and the cases dragged on and on. Many of them were still in court when the Great Drought came — and the great hush fell over the ranchos.

Finally, there was the tricky matter of water and mineral rights, of which the early grants made no mention. Don Nicolàs Den suspected that there were deposits of oil beneath some of his land, and he was right.

Considering all this, it is astonishing that any of California's earliest Spanish aristocracy should have been able to hold on to any of their land at all, and yet, miraculously, some did — if not to all of it, at least to some of it. Bernardo Yorba is a handsome, dark-haired, olive-skinned man in his fifties who still speaks with a trace of a Spanish accent and who has made quite a lot of money in Southern California real estate. He is the great-great-grandson of Don José Antonio Yorba, who came in the original party with Gaspar de Portolá and Father Serra in 1769. His cousins are Peraltas, Carrillos, Sepulvedas, Serranos, and a great many other Yorbas, since his great-grandfather, also named Bernardo, sired twenty-three children. Fecundity being a Yorba family tradition, the present-day Bernardo Yorba is the father of ten. In addition to the family's paternity record, Bernardo Yorba is proud of the fact that his estate in the Santa Ana Canyon, outside Anaheim, stands on part of the original land granted to his great-great-grandfather by the Spanish king. This was sixty-two thousand acres, *mas o menos,* which Don José Yorba christened Rancho Santiago de Santa Ana and which was large enough to permit the don to ride twenty miles in any direction and not leave his own property. Much of the Yorba land was lost after the Great Drought, scooped up by a canny Scotsman named James Irvine who was putting together his vast Irvine Ranch. But the family held on to some of it, turned from cattle raising to citrus growing, and prospered raising the crop for which Orange County is named. Bernardo Yorba still has orange trees on his property — "but only enough to squeeze into my vodka," he says with a wink.

Bernardo Yorba still speaks bitterly about the Anglo bankers who moved in "like buzzards on a kill," tempted his forebears with mortgages in their time of need, and then, when they could not pay them off, ruthlessly foreclosed and evicted them. He also deplores the fact that so much of the land that once belonged to hardworking rancheros has ended up the property of the U.S. government. "The government does *nothing* with it, *nada*. That land could be made productive, but the government just lets it *sit* there," he says. But he is at all times fiercely proud of his Spanish heritage. "Of course we form an aristocracy here," he says. "Spain's is an ancient culture and civilization — much older than the English. *Dios mio,* in cities like Cordoba and Granada and Seville they had indoor plumbing and flush toilets in the fifteenth century, when Londoners were still throwing their slops into the streets!"

Don Bernardo, as his family and friends still call him, is also proud of his Mexican ancestry. "My mother used to say, 'We're Spanish, not Mexican,' " he says. "It was sort of a snobby thing with her, as though being a Mexican was somehow an inferior thing to be. But we came up to California, on horseback, from *Mexico*. When people ask me, I say I'm a *Mexican*. The Mexicans are a proud, hardworking people, with a culture even older than the Spanish. Look at the color of my skin — don't you suppose there's the blood of some old *Indio* or *mestizo* in me from way back? Of course there is. We're an aristocracy because we descend from a superior *people*. Look at the way my ancestors treated the native Indians when we first came to California — much better than the English, Scotch, and Dutch settlers did back East. We tried to convert them to Catholicism, yes. But that was an effort at assimilation, as a way to lift them up to our level of culture. We didn't go out and massacre them, or try to turn them into slaves, or herd them onto reservations the way the Yankees did."

Because of his loyalty to Mexico, Bernardo Yorba is the only American member of the Congress of Charros, a patriotic-historic Mexican equestrian group that, in traditional *charro* garb, demonstrates precision horsemanship at such events as the Rose Bowl Parade. In addition to his various enterprises — chiefly building and developing shopping centers — he is also properly civic-minded and has headed various projects to improve Orange County schools. He is executive vice-president of the children's hospital and is a director of the Angels Stadium Corporation. "We Yorbas are still doing our share, pulling our weight," he says. "My wife and I want to set that kind of example for our children."

"We families are all mixed together," says Conchita Sepulveda Chapman Raysbrook, whose mother, Princess Pignatelli, was for many years the popular society columnist for the *Los Angeles Examiner.* "The members of those few original clans all married into one another's families, which explains why so many of us are interrelated. Our family records show that we're related to the Avila, Serrano, de la Guerra y Noriega, Verdugo, and Dominguez families — so I guess we're all cousins somehow." If Mrs. Raysbrook has Serrano cousins, so does Bernardo Yorba, which would probably make him and Mrs. Raysbrook cousins, though at this point neither of them could tell you how.

But at the mention of their Dominguez cousins, the eyes of both Mr. Yorba and Mrs. Raysbrook will light up perceptibly. The Dominguezes have the honor of being not only the very first of the Spanish families to have been given a grant by Carlos III of Spain, but also of being one of a painfully short list of families who have been able to hold on to *most* of it. The grantee was the pioneering Don Juan José Dominguez, and that much of his original grant is still owned by his heirs is due to the tireless efforts of his great-nephew, Manuel Dominguez, who spent most of his lifetime fighting to have his family's claim to the land recognized by the U.S. courts. In the end, he won, and his deathbed words to his large family are said to have been "*Hold on to it!*"

The only trouble was that, at the time of Don Manuel's death, the land he had secured didn't appear to be worth much. But his heirs followed his instructions, and today the situation is quite different. The land, most of it in the South Bay area, extends on either side of the San Diego Freeway, that booming northwest-to-southeast corridor that has become so hectic with development that it threatens, in time, to turn the cities of Los Angeles, Long Beach, and San Diego into one contiguous, indistinguishable megalopolis. Along much of the distance, little pumps bob cheerily up and down, looking very much like ponies on a merry-go-round, pumping oil from the ground. Yes, Don Manuel was also able to secure the mineral and water rights, and many grateful Dominguezes find lovely royalty checks in their mailboxes every month. "Thank you, Don Manuel," whisper his heirs on their way to the bank. Today, the land around what was

Rancho San Pedro is selling for as much as $100,000 an acre. It will probably go higher. "Never sell — *lease,*" was another of Don Manuel's parting shots. Thank you, Don Manuel.

Profits from the family-controlled Dominguez Water Company, which started supplying water to once arid Torrance in the 1920s — opening up that city to agriculture and development — are still flowing in to this day. As they say in California, "Civilization begins at the end of the water hole." Other Dominguez enterprises include the Carson Estate Company, the Watson Land Company, and Dominguez Properties, Inc. Though there are many Dominguez heirs to share, in varying degrees, the income from these operations, the family collectively today is worth easily a billion dollars.

Another Spanish family that has managed to hold on to a good deal of its land is the Camarillos. The Camarillos are not to be confused with the Carrillos. The Carrillos are a true first-cabin family. The Camarillos are not quite, having arrived in California a little later. But the Camarillos had the good sense, in the 1870s, to buy Rancho Calleguas from Don José Gabriel Ruiz, the original grantee, and to turn its acreage into citrus groves and fields of beans and strawberries, which have been flourishing very profitably ever since. One of the features of Santa Barbara's annual August Fiesta has been the sight of members of the Camarillo family, in Spanish costume, seated in silver-studded saddles astride their pure-white Camarillo horses — a special breed developed by Don Adolfo Camarillo in the 1920s. The dowager of the family today is Doña Carmen Camarillo de Jones, Don Adolfo's daughter, a sprightly octogenarian who rode in the Santa Barbara Fiesta for sixty-three years. Many of Doña Carmen's children and grandchildren live in the nearby town of Camarillo that has sprung up around the ranch. Asked how many of Rancho Calleguas's original acres the Camarillo family still controls, Doña Carmen replies with aristocratic vagueness (and Spanish indifference to such mundane matters as figures), "Oh, about a thousand." "Actually, about five thousand," corrects her nephew, Gerald FitzGerald, who manages the properties, "among various family members. Carmen herself has about twenty-five hundred, mostly leased."

The town of Camarillo, like so many others in California, is growing rapidly, with a population now nudging fifty thousand, and Doña Carmen is under constant pressure to sell her land. "The developers call me up all the time and say, 'Don't you want to sell, Mrs. Jones?'

And I say, 'No, I don't. You know perfectly well I don't.' " And that has been that.

It often comes as a surprise to some easterners to learn that one of the oldest hereditary societies in America — older than the Colonial Dames of America, as well as both the Sons and Daughters of the American Revolution — was organized in California in 1850.* This is the Society of California Pioneers, known more informally as the Pioneers Club. To join the all-male Pioneers, a prospective member must produce a male or female antecedent who set foot on California soil prior to midnight, December 31, 1849, and be able to prove it. Since 1849 was the height of the gold rush, a number of present-day Californians manage to qualify. But some very prominent others do not. Members of San Francisco's Crocker family have applied in vain; the first Crocker was not there in time. Similarly the De Youngs, who gave San Francisco its leading newspaper, the *Chronicle,* as well as its De Young Museum, have been disqualified, though one De Young grandson, Michael de Young Tobin, was able to join when he produced an ancestor on the distaff side named Oliver who just made it under the magic wire. The Floods also just managed to make it by a hair, but not the Fairs, Mackays, or O'Briens. The great California publishing families — the Hearsts, Otises, and Chandlers — cannot join. Neither can most of San Francisco's great Jewish families — the Magnins, Haases, Koshlands, Dinkelspiels, Fleischhackers, Hellmans, and Schwabachers. The Zellerbachs, on the other hand, met the deadline.

The membership committee of the Pioneers has always been relentlessly strict. Not long ago, one applicant produced records to

*A hereditary society, of course, differs from a social club in that ancestry is the sole criterion for membership. Over the years, a number of these have evolved and have received national recognition. The most prestigious is probably the Society of the Cincinnati, which requires that one prove descent from an *officer* in the Revolutionary Army (fighting on the American side, naturally, and honorably discharged). To be a member of the Society of the Cincinnati is considered the American equivalent of being made a Knight of the Garter in England and is taken very seriously. Other hereditary societies have somewhat more quaint, even whimsical, genealogical criteria. There is, for instance, the Flagon and Trencher Society, whose membership is restricted to descendants of colonial tavern keepers. There is also the Descendants of the Illegitimate Sons and Daughters of the Kings of Britain, where one must produce an ancestor who was a bastard offspring of any king or queen of England, Scotland, or Wales. There is even a national society called Son of a Witch, with members whose ancestors were either accused, tried, convicted, or hanged for witchcraft. (The society will provide a list of "recognized" witches, most of whom operated in the vicinity of Salem, Massachusetts, in the 1690s, to interested applicants. Why the society's national headquarters are in Arizona is unclear.)

show that his ancestor, headed for San Francisco by ship and due to arrive within the December 31 deadline, had been delayed by a storm that forced his ship to drop anchor off the Farallon Islands, outside the bay. As a result, he did not arrive until the morning of January 1, 1850. Not good enough, said the committee in its rejection of the application. Even though the Farallons are part of the state, the ancestor had not *set foot on California soil* until after the witching hour had passed. Dropping anchor offshore did not count. Still another would-be Pioneer tried another tactic. He produced documents showing that his ancestor had left New England in October 1849 and other records showing that the same man had become gainfully employed in Sacramento by mid-January 1850. That meant, he claimed, that his ancestor *had* to have crossed the state line some weeks earlier, within the time requirement. This argument cut no ice with the committee. Though technically enough time had passed between the eastern departure and a California arrival two or three months later, the committee pointed out that the ancestor had made his westward trek during winter months, when snows in the high Sierra would most likely have slowed him down.

The Society of California Pioneers is headquartered in San Francisco, where it maintains a handsome clubhouse on McAllister Street, part of which is devoted to a museumlike collection of Old California artifacts, including gold and silver household utensils from the adobe haciendas of the old Spanish dons. But the society's 1,300-odd members are scattered all over the United States, Canada, Mexico, and Europe. The Pioneers considers itself a truly international assemblage, far from parochial.

Mr. George T. Brady, Jr., of San Francisco is a small, compactly built, handsome, and dapper man in his seventies who never steps out-of-doors without donning a spotless, gray felt homburg. He is the kind of man who, even when he is not wearing one, exudes the air of sporting a small fresh flower in his buttonhole. Yes, Mr. Brady is a dandy and would be the first to concede this fact. He is also the sort of man who, in his mature years, has never missed the gala opening night of the San Francisco Opera, the city's premier social event. Mr. Brady was raised to the music of his mother's singing and piano playing. For opening nights, though black tie suffices for most gentlemen these days, Mr. Brady prefers to dress in full fig, in white tie and tails and a tall silk hat and immaculate white gloves, plus a crimson sash across his chest on which to display his various medals and decorations. These include honors earned as a lieutenant commander in the U.S. Navy in both World War II and the Korean conflict, as well as the jeweled medal he is proudest of, which shows him to be a Knight Commander of the Order of Isabella Católica, an award bestowed upon him by King Juan Carlos of Spain in return for Mr. Brady's achievements in stimulating and maintaining interest in the Spanish exploration and colonization of California.

Mr. Brady is an unabashed San Francisco aristocrat: "If I'm not one, who is? It comes in one's mother's milk." His father, George T. Brady, Sr., was a noted San Francisco physician. He himself is a semiretired San Francisco attorney whose specialty was international law, and his wife is a Denby of Rhode Island whose ancestor Thomas Harris was among the first band of colonists to come down from Massachusetts by canoe with Roger Williams. His mother, meanwhile, was the late Doña Francesca de Ortega de Brady, who in her youth, was one of San Francisco's great beauties, and, in her old age, was one of the city's revered *grandes dames.* This makes George T. Brady, Jr., the great-great-great-great-great-grandson of Don José Francisco de Ortega, who married Maria Antonia Carrillo and who is credited with being the first white man to set eyes on San Francisco Bay and the Golden Gate — and who died a bit disappointed that he had not discovered a grander bay for his king.

"Of course in California now there are Ortegas, and there are other Ortegas. In Spain and Mexico, the name Ortega is about as common as Smith or Jones," Mr. Brady says. "But we are the genuine article, and we all know who each other are. There are quite a lot of us around. Alas, Don José's lands were all lost after the Great Drought of the sixties. But most of us have done well for ourselves, nonetheless. Success is in our blood. Some of my Vallejo cousins married Ganters, who make swimsuits. Others married McGettigans. Don José's rancho was about eighteen square miles, and was called Rancho Nuestra Señora del Refugio. It was the twelfth Spanish land grant in the state, and one of the first five in Santa Barbara County. The land may be gone, but in Santa Barbara there are an Ortega school, a library, and a street. There *may* have been an Ortega who came over even earlier, with Cortés, and he *may* have been an ancestor, but we can't prove it. Which is the grandest of the old Spanish families? There's only one rule — never be the first to leave a party of old *Californianos.* The others will all start saying how much more of the *sangre azul* they have in their veins than the fellow who just left!"

Needless to say, George Brady, as a direct descendant of one of the first settlers, is a member in good standing of the Society of California Pioneers, along with a profusion of his cousins. He is also a past president of the organization and remains on its board of directors. Civic-minded, as an Ortega should be, he is also on the boards of Mount St. Joseph's and Mount St. Elizabeth's Home for Wayward Girls, the Proctor Library Foundation, and the Glaucoma Foundation. "We've always tried to do our duty," he says. "That's in the blood, too."

The Ortegas may have lost their land, but the family has held onto other heirlooms: the heavy silver table service, antique lace mantillas, combs, military uniforms, and Mr. Brady's four-times great-grandfather's sword, emblazoned with the family's motto, which, translated from the Spanish, is "Never draw me without reason, never sheathe me without honor."

George Brady had the fact that he was an Ortega, and an aristocrat, drummed into him "from the time I was old enough to talk." One of his earliest memories is of being taken, by his nurse, to visit a young cousin — "fourteen times removed, I think" — and of being presented to his cousin's grandmother, "a little old Spanish lady, dressed in black widow's weeds." Young George was introduced to her, and she responded with a little sniff. Obviously, the name Brady meant nothing to her. A little later, Brady's mother dropped by to pick him up, and she was introduced to the little Spanish lady as Doña Francesca de Ortega de Brady. Slowly, the little lady rose to her feet, extended a jeweled hand, and said, "I rise to greet an Ortega."

Then she performed a deep curtsy.

PART THREE

Heirs Apparent

18

Secret Society

> Only recently a New York woman, who can trace her lineage to the gracious Dutch women who founded Society in New York, gave a dinner for fifty of her friends. Practically all of them came of families antedating the arrival of the British fleet that turned Nieuw Amsterdam into New York. No mention was made of the affair in any paper in New York City, first, because the old regime did not and still does not believe that publicity is necessary to social success, and second, because the city at large has forgotten the families who built it.
>
> Yet these families endure, submerged, and women whose ancestors have directed the social life of New York for ten or more generations still continue to entertain and be entertained without the blare of publicity.

These words, from Mrs. John King Van Rensselaer's book, *The Social Ladder,* were penned in 1924. But they could just as easily, and accurately, have been written in 1987, and about private enclaves of New York gentlemen. Few New Yorkers today are probably aware of the existence, in their very midst, of a small, elite men's club called The Zodiac. It is typical of America's secret aristocracy that The

Zodiac should have been created, in a very real sense, in secret, that it should have passed its hundredth anniversary several years ago without anyone but its members knowing, and that even the *Social Register* — which publishes the names, addresses, telephone numbers, and officers of all the elite clubs in the country — should be unaware of The Zodiac. The Zodiac has no clubhouse, and no address, and no telephone. It has no bylaws and no president, and no list of its members has ever been published. And yet it is easily the most exclusive club in the United States. As its name implies, its membership is restricted, at any given time, to only twelve male members.

The Zodiac was founded in the 1870s by the elder J. Pierpont Morgan, and to understand the principles behind The Zodiac it is first necessary to understand Mr. Morgan. J. P. Morgan has enjoyed, for some reason, the worst posthumous reputation of any man in the history of American banking and finance. History has portrayed Morgan as vain, autocratic, stingy, curmudgeonly, and money-mad. He was in fact none of these things. What he was, was an aristocrat to the marrow. When Morgan died in 1913, much was made in the press of the fact that, out of his $69.5 million fortune, only a small portion of his estate — about $700,000 — was left to charities, giving the impression that the public weal was one of the last things Morgan cared about. What was overlooked was that, during his lifetime, Morgan had contributed vast sums to a wide variety of causes. He was a notable collector of rare books, paintings, and other art objects, and many of these were given to the Metropolitan Museum of Art, of which he was president. Over the years, he had made large financial gifts to this museum, as well as to the American Museum of Natural History, Harvard College (especially to its medical school), the Lying-in Hospital of New York, and the New York trade schools. He was also the principal financial backer of the Groton School, in Massachusetts. It has also been forgotten that, in 1895, when the U.S. Treasury's gold reserves had sunk dangerously low, Morgan's bank loaned the government $62 million in gold to shore up the gold reserves to the $100 million level, thereby supporting the country's currency and averting a financial panic. In his will, furthermore, Morgan stipulated that his son and principal heir, J. P. Morgan, Jr., should make regular annual gifts to designated charities.

At the time of Morgan's death, the "huge" size of his fortune was drawn to public attention. In fact, his fortune, though respectable, was far smaller than those of Henry Frick, E. H. Harriman, or Andrew Mellon and even smaller than those of Thomas Fortune Ryan and Payne Whitney. And Morgan's money was as nothing compared with that of the Du Ponts or John D. Rockefeller. It was Andrew Carnegie who, commenting with surprise on the quality of Morgan's art collection, said, "And to think — he wasn't even a rich man!"

Perhaps Morgan's most famous comment was his laconic reply to a man who asked him how much a yacht cost. "If a man has to ask," he answered, "he can't afford it." At the same time, as an aristocrat who believed that sailing provided the truest test of a man's character, he also once said, "You can do business with anyone, but you can only sail a boat with a gentleman." Also memorable was his humorous reply to a friend who had asked him to lend him some money. "No," replied Morgan, "but I'll let you walk down the street with me."

Admittedly, Morgan had a crusty, distant personality and never made a fuss over other people. He disliked being fussed over himself and, in his London office, became so annoyed with the European practice whereby underlings bowed themselves in and out of the offices of their superiors that he ordered the practice stopped on pain of dismissal.

Like an aristocrat, Morgan observed a strict, almost puritanical code of behavior. No scandal, romantic or otherwise, ever attached itself to his name, even in an era where every rich man was expected to have a mistress. Once, when Morgan was taking to task an associate whose love life was becoming the stuff of drawing room gossip, his associate replied that he was doing nothing more than what everyone else was doing "behind closed doors." "That, sir," countered Morgan, "is what doors are for." According to Morgan's rigid standards, the worst thing a man could do was to break his word. Once, when a man who had been a longtime friend and business associate and was even a relative by marriage, broke his word over a relatively trivial matter, Morgan never spoke to the man again.

John Pierpont Morgan was a prototypical patrician Yankee. He was born in 1837, the son of Junius Spencer Morgan, who, with his partner George Peabody of the Salem Peabodys, formed what eventually became the international banking house of J. S. Morgan & Company in London. The banker's son was splendidly educated at the private English High School in Boston and at the University of Göttingen, in Germany. Throughout his life, J. P. Morgan remained very England-oriented. His suits, shirts, cravats, hats, shoes, walking sticks, and even underwear were custom-made for him in London. He admired the stiff-upper-lip *nil admirari* quality of the upper-crust Britisher's famous reserve, and for this he was thought to be a very cold fish indeed. On the other hand, to the few men whom he considered his true friends, he was intensely and almost sentimentally loyal. When Morgan built and established New York's imposing Metropolitan Club at the corner of Fifth Avenue and Sixtieth Street in 1891, it was widely reported that he had done so to spite the older (1836) Union Club, which had slighted him. In fact, spite had nothing to do with it. Morgan had proposed a friend of his for membership in the Union, but the club had blackballed him. Acutely embarrassed that a man whom he had endorsed should have received such humiliating treatment from his fellow clubmen, Morgan decided to create a new club for his friend by way of atonement. The Metropolitan Club that resulted was a far more luxurious facility than the proud but somewhat dowdy Union Club.

One reason J. P. Morgan was vilified by the press after his death was that, throughout his life, he had an aristocratic disdain for — even loathing of — publicity. Though his name was known all over the world, he never made a speech or attended a public meeting. He never granted interviews to reporters, and he dodged photographers. When Harvard, to whom he had been so generous, wanted to give him an honorary degree, he declined the honor, knowing that receiving it would involve an acceptance speech and dealing with the press. Publishers offered him huge sums for his autobiography, but he turned them all down and refused to authorize any book to be written about him in his lifetime. Even his son-in-law, Herbert Satterlee, was unsuccessful in trying to persuade him to be interviewed on the subjects of his life and business philosophy for posthumous publication. "He had," said one of his former associates, "the instinctive shrinking from publicity of the man of breeding." The closest thing to a public statement of his code occurred a year before his death, during the monetary trust investigation of 1911–1913 by a House committee, when Samuel Untermyer asked him whether commercial credit was based primarily on property or on cash. "The first thing," roared Morgan in reply, "is *character*. A man I do not trust could not get money from me on all the bonds in Christendom."

By the 1870s, Morgan had begun to question the role of the private men's clubs in the city. Their original purpose, he felt, was being subverted. Men's clubs in New York and elsewhere had been originally founded on the model of the men's social clubs in London, designed as places to which men of similar backgrounds and interests could repair at the end of a business day and enjoy an hour or so of companionship unrelated to business. The Union Club had been organized on this principle, and indeed, during the early days of this so-called Mother of Clubs, it was considered poor form to discuss business on the club's premises. This had also been the basic tenet on which the oldest club in America had been established, the Fish House in Philadelphia, which was founded in 1732. To assure that the Fish House would always be assertively social, and nonbusiness, it was formed as a men's cooking club, with members taking turns preparing meals for the membership. (The Fish House, also known as the State in Schuylkill, was indeed a separate state in colonial times and was so recognized by colonial governors. For nearly two hundred years, the club kept the recipe for its famous Fish House punch — a potent mixture of rum, brandy, peach liqueur, sugar, and lemon juice — a closely guarded secret.)

Other New York clubs had followed the Union Club's example and were, in a sense, all offshoots of the Union. The Union League Club was organized in 1863 by disgruntled Union Clubbers who objected that the Confederate secretary of state had been allowed to resign from the club when he should have been expelled. The Knickerbocker Club had been formed in 1871 by ex-Unionites who felt the Union was taking in too many out-of-towners and not giving proper preference to members of Old Knickerbocker families. The Brook Club was founded in 1903 by two young Turks who had been ousted from the Union Club for attempting, or so they said, to fry an egg on the bald head of one of the Union's most venerable members.

But it was not frivolity or politics that Morgan found objectionable about New York's men's clubs. It was a trend he spotted developing in the post–Civil War era of capitalist expansion, in which the clubs were abandoning their initial precepts of gentlemanly good-fellowship among peers and were becoming places where business deals were put together. In this, he was foresighted, for this is exactly what the men's clubs have become, particularly in a financial city such as New York. The clubs have certainly wandered far from their original goals. The Links Club, for example, was first organized, as its name implies, "to promote and conserve throughout the U.S. the best interests and true spirit of the game of golf." Today, the Links, on East Sixty-second Street in Manhattan, is far from any golf course and has become a club whose membership consists of business leaders from all over the country — Minneapolis Pillsburys, Beverly Hills Dohenys, Dorrances from Philadelphia, and Kleenex-making Kimberlys from Neenah, Wisconsin.

The commercialization of the private clubs is now almost complete. As one New York clubman put it recently, "If I have a hundred-thousand-dollar deal to put together, I'll take my client to lunch at the Union or the Knickerbocker. If it's a million-dollar deal, I'll take him to the Brook. If it's ten million, we'll go to the Links. If there's no deal to discuss, we'll go to the University Club."

To offset what seemed to Morgan such an alarming and unaristocratic trend, his answer was the tiny Zodiac club: twelve gentlemen selected on no other basis than, as one member has put it, "good-fellowship and good genes." For nearly a hundred and fifteen years, twelve Zodiac members have met on no regularly scheduled basis, but at least two or three times a year. For each gathering, a member is designated "caterer" to the other eleven and is expected to provide a dinner, either in his own home or in one of the private rooms of one of his clubs. No female guests have ever been invited to meetings, though once a year a dinner is held to include the wives of members. For years, Zodiac members met in full evening dress, white tie and tails, wearing medals and decorations where appropriate. Today, that dress code has been relaxed somewhat, and Zodiac dinners are black-tie. Conviviality and conversation are the only orders of the evening. Business is never to be discussed.

Not that Zodiac members are necessarily men who lead lives of idleness. Their gatherings are intended to be marked only by "congeniality and conviviality," but there is an underlying, more serious theme: the cultural and civic betterment of the city of New York. Membership in The Zodiac is supposed to be kept very secret, as Mr. Morgan wished it, but this author has been able to ascertain the names of ten of the current dozen members. These are:

• Robert G. Goelet, of the old New York real estate family, related to Astors as well as to Vanderbilts, a trustee of the American Museum of Natural History and former president of the New York Zoo.

- John Jay Iselin, descendant of John Jay and former president of New York's WNET/Channel 13 public television station.
- S. Dillon Ripley, retired head of the Smithsonian Institution and married to a Livingston.
- Schuyler G. Chapin, former dean of the Columbia University School of Arts and a Schuyler descendant.
- Daniel G. Tenney, Jr., a descendant of Massachusetts Sedgwicks, married to a Philadelphia Lippincott, a partner in the old New York law firm of Milbank, Tweed, Hadley & McCloy, and a trustee of the Russell Sage Foundation.
- Robert S. Pirie, president of L. F. Rothschild & Company.
- August Heckscher, former New York City Parks commissioner and The Zodiac's secretary and only officer.
- Arnold Whitridge, occupation "gentleman," and the club's oldest member.
- Howard Phipps, Jr., of the Pittsburgh steel family.
- J. Carter Brown III, director of Washington's National Gallery of Art.

The observant will note a preponderance of Harvard and Yale alumni among The Zodiac's membership. The even more observant will spot the fact that many of these men are graduates of the Groton School. Mr. Morgan would have approved of that, too.

Today, only three men's clubs in America survive that are dedicated principally to good-fellowship and good times. There is the ancient State in Schuylkill, still a men's cooking club, which was obviously the inspiration for Morgan's Zodiac. The State in Schuylkill calls itself "The oldest formally orgainized men's social club in the Anglo-Saxon (which is to say civilized) world." The governing qualifiers here are the words "formally orgainized." Such famous London clubs as White's, Boodle's, and St. James's would appear at first glance to be older, but State in Schuylkill members point out that these private clubs started out as public coffeehouses, until White's became "formally orgainized" in 1736, thus making the State in Schuylkill four years older. As for its informal name, the Fish House, this stems from the fact that the club was originally a "Fishing Company" of Philadelphia men who fished the banks of the Schuylkill River in the eighteenth century and enjoyed cooking their catches afterward.

The Fish House meets thirteen times from May to October for its home-cooked luncheons, and periodically during the winter months for dinners. Each course of each meal is the responsibility of an individual member, meaning that members get a chance to try their hand at various dishes — with an emphasis on hearty, outdoorsy fare such as boola-boola soup (made with mussels), planked shad, and pressed duck — throughout the year. As with The Zodiac, there is a dress code at the Fish House. Preparers of the dishes don long white aprons and odd-looking wide-brimmed straw hats called boaters, but which look more like Chinese coolie hats. Members explain that "these hats are of a pattern brought from China early in the last century, and were worn by a high Mandarin caste."

The State in Schuylkill clings determinedly to the notion that it is a separate state, and no part of Pennsylvania. Its members are called Citizens, and among its elected officials are a secretary of state, a secretary of the treasury, a governor, counselors, a sheriff, and even a coroner. Meals traditionally begin with a toast — "To the memory of General Washington" — followed by a second, "To the memory of Governor Morris," who was Samuel Morris, Jr., governor of the State in Schuylkill from 1765 to 1811. After other past governors have been toasted, there is a toast "To the President of the United States," though during the presidency of Franklin D. Roosevelt this part of the ritual was conspicuously omitted. The club's bylaws permit no more than thirty Citizens, or members, at any one time, though at its meetings a certain number of carefully screened Apprentices — or hopeful members-to-be — are invited. While the Citizens do the cooking, the Apprentices do the serving. As a result of the thirty-Citizens-only rule, there have been fewer than five hundred Citizens of the State of Schuylkill in the more than two hundred and fifty years of its existence. Citizenship, it may go without saying, is nearly always conferred upon members of old Philadelphia families.*

During Prohibition, the State in Schuylkill reminded itself that it had never actually ratified the U.S. Constitution. Therefore, it saw no reason to be bound by the strictures of the Eighteenth Amendment.

Then there is San Francisco's remarkable Bohemian Club. Since San Francisco is a much newer city, the Bohemian Club cannot claim the great age of many eastern men's clubs, but it is nonetheless a spiritual descendant of both the State in Schuylkill and New York's

*Membership is supposed to be a closely guarded secret, but who belongs can be ascertained by consulting the *Social Register*.

Century Association, which in turn was another of the splinter groups to emerge from the old Union Club. Formed in 1847, the Century's first membership consisted of gentlemen who felt that intellectual and artistic endeavors were being slighted by the Union. (At the time, one Union Club member grumbled, "There's a club down on Forty-third Street that chooses its members mentally. Now isn't that a hell of a way to run a club?") From the State in Schuylkill, the Bohemian Club has borrowed its emphasis on the great outdoors. From the Century, the Bohemian has taken its emphasis on matters of the mind, or at least the imagination.

Every Bohemian Club member is expected, no matter what his actual calling or profession, to demonstrate some sort of artistic talent — whether it be writing doggerel, playing a musical instrument, or singing a passable baritone. When "other qualifications have been met," a candidate for Bohemian membership can even make a willingness to paint flats for the scenery of the club's stage shows pass for a "talent." In the city, the Bohemian Club occupies a handsome red brick Georgian clubhouse on one of the flanks of Nob Hill, and among the facilities here is a 750-seat theatre, where members prepare and present regular amateur theatricals. But the club's most celebrated institution is its annual two-week summer "encampment" at Bohemian Grove, a twenty-eight-hundred-acre tract it maintains high in the Sierra wilderness. Each Bohemian encampment begins with a campfire ceremony called The Cremation of Care and continues with such events as lectures, poetry readings, musical productions, spectacles of *son et lumière,* and concerts presented by the club's own seventy-piece symphony orchestra. All these productions are written, produced, directed, and performed by the club's membership, and a high degree of professionalism is expected and often achieved. In between these cultural events, there is plenty of time for entertainment of a more bibulous nature.

By eastern standards, the Bohemian Club is large, with some twelve hundred members, but it is also in one sense exclusive. Because social San Francisco has been accused of being both parochial and provincial (as well as a bit *nouveau*), and to offset the fact that some older-established eastern families still tend to think of San Francisco as being at the end of the Anglo-Saxon (which is to say civilized) world, the Bohemian Club likes to think of itself as a national, not just a city, club. Though plenty of Old Guard (which is to say late-nineteenth-century) San Francisco names such as Crocker, Flood,

Spreckels, and de Young are represented in its membership, the Bohemian Club welcomes members from other cities. Thus, while prominent San Franciscans and other Californians often have to wait for years to be invited to join, men from Detroit, Atlanta, Chicago, and Washington go sailing in with no delay at all. The club also has members from Canada and from European cities. To each encampment, a small, carefully screened list of out-of-town guests is invited. These have included Presidents Eisenhower, Nixon, and Reagan. But otherwise the encampments are members-only, and assertively all-male.

For a long time, the location of the Bohemian Grove was a jealously guarded secret, which led to stories and speculation — particularly among wives of members — about wild goings-on, involving loose women, at the grove. Naturally, members did nothing to scotch these lurid tales. But eventually the secret leaked out. Today, wives and children of Bohemian Club members are permitted to visit the grove, though never during an encampment. They find it a peaceful spot for picnics, and if there were ever orgies there, no sign of them remains.

Then, finally, there is the little Zodiac club of New York, the most secret of them all. Aside from its once-yearly nod to spouses, women are never included at its gatherings, nor have outside guests ever been invited. With only twelve members, a member must die or otherwise be placed *hors de combat* before a new member can be taken. As a result, only about fifty men have belonged since J. P. Morgan started it more than a hundred years ago.

"Part of the fun of belonging to The Zodiac," says John Jay Iselin, one of the club's newer members,* "is that nobody else knows about us and, because nobody else much cares, they can't call us 'exclusive.' We're just a bunch of friends who like to get together and enjoy each other's company."

And to enjoy the company of good genes.

*An opening slot for Iselin appeared upon the death of James Bryant Conant, former president of Harvard, later U.S. high commissioner for West Germany, and still later American ambassador to West Germany.

19

Old Guard Versus New

In New York, where money has become the main municipal product and preoccupation, members of the old-line families have responded to the often voracious social onslaughts of new wealth by collectively (and politely) withdrawing into a common protective shell such as The Zodiac. Tortoiselike, they have tucked their heads inside the carapace of family blood and family name. While leading active business lives, they have, in a social sense, become like cave dwellers in the city their ancestors built. They have gone underground. After all, they all know who each other are, and they no longer feel the need to prove or promote themselves in any public way. They cannot properly be called snobbish, because a snob is defined as a person who aggressively seeks out the company — and *only* the company — of the wealthy or well known. Faced with social climbers, the Old Guard families have tended to respond with passive, and again polite, rather than active resistance. A case in point would be the Old Guard's reaction to the arrival of the first August Belmont in its midst.

John Jacob Astor was not a social climber. August Belmont was. Indeed, he may have helped invent the term in New York. He was social climbing personified and a snob *par excellence*. He had appeared suddenly in New York in 1837, with money in his pockets, to take advantage of one of the financial community's periodic panics. Buying up stocks at bargain-basement prices and then watching them rise again, he quickly succeeded in his mission. Belmont was Jewish, but that fact alone would not have amounted to a social demerit at the time. He announced himself as the new American representative of the European banking house of Rothschild, and the Rothschilds were by then internationally respected and in several cases bore European titles. But Belmont denied his Jewishness, and somewhere during his journey from his native Germany to America his original name of Schönberg — "beautiful mountain" — had been more or less Frenchified into Belmont.

But there was something peculiar about all this, beyond the name change. The Rothschilds almost never sent a representative to open up new banking territory who was not a family member, yet they did seem to be on very close terms with Mr. Belmont. And the rumor circulated to the effect that, in Europe, whenever a male Rothschild traveled with a lady who was not his wife, the pair would traditionally register at hotels as M. et Mme. Schönberg. Thus the possibility presented itself — though it would never be proven — that August Belmont was an *illegitimate* Rothschild, an embarrassment to the family at home but trusted sufficiently to be dispatched to conduct family business on the other side of the Atlantic. This was the enigma of August Belmont: a man who looked like a German, spoke with a precise, if stilted, British accent, had a French name, and wanted to become an American aristocrat.

Belmont had not been able, as the Astors had done, to ally himself maritally with one of the Old Guard families. But he did the next best thing. He proposed to, and was accepted by, the daughter of an American war hero. She was the beautiful — if, by some accounts, dull-witted — Caroline Slidell Perry, the daughter of Commodore Matthew Calbraith Perry, distinguished officer in the Mexican War and the man credited with having opened Japan to the West. Her uncle was another naval commander, Oliver Hazard Perry, hero of the War of 1812 and the Battle of Lake Erie. The Belmonts were married grandly in the Episcopal Church.

But from that point onward August Belmont began doing everything on almost *too* grand a scale, which left New Yorkers more aghast than impressed. He and his new wife established themselves in a new house on lower Fifth Avenue that was bigger and more elaborate than anything the Astors had ever owned. It was the first house in New York to have, among other things, its own ballroom, a room set aside solely for the annual Belmont ball. As Edith Wharton commented later, in her novel *The Age of Innocence,* this room "was left for three hundred and sixty-four days of the year to shuttered darkness, with its gilt chairs stacked in a corner and its chandelier in a bag." The Belmonts were also the first couple in New York to have their own red carpet, to be rolled down the marble front steps and across the sidewalk, for parties, instead of renting one from a caterer along with the gilt chairs.

Everything the Belmonts did seemed larger than life, and so naturally it was talked about and written about. August Belmont may have been New York's first, and was certainly its most ardent, publicity seeker. When he imported a French chef from Paris, the news made the papers. August Belmont's art gallery was the first in the city to be lighted from a skylight in the roof, and the collection of art it housed was remarkable, including works by Madrazo, Rosa Bonheur, Meissonier, Vibert, and — truly scandalous — an assortment of voluptuous and oversize nudes by Bouguereau. Most scandalized by the last was an Old Guard New Yorker named James Lenox, who lived directly across the street from the Belmonts. Learning of Mr. Lenox's objections to the Bouguereaus, Belmont defiantly hung the largest and most explicit of the nudes just inside his front door so that it would be in full view of the Lenox front windows every time the Belmont front door was opened, which, in light of the amount of entertaining Belmont did, was often. Mr. Lenox would become almost apoplectic at the mention of the Belmont name, and according to Lucius Beebe, when Lenox was told that Belmont spent twenty thousand dollars a month on wines alone, Lenox collapsed of a heart attack and died.

The press happily chronicled the extravaganza of Belmont's high living. Two hundred people could be comfortably seated at table in the Belmont dining room, with a footman behind each chair, to dine off the Belmont gold service. Belmont had taken up the sport of kings, and the regal Belmont racing colors — scarlet and maroon — had been established. The livery of Belmont's coachmen and footmen consisted of maroon coats with scarlet piping and silver buttons embossed with the Belmont family crest (which, it was said, Belmont had himself designed after studying various royal European coats of arms), along with black satin knee breeches, white silk stockings, and patent-leather slippers with silver buckles. All his carriages were painted maroon with a scarlet stripe on the wheels. His chief steward, it was said, was required to go through five complete changes of uniform each day.

At the same time, there were some decidedly odd stories that also circulated about August Belmont. It was said that he washed, combed, and set his wife's hair, and chose all her dresses from her dressmaker. It was said that, despite his stable of Thoroughbreds, he himself could not sit a horse. It was said that he eavesdropped on his servants and blackmailed them into accepting the lowest wages in the city. Heroism had not made Commander Matthew Perry wealthy, and when Mrs. Belmont's father came to live with the Belmonts, it was said that August Belmont treated his father-in-law like a servant, giving him menial household chores to perform and sending him out on petty errands. These activities did not sound like those of the kind of gentleman August Belmont seemed to want to be.

In *The Age of Innocence,* Edith Wharton presented a thinly veiled portrait of August Belmont in the fictional character of Julius Beaufort, a man whom, as one of Mrs. Wharton's characters put it understatedly, "certain nuances" escaped. As Mrs. Wharton wrote:

> The question was, who *was* Beaufort? He passed for an Englishman, was agreeable, handsome, ill-tempered, hospitable and witty. He had come to America with letters of recommendation from old Mrs. Manson Mingott's English son-in-law, the banker, and had speedily made himself an important position in the world of affairs; but his habits were dissipated, his tongue was bitter, and his antecedents were mysterious.

Like Caroline Belmont, Julius Beaufort's wife (who "grew younger and blonder and more beautiful each year") always appeared at the opera on the night of her annual ball "to show her superiority to all household cares." To explain why she accepted invitations to the Beauforts' dinner parties, one of Mrs. Wharton's characters said airily, "We all have our pet common people." But, Mrs. Wharton added, "The Beauforts were not exactly common; some people said they were even worse."

August Belmont had gone a long way toward going too far with New York society, but he had not yet made his final, fatal step. That was yet to come. For years, the most important social event in New York had been the annual Assembly, held at Delmonico's. And, for years, invitations to the Assembly had been rigidly based on the standards of "birth and breeding." An invitation to the Assembly was the ultimate proof of social rank. Year after year, August Belmont had dropped broad hints to various of the all-male members of the Assembly Committee that he and his wife would like to be invited. The hints had been politely ignored.

Finally, August Belmont decided to pull out his heavy artillery. He appeared before several members of the committee and stated firmly that this year the Belmonts expected an invitation. The men replied that they were sorry, but that it was quite impossible. Belmont then allegedly told the committee members, "I think it's not only possible, it's also extremely probable. I have been investigating the accounts of you gentlemen on the Street. I can assure you that either I get an invitation to the Assembly this year, or else the day after the Assembly each of you will be a ruined man."

The Belmonts received their invitation, but the story of the means by which it had been procured got around. The following year, the Belmonts were also prominent guests at the Assembly. They were particularly prominent because nearly everyone else who had been invited stayed home. The Assembly was never held again.

Thus did the Old Guard deal with climbers, not by battling them but simply by withdrawing from the arena. Of course the result would be that the climbers had the arena to themselves. But the Old Guard would never view this as weakness on their part, or as a signal of abdication or defeat. On the contrary, they saw it as a kind of victory of principles over sheer power. Was there any other gentlemanly or ladylike way to deal with social ruffians?

Margaret Trevor Pardee grew up next door to August Belmont's son, August Belmont, Jr. Her father's big house took up half the block on Madison Avenue and Fifty-second Street, and the Belmont house stood on the other half. "Mother told us that of course we were to be civil to the Belmonts," she says, "but we were not to get involved with them." The tiny nonagenarian with twinkly blue eyes and auburn hair ("I give it a little help from a bottle") recalls a turn-of-the-century New York girlhood and upbringing quite different from that of her neighbors. "Goodness, I couldn't tell you how many servants Mother had as opposed to the Belmonts," she says. "They were hard to count, because we children were not permitted in the kitchen. This was not for a snobby reason. It was because we were told that we would be underfoot and in the way while the kitchen staff had important work to do. Of course, when

Mother was out, we'd sometimes sneak in. But we didn't count because we were taught that it wasn't nice to talk about how many servants one had. It would be like boasting, and it was bad manners to boast."

The strictures of Margaret Trevor's girlhood read a bit as though they were taken from a Renaissance manual for the training of a princess: You are to rule your kingdom, but to be served you must also know how to serve. "Everybody we knew was taught the same thing," she says today. "We were taught never to ask a servant to do something you wouldn't be perfectly willing and able to do yourself. You might never have to scrub a toilet, but it was important that you know how to do it. You might never have to change a tire on an automobile, but that didn't mean you weren't taught to do it properly. My children were taught the same things, and now their children are teaching *their* children.

"Of course, a lot has changed. Mother started her day early, with her breakfast brought to her on a tray in bed. While she ate, she and the cook went over the day's menus together. Then she read and answered her mail, and paid the bills that had come in that day. Then she rose and bathed, and went out visiting or shopping. My children and grandchildren can't get that kind of service today, but I'm happy to say they still observe the rules that my mother laid down to me. Two of them were: Never leave your house until all the day's bills have been paid; and, a lady isn't a lady if her bed isn't made by noon."

Like others in her circle, Margaret Trevor was raised by governesses and educated by private tutors until she was twelve years old. "The governesses were usually English, and *very* strict on manners. The chauffeurs were usually Scotsmen — don't ask me why — and the maids were Irish. It sounds extravagant, I know, but in those days it wasn't — it just wasn't. There was a steady supply of Irish girls who were eager to get the work, who were clean and honest and loved children, and who would work for very little — seven days a week, with an hour off on Sunday to go to mass — just to have a roof over their heads. They didn't act as though we were exploiting them — they felt we were *helping* them! In those days, every lady had a personal maid as well. Oh, my, it all seems so long ago!

"But we children were never allowed to have a maid pick up after us the way" — she sniffs — "*some* people did. I'm thinking of the

Belmonts. Oh, no, that was taboo. We had to keep our rooms tidy and make our own beds. Our clothes had to be all folded and put away at night before we went to bed. We ironed our own middy blouses — middy blouses were the big thing. Oh, I suppose it was all very rigid, very formulated, very *comme il faut,*" she says of the kind of girlhood that has been compared to the binding process that was used to form the Chinese lotus foot, "but we didn't think so at the time. We lived the way everyone else we knew lived."

As she talks, Margaret Pardee's voice is full of little trills and crescendos, punctuated with tremolos and staccato passages. It is a voice that seems to have been trained for the theatre, and it almost was, for Margaret Pardee at one point threatened to rebel against her aristocratic training in order to become, of all things, a show girl. "But wiser heads prevailed. As children, you see, our upbringing was very strict. From nine in the morning until one in the afternoon, my brothers and sisters and I had our lessons with our governesses. But then, for two whole hours we had freedom! Freedom. We'd put on our roller skates and skate up Fifth Avenue to Central Park, and down the Mall — our governesses tagging along, of course, a block behind us, not because the park was dangerous, but because it was *comme il faut,* you see. When I was twelve I was sent to a real *school,* and that was to Spence when it was still called Miss Spence's Classes. Miss Spence's school was on West Fifty-fifth Street then, and my brother went to the Browning School, which was also on West Fifty-fifth, just across the street. My brother and I would walk to Fifth Avenue, and there we'd pick up our friend Dickie Babcock, and walk north to Fifty-fifth. But there we'd have to part company, because Spence girls weren't allowed to be seen walking down the street with boys. Oh, *my!* So the boys would walk down the north side of the street to Browning, and the girls would walk down the south side to Spence. In good weather, at recess time, we liked to go up on the roof, where there was a sort of playground. Across the street, the Browning boys would be up on their roof, and we would look at them from across the street. But we weren't allowed to wave at each other. All we could do was *look.* Oh, my!

"And, oh, my, there were all sorts of rules at school. We were only allowed to wear one simple ring, and one simple pin, no other jewelry, and no more than *two hats at a time.* You see, it was fashionable for women to change their hats several times a day — even in their own houses ladies wore hats — but at Spence we could only change hats once a day! And there was a rule that the hats must be 'inconspicuous and not costly.' We didn't have uniforms, but I used to wish we did. Even though Spence girls weren't supposed to wear expensive dresses either, some girls did. The Bishop girls! Oh, my, I remember how I envied their velvet dresses! Nowadays, I suppose you'd call the Bishops *nouveaux riches,* but we didn't call them that, though the Bishop girls were considered rather *fast.* Money didn't matter to people in those days the way it does today, or at least we never talked about it. What mattered was *breeding,* and whether we *liked* someone. And breeding didn't just mean old family, or pedigree. It meant people who behaved in a well-bred way — who were *nice,* you see.

"And my Spence graduation! It was held at the old Sherry's at Forty-fourth and Fifth. We marched down the aisle to the strains of "Pomp and Circumstance." Oh, my, and Miss Clara Spence herself — a steely-eyed Scotswoman! Excellence, excellence — that was her credo! Better grades, better grades! 'Come now, Miss Trevor,' she would say to me, 'you can do better than that!' At night, I used to stuff cotton around the cracks of my bedroom door so my father wouldn't see how late I was staying up, studying. But I got good marks, and when I graduated I was one of the top ten in my class. It was unusual for a girl to go to college in those days, but I begged my father to let me go to college. He turned thumbs down on that. College was for boys, not girls. It sounds unfair, I know, but there was a reason for it. In those days, if a girl went to college there was nothing she could do with her education except become a schoolteacher. And schoolteachers were not permitted to marry, and so that meant becoming a spinster. Every father wanted his daughter to marry, and to give him grandchildren. In those days there was always a good reason for everything."

A young woman of good family was not only expected to marry. She was expected to marry *well.* "This was drummed into us," and so this Margaret Trevor did in 1917, when she married Dr. Irving Pardee, a prominent neurologist and himself a member of an old-line New York and New Jersey family. Margaret Pardee's younger sister, Louise, married even better. Her first husband was J. Couper Lord, of the family that founded Lord & Taylor, who died. She married, next, Lewis Morris, a grandson of the Declaration of Independence signer. He also died. She then married, third, Henry Mellon of the Pittsburgh Mellons, who suffered a heart attack in

Florida, became paralyzed, and eventually died. "So she managed to marry and bury three rich husbands," Mrs. Pardee says with a sigh.

Between her graduation from Miss Spence's and her marriage to Dr. Pardee, however, Margaret Trevor was required to fulfill another social obligation to her class — the proscribed ritual of becoming a debutante — in the 1912–1913 New York winter social season. There were the balls, parties, luncheons, and *thés dansants* at which she was officially presented to her parents' friends as their social peer. She herself was presented to society at a tea dance for several hundred people held at her parents' Madison Avenue house.

"I loved to sing, and I loved to dance," she says. "My father used to sleep with his bedroom door ajar, and my sister Louise and I used to tiptoe past his door when we came in at night, so he wouldn't know how late we'd been out. Oh, my, but he was strict with us! Not with himself, of course — he had French blood, and loved a good time. But with us he was so straitlaced! My mother was much more laissez-faire. She didn't care how late we danced, because she knew that we wouldn't do anything *wrong*. There were some dances that were frowned upon. The turkey trot and the bunny hug, for instance. We didn't do those dances. The tango was a *problem*. Some people thought it was very elegant and beautiful. Other people thought it was downright *naughty*. I loved to dance the tango! And the Yale Prom — *that* was *the* party of the entire season. Everyone went up to New Haven and stayed at the Taft Hotel. The prom started on Saturday night, and by Sunday afternoon people were still dancing! The next year, they were still dancing on *Monday*, and it became a *thing* to see how long the dance could last! It went on all day Monday, and Monday night, and then all day Tuesday, and Tuesday night! People were still dancing on *Wednesday!* It became something of a scandal, and all the newspapers wrote it up, and the Yale authorities issued a statement to the press that such a thing would never be permitted to happen again! Oh, my, but how I loved it!"

Currently, Margaret Trevor Pardee is in the process of sorting out the family papers in order to prepare a scrapbook of family memorabilia for each of her grandchildren. Old newspaper clippings, diaries, journals, and family bibles — plus one fat scrapbook of clippings from her own debutante year — are being sorted through, arranged, and filed in appropriate folders. Into each grandchild's scrapbook will go copies of the interwoven family trees of the Schieffelins, Pardees, and Trevors, and her own genealogy, which wanders backward through eighteen generations of Trevors, Stewarts, Lispenards, Roosevelts, Barclays, Bownes, more Barclays, more Stewarts, back to the turn of the fifteenth century — showing her direct linear descent from Mary Stuart, Queen of Scots.

What is it that she hopes to transmit to her grandchildren, and on to their grandchildren after that, through the medium of these family-memory books? "Pride," she says. "The things I was taught. Poise and pride. Pride of our place in American history. The things that knit a family together. We were always very proud of being *Americans,* you see. Even though a Schieffelin ancestor fought on the side of the British in the Revolution, he was part of American history.

"I suppose that was one of the troubles with the first August Belmont. He was a foreigner. He didn't understand America, and he didn't understand New York. Our ways were foreign to him. He had no background, no roots to fall back on. He thought he could buy it all with money, but you just can't. He had plenty of money, but he had no pride."

20

The Gospel of Wealth

In Margaret Pardee's scrapbooks, files, and collections of family-related newspaper clippings, there are occasional items which indicate that life for privileged early-twentieth-century New Yorkers was not entirely one of ease and comfort and night-and-day-long dancing. There were certain vicissitudes as well. Automobiles, for example, were still something of a novelty, and automobile accidents made headlines on the front pages of the New York papers. Since motorcars were still affordable only to the wealthy, the accidents usually involved a prominent citizen.

Such an occurrence involved Margaret Trevor Pardee's great-aunt, Mrs. Hamilton Fish, who, with a friend, Miss Emily Van Amringe, was being driven down Riverside Drive in Mrs. Fish's landaulet when their car struck a Fifth Avenue southbound motor stage at 101st Street. In this accident, the omnibus was not damaged, but the landaulet lost a wheel, and the ladies were thrown against the windscreen that separated the driver from his passengers. The chauffeur, Henry McEwen, was unhurt, but the ladies were taken to St. Luke's Hospital for treatment of cuts and bruises. To a policeman who came to the scene, Mrs. Fish commented, "If anybody is to be hurt by these accidents, I wish the chauffeur would suffer once in a while." The *New York Sun* agreed with her.

America, after all, was a democracy, where everyone was entitled to equal treatment.

Despite the aura of languor and complacency that seems to have hung around this era like a perfumed breeze, as the *belle époque* glided to its close and the twentieth century entered its teens, there were disquieting signs of social unrest in the country that were hard for even the most gently bred and carefully sheltered to ignore.

The first of these warnings had appeared in 1899, with the publication of Wisconsinite Thorstein Veblen's *Theory of the Leisure Class,* with its introduction of such phrases as "conspicuous consumption" "conspicuous leisure," and "the pecuniary standard of living." Veblen was no marxist or socialist, but his treatment of the leisure class was definitely impious and mocking. He placed clergymen, for example, in the servant class, pointing out that they put on elaborate uniforms in order to perform ritual duties to a superior master. He also — perhaps intentionally, or perhaps not — managed to misquote Shakespeare when he spoke of people who were "to the manor born." What Hamlet actually said was, ". . . though I am a native here and to the manner born. . . ." Hamlet was talking about aristocratic attitudes and deportment, but Veblen left the impression that the subject was rich people who lived in manor houses. This confusion over the meaning of the term has persisted ever since. In any case, Veblen's book, which was widely read and discussed, left the distinct impression that the leisure class was frivolous and silly. Was the American aristocracy in danger of becoming a laughingstock and being ridiculed out of existence? Some people interpreted Veblen just that way.

Fourteen years later, in 1913, the American rich found themselves under attack from several different directions at once, and there were ominous signs that the American public in general was growing less and less tolerant of the well-to-do. That year, the Sixteenth Amendment to the Constitution went into effect, empowering Congress to levy a graduated income tax on all incomes over three thousand dollars a year. This, it was proclaimed, would equal things out and require that the rich contribute a fuller share of their wealth to the public coffers — though the rich would soon devise loopholes and shelters against the tax laws that would leave most of them just as wealthy as before. And, also in 1913, a Columbia University professor named Charles A. Beard published *Economic Interpretation of the Constitution* and pointed out that America's founding fathers who drafted the Constitution in 1787 were all men of considerable property — colonial aristocrats. This fact, Beard suggested, had led to certain economic inequities in the years since then.

These vaguely unsettling noises did not go unheard among the upper echelons of society in New York and elsewhere. The ideas had begun to take hold that, though some Americans were quite fortunate, there were many more who were less so; that though a privileged class had definitely evolved, there was another that was just as definitely underprivileged; that with great wealth there went proportionately great social responsibilities; and that there might be more important things to think about than the morality of the tango and the duration of the Yale Prom. Part of this sobering sense was inherited from the European concept of *noblesse oblige* and from the motto of the British monarch, *Ich dien,* "I serve." But even more of it seems to have involved a very American capitalist sense of Protestant guilt.

On the heels of Mr. Beard's published thesis came the House Committee on Banking and Currency's report on the "money trust," a loosely organized but highly effective cabal of bankers and industrialists, led by J. P. Morgan, that controlled financial power in the United States. And, to bring home the notion of the enormous power held by the rich in a violent and frightening way, 1913 was also the year of the bloody strike called by the United Mine Workers at the Colorado Fuel and Iron Company, protesting the policies of the firm that was headed by John D. Rockefeller of Standard Oil. Twenty-seven strikers were killed, and Mr. Rockefeller, whose attitude up to that point had been one of simple arrogance, found it wise to enlist the services of one Ivy Ledbetter Lee, a pioneer in the new "science" of public relations. It was Mr. Lee who counseled Mr. Rockefeller to travel to Colorado and to personally address the striking miners, a gesture that had an immediately calming effect on the highly charged situation. It was also Mr. Lee's suggestion that Rockefeller adopt the tactic of handing out shiny new dimes to bystanders wherever he went, helping to create the illusion that the ruthless oil tycoon was not a curmudgeonly despot at all but a kindly national Santa Claus of sorts. At the same time, Lee was helping Rockefeller lay the groundwork for the vast Rockefeller Foundation, which would become a major force in improving world health, world agriculture, and education. It is thanks to the foundation, rather than to any individual family member, that the Rockefellers today have been admitted, albeit begrudgingly, into the ranks of the American aristocracy — though to members of the Old Guard they will perhaps always be regarded as newcomers.

Ivy Lee had to teach John D. Rockefeller that "rich" and "responsibility" began with the same letter of the alphabet. Lee himself was born with the knowledge. Six feet tall, lean and erect and handsome, he bore himself with the courtliness and dignity of a southern gentleman, which, indeed, he was. A childhood accident had left him with a slight limp, which only managed to add to his kindly, decorous demeanor. Though he had started his career in the somewhat raffish world of newspaper reportage, his presence added a touch of unexpected class to that profession, and it was the kind of class that Lee owed both to his heritage and to his education.

On his father's side, the family could trace itself back to the first Richard Lee of the Lees of Virginia. On his mother's side, he was descended from George Washington's father and, beyond the Washingtons — admittedly with a slight genealogical hiccup* — to Margaret Butler, whose illustrious ancestors included nearly all the kings of Europe, including Charlemagne. Ivy Lee's grandfather Zachary Lee had been a wealthy Georgia planter and gristmill owner, and Ivy Lee's father, James Wideman Lee, had been privately educated at Bawsville Academy before the Civil War. But the family fortune was lost when General William Sherman put a torch to the Lee plantation and mill on his march to the sea, and so James W. Lee chose the best occupation that was open to a newly impoverished gentleman and became a Methodist Episcopal clergyman. Soon he was one of the most popular ministers in Atlanta.

For his time, James Lee was an altogether remarkable man, and Ivy Lee grew up listening to his father's sermons, which were about love, racial and religious tolerance, thrift, hard work, and moral duties. He was an early southern advocate of civil rights for blacks and for government programs that would improve the quality of black education in the postwar South. Following an anti-Semitic incident in St. Louis, the Reverend Lee preached a sermon that made national headlines: "METHODIST PASTOR LAUDS JEWISH RACE." Later, he led a campaign to admit Jews, Catholics, and blacks into the YMCA and proposed a "Cathedral of Cooperation" in Atlanta that would welcome all faiths, Protestants, Catholics, and Jews. Ivy Lee's

*George Washington's father, Augustine Washington, married twice. His first wife was a Butler. His second wife, the former Mary Ball, was the mother of George.

mother was equally extraordinary. Born in the middle of the War Between the States, and growing up in the southern poverty that followed, she had no opportunity for any education whatsoever. Yet she taught herself to read and write, and became an eloquent public speaker, traveling widely about the United States lecturing at women's clubs and church functions. Like her husband's, her themes were tolerance, compassion, humanity, and duty. With their combined incomes, the Lees were able to send their firstborn son north to be educated at Princeton.

At Princeton, Ivy Lee came under the influence of the university's then president, James McCosh, a leading exponent of the Scots philosophy of common sense. According to McCosh, individualism, freedom from government interference, the rights to acquire and own property, and the right to amass wealth were basic tenets. Not long before Ivy Lee arrived at Princeton, President McCosh had written that "God has bestowed upon us certain powers and gifts which no one is at liberty to take from us or to interfere with. All attempts to deprive us of them is theft. Under the same head may be placed all purposes to deprive us of the right to earn property or to use it as we see fit." Poverty, in McCosh's view, was simply the result of laziness. Wealth resulted from hard work and thrift, and from hard work and thrift came civilization. Wealth was a kind of divine reward.

By the early 1900s, however, this somewhat harsh and simplistic view required some sort of tempering. The era of the robber barons that had followed the Civil War had produced fortunes far more vast than any America had ever seen — fortunes that were patently out of all proportion with any intellectual, moral, or even business capacities on the part of the individual entrepreneurs who made them. While a handful of Americans had become enormously wealthy, the other side of the coin was displaying an alarming spread of urban slums, destitution, and disease. The gulf of disparity between the very rich and the very poor had become so yawningly wide that some sort of explanation seemed needed. Could it all be written off as the will of the Almighty? How did one reconcile the pursuit of wealth with the spread of social ills that seemed to accompany it? How, in short, could the obvious success of American capitalism be credibly advertised as being for the common good?

One answer had been proposed a few years earlier by Andrew Carnegie, one of the richest men of his day and one of the few new

American millionaires who actually appeared to possess such a thing as a social conscience. Carnegie had given the matter of excessive riches serious thought. In 1889, in the *North American Review,* he had published an article titled, simply and honestly, "Wealth." And out of this had evolved what came to be known as "the gospel of wealth." Soberly and painstakingly, Carnegie had outlined what he felt to be the duties and responsibilities of the man of wealth, and how he felt that wealth must be used to ease the social ills of the world.

The first duty of the man of wealth, Carnegie wrote, was

> to set an example of modest, unostentatious living, shunning display or extravagance; to provide moderately for the legitimate wants of those dependent upon him; and after doing so to consider all surplus revenues which came to him simply as trust funds, which he is called upon to administer, and strictly bound as a matter of duty to administer in the manner . . . best calculated to produce the most beneficial results for the community.

Needless to say, very few of the new millionaires of the era were living their lives according to this gospel — though some were, and most of these, interestingly enough, were members of the newly rich American Jewish community, led by such eminent and conscientious men as the banker Jacob H. Schiff and the lawyer Louis Marshall. Schiff, for example, believed in the principle of tithing, and at least 10 percent of everything he made went somehow or other toward the public weal — to Jewish and non-Jewish causes alike. Schiff, furthermore, believed in the Talmudic doctrine that "Twice blessed is he who gives in secret," and so most of his major benefactions were made anonymously. When his son-in-law, Felix Warburg, embarked on a project to build himself an elaborate mansion on Fifth Avenue, a display of extravagance if there ever was one, Schiff stopped speaking to him.

But in the case of men like John D. Rockefeller and others who were busily erecting vast, showy mansions in Newport, on Long Island, in Bar Harbor and Palm Beach, there was a need by 1913 — as Ivy Lee saw it — for the very rich to at least pay lip service to the gospel of wealth, if their gilded gates were not to be stormed by the hungry rabble. Following his graduation from Princeton, and a few years as a newspaperman, which taught him the importance of having "a good press," Lee moved into the world of the rich, where, with his looks and manners, he seemed more than at home and where he offered his services as a polisher of seriously tarnished images. One after another, he became adviser on what he dubbed public relations to such men as George Westinghouse, Thomas Fortune Ryan, Charles Schwab, Walter Chrysler, Harry F. Guggenheim, Alton B. Parker, John W. Davis, Henry P. Davison, Dwight Morrow, Otto Kahn, Winthrop Aldrich, and the Rockefellers.

In the process, to be sure, Ivy Lee himself would become a moderately rich man. Still, he remained true to the gospel. When universities, foundations, charities, or churches sought his services, he offered them for nothing.

But he had discovered that there was money to be made in teaching new money how to behave like old money. And he was so successful at it that the general public would begin having trouble distinguishing which kind of money was which — a fact that would have the effect of driving the old money even deeper into its cave, licking its wounds, cringing at the thought of having names such as Rockefeller and Vanderbilt uttered in the same sentence as Livingston or Jay.

21

Comme Il Faut

Considering the opulence of some of the private entertainments that had been put on in the 1880s and 1890s, it was not hard to see how Thorstein Veblen had come up with the term "conspicuous consumption." In fact, by the time James L. Breeze gave his notorious "Jack Horner Pie" dinner for twelve gentlemen in honor of Diamond Jim Brady — conspicuous by virtue of its human party favors — the scale of that party seemed rather modest. In Washington, Mrs. George Westinghouse had already topped him. As a countermeasure to Caroline Astor's New York Four Hundred, Mrs. Westinghouse decided to give a party for the capital's One Hundred. Exactly one hundred guests were invited, and folded into the napkin of each guest as a party favor was a crisp one-hundred-dollar bill.

Large sums of newly acquired money were tossed about in even more outlandish ways. There was, for instance, Mrs. Stuyvesant Fish's infamous "Monkey Dinner," at which guests were invited to meet a visiting guest of honor billed as Prince del Drago. Prince del Drago turned out to be a monkey attired in full evening dress that scrambled about the tabletops hissing and grimacing at the guests. Public hilarity at Mrs. Fish's great "joke" was somewhat muted. Animals suddenly became popular honorees at formal dinners, and there was a "dogs' dinner," at which every guest was required to bring a canine pet, appropriately costumed and bejeweled. This fad came to its silliest climax with Mr. C.K.G. Billings — a gasworks heir from Chicago — who came to storm New York society with a "Horseback Dinner" in 1903. Here is how Albert Stevens Crockett recalls that memorable evening in *Peacocks on Parade:*

> The choicest mounts from Billings' stable were taken to Sherry's rear entrance and carried by elevators upstairs to the big ballroom on the fourth floor, which had been completely disguised as a woodland garden, with trees and shrubs apparently growing, and the floor sodded. In the centre was a great manger, where the blue-bloods of the equine world were hitched, their part being to stand and contentedly chew sweet hay. Overhead, an effect of clear blue sky had been achieved, with twinkling stars and a harvest moon, and real birds twittered in the shrubbery. Waiters were dressed as grooms, in scarlet coats and white breeches. Over each horse was slung a table, securely anchored to the animal's flanks, and from its shoulders dangled two saddle-bags, stuffed with ice-buckets of champagne. The guests came in riding costume. Each mounted the charger assigned to him, and in his saddle ate a bewildering array of courses, cooled with sips through long, nippled rubber tubes that led to the champagne bottles in the saddle-bags.

Coming-out parties, which before the Civil War had always been sedate, quiet, and unpublicized affairs attended only by family and close friends, became occasions for the lavish display of wealth and nothing more. In New York, George Jay Gould spent $200,000 in 1909 on the debut of his daughter Marjory. ("How does the American press find out the costs of these parties?" a visiting British journalist mused. The answer: Their hosts cheerfully supplied them.) The flowers alone at the Gould gala included 5,500 lilies of the valley, 1,500 white roses, and "every American beauty rose in the East."

At Sherry's again, Mrs. W. Watt Sherman gave a party for her daughter Mildred where a huge swan floated on an artificial lake among 1,300 guests and where, when the debutante took her bow, the swan exploded, scattering 10,000 pink roses into the air. Less successful was the "Butterfly Ball" given by the James Pauls of Philadelphia for their daughter Mary. For this affair, some 10,000 exotic live butterflies had been imported from Brazil and collected in a decorative bag suspended from the center of the ballroom ceiling.

As the debutante curtsied to her peers, the bag was to burst open, releasing the butterflies to fly prettily about the party. Unfortunately, in those days before air-conditioning, the heat at the ballroom ceiling rose to surpass even that of the Amazonian jungle, and when the bag was opened, out tumbled 10,000 butterfly corpses.

In Newport, the Norman de R. Whitehouses hired the U.S. Navy for the coming-out party of their daughter Alice. While the guests danced under the stars, warships moored offshore played their searchlights on the partygoers. On Long Island, the banker Otto Kahn, in his pre–Ivy Lee days of big spending, paid the tenor Enrico Caruso ten thousand dollars to sing two songs for his daughter's party. (In his post–Ivy Lee period, Kahn would be persuaded to dip into his ample pocketbook for civic and cultural events instead, and when New York's Metropolitan Opera Company was in financial straits, Kahn simply bought the opera to keep it going.)

All this party giving, of course, had been without redeeming social value and could be excused only with the often trotted out, but rather lame, claim that it provided "needed employment" for caterers, waiters, florists, musicians, and the like. A particularly sorry result of one of these affairs had occurred in the case of Mr. and Mrs. Bradley Martin, who, on their social voyage from the hinterlands of Troy, New York, to Manhattan, had acquired an Englishy-sounding hyphen to their name and become known as Mr. and Mrs. Bradley-Martin. It was the era, also, of the great American title search, when newly rich American mothers packed their nubile daughters off to Europe in hopes of trading an heiress's expectations for a European title or even a coronet, thereby achieving instant aristocracy. (Unfortunately, it wouldn't work the other way around; if an American male married a duchess, his wife became an ordinary Mrs.) The Bradley-Martins were celebrating their sixteen-year-old daughter's recent marriage to Britain's Lord Craven.

The Bradley-Martins' 1897 winter ball, given at the height of a deep financial recession "as an impetus to trade," was widely criticized by the press and public for its poor timing and poor taste. Even the host's brother, Frederick Townsend Martin, complained that "the power of wealth" and "vulgarity" was "everywhere." In the wake of this disaster, the Bradley-Martins found themselves so ostracized that they moved permanently to England. Similarly banished was James Hazen Hyde, whose $200,000 ball at Sherry's — at which the restaurant was transformed into an exact replica of the Hall of Mirrors at Versailles — resulted in an investigation of his Equitable Life Assurance Company of America that revealed some bookkeeping which was exceptionally imaginative, to say the least. Obviously, party giving that was no more than an end unto itself was coming under close public scrutiny.

In 1901, two young debutantes-to-be seemed to have suddenly been struck with the uneasy notion that the round of private galas they would be facing in the coming year might be viewed less than charitably by people outside their own moneyed circle. In a sense, the two were a decade or so ahead of Ivy Lee with the idea that along with great wealth should go at least *some* sense of civic responsibility. The two young women were Miss Mary Harriman and Miss Nathalie Henderson. Miss Harriman had particularly good reasons for feeling apprehensive: Her father, Edward H. Harriman, was one of the most hated and feared railroad tycoons of his day. (When workers on one of his railroads had threatened to strike, Harriman sent in goons armed with machine guns who had orders to fire at will if any work stoppage occurred.) According to Miss Henderson's later account, she and Miss Harriman had been driving down Riverside Drive in a snappy four-wheeled sulky behind Miss Harriman's trotting horse, Gulnair, when Mary Harriman suddenly exclaimed — in the somewhat stilted language attributed to her by Miss Henderson — "There is an exceptionally large number of debutantes coming out our year. What can we do to make it a particularly good year, and to show that we recognize an obligation to the community besides having a good time?" Miss Harriman promptly answered her own question. She had read about the College Settlement House on Rivington Street, and said, "We will work for the benefit of the College Settlement." The Junior League for the Promotion of Settlement Houses "for the benefit of the poor and the betterment of the city" — later abbreviated to the Junior League — was born.

The College Settlement was an unusual choice for a beneficiary. Rivington Street was in the untidy heart of New York's Lower East Side, and the settlement houses that had been established there were designed to "Americanize" the immigrants who were pouring into New York Harbor by the tens of thousands, most of them Jews fleeing from Eastern Europe. Originally, the settlement houses had been little more than delousing stations, but the young women seemed to have been determined to show that the Junior League was not afraid to get its fingernails dirty. That first year, the Misses Harriman and Henderson and several of their friends wrote and staged a little musical entertainment, put on at the house of another debutante, and raised about a thousand dollars for the College Settlement.

Considering the fact that Miss Harriman's father was said to be worth $200 million, it was perhaps a small sum and may have represented no more than the girls' mad money. But the idea caught on and quickly spread — first to Boston and then, in rapid succession, to Brooklyn; Portland, Oregon; Baltimore; Philadelphia; and Chicago, as debutantes clamored to form Junior League chapters of their own. Today, there is hardly an American city of any size that does not have its Junior League chapter, and there are leagues in both Canada and Mexico. Across the countryside, roughly a hundred thousand Junior League volunteers manipulate puppets in school classrooms, restore historic houses, operate mobile museums, push book and art carts through hospital corridors, sing Christmas carols to shut-ins, plan children's concerts and zoo trips, stage operettas and plays, produce educational films and organize educational television stations, teach arts, crafts, science and language courses, cheer the wounded and dying, and uplift the imprisoned. "We had made it amusing," Nathalie Henderson wrote modestly, "and also *chic* to belong."

Of course some of the Old Guard would argue that they made it *too* amusing and *too* chic, and that the Misses Henderson and Harriman would be appalled at the huge, catchall organization the Junior Leagues of America have become today. Their intention had been to demonstrate that debutantes were not empty-headed social butterflies but had social consciences as well, and originally the league's membership was restricted to debutantes and debutantes only. Jewish girls were not invited to join the league, and certainly no blacks were. Today, all those barriers have fallen. In many cities, including New York, the Junior League holds a fund-raising ball where debutantes are presented. Any set of parents willing to contribute sufficiently to a league-approved charity can make their daughter a tax-deductible debutante. Similarly, any young woman (debutante or not) who is willing to undergo the league's rigorous training program and who agrees to devote the prescribed number of hours a week as a league volunteer can join. Some would say that in the process of democratization, the whole point of joining the league and the whole point of being a debutante — even the whole point of charitable work and giving — have been lost.

But the idea of a huge, high-ticket, commercially underwritten function for charity was born with the Junior League. In a sense, though it was clearly not Miss Harriman's or Miss Henderson's intention, what they were doing was opening up the private world of metropolitan high society to the entire outside world. Today, anyone with the price of a ticket can go to a charity ball.

22

"To Serve . . ."

In January 1936 (which, we need hardly be reminded, was the height of the Great Depression) *Fortune,* by then the self-appointed mouthpiece of the American moneyed, if not necessarily the upper, class, was casting about for social institutions that might be blamed for the country's economic woes. The magazine hit upon the nation's dozen most prestigious college preparatory schools and chose to attack them in two major articles. "They have produced," the series led off, "from among the privileged youth of the country 67,000 Old Boys — but in all their history only twenty-seven U.S. Senators, one member of the U.S. Supreme Court, and one President of the U.S."

This harsh judgment was based almost entirely on what the magazine saw as the failure of the elite schools to produce graduates who would enter public service, as their equivalent schools had traditionally done in England. American private schools, the articles claimed, had failed to train their students for leadership in a democratic country. Thus the Depression was probably their fault. *Fortune*'s anonymous writer concluded: "The American ruling class may quite possibly be taxed out of existence in the next few decades because the American ruling-class schools have not educated rich men's sons to political superiority — have not presented the country with any logical reasons why the class should *not* be taxed out of existence."

Fortune's argument, however, was more emotional than logical. Nor was its crystal ball unclouded. In the decades to come, it would be the British ruling class that would be threatened with extinction by taxation, and it would be the British public schools that would be brutally forced to relax their elitist admissions standards during the fifties, sixties, and seventies. Furthermore, the magazine overlooked the fact that American prep schools were designed only to prepare young people for college and, though they offered courses in government, history, and political science, had provided no guarantee of entrée into a ruling class, the way Britain's public schools had virtually done for years.

Finally, the magazine's arithmetic was off. The "one President of the U.S." referred to was probably intended to be Franklin D. Roosevelt, a graduate of Groton, but *Fortune* had forgotten FDR's relative President Theodore Roosevelt, who was also Groton-educated, as well as the similarly private-school-educated William Howard Taft. Also, though prep schools as such didn't exist at the time, Presidents Washington, Jefferson, and both Adamses were all the products of decidedly upper-class private educations. In the years since the *Fortune* articles appeared, a number of other political leaders have emerged from a prep-school milieu, including John F. Kennedy, a graduate of Choate.

Part of the trouble has been that, in terms of American politics, no one has been quite able to decide whether an upper-class education is an asset or a liability, and so campaign managers have tended to shy away from the whole issue. Franklin D. Roosevelt, for example, whose popularity was said to be based on his appeal to the common man, was advised to play down his privileged schooling at Groton and Harvard. Indeed, his Groton classmates were grateful that he did, since they considered FDR and his New Deal a blot on the school's escutcheon and threatened to boycott a school reunion if the president were also planning to attend. Adlai E. Stevenson's Choate and Princeton background did not seem to be held against him when he campaigned successfully for the governorship of Illinois. But, in his two campaigns for the U.S. presidency, his advisors recommended soft-pedaling his boarding-school credits, and he lost both times. On the other hand, during William W. Scranton's gubernatorial campaign in Pennsylvania, it was also deemed wisest not to mention Scranton's fine record at Hotchkiss and Yale, and Scranton won.

In American politics, as well as in business life, the feeling seems to have developed that while it is acceptable to have gone to college, to have attained a prep-school diploma in addition is somehow unacceptable, an unnecessary gilding of the lily. Men in particular seem embarrassed by their prep schools, as though there were almost something sissified about the whole thing, something dandified and effeminate. The term "preppie" is used derisively, and the question "Where did you prep?" when asked in a drawing room comedy will inevitably get a laugh from the audience, for the fop who would ask such a question doubtless also has the sexual proclivities of an Oscar Wilde. The good manners and speech and poise that boarding schools tend to instill are something like upper-class values — one has them but doesn't talk about them. One has them, but one doesn't let them show too much. They are private secrets, shared with a private world of one's private-school social peers. Adlai Stevenson's private-school training was visible in his upper-crust manners and audible in his upper-crust speech, and in an interesting lapse of manners, John F. Kennedy once referred to his fellow Democrat and fellow boarding-school alumnus as "that faggot."

Still, in Rhode Island, Senator Claiborne Pell decided to make no bones of the fact that he had been privately educated at St. George's School and Princeton, nor of the fact that he was descended from one of America's oldest and most aristocratic English manorial families, the Pells of Pelham. Yet Pell remains one of the state's most popular figures in Democratic politics. Also in Rhode Island, William H. Vanderbilt — perhaps acting on the theory that, being a Vanderbilt, he would have *had* to have had a fancy education — decided to neither disown nor flaunt the fact that he had attended the same schools as Claiborne Pell. He won one term as Republican governor of the state in 1939 but lost his bid for a second term. Bitter in his defeat, he pulled up stakes and moved to Massachusetts, where he went into real estate. John D. Rockefeller IV, campaigning for the governorship of West Virginia, affected scuffed sneakers, faded blue jeans, and a down-home Appalachian manner, and apparently got voters to forget that he was a Rockefeller and had any sort of education whatsoever. Others have buried the shameful secret of their prep-school pasts even more cleverly. Mayor John V. Lindsay of New York City chose the tactic of referring to his boarding school as "my high school" — a ploy that amused those who knew the high school was snobbish St. Paul's, in Concord, New Hampshire. And, meanwhile, who ever suspected that Lindsay's tough-talking predecessor, Robert Wagner, Jr., was a graduate of the Taft School? That Supreme Court Justice Potter Stewart was an alumnus of Hotchkiss was never advertised until it appeared in his obituary.

But the results of confessing to an upper-class upbringing remain unpredictable. In 1938 — Depression days again — Mrs. Robert A. Taft made a startling speech to a gathering of Ohio mine workers in which she said, "My husband did not start from humble beginnings . . . he had a fine education at Yale." Her husband's Republican backers wrung their hands, and it was widely assumed that she had dealt him a political death blow in his senatorial campaign. But she hadn't, and Taft went on to win his Senate seat handily.

Another thing that *Fortune*'s writer seemed to have overlooked is that there are other forms of public service, outside the realms of government and politics, where citizens can prove themselves useful. And at a number of these endeavors the alumni of America's private schools seem to have acquitted themselves rather well. Philanthropy and patronage of the arts come first to mind. New England boarding schools have turned out such art patrons as Seymour H. Knox, whose benefactions to the city of Buffalo have included its Fine Arts Academy, and the late Robert Lehman. When Mr. Lehman's princely collection was turned over to New York's Metropolitan Museum of Art for the public to enjoy, a whole new wing for the museum was required to house it — a wing donated by Mr. Lehman, of course.

Walter Chrysler's art collection has similarly benefited the city of Detroit, and in the meantime, many prep-school graduates have gone on to careers in the arts. These, in a very random sampling, would include Craig Smith, head of the Department of Fine Arts at New York University; Henry Gardiner, designer of exhibits at New York's Museum of Natural History; Samuel Wagstaff, Jr., curator of the Wadsworth Atheneum in Hartford; Gray Williams, a curator of the Metropolitan Museum of Art in New York; William Hutton, curator of the Toledo Museum of Art; artists Tony Vevers, Jerry Pfohl, Denver Lindley, and the *New Yorker* cartoonist Peter Arno; director John Frankenheimer; composer Stephen Sondheim; and novelist Louis Auchincloss.

The list could go on and on, including newspaper editors, scientists, doctors, lawyers, clergymen, and educators. Surely *Fortune* sadly underrated the contributions of America's upper-class schools when it accused them of creating nothing more than a network of sixty-seven thousand "Old Boys."

But what the system did create was sixty-seven thousand individuals who, though intensely proud of their upper-class education, have been a little shy when it comes to talking about it — except, of course, among themselves.

Meanwhile, it would seem to be a fact that, out of even the most pampered and protected of environments, certain notions of behavior — of propriety, or duty, whether spoken or unspoken — become instinctual, almost automatic responses. This is not to say that a genteel upbringing and schooling will guarantee worthwhile citizens, or even ladies and gentlemen, as an inevitable result. The American upper-class educational system has produced its share of cads and bounders, and one of the most notorious of these was perhaps Richard Whitney, who "betrayed his class" in the 1930s. After being splendidly educated at Groton and Harvard, he went on to become president of the New York Stock Exchange and, in 1938, was sentenced to Sing Sing for defrauding not only the American public and the state of New York but also his business partners and the treasury of his own New York Yacht Club. And yet even the Whitney case offered an example of upper-class values at work. While Whitney served his prison sentence, he received regular visits from the Reverend Endicott Peabody of Groton, his old school headmaster. It simply seemed to the Reverend Peabody the gentlemanly and proper thing to do for a Groton boy who had, alas, become a felon.

Groton is often cited as the most aristocratic of New England's private schools, and though it is by no means the oldest (both Exeter and Andover were founded more than a hundred years earlier), it came into existence in 1884 with excellent credentials, both social and financial. Its founder, the Reverend Peabody, was connected with a variety of old New England families, including the Lawrences and the Parkmans, as well as the Endicotts — an ancestor was Massachusetts Bay Colony Governor John Endicott — and Peabodys of Salem, where, it was said, even the peeping frogs in ponds on summer nights sang a chorus of "Peabody, Peabody, Peabody." The school's chief financial backer was J. Pierpont Morgan, who at the time ran what amounted to his own federal reserve system before there was such an institution. Both Peabody and Morgan had been educated at select "public" schools in England, where Peabody's father had been a Morgan partner in London, and their intent with Groton was to create a school in America that would follow the English upper-class mode as closely as possible. Their models were such schools as Eton, Harrow, and Cheltenham, and since Peabody was an Episcopal clergyman, their goal was to educate "Christian gentlemen" and to develop "manly Christian character." Religious services were an important part of the school's curriculum. In addition to church on Sunday, compulsory chapel services were held twice daily, in early morning and at vespers. The school's motto, created by the rector, was *Cui servire est regnare* — "To serve Him is to rule."

The Rector, as the Reverend Peabody was always called, was a strapping, handsome six-footer with piercing eyes and a long, thin, aristocratic nose. Standing behind his pulpit in his flowing white robes, he was a commanding figure as he delivered one of his impassioned sermons on the subtleties of a Satan who could tempt a boy into the paths of unrighteousness through such a simple technique as permitting him to mouth the prayers and liturgical responses with his lips, rather than in full, strong, manly voice. But there was more to the Rector's emotional appeal than that. His goal was to make his school quite literally a spiritual extension of a well-born boy's own family. A Groton boy was intended to feel as loved and needed while away at boarding school as he would feel at home, and like the fictional Mr. Chips, the Rector referred to all Grotonians as "my boys."

As an affectionate biographer of the Rector wrote, "It was the most natural thing in the world for him to think of his school as being simply a large family. . . . At the center of the big school family his own family grew and the beautiful home and family life was presided over by Mrs. Peabody, the most gracious and beautiful of wives and mothers." Every night, the Rector and Mrs. Peabody would say individual good nights to each and every boy as he trooped off to bed, and on the foreheads of the younger lads Mrs. Peabody would bestow a kiss, along with a sweet-dreams wish.

From the outset, the Rector adopted the habit of following his boys throughout their careers and lives. He was frequently called upon to marry them (he officiated at the wedding of Franklin and Eleanor Roosevelt) and, toward the end of his long tenure at Groton, occasionally to bury them. For fifty-six years, until his retirement in 1940 at the age of eighty-four, and continuing until his death four years later, every Groton graduate received a handwritten letter on his birthday from the Rector — even when the list of the school's alumni had swollen to include thousands of names. Writing from the White House in 1936 to thank the Rector for his annual message, Franklin D. Roosevelt told him that he had saved every one of the birthday letters since his graduation.

On the other hand, some of the Reverend Peabody's Brahmin borrowings for Groton from the British public-school system seemed so abject as to be anachronistic. He always used British spellings, for example, of such words as *colour, honour, favour, centre,* and *realise.* Bruised knees of Grotties were treated with sticky plasters, not Band-Aids. Cheers for the school's athletic teams were not of the one-two-three-four-siss-boom-bah variety, but were hip-hip-hurrah. Some of the Rector's Briticisms drew snickers from the boys. Criticizing a messily erased theme paper, for instance, the Rector might say, "You need to get yourself a good rubber."

At Cheltenham and Cambridge, where he himself had been educated, the Spartanness of damp and drafty eleventh-century corridors and chambers had been touted as character building, and a certain amount of physical discomfort was considered good for spiritual and moral growth. Thus, at Groton, undergraduates slept in unheated cells without doors, washed up at long communal black sinks with cold water and slabs of yellow kitchen soap, and ate meals that featured such items as cold poached cod and "sure-death hash." Groton boys wore stiff white collars and black patent-leather pumps to dinner, and there were other rules laid down by the Rector. The purpose of these may have seemed mysterious to many of the boys. It was against the rules to walk or stand with one's hands in one's pockets. Close friendships were discouraged, and it was also against the rules to walk or sit about the school in groups of twos. (Male adolescent crushes, the Rector seemed to feel, which might lead to the vice that dare not speak its name, could this way be discouraged.)

Much emphasis was placed on vigorous outdoor exercise, and Grotonians played fives, an Etonian form of handball. "Leadership" was another of the Rector's favorite nouns, and boys were taught that to become a sixth-form prefect was perhaps the most splendid achievement a young man could hope for in his scholastic life. The British custom of "fagging," in which upperclassmen used lower-classmen as their personal servants, was not allowed, but the Rector did believe that senior boys should be allowed to discipline their juniors when they misbehaved or failed to achieve that ineffable quality known as the Groton "tone." (That tone might be defined as an air of perpetual self-assurance, combined with an attitude of distrust toward anyone who was not a fellow Grotonian.) A favorite form of punishment was known as pumping, where an errant youth was taken into the lavatory and literally pumped full of water. Over the years, there were several near-drowning episodes, where artificial respiration had to be applied, from pumpings.

All of this made the Groton School seem, to outsiders, a very peculiar place as the school moved into the twentieth century. But that was perfectly all right with the Rector. "Groton School," wrote William Amory Gardner, one of the school's early trustees, "is perfectly incomprehensible to those who have not belonged to it," and the Rector kept it that way through the force of his personality.

Meanwhile, in such matters as imparting actual knowledge, much less scholarship, the Rector had less interest. More emphasis was placed on godliness and cleanliness (of mind and body) and good sportsmanship. Peabody's biographer summed it up politely, saying, "He never seemed to enter wholeheartedly into the field of theory, as he always fought the idea that teaching can or should be limited to the mind alone. He was primarily a personality, interested in persons, each of whom he saw most importantly as a child of God." Despite such pieties, the Rector turned Groton into the most openly snobbish school in America.

And yet Groton is the only private boarding school in America to have turned out two U.S. presidents, both of them named Roosevelt. This was Endicott Peabody's greatest source of pride. Again and again in his sermons the Rector stressed his belief that Groton's students composed the future leadership of the country. Public service was held up as a noble goal. His boys represented the cream of America's youth, and after Groton — and Harvard — his boys were to go forth and serve their nation with the same dedication and devotion as they gave to their daily prayers. With such dedication and devotion to God and country, Grotonians could only be expected to rise naturally into the highest ranks of government. Hadn't they harkened to the school's proud motto that to serve God was to rule?

His shining example was Teddy Roosevelt. Roosevelt was his flagship Groton student: a man of fine family and distinguished ancestry, an American aristocrat, a bold war hero who had gone on to seek and obtain the highest office in the land and become a fine and upright and beloved president. Over and over, Teddy Roosevelt was offered up to Groton boys as their ultimate ideal. Roosevelt, in turn, had sent his two sons to Groton and made frequent trips to the school to address the students, to regale them with stories of his adventures in the worlds of the military, big-game hunting, and politics, and to provide them with solid, in-the-flesh inspiration.

The Rector once said, "If some Groton boys do not enter political life and do something for our land it won't be because they have not been urged." One person who obviously listened to these exhortations very closely was the young Franklin D. Roosevelt, Teddy Roosevelt's distant cousin. For despite the egalitarian thrust of the New Deal, his apparent deep concern and sympathy for the poor, the blacks, the laborers, and the unemployed, and what seemed to be his determination to tax the rich out of existence, FDR was an aristocrat to the core. He had merely adopted the tactic of some of his peers by making a secret of it. He had been raised in a world that had been neatly divided between servants and masters, and it was a world he was used to and comfortable within. Writing home to his mother from Groton, and commiserating with her on the loss of a butler (Sara Delano Roosevelt perennially had difficulties keeping servants), he said, "Don't let Papa worry about it, after all there are plenty of good butlers in the world." And when it came time for him to marry, he did not choose a woman he had fallen in love with — as his wife would learn, in time, to her sorrow. He married another Roosevelt, his own kind, because it was the familiar, the traditional thing to do. At the same time, with a relative in the White House, FDR had certainly been given a special impetus to enter politics. He was a frequent White House guest, had attended Cousin Alice's coming-out party, and had been given a firsthand taste of the pomp and privilege and perquisites and glamour that went with being president. The excitement . . . the power.

But, alas, for the great majority of Groton's graduates, the urgings of the Rector and the leaders of the community whom he imported as lecturers fell on deaf ears. Most Groton boys had come from families who had taught them that politics was dirty and that politicians were not gentlemen. (Franklin Roosevelt's father believed the same thing.) In 1881, Henry Adams had told his Harvard pupil Henry Cabot Lodge, "I have never known a young man to go into politics who was not the worse for it." Oh, there were a handful — a very small handful — of Groton-educated men who became public figures: Senators Bronson Cutting and Frederick Hale, Congressman Jonathan Bingham, Dean Acheson, Francis Biddle, Averell Harriman, and Sumner Welles, in addition to the two Roosevelts. But that is about the end of the list. Most of the other Grotonians went into family businesses, or became lawyers or bankers, or "went down to Wall Street," where the benevolent and paternalistic J. P. Morgan — who always had a special fondness for Groton boys — usually could be depended on to find them places at his bank. After all, politics did sound like hard work — all that campaigning. And, unless one went into politics dishonestly, as most Groton boys would be loath to do, there was very little money in it. Going down to Wall Street was easier. Again, it was the traditional, the familiar, the more expected thing to do.

While the Reverend Peabody at Groton longed, perhaps naively, to have his school produce America's leaders — *Christian* leaders, it might be added — the way Eton and Harrow had for centuries turned out England's ruling class, George Van Santvoord at the Hotchkiss School in Lakeville, Connecticut, had a somewhat different goal for the school that he headed from 1926 to 1955. His concern was the development of *character,* and not so-called Christian character, either. Both the Talmud and the Koran, he often pointed out, as well as Confucius, had something to say about character. If Hotchkiss educated young men who turned out to be leaders, that was fine with him. But, to him, a leader with a flawed character was worse than no leader at all.

At the time of Van Santvoord's appointment by the school's board of trustees, this choice was considered peculiar. For one thing, though the history of the world's religions was a subject that interested him — he even taught a course about it at Hotchkiss — he was not a clergyman. He was, on the other hand, better educated than Peabody, having earned Bachelor's, Master's, and Bachelor of Letters degrees and being a graduate of Yale, a Rhodes scholar, and a winner of the croix de guerre in World War I. Tall, erect, broad-shouldered, and patricianly handsome, with an Old Knickerbocker, Hudson Valley name, he looked every inch the American aristocrat.

At the same time, he believed in common sense. "In fact," he would say with a little sniff, "I've never understood why it's called *common* sense, because to find anyone using it is quite uncommon." If a distinction can be made between commoner and aristocrat, then

Van Santvoord believed in aristocratic sense. When one of his students came to him with a problem, his usual response was, "Well, what do *you* think?" Or, "How do *you* think this problem should be handled?" On the subject of morality, he often said, "One way to decide whether an act is moral or immoral is to ask yourself what the world would be like if everybody did it."

The Hotchkiss School first opened its doors in 1892, the gift of Mrs. Maria Bissell Hotchkiss, a former schoolteacher whose late husband, Benjamin Berkeley Hotchkiss, had made a fortune as a munitions manufacturer. Among Mr. Hotchkiss's inventions had been one that perfected the machine gun, and Mrs. Hotchkiss may have wanted to donate a school for boys to atone for the many young male lives her husband's device had dispatched in wars. Before George Van Santvoord's arrival, Hotchkiss had been a school much like other prep schools in New England of the era: a school for the pampered sons of the rich.

But Van Santvoord decided to change all that, and he was immediately branded — by trustees, alumni, faculty, and students alike — as an iconoclast, a radical, a shatterer of sacred traditions, even a bolshevist. One of the first things he did was to abolish the practice of hazing new boys. Up to then, the lowerclassmen had been ruled despotically — often savagely — by members of the senior class. When speaking to seniors, new boys were required to call them Sir, and then were only to speak when spoken to. Among the rules set down by seniors for new boys were:

No whistling
No loud ties
When walking down corridors new boys are always to keep elbow or finger touching wall furtherest from windows
Keep out of corridors except on business
As much as possible keep out of sight of Seniors

Violations of these rules could lead to brutal corporal punishment. All this was outlawed by Van Santvoord. Also outlawed were the fraternities and secret societies that, in such schools as Groton and St. Paul's, had taken such a firm grip on student life that they were completely beyond administrative control. Prior to Van Santvoord, the school had placed much emphasis on athletics. Students had been selected for brawn as much as brain, and alumni were horrified at

George Van Santvoord's announcement that sports were to be downplayed in favor of more intellectual activities. Saturday nights at the school had been traditionally given over to movies. Van Santvoord decided to vary this fare with periodic piano or violin concerts and readings from visiting novelists and poets, including the "controversial" Vachel Lindsay. He discovered that the school had a cache of reasonably good paintings, and art and sculpture exhibitions were displayed in the corridors. Boys were encouraged to decorate their rooms with paintings rather than the customary pennants and pinups.

Under the Van Santvoord regime, the school added its own infirmary and its own full-time physician. The school library more than doubled its number of volumes and included the writings of Karl Marx, Friedrich Engels, Sigmund Freud, and Carl Jung, writers whose thoughts had been considered "dangerous" to well-born American youths. When asked by a worried alumnus whether some of his students might be being exposed to "improper books," Mr. Van Santvoord replied that he was more interested in dealing with improper fractions. His own personal store of knowledge was formidable. He was scholastically equipped to teach — and often did — courses in Latin, Greek, French, German, Spanish, Italian, English, and history, as well as comparative religions. Though he had never formally studied it, in his spare time he taught himself Russian. He could converse knowledgeably about Confucius and Mencius and Lao-tse, as well as on the great violin makers Guarnieri, Amati, and Stradivarius. Once, when asked by a student if there was an encyclopedia handy to look something up, Van Santvoord replied coolly, "What is it you want to know?"

Though the Sunday services in the school's chapel were basically Church of England, Mr. Van Santvoord had a broader, more ecumenical outlook. He frequently invited rabbis, priests, and clerics from other Protestant denominations, as well as lay speakers, to visit the school and deliver the Sunday homilies. He occasionally took the pulpit himself to talk about whatever was on his mind and encouraged members of his teaching staff to do the same.

In terms of teaching, Van Santvoord once remarked that he cared less about whether a student knew the dates and generals of the War of 1812 than whether the student knew why that war was fought. In teaching English, he felt that it was less important for a boy to know how to parse a sentence than to be able to speak and write the language gracefully and correctly. In other words, he had the revolutionary notion in private-school education that a young man should be taught to *think*.

In manner and bearing, Van Santvoord was aloof and somewhat distant, though the faint traces of a smile usually hovered tentatively about the corners of his mouth, and when truly pleased, he fairly beamed. Still, he frightened many boys and often offended parents — doting mothers in particular. When they came to him with trivial questions about their sons' progress in school, he gave them short shrift. Their progress in school, he implied, was his business, not theirs. He particularly disliked parents who were divorced or separated, feeling that these couples had abandoned *their* job — raising a son — before they had finished it. Once, after expelling a boy and learning that neither parent was available to collect their son (a chauffeured car was being sent instead), he announced that such parents didn't deserve to have their son back, and the boy was reinstated in the school. Outspoken, a touch autocratic, regal but usually fair, he quickly earned the nickname that would stick to him throughout his thirty-year Hotchkiss career: the Duke.

His school, the Duke used to say, had only one rule, and that was "Be a gentleman." How he defined what a gentleman was he did not say, but what a gentleman was usually became clear when you discovered what a gentleman wasn't. A gentleman didn't cheat. He didn't lie. A gentleman wasn't petty. A gentleman wasn't intolerant of others' shortcomings. A gentleman wasn't a whiner, wasn't a gossip, wasn't a boor, wasn't inconsiderate of others' feelings. Once, in a discussion of what the most serious of human crimes might be, he said that he felt the worst was deliberate cruelty. But a close second, he added, was boredom.

The Hotchkiss curriculum was both loosened and expanded under the Duke. If, for example, a boy could pass the examination for French I, he was not required to take that course and could move directly on to French II. A teacher was hired to teach art and art history, another to teach music and music appreciation, and still another to teach drama. Though alumni moaned that the school was teaching "sissy courses," the Duke remained unfazed. It was clear that, in his opinion, a gentleman was a man of taste and culture. He offered prizes for the most tastefully decorated dormitory rooms, which, he made clear, did not mean the most expensively decorated.

In the winter of 1945 a young teacher, recently hired by the school, chose to commit suicide in his campus apartment by hanging himself with his bathrobe cord. When his body was discovered long after lights out, the entire school was awakened by the sounds of ambulance and police sirens and the lurid flashing of red and blue bubble lights. The next morning, since the school was agog with what had happened, the Duke felt it necessary to address the situation at the students' daily assembly in the chapel. The expression on his face was one of extreme distaste, and his remarks were very brief. Obviously, some sort of standard had been betrayed. It was clear from his icy look that he disapproved of suicides in general, and also that he found the young teacher's choice of venue unpardonable. That was the worst sin — to commit such an act within the confines of a school for boys whom he had been employed to teach and guide. The Duke, however, said none of this, while conveying it all in his eyes and in his voice: overwhelming disappointment that a man he had counted upon to be a gentleman had turned out not to be one after all. What he said, after making a few routine announcements, was this: "I am sure you have all heard by now that Mr. ____ chose to take his own life last night. I do not know why. He came to me yesterday afternoon with some problems that didn't seem to me terribly important. I suppose one way to think of this is that there are interesting novels, and interesting short stories. Mr. ____ chose to make a short story of his life."

Be a gentleman! Oh, there were other rules, most of them sensible. Drinking and smoking on the campus were grounds for expulsion. So were swimming in the lake at night and accepting rides in automobiles from anyone who was not a faculty or family member. Jackets and ties were required in classrooms and in the dining room, and there were some quaint exceptions to this dress code. On hot days, for example, boys would be permitted to remove their jackets in the classrooms but only provided that they were not wearing suspenders, which the Duke called galluses. But otherwise the only duty was to that unwritten code.

"To be a gentleman, to be a person of character — that is the most important thing we can teach you here," Van Santvoord often told his boys. In his notes and in his office sessions, the Duke kept stressing character; how we must always be on guard that we do and say only those things that are truly worthy of a gentleman — regardless of whether anyone finds out or we get caught. We owe it to others, the Duke wrote, to do what is truly right. And, above all, we owe it to ourselves. For only that way can we truly live with ourselves in peace. A gentleman was defined by his strength of character.

Though he never came right out and said so, George Van Santvoord was emphasizing the true standards of a true aristocracy — standards of cultivation, of intellect, of duty, of generosity of spirit, standards of doing one's best. The fact is that out of schools like Groton and Hotchkiss, out of even the most hothouse-seeming notions of how the children of the American rich should be educated, would emerge people who, when the chips were down, would manage to rise to occasions and do the things that were expected of them. It is as though this instinct had been somehow absorbed by osmosis from the attitudes of parents, or grandparents, or teachers, or a combination of all these influences. It is as though service in a time of need were an almost atavistic response, the way an English gentleman will sit for hours waist-deep in the icy waters of a duck blind on the chance of bringing down a single bird, not because he enjoys it so much but because his family and friends all do it, have always done it, and it is the thing that, if one is an English gentleman, *one does*.

"Where did it come from, I often wonder?" mused the late Mr. Wilmarth S. Lewis, Yale alumnus ('18), Horace Walpole scholar, and gentleman farmer of Connecticut. The subject of Mr. Lewis's musings was his adored wife, the former Annie Burr Auchincloss, one of the most gently bred, gently spoken, and gently featured of women, whose chief preoccupation and talent had always appeared to be tending her extensive flower gardens, taking cuttings, and creating hybrid roses. And yet, for all her apparent delicacy, she had emerged during World War II as something of a heroine. Mrs. Lewis had had, as her wondering husband explained it, "the most restrictive, blindered sort of childhood," raised in New York by nurses and governesses, privately tutored and schooled, shielded from such realities as poverty and crime and mortality, never permitted to forget that she was a Burr. Her education had ended, in the manner of young women of her day and social class, at a finishing school — in her case, Miss Porter's, at Farmington, Connecticut, a school many girls attended accompanied by private detectives serving as bodyguards, and a school so discreet that the young Gloria Vanderbilt was asked not to return because it was felt that her presence generated "too much publicity."

At Farmington, young ladies were expected, if they did not know how to do so already, to learn to play tennis, to curtsy, to pour tea, to remove the finger bowl *with* the doily and place these at eleven o'clock before separating the dessert spoon and fork. Girls were not permitted to wear high heels because of Miss Porter's arcane belief that high heels damaged a woman's child-bearing ability. A bit of art, a bit of music, a bit of American history, and a bit of French were taught for good measure. The school also employed a riding mistress and arranged for stables for the saddle horses that some girls might wish to bring along with them. The school's greatest honor was for a girl to be asked to help carry the daisy chain.

And yet, despite this swaddled upbringing and an education that was insular to say the least, no sooner had the first Japanese bombs fallen on Pearl Harbor than Annie Burr Lewis was galvanized into action — volunteering for Red Cross work, driving an ambulance in France, changing tires and spark plugs, caring for the sick and wounded, and winding bandages, much of this activity behind enemy lines.

Where had this extraordinary ability come from, her husband wondered? Surely not from Miss Porter's School. Might he be suggesting, Mr. Lewis was asked, that there were such things as "American aristocratic values" that sprang to the fore in times of crisis — an intuitive, inherited knowledge that when service is needed from one, one must serve, and that when duty and country call, the dutiful and patriotic must respond? Would this account for his wife's volunteer service in the war?

Mr. Lewis looked briefly alarmed at this suggestion. Then, lowering his voice, he murmured, "Oh, yes, of course — of course there are. But one isn't supposed to talk about such things. Once you mention them, then the hackles begin to rise. . . ."

23

The Bogus Versus the Real

In the early 1960s, the American public was introduced to a woman who was advertised as a true aristocrat and one who would become — for a while, at least — an American heroine. She was Jacqueline Bouvier Kennedy, and she was unusual because her aristocratic background, it was said, was French. Mrs. Kennedy's ancestors, it was widely reported, were almost without exception members of the French nobility: ducs and duchesses, comtes and comtesses, a prince here and a king there. Even the famously nit-picking *New Yorker* magazine, whose staff of fact-checkers utters wild cries of glee whenever a fact turns out, in fact, to be a fiction, was taken in by the deception and soberly printed Mrs. Kennedy's Bouvier "genealogy."

The trouble was, it turned out, that none of it was true. It seemed that Mrs. Kennedy's Bouvier grandfather had made the whole thing up, created bogus ancestors out of thin air, and drawn up a Bouvier family tree that had no relation to fact whatsoever. He had then had the fictional family history privately printed as a small book titled *Our Forebears,* had distributed it to family members, and had presented copies to various libraries and historical and genealogical societies, which had dutifully filed it away. To make the whole thing "official," Grandpa Bouvier had cleverly given a copy of *Our Forebears* to the Library of Congress, which will file any piece of printed matter it receives. None of Mr. Bouvier's family, including Mrs. Kennedy, ever thought to question the validity of the patriarch's researches, and all his descendants grew up believing that the blood of French nobles coursed in their veins.

Why had Grandpa Bouvier lied? Simply to enhance his family's, and his own, prestige in others' eyes, of course. A psychologist might suggest that he suffered from certain insecurities and feelings of inferiority and low self-esteem, unwilling to accept the truth, which was that the Bouviers were descended from peasant French carpenters and cabinetmakers.

Why do some families find it necessary to invent a grander heritage than that to which they are actually entitled? Grandpa Bouvier's is not an isolated case by any means. Hammersmith Farm, the Newport estate where Jacqueline Bouvier spent most of her growing-up summers and where she was married to John F. Kennedy, was the family seat of Hugh D. Auchincloss, who was Mrs. Kennedy's mother's second husband. After Hugh D. Auchincloss's death, Hammersmith Farm was sold, and today the estate is open to the public. Every day, busloads of tourists troop through the former Auchincloss house and are informed, in the tour guides' spiel, that Jacqueline Kennedy's mother, the former Janet Lee, is "one of the Lees of Virginia." This is not true, either. She is, in fact, one of the nineteenth-century Irish immigrant Lees, whose grandmother never lost the brogue she was born with. But if the former Miss Lee, who still owns a smaller house on the property, is aware of the misinformation about her that is being given out, she has done nothing to correct it.

She is a woman, however, who has always made upwardly mobile marriages — first to the French "aristocrat" John V. Bouvier, second to the wealthy Mr. Auchincloss, and, most recently, to Mr. Bingham Morris, a descendant of Lewis Morris, one of the two Morris signers of the Declaration of Independence. In an age when it has been reported that women over thirty have scant chances of ever finding husbands, Janet Lee Bouvier Auchincloss Morris has proven that finding a well-placed husband is not impossible even in one's seventies.

And so that is the aristocratic background of Jacqueline Lee Bouvier Kennedy Onassis, the daughter of a father and a mother who both had fancily fabricated family backgrounds. Yet she is a woman of obvious taste and refinement, displaying many of the characteristics normally associated with "good breeding." That she is a woman capable of rising to great and terrible occasions with dignity and courage was demonstrated before millions of television viewers at the time of President Kennedy's murder in Dallas and during the state funeral that followed. (To lesser occasions, to be sure, she has risen with less dignity; angered by a photographer who she claimed was pestering her, she became petty and vindictive.) One of the reasons John Kennedy — as well as Aristotle Onassis — married Jackie is that she seemed to both men the embodiment of "class." She has become the most publicized woman in the world and yet has managed to conduct her private life with singular propriety and discretion. Where, then, did this exemplar of good breeding acquire it? From socially ambitious parents? From her understandably innocent belief in aristocratic bloodlines on both sides? From growing up in the mannered elegance that befitted an Auchincloss stepchild? Or from her education at Miss Porter's School?

The Auchinclosses, meanwhile, though not a particularly old American family, have managed to enter the American aristocracy through the familiar doorway of marriage. (Hugh D. Auchincloss's money came from his mother, the former Emma Jennings, whose father, Oliver B. Jennings, helped John D. Rockefeller found the Standard Oil Company.) The first Hugh Auchincloss arrived in America from Scotland in 1803, and the Auchinclosses became thread merchants — or, rather, they married thread merchants when they became maritally allied with the Coatses of the Coats Thread Company. Since then, Auchinclosses have married Colgates, Rockefellers, Sloans, Winthrops, Saltonstalls, Frelinghuysens, Van Rensselaers, Cuttings, Du Ponts, Grosvenors, Tiffanys, Burdens, Ingrahams, Vanderbilts, Adamses, and Burrs — to list just a few of their connections — and have become what is called the best-*connected* family in New York. And, since they have proven to be excellent at producing male heirs, Auchinclosses now have more listings in the *Social Register* than almost any other family in America, even nosing out the ancient Livingstons by a score of Auchincloss 21, Livingston 18. And yet, with the exception of the novelist Louis Auchincloss, there has never been a true Auchincloss of distinction.

The older families, more secure and sure of their position, have been less preoccupied with marrying upward in recent years, have become more honest about their forebears (the Livingston connection with the earls of Callendar, very remote to begin with, is today treated almost — but not quite — as a family joke) and even more tolerant of family black sheep as they have appeared.

Mabel Seymour Greer had always seemed the very model of a proper New York society matron. In old age, she had reminded many people of Queen Victoria. Since marrying Louis Morris Greer, she had devoted her life to charity work. Her late husband, a top executive with the Consolidated Edison Corporation, had been a rather stiff and formal gentleman who usually wore a tall silk hat and carried a walking stick. The two had met in the spring of 1908, it seemed, when Mr. Greer had gallantly come to the aid of a pretty young woman who was trying to cope with a broken carriage wheel. He had taken her for tea at Sherry's and married her the following fall. Of Mabel Greer's prior history, little was known. She spoke with an attractive English accent and claimed England as her birthplace. At the time of the marriage, Mabel Seymour Greer was known as the girl who had come out of nowhere and snapped up one of the town's most eligible bachelors. But the pair had embarked upon such eminently respectable lives together that they were quickly accepted everywhere, and the new Mrs. Greer's name entered the *Social Register*. The Greers established themselves properly in a mansion on Fifth Avenue and in a summer place on Long Island.

At the time of Mrs. Greer's death, her husband had been dead only a few months. The couple had been childless, and when Mrs. Greer's will was read, her entire fortune was bequeathed to Harvard College, her late husband's alma mater, which had also been a major beneficiary under Louis Greer's will. The trustees of Harvard rubbed their hands. From both Greers, Harvard stood to receive well over a million dollars.

There was, however, one small complication, which Mrs. Greer's lawyer and executors felt it their duty to reveal at the time her will was filed. Not long before her death, Mabel Greer had told her lawyer that, years before meeting Mr. Greer during her carriage accident, she had given birth to an illegitimate son by a young medical student named Willard B. Segur. She had given up the child to its father, who had adopted it. She was, she explained, "terribly young and innocent" at the time, had been seduced by Segur without knowing what might be the consequences, and had often wondered what might have become of her baby. No sooner had this titillating news reached the newspapers than one Harold A. Segur of Worcester, Massachusetts, the adopted son of Dr. Willard B. Segur of Ware, Massachusetts, who had died in 1939, appeared to claim that he was Mabel Greer's long-lost son. Under law, a woman could not disinherit a living child by leaving more than half her estate to charity. Furthermore, since Mrs. Greer's last will was executed within months of her death, Harold Segur had been advised that he could argue that his mother had not been in full possession of her faculties at the time. Thus, if Harold Segur could prove that Mrs. Greer was indeed his mother, he stood to inherit at least half, and possibly all, of her estate.

During the lengthy court proceedings that followed, the question became not so much Who was Harold Segur? but, Who was Mabel Seymour Greer? For one thing, it turned out that in a series of legal documents, including her marriage license to Mr. Greer, Mabel had consistently lied about her age, making herself at least ten years younger than she actually was. That a woman should falsify her age in this fashion was not particularly astonishing, but it was important to the case. Harold Segur had been born in 1888. Mrs. Greer had always given the year of her birth as 1881, which would have made the "young and innocent" mother a child of not quite seven, an unlikely age for parenthood. Moreover, it appeared that Mrs. Greer had not been quite candid with her lawyers when she confessed the existence of an illegitimate son. Dr. Willard Segur had not been a young medical student when he adopted Harold but in fact had been in practice for several years.

New and untidy facts kept emerging about the woman who had introduced herself at curbside to Louis Greer as Mabel Seymour. She seemed to have operated under a variety of aliases, for one thing. Also, before settling into the life of a New York society lady, she had variously given her place of birth as England, Canada, Philadelphia, and Spain. As a Spanish woman, she used the name Mabel (and sometimes Mabelle) Arevalo. At the alleged time of her first encounter with Dr. Segur, she would hardly have been young and innocent, since it was discovered she had been working as a trained nurse, who should have known the facts of life.

To further complicate matters, a search of birth records in Massachusetts turned up a birth certificate in Boston recording the birth in 1894 of one Willard B. Segur, Jr. This child's father was listed as Willard Blossom, occupation physician, and its mother as Mabel Arevalo, birthplace Spain. Adding to this mystery was the fact that after Mabel Arevalo's name had been added the name Seymour, in parentheses and in an obviously different handwriting, and after Willard Blossom's name had been added — in still a different hand —

the name Segur. On top of everything else, the middle initial *B* in the baby's name had been scratched out on the certificate, and in yet another handwriting had been written the name Blossom.

Harold Segur of Worcester, meanwhile, claimed to be unaware that he had had a six-years-younger brother Willard, but at least the problem of Willard, Jr., coming forth to claim an inheritance from Mabel Greer was eliminated when other documents turned up to reveal the following facts about this second child: He had initially been placed in a private orphanage in Boston and then been retrieved two years later by his mother. There followed a bastardy suit initiated by Mabel Arevalo Seymour in which Dr. Willard Segur, Sr., denied the child's paternity. This case was settled out of court, and little Willard was returned to the orphanage. Over the years, employment records and the social security number of Willard B. Segur, Jr., showed him working at various odd jobs in the Boston area and, finally, his death in a Boston poorhouse. Meanwhile, the woman who appeared to have been his mother turned up in various guises as Mary Everett, Mary Ernest, and Mabel Arevalo until that fortuitous spring day in 1908 when, as Mabel Seymour, she met her wealthy future husband.

In the end, the courts decided that Harold Segur had been unable to prove that Mabel Greer had been his natural mother. Harvard got its money. But a couple of conclusions seemed more than likely from the evidence: Mabel's affair with Dr. Segur had been more than a one-night fling, had probably lasted for at least six years, and had resulted in the birth of at least two sons, both of whom she had abandoned. With all the principals now dead, the exact truth of the matter would probably never be known. Two questions, however, would nag at the minds of members of the Morris family: How much had Louis Morris Greer known of his wife's cluttered past when he married her, and what version of those years had she given him? One thing seemed quite certain. During her long career as a respectable society matron, patroness of the arts, and Lady Bountiful, Mabel Seymour Greer must have been one of the most frightened women in the city of New York. At least she had not lived to see the details of her past come tumbling down upon her.

And at least the Morrises, though they may not always know who their in-laws are, will always know who *they* are.

24
Family Curses

Even in colonial times, the notions flourished — among the moneyed, at least — that prosperity was the reward for goodliness and godliness, that the success of the capitalist system was based on divine will, and that the rich became rich because they were better, more virtuous, people. Rogues and scoundrels would be punished on earth as they would be in the afterlife, while the virtuous would be repaid with cash and property, as was their due. The reverse tenet was also an article of faith. If the goodly and godly were rewarded with a high station in the scheme of things, those who were of high station were expected to be even goodlier and godlier as a result. If money were virtue's natural reward, then money's natural reward was further virtue. It was a dogma, simple enough to follow, on which an American aristocracy would be built.

To detractors of John D. Rockefeller's outrageous-seeming fortune, an Ivy Lee could point out that, through Rockefeller-devised technology, the cost of kerosene to the American consumer had been reduced by 66 percent in three short years. Andrew Carnegie might have made a fortune beyond most men's wildest dreams, but his gift to the world was more than his well-publicized charitable benefactions. In twenty-five years' time, his companies had lowered the cost of steel by nearly 90 percent. Capitalism was a simple matter of give-and-take, a gentlemanly handshake, a deal in which everyone came out ahead — the capitalist a little further ahead, of course.

It became an article of faith that members of the American upper crust would be offered an automatic admission into heaven. It even came as no surprise that one of the elite should be beatified. It seemed perfectly fitting, to members of America's old and distinguished Ijams family, that one of their ancestors should have become a saint. Great-great-grandmother Elizabeth Ann Seton was, after all, a *Seton,* a member of a great and noble family originally from Scotland. To be sure, she had broken with family tradition somewhat when, as a mother of five, she converted to Roman Catholicism, founded the first parochial school in America in 1809, and began performing miracles for which the Church could find no temporal explanations. But when Mother Seton was canonized in 1975 as the first American to be registered in the Calendar of Saints, one of her descendants, Mrs. J. Horton Ijams of New York, announced, "I happen to be a good Episcopalian. But if an ancestor of mine is going to be made a saint, I intend to be there." Mrs. Ijams took her whole family to Rome for the occasion.

According to the gospel of wealth, freedom was good and therefore ordained by God, including freedom of enterprise. The Declaration of Independence bristles with references to God and the Creator, and from a tone of self-congratulation that creeps into this document it is possible to suspect that its framers viewed themselves as God's earthly archangels. And, if America's revolt from England and eventual independence were endorsed by God, it was not too great a leap of logic to assume that America's development into the richest country in the world was also God-ordained.

Capitalism — free enterprise — would succeed, according to the gospel, because it was based on reliable and homely values: thrift, industry, honesty, and the keeping of promises. This last was perhaps most important: trust, which might be called capitalism's key concept. It is probably no coincidence that so many of America's banks call themselves trust companies, or that every piece of American currency, and every coin, is emblazoned with the words "In God We Trust." Or that those inviolable legal instruments through which fortunes are passed on from one generation to the next are called trust funds. With each trust fund, in addition to property and cash, is passed the implicit wish that each member of each succeeding generation will carry the family name onward to greater riches, and greater glory.

But, to some descendants of America's oldest families, the weight of upholding such a gospel could be just too much to bear. It could sometimes seem as though one were being required to bear the weight of God himself. Added to this weight was the heavy onus of family traditions, the weight of ancient heroism, the weight of leadership, the weight of past achievements, of excellence, the weight of nearly three hundred years of proud American history. In some families, inheriting great wealth (the Kennedys are conceivably a case in point) can seem to bring with it a kind of bane. But in others, the curse can come from inheriting — and being expected to live up to — a prestigious ancestral name. When one was born, say, a Livingston or a Jay, so much was expected of one from the outset. The past cried out to a Jay heir to match or even transcend his ancestors' mighty, godly, patriotic deeds. Sometimes the results of bearing such inherited burdens would be positive in terms of strengthened character and backbone. But, to the frail or the uncertain or the neurasthenic, the results could just as easily be harshly negative. For the uncertain child, being born into a proud old family could be less a blessing than a family curse, as the struggle to uphold the family name and honor becomes unbearable and finally impossible, and the child turns from uncertainty to rebelliousness, from rebelliousness to eccentricity, and from eccentricity to madness — while, all the time, his family keeps insisting that this disaster cannot be happening to *them*. This, at least, is one explanation for the tortured life of John Jay Chapman. The burdens of aristocracy were more than he could shoulder. But who knows for sure?

Henry and Eleanor Jay Chapman had raised their children in Manhattan and at Jay Farm, the thousand-acre family spread in suburban Bedford, New York, which the first John Jay's grandfather Jacobus Van Cortlandt bought from the Indian chief Katonah in 1703. Jay Farm was — and still is — an idyllic place consisting mostly of rolling woodlands, old stone walls, and ancient bridle paths. From the crest of the highest hills, it was possible to see across the Kisco and Croton valleys (both turned into reservoirs now) to the town of Dunderberg on the Hudson River. It was to the farm that John and Sarah Jay retired after his long career in public life.

In addition to the old frame farmhouse itself, there were stone cottages and outbuildings, a cider mill, an ancient rose garden, a pond, barns and haymows, and stables filled with horses, Shetland ponies for the children, old hacks, dog carts, sulkies, carriages, and tack that had been used by generations of Jays. At the same time, by the end of the nineteenth century, the farm had become a repository of old memories and, to the Jay children at least, a somewhat spooky place. The Jays were another family who never threw anything away, and there were more than two hundred years' worth of family silver, furniture, books, mementos, trunksful of Revolutionary uniforms and the dresses Sarah Jay brought home from Paris, and, outside in the yard, the grave of Old Fred, the horse that carried Colonel William Jay in the Civil War. And of course there were the family portraits gazing down from the walls, by Stuart and Trumbull, of Washington, Hamilton, Egbert Benson, as well as the remarkable Stuart of the Chief Justice himself and a bust of him by Ceracchi, and the portraits of William Jay and his wife by Vanderlyn. Jay Farm had become more like a family museum, or even mausoleum, than a home, and even before John Jay Chapman's departure for St. Paul's, the boy's head was filled with thoughts of darkness and death, of ashes to ashes and dust to dust. Still, more than anything else, this brooding, temperamental child wanted to play the violin.

If there was one message conveyed by Jay Farm — particularly to the younger, more impressionable members of the family who gathered there every summer — it was: *Excel, excel. You are a Jay, and we are your ancestors, and look what we managed to accomplish on less than you have inherited from us. It is up to you to do as well as we did, or better, and to bring more honor and glory to the Jay name.* And there was also a religious message, as the family trooped off every Sunday morning dutifully to worship at St. Matthew's Episcopal Church, where there were more reminders of the family's long prominence in the region: stained-glass windows, pews, altar decorations, a reredos, all benefactions from the Jays. The Jays, the message read, had been generous to God, and therefore God had been generous to the Jays.

There are several family theories about what was wrong with John Jay Chapman, other than that the clustering of Jay family genes over so many generations had resulted in too rarified a mixture — so rarified that it became explosive. "He was my grandfather's first cousin," says one of the contemporary Jays. "By then, there was a family tradition that one studied law, but one didn't practice it. Instead, one was supposed to sit down and carpenter some great social document, like the United States Constitution, and pass into history. John Jay Chapman wrote . . . and wrote . . . and wrote, and nobody had the slightest idea what he was writing about. He became a professional dilettante, an aristocratic nut."

Another family member disagrees. "It was his mother's fault," this woman says. "She indulged him, encouraged him to be what she called an *enfant terrible*. Because he was a Jay, she assumed he had to be a genius, and because he was a Jay, he could do no wrong. She had heard about aristocratic English eccentrics. That was what she allowed her son to become. In today's terms, we'd call him a spoiled brat. Whenever things didn't go exactly as he thought they ought to go, *for a Jay,* he'd throw one of his fits."

Certainly aristocratic eccentrics were nothing new in the Jay clan. In a family of dedicated equestrians, one Jay — as a kind of reverse snobbery — insisted on riding a white mule and even taught the animal to jump fences. Eleanor Jay's grandfather had raised eyebrows when he wore a bright red necktie to his wife's funeral. This same old gentleman, when a visiting Englishman had innocently proposed a toast to the president of the United States (James Buchanan, of whom the host disapproved), had overturned his wineglass on the dinner table and announced, "I won't drink it." Even before it was fashionable, the Jays had been staunch abolitionists, and one Jay grandmother had startled her friends and social peers by actually inviting "Negro females" to her house and seating them at her table. Nonconformity, furthermore, was a trait that the Jays encouraged. As a result, when Eleanor Jay Chapman's younger son John threw violent temper tantrums in front of guests when he did not get his way, this behavior was dismissed by his indulgent mother as simply "Jack expressing himself."

Another family member says, a little sadly, "All he wanted, really, was for someone to pay attention to him, someone to listen to him. He was like an Old Testament prophet — even looked like one after he grew that dreadful beard — roaming through the streets, crying, 'The Messiah has come! The Messiah has come!' But no one listened to him, not even his mother. He led a miserable life."

What John Jay Chapman was to become was a champion of lost, losing, or simply hopeless causes, or Causes.

At St. Paul's School, Chapman was not popular with his schoolmates. It was what seemed to be his excessive religiosity that was most off-putting. He had a habit of suddenly falling to his knees, in prayer, in the classroom or on the playground, and his classmates learned that in the woodlands behind the school John Chapman had created a secret shrine of his own to which he would repair for private religious rites. In his third year at St. Paul's, he began to complain of mysterious physical ailments. He was losing his eyesight. His back was so weak that he could not stand up. He was examined by the school physician, who could find nothing wrong with him and who recommended "any employment which will make him forget himself." But, in the end, this difficult student was too much even for the formidable headmaster, the Reverend Dr. Henry Augustus Coit. Writing to Chapman's parents that their son was "very morbidly conscientious," Coit recommended that he leave the school and return home. It was the beginning of one of the long series of nervous breakdowns that would plague Chapman for the rest of his tormented life.

At home, he was lovingly nursed back to health by doting family servants, and it was decided that he would continue his education, and preparation for Harvard, under the less stressful guidance of private tutors.

There was never any question but that the boy would go to Harvard. Jays *always* went to Harvard. At Harvard, John Jay Chapman was expected to, and did, join the Porcellian Club, that famously elite institution that has, for its front window, a one-way mirror, allowing members of Porcellian to look out on the campus, while outsiders looking in can see only their own reflections. Chapman was taken into Porcellian not because he was well liked but simply because he was a Jay, an aristocrat or, as he himself liked to call himself, an "aristophil" — a lover of aristocracy. As he wrote later, "Come down to it and you find the paradox that only aristocrats are truly democratic in their social conduct and feeling. They only are simple — they have nothing to gain and nothing to lose, and have the freedom and simplicity of human beings."

At Harvard, because of who he was, Chapman was invited to the proper Bostonian homes of such Brahmin families as the Cabots and Lawrences and Lowells and Saltonstalls and Russells and Sargents and Searses. It was a milieu that Chapman seemed to enjoy for the first time in his life. As he wrote home, "Certainly it is not respectable not to have money, and all the tribute paid to wealth has its foundation in right. Not to have it shows a lack of force of character — either in yourself or in your fathers — coming sooner or later from vice or disregard of law. If this is not so, morality has no foundation." It was the gospel of wealth, phrased another way.

At Harvard, too, Chapman pursued his dream of becoming a great American concert violinist and at the same time displayed that recurring theme of violence and self-destruction that seemed periodically to haunt his thoughts. After hearing a child prodigy perform at a Boston concert, Chapman wrote to his mother:

> To play like that I'd cut off my foot with a hatchet, I'd pull off my ear by main force, I'd walk naked nine times around Boston, I'd swallow a fishing hook, I'd throw President Eliot out of his own parlor window sash and all — I'd go ten days without eating and before touching a morsel, I'd seize a violin and say, "Now! Listen!"

Alas, many of his fellow Cantabrigians were forced to listen to his discordant scrapings on the instrument. They threw rocks and lumps of coal at his door and hurled alarm clocks through his window at Thayer Hall to get him to stop, but despite everything he played obsessively on. *Excel! Excel!* his ancestors were crying out to him. He also decided that he might become a great American playwright or perhaps a great violinist *and* a great playwright, and he wrote in his diary, "The English stage stands in great need of a Dramatist whether comic or tragic — something real, of definite character. Perhaps I am the man. I've always thought the stage my vocation." It became another of Chapman's obsessions that would recur throughout his life, with the onset of another period of frenzied and obsessive behavior, usually signaling the coming of another of his breakdowns.

And it was at Harvard that John Jay Chapman committed the bizarre and grisly act that would indeed make him famous, in a limited sort of way, within his own circle, but for all the wrong reasons and not for anything he himself could have wished to be famous for. He had fallen madly in love with a young woman named Minna Timmins, the daughter of a wealthy Bostonian, George Henry Timmins. Minna, it seemed, had fallen in love with him. The two would eventually marry. But love, according to those who observed him that autumn of 1886, had made him moody, withdrawn, and forgetful — even forgetting dates with his beloved, which must have made Minna wonder how sincere his protestations of love might really be. He brooded and walked about the Harvard campus talking and arguing with himself over arcane matters no one could understand, while Minna's parents (who were rich but not quite Brahmins) waited breathlessly for the romance to develop further. After all, their daughter was not exactly pretty and was a bit on the plump side, but she was being courted by a *Jay*. Yet to those who had observed Chapman's behavior in the past, there were ominous signs that an explosion was coming.

The occasion for it was a black-tie soirée at the Brookline home of Mr. and Mrs. Walter C. Cabot. John Jay Chapman had of course been invited and was already in attendance. Up the Cabot front walk strolled another male guest in full evening dress. He was Percival Lowell, aged thirty-two — seven years Chapman's senior — handsome, urbane, and considered one of Boston's great bachelor "catches." His brother Abbott Lawrence Lowell would become president of Harvard, and his sister Amy would become a leading Imagist poet. Percival Lowell himself would go on to become a leading astronomer whose controversial theories about intelligent life on Mars would be widely circulated. All at once, out the Cabots' front door and down the front steps charged John Jay Chapman, brandishing a heavy walking stick; to the horror of other guests who watched the scene from the doorway, he began beating the more slightly built Lowell over the head with the stick. When Lowell finally fell, bloodied, upon the walkway, Chapman ran off into the night.

The attack, and the viciousness of it, seemed totally unprovoked. It was true that Lowell was considered something of a ladies' man and belonged to the same dramatic club as Minna Timmins. But if it was jealousy that provoked Chapman's murderous rage, there was no foundation for it. Percival Lowell had not been a suitor of Minna's. In fact, he had not shown the slightest interest in her. Lowell was picked up and carried into the house, and his cuts and contusions were bathed and bandaged. As for Chapman, he had disappeared and for the next two days could not be found — two days about which, as he later recounted, he had absolutely no recollection.

Naturally, no charges were pressed against Chapman for the assault, nor was the incident reported in the newspapers. It was written off as simply an altercation between two gentlemen of the same social class who were both members of Porcellian, though Mr. Lowell was no longer an undergraduate.

Since the attack on Lowell seemed so mindless, it would soon be forgotten, but what happened in its aftermath would never be by those who knew John Jay Chapman. After his two "lost" days, as Chapman wrote almost matter-of-factly in his memoir, "Retrospections":*

> The next thing I remember is returning late at night to my room. At that time I was rooming alone in a desolate side-street in Cambridge. It was a small, dark horrid little room. I sat down. There was a hard-coal fire burning brightly. I took off my coat and waistcoat, wrapped a pair of suspenders tightly on my left forearm above the wrist, and plunged my left hand deep in the blaze and held it down with my right hand for some minutes. When I took it out, the charred knuckles and finger-bones were exposed. I said to myself, "This will never do." I took an old coat, wrapped it about my left hand and arm, slipped my right arm into an overcoat, held the coat about me and started for Boston in the horsecars. On arriving at the Massachusetts General Hospital I showed the trouble to a surgeon, was put under ether, and the next morning waked up without the hand. . . .

Chapman added that he found himself the next morning feeling "very calm in my spirits." In his macabre act of self-mutilation, he had had what amounted to a religious experience. It had been a rite of exorcism, and he had heeded the biblical injunction "If thy right hand offend thee, cut it off." Of course Chapman, who was right-handed, had cut off his *left* hand. In the course of his hospital stay, Chapman wrote, he was visited by "the great alienist Dr. Reginald Heber Fitz, an extremely agreeable man. He asked me among other things if I was insane. I said, 'That is for you to find out.' He reported me as sane. . . ."

To his mother, Chapman wrote home about the amputation with the unlikely explanation that his hand had been run over by a streetcar. "I am perfectly well and happy," he added. "Don't mind it a bit — it shall not make the least difference in my life."

In his own, almost breezy account of the episode, Chapman omitted only one fact, which was that during his two days in an amnesiac state Minna Timmins had written him a letter demanding that he apologize to Percival Lowell. It may have been the effect upon him of this letter, more than contrition, that caused him to plunge his hand into the blazing coals.

*"Retrospections" is a fragment of an autobiography that Chapman began in 1931. Most of it appears in *John Jay Chapman and His Letters* by M. A. DeWolfe Howe.

Unfortunately perhaps, the loss of his hand, as Chapman had assured his mother, did not make the least difference in his life as it continued in its erratic course. Following his graduation from Harvard and its law school (as a Jay, he would be expected to practice law only in a most dilatory way) and his marriage to Minna, Chapman was still not ready to settle down. As for Minna, the advantages of being married to a Jay seemed to outweigh the vicissitudes of being the wife of a man who, from time to time, behaved like a lunatic. Her husband continued to be subject to emotional outbursts and tantrums. He still dreamed of lighting up the skies in some important and dramatic way. With only one hand, he had pretty much abandoned his hopes of becoming a concert violinist, though he would never give up trying to be a playwright. Then, in 1890, he had a new idea. He would become a great reformer.

New York, in the 1890s, was very much in the political grip of the Tammany Hall machine, and to reform that situation became Chapman's goal. With others of similar bent, Chapman helped form the People's Municipal League, whose aim was to defeat the Tammany candidate in the 1890 mayoralty race. Though the league succeeded in exposing the huge bribes that the candidate had paid to Tammany's chiefs, the result of their efforts was that the candidate was reelected by a sizable margin. In defeat, the league consoled itself with the fact that it had probably given the Tammanyites a good scare.

Chapman's next targets were New York City's saloons. Chapman was not a Dry, but many saloons had become centers of Tammany influence, and since saloons were subject to licensing and inspections, they offered splendid opportunities for bribery and graft. Liquor regulation, blue laws, and Sunday closings of bars had become powerful political weapons used by both parties, and there were certainly a great many saloons in the city — by 1890, there was one for every two hundred citizens. In 1896, the Republican administration of the state had pushed through the Raines Liquor Law to meet the demand for Sunday closings. According to the new law, only hotels and restaurants serving food could serve liquor on the Lord's Day. To comply with this law, saloons merely began calling themselves restaurants and offered "Raines Law sandwiches" of cheese or peanut butter, which no one ever ate. Others restyled themselves hotels and let out upstairs rooms at hourly rates to prostitutes and other guests without luggage.

As secretary of the Excise Reform Association, Chapman toiled for the repeal of the Raines Law. He published and passed out pamphlets and screeds and wrote letters to the editors of newspapers, itemizing the abuses of the Raines Law. He traveled to Albany to address the state legislature on the problem. He even managed to write and have published in the *New York Times* a new and more workable liquor law of his own devising. But after six years of feverish activity on Chapman's part, the Raines Law remained the law of the land, and it would remain so until the advent of Prohibition in 1919.

It had to be admitted that there was a certain logic to Chapman's enthusiasms as he moved from one crusade on to the next. By his interpretation, his failure to defeat Tammany Hall was due to the situation in the saloons, and his failure to remodel the liquor law was due to — what else? — commercialism. Commercialism became his new villain. Everything that was wrong in America was due to the country's overemphasis on commercialism. Commercialism explained why saloon keepers wouldn't close their bars on Sunday. Publishers published bad books because trash made money. Artists painted banal and sentimental pictures because that was what sold. Cheap music made its way to vaudeville stages because that was what sold tickets, and so on. Culture in America was being defeated by commercialism. More pamphlets and screeds and handouts and letters to the editor appeared over John Jay Chapman's signature decrying Americans' submission to the Baal of commercialism, the false god Mammon. Of course, in a capitalist economy based on supply and demand, there was little hope that Chapman's righteous indignation would have much effect on the scheme of things. And, after the failure of each new campaign, there was usually a breakdown.

Minna Timmins Chapman died from complications following the birth of the couple's third son, and for a while Chapman's life seemed to have lost its emotional footing. But then he married the former Elizabeth Chanler, an old friend of the family. Elizabeth Chanler was a cripple and walked with a pronounced limp, but at least Chapman and Elizabeth became two disabled people who could lean on one another. Elizabeth had an additional, much more pleasant attribute. She was an Astor. Her mother, Mrs. Winthrop Chanler, was the granddaughter of William Backhouse Astor and his Livingston bride, and she brought Chapman financial independence from his parents, who had largely supported his activities up to then.

She also brought with her a high-living, convivial, and somewhat dotty brother, William Astor Chanler, who had some ideas that immediately interested his new brother-in-law. Among Chanler's theories were these: that President Wilson had promised to support the Pope and make Catholicism the official American religion in return for the use of the Vatican's spy system; that the League of Nations was a Jewish plot to rule the world; and that Wilson's Fourteen Points had been written by Jacob Schiff, Judge Louis Brandeis, and the Jews.

Chanler's rantings served to uncover in Chapman an unpleasant streak of anti-Semitism that had always been seen lurking there. To be fair, however, social anti-Semitism was commonplace in America in the 1920s, and even the famously democratic Eleanor Roosevelt had been known to make slurring comments about Jews. But what really excited Chapman most were his brother-in-law's sentiments about the Catholic Church. Anti-Catholicism became his new crusade, and a new barrage of literature and letters emerged from Chapman's pen. Catholicism, with its emphasis on commercialism — think of all those religious stores that sold crucifixes and rosaries and votive candles and icons depicting the Blessed Virgin! — was to blame for America's dangerous swing toward commercialism. The Pope wanted to take over America! Because of its anti-Catholic stance, Chapman found himself publicly praising (of all things, for a member of a great abolitionist family) the activities of the Ku Klux Klan.

The Klan, he felt, could profit from a bit of refinement and gentrification, and a coalition between the Klan and the eastern establishment might accomplish this. Wrote Chapman, "Being an old agitator, I see the game so clearly — the needs of the moment — i.e., to connect up the Ku Klux element with the better element in the East. The K.K. are on the *right track,* i.e. open war, and the rest of the country is in a maze of prejudice against the K.K. due to R.C. manipulation of the Eastern Press."

Naturally, the Klan was delighted with this praise from a member of the eastern aristocracy. And yet, as Emerson wrote, a foolish consistency is the hobgoblin of little minds, and Chapman could be nothing if not inconsistent. While extolling the wisdom of the Ku Klux Klan, he was simultaneously taking up the cudgel against his alma mater, Harvard, for its refusal to let a Negro student live in a freshman dormitory. In a letter to the *New York World,* Chapman accused Harvard of trying "to keep alive the idea of white supremacy," and added that "such negroes among us as can receive a college education must be offered one that is without stigma."

There is also the touching episode of his pilgrimage to the little town of Coatesville, Pennsylvania, in the summer of 1911. Reading an account of the lynching of a black man named Walker, John Jay Chapman was so moved that he decided to journey immediately to Coatesville and to conduct a memorial prayer service there for Mr. Walker. Arriving in the still-tense town the day after the lynching, the outsider Chapman, and his mission, were viewed with understandable wariness. The local newspaper refused to print an announcement of the prayer service, but Chapman went gamely around the town tacking up notices announcing it anyway, despite the fact that his posters were quickly torn down. He rented a vacant storefront, brought in chairs, and labored with his usual fervor over the sermon he planned to deliver.

Two people — an aged black woman who may have been a relative of the victim and a white man who had been appointed as the town spy to report on what went on — attended the service.

Chapman had just recovered from his longest and most severe breakdown. It had begun in 1902, when he was forty, and lasted nearly a decade. Most of this period he spent at Rokeby, the Chanler family estate on the Hudson. (Originally, Rokeby had been a Livingston house, but with the Livingston-Astor union it had passed into the hands of Astor heirs.) During much of this time, Chapman was bedridden, claiming he had lost the use of his legs, curled in a fetal position, his legs drawn up under his chin, babbling incoherent prayers, quoting snatches of poetry, demanding absolute silence, solitude, and darkness. For most of this time, he was unable to feed, clothe, bathe, or otherwise care for himself, and it must have been painful for his long-suffering wife to see her husband, when he did emerge from his bed, crawling about naked on the floor on all fours like a baby. Why he was never hospitalized during these years is unclear, except that perhaps his Astor in-laws' declaration that Chapman was "sane, though imaginative" carried some weight. If it was just imaginativeness that pushed the man into these horrible straits, his must surely be the longest case of feigned insanity in history. During these years he grew his long, black beard that made him look like Jove or a Hebrew prophet from the Old Testament.

Following the Coatesville fiasco, it might be presumed that John Jay Chapman would have felt utterly defeated by life. But he was not. He went on writing letters to editors, putting out pamphlets, writing essays and poetry (paying for the publication of much of this himself), turning out his curious plays about fairy princesses, ogres, and fire-breathing dragons, translating and adapting Greek classics. He managed to meet, and be impressed by, a number of leading figures of his day, including the analyst Carl Jung and the philosopher-mathematician Alfred North Whitehead. Henry James was his friend, and the novelist admired him as an American original, which indeed he was. During the 1920s, Chapman and his wife made several trips abroad, where — as an Astor and a Jay — they were welcomed at a number of stately homes, châteaux, and palazzi. In between, to be sure, there were more bouts with that undiagnosed "illness" that Chapman had always suffered from, whatever it was.

In 1933, though, when he was seventy-one, there was something at last diagnosable — cancer of the liver. He died in November of that year, with his ever-loyal Elizabeth at his side. In his final moments, his thoughts seemed to have returned to his first obsession, the violin. Half conscious, he clutched at Elizabeth's hand and said, "I want to take it away, I want to take it away!" "What," she asked him, "the pillow?" "No," he said, "the mute, the mute. I want to play on the open strings."

And so, in the end, he died not defeated in his ambitions, but *by* them. He was always haunted. But that was perhaps the price one had to pay for being born a Jay. It was as though those mighty ghosts from the past that possessed Jay Farm kept rising up to say to him, "*Excel . . . try harder . . . do more . . . no, you STILL haven't got it right!*"

John Jay Chapman's widow had already brought some peculiarly haunted characters with her into the Jay family circle, though her relatives did not display the aristocratic curse as violently as her late husband did. And Rokeby, the estate on the Hudson, had already been put to some unusual family uses before it became a sort of private sanatorium for John Jay Chapman. Elizabeth Chanler Chapman had been one of the famous "Astor orphans," the nine great-grandchildren of John Jacob Astor who, when their parents both died young, each fell heir to roughly one million dollars. Rokeby had then been turned into a luxurious private orphanage where the children were raised by nurses and governesses and private tutors and where, since the nurses and governesses and private tutors were, in a very real sense, the employees of the children, the orphans were allowed to lay down the rules. The results of this form of upbringing were some rather unusual — to say the least — adult human beings. It is said in the Chanler family that there was nothing wrong with the blue of the Chanler blood until it became mixed with the yellow of the Astor gold. Yellow mixed with blue of course results in green, and in the case of the orphans it was not always an attractive shade of green.

John Jay Chapman's brother-in-law, William Astor Chanler, when not spouting international Jewish-Papist conspiracy theories, was fond of big-game hunting in Africa, buying and selling racehorses, and enjoying the good life in general. He had lost a leg: not in a war but, it was said, as the result of a bordello brawl. During the 1920s, he was a well-known figure at Maxim's in Paris. Entering the restaurant one day at lunchtime with a friend, he explained to the waiter that he would have to be served promptly, since he had a horse running at Longchamp that afternoon and needed to get to the track. When the service was not as speedy as he wished, African Willie, as he was known in the family, began to grumble, and presently his companion noticed him fumbling with something under the table. What emerged from below was African Willie's artificial leg — shoe, sock, garter, and all — which he proceeded to hurl across the room at the waiter's back, shouting in French, "Now may I have your attention!"

People usually had no trouble paying attention to William Chanler's brother, John Armstrong Chanler. Known as Uncle Archie, John Armstrong Chanler always wore a pair of binoculars in restaurants to keep track of waiters. His table manners, too, were hard to ignore. He would eat a piece of fish as though playing a harmonica or he would take a dozen pancakes, douse them with melted butter and maple syrup, and then drape them behind his ears like hibiscus blooms. Uncle Archie often dressed up as Napoleon, slept wearing a saber, and carried a silver-headed cane engraved with the words "Leave Me Alone." At length, his brothers and Stanford White, a family friend, succeeded in having Uncle Archie declared insane and placed in Bloomingdale's lunatic asylum in White Plains, New York. When Uncle Archie managed to escape from Bloomingdale's in 1900, he wrote a courtly note to the superintendent, saying, "You have always said that I believe I am the reincarnation of Napoleon Bonaparte. As a learned and sincere man, you therefore will not be surprised that I take French leave."

A number of the Astor orphans and their descendants remained in the vicinity of Rokeby, in the village of Barrytown, New York, where they had the advantage of living in a community of townsfolk who were used to them and took the family's eccentricities in stride, while Rokeby itself — once one of the statelier Hudson River mansions — began to show the signs of benign neglect. For years the official manager of Rokeby has been Richard Chanler Aldrich, a grandnephew of Uncle Archie and a grandson of Margaret Livingston Chanler Aldrich, who fought for the establishment of the U.S. Army Nursing Corps in World War I. Ricky, as he is called, has two principal hobbies. One is collecting and restoring antique iceboats. The other is studying Serbian, Croatian, and Polish grammar, an intricate and time-consuming occupation. Ricky actually studied in Poland for a while. Ricky's other, and most legendary, characteristic is that he rarely bathes. Ricky is much loved in Barrytown, where it is often said, "Ricky would give you the shirt off his back, but who would want it?"

Then there was John Jay Chapman and Elizabeth Chanler Chapman's son, Chanler Chapman, who was Ricky Aldrich's first cousin once removed. In Barrytown, Chanler Chapman invariably wore bib overalls and carried a slingshot. When asked to explain his slingshots, Chanler Chapman would reply, "They don't make any noise." He had been using ball bearings for ammunition but found them too expensive. So, for four dollars, he bought six hundred pounds of gravel. Armed with his slingshot and his gravel, he enjoyed taking aim and inflicting dimples on the bodywork of various of his relatives' automobiles. Actually, the townspeople were relieved when Chanler Chapman converted to slingshots from guns. He at one point had a collection of 115 of these and liked hunting. But few of his neighbors cared or dared to go out hunting with him because of his habit of firing at anything that moved, even if it was another hunter. Fortunately, Chapman was a poor shot, and so a number of hunters' lives were spared.

For years, Chanler Chapman published the monthly *Barrytown Explorer,* a journal that most people in the village bought since it sold for only twenty-five cents an issue, cost four dollars for a year's subscription, and was full of surprises. Chapman was the *Explorer*'s publisher, editor, and principal contributor, and you never knew what you might expect to read in the *Explorer,* whose slogan was "When you can't smile, quit." Readers would be treated to Chapman's salty, if a little hard to follow, opinions such as, "You can abolish rectitude, you can abolish the laws of gravity, but don't do away with good old American bullshit."

Each issue of the *Explorer* usually contained a sampling of Chapman's output of poetry, which always gave the place and date of each composition — e.g., "Kitchen, Sept. 13, 7:15 A.M." What might be called an advice column was another regular feature of the paper, where readers might encounter such a nugget as this: "Close the blinds at night, and lower the chances of being shot to death in bed." Chapman was inordinately fond of W. C. Fields and ran photographs of the comedian in the *Explorer* from time to time for no particular reason other than as tributes to the star.

Chanler Chapman's first wife was the former Olivia James, a grandniece of Henry and William, and a son of this union, Robert Chapman, lives in Italy where, for a time, he lived in a cave and made kites, becoming the first troglodyte in the *Social Register.* Another son, John Jay Chapman II, graduated from Harvard and then went to Puerto Rico, where he became a mailman. In Puerto Rico he met and married a black woman by whom he had several children. When one of his daughters was ready for boarding school and had applied to St. Paul's, which had recently gone coeducational, Chanler Chapman ticked off the list of reasons his granddaughter was bound to be accepted: "She's a she, she's a Chapman, she's a Chanler, and she's black."

In 1972, John Jay Chapman II returned from Puerto Rico to his hometown of Barrytown and became a mailman there. Said cousin Winthrop Aldrich — known as Winty — to Chanler Chapman of his son's chosen occupation, "Isn't it remarkable — Edmund Wilson called your father the greatest letter writer in America, and now your son may be the greatest letter carrier!" Chanler Chapman was not amused. "Winty knits with his toes," was his only comment.

In the meantime, Uncle Archie, gone from the lunatic asylum but not forgotten by the New York State police, who had a statewide warrant for his return, had gone to Philadelphia for a while, where he had himself examined by his relative by marriage William James in an effort to get himself declared sane in New York. The results of the psychological tests were mixed, and Uncle Archie then moved to an estate in Virginia called Merry Mills, changed his name to Chaloner, and continued his fight to be pronounced legally sane. In Virginia, he was just as noticeable as he had been elsewhere. Like many of his relatives, Uncle Archie loved horses, and managed to unearth an obscure Virginia statute that required automobiles to "keep a careful look ahead for horseback riders. . . . If requested to do so by said rider [said driver] shall lead the horse past his machine." To enforce this law, Uncle Archie, dressed in an Inverness cape, patrolled the roads outside Merry Mills on horseback. A green umbrella was affixed to the cantle of his saddle, a horn was attached to the pommel, and a revolver was tucked in Uncle Archie's belt. After dark, he had port and starboard running lights hung from his stirrups, and what amounted to a riding light hung from the girth. To unobliging motorists, the horn was his warning. The revolver was his ultimatum.

In 1909, Uncle Archie shot and killed an intruder at Merry Mills — a man who had a long local record as a wife beater. To memorialize his feat, Uncle Archie had a silver plaque sunk in the floor of his house, marking the spot, which was inscribed with the cryptic message "He Beat The Devil." This was not long after Harry Thaw shot Stanford White, and the *New York Post* noted, "The latest prominent assassin has taken the precaution to have himself judged insane beforehand." Uncle Archie, not amused, promptly sued the *Post* for libel. The lawsuit dragged on for nearly ten years, but, in the end, Uncle Archie won it, and he also won his battle to have himself declared sane in New York State.

Chanler Chapman admired his uncle Archie for his spunk, and he also admired his uncle Bob, Robert Winthrop Chanler, another of the colorful orphans. Uncle Bob ran for, and was elected, sheriff of Dutchess County. On the job, Uncle Bob wore cowboy suits and ten-gallon hats, and he hired Richard Harding Davis as his deputy. After divorcing his first wife, Uncle Bob declared that he was going to marry the most beautiful girl in the world. He went to Paris and married an opera singer named Lina Cavalieri, who, if she was not the most beautiful girl in the world, was certainly one of the most calculating. After a week of marriage, Lina left Uncle Bob to live with a lover, whereupon it turned out that Uncle Bob had signed over his entire fortune to her. Asked by the press to comment on his brother's plight, Uncle Archie — still in the midst of his sanity fight — delivered a much publicized quote: "Who's loony now?"

Uncle Bob, however, managed to get most of his money back.

He returned to New York, bought three adjoining East Side brownstones, threw them together, and created what he called a House of Fantasy, filled with parrots and other tropical birds, where he held orgies. Invited to one of Uncle Bob's parties, the young actress Ethel Barrymore said, "I entered his house one evening an innocent girl, and left the next morning an old woman."

But despite the vagaries of his various uncles, it was Chanler Chapman who was proud to lay claim to the title of the most eccentric man in America. He had embarked on this career early, at St. Paul's, where his antics quickly earned him the nickname Charlie Chaplin. At St. Paul's, among other things, he collected a $100 purse for throwing a clandestine prizefight in which he was knocked out. He would do anything on a bet — such as hurling himself into an icy pond. He charged 50 cents admission for a show in which he took a mouthful of kerosene, lit a match, held the match close to his mouth, and shot flames across the room. On the side, he dealt in firearms, selling the same Smith & Wesson .32 over and over again. It inevitably jammed after a few rounds, and so Chapman would buy it back from the purchaser at a reduced price. Entering Harvard in 1920, at the outset of Prohibition, he quickly set himself up as a bootlegger and was soon bringing in $300 to $400 a week selling liquor to students at Groton, St. Mark's, St. Paul's, and other elite boarding schools in the area.

When his uncle Archie returned to Barrytown, Chanler Chapman was one of the first to welcome him back into the family fold and to insist that the other relatives do likewise — and to politely pretend not to notice Uncle Archie's new diet: ice cream and grass clippings. Uncle Archie had the back half of his Pierce Arrow limousine converted into a field kitchen, and he and his nephew went on many pleasant outings to New York City, where they enjoyed riding from one end of Manhattan to the other and back again, with ice cream stops along the way. Uncle Archie had passed out of his Napoleon phase and now declared that he was the reincarnation of Pompey and had plans to take over the world. He was already in control of New York City's traffic system, an important first step. Whenever his chauffeur came to a red light and stopped, Uncle Archie would furiously rub his big emerald ring for several seconds. Then he would cry, "See? It turned green!"

In the end, everyone in the family grew to love Uncle Archie. An aristocracy, after all, is tolerant of its oddballs.

25

The Great Splurge

In a sense, Mrs. Elizabeth Ellet was correct when, in 1867, she predicted that the new "fast people," whose gaudy fortunes came directly or indirectly out of the profiteering that went on during and after the Civil War, would never be fully accepted by the old aristocracy and that "the really excellent will never mingle with them." But there was more to it than that. It was not just that the old aristocracy adopted a snooty and superior attitude toward the newcomers. And it might have been more accurate if Mrs. Ellet had said that the Old Guard would never fully comprehend, or accept, the behavior and values of such later-arrived families as the Vanderbilts, Rockefellers, Goulds, Harrimans, Belmonts, and such. These "new rich" seemed to have standards and priorities that were totally at variance with those the Old Guard had always believed were appropriate to an American upper class. The newcomers seemed to have rewritten the gospel of wealth entirely.

The Old Guard had always believed that Christian character was based essentially on the golden rule and that strength of character involved a willingness to pull one's weight and an ability to handle situations, even when they involved getting one's fingernails dirty. The New Guard, faced with nail-dirtying chores, believed in issuing orders to underlings. The Old Guard worshipped their ancestry and their families' places in history and tradition. The New Guard seemed to worship only money and those who had it. The Old Guard had accepted, as an article of faith, that wealth was to be used to enjoy learning, travel, culture, animals and nature, family pleasures, and philanthropies. The New Guard seemed to use money for ostentation, self-promotion, and as a means of wielding power and control over others. In Chicago, John D. Rockefeller's daughter, Edith Rockefeller McCormick, refused to learn her servants' names as they came and went in her imperial household. The servants were not even permitted to speak to her, and all communications with the mistress of the house had to be directed, through a lengthy chain of protocol and command, to her private secretary. The Old Guard had faith in the superiority of conscience and breeding. The New Guard's creed was superiority of position and possessions. The differences between the philosophies of the Old and New seemed so vast as to be irreconcilable. It was as though a whole new era, or Era, had come into being.

The years between 1890 and 1930 in the United States might be called the Era of the Great Splurge, when newly rich Americans embarked upon a period of aggressive and competitive spending that the country had never seen before and may never see again. It was during this period that the sleepy seaport of Newport, Rhode Island, was transformed into one of the grandest and most pretentious summer resorts in the world. So in demand did waterfront properties become on this relatively small island that Newport today presents a strange spectacle indeed: Palaces and châteaux whose architecture would normally demand sweeping vistas and long approaches have been set down, cheek by jowl, on one-acre or half-acre plots and look, to at least one observer, like a collection of "very large hats on very small boys," all in an assertive row down the length of Bellevue Avenue. In the Long Island beach resort of Southampton, where certain Old Guard families had long kept modest summer homes to escape the heat of Manhattan and where activities were seldom more socially ambitious than swimming, canoeing, and games of bicycle polo, the same thing happened. But in Southampton there was more elbow room, and so the new estates sprawled outward, surrounded by rolling lawns and gardens, and in the Era of the Great Splurge the bays and inlets of Southampton filled with ocean-worthy yachts. Into Southampton, furthermore, came a new wave of wealthy immigrants from as far away as Pittsburgh, Cleveland, and Chicago. Closer to Manhattan, the private, guarded enclave of Tuxedo Park was created, with more estates and three man-made lakes: one for boating, one for fishing, and one for swimming. Tuxedo Park, according to the doctrine of the Great Splurge, was for autumn weekends, when the foliage of Rockland County was at its best.

In all three of these places, the local townsfolk were expected to supply a cadre of willing and obedient servants; local merchants were treated as private caterers; and the local police were used as a private security force. Since the Era of the Great Splurge lasted a full forty years and more, a whole generation of rich children was born and raised unaware that they might ever expect anything less.

Meanwhile, the more conservative Old Guard families, who not only had had their money longer but who were also more experienced with the job of tending and nourishing their fortunes — as well as with the ordeal of losing them — found the Great Splurge phenomenon not merely distasteful. They found it incomprehensible and full of hidden warnings. "Watch out," they cautioned their children, "for that sort of thing."

The famous 1906 murder of the architect Stanford White by Harry K. Thaw of Pittsburgh was a case of old money versus new. Ostensibly, Thaw's motive for shooting White that summer evening at Madison Square Garden was Thaw's discovery of an earlier dalliance between White and Thaw's wife, a former show girl named Evelyn Nesbit. But there was more to it than that, and Thaw had hated White long before Thaw and Miss Nesbit ever met.

The Whites were an aristocratic family with roots both in Old New York and Old New England. The first American White arrived in Massachusetts in 1632 with John Hooker's Puritan congregation. He had a large farm in Cambridge on what is now the site of Harvard's Houghton Library, but because of theological disputes with Boston's theocracy, he sold his farm and, with a small band of others and 160 head of cattle, moved down the Connecticut River to found the city of Hartford. Whites had gone on to produce generations of Episcopalian, Presbyterian, and Congregationalist clergymen — though one apostate White cleric converted to Catholicism — who founded other New England towns as well as Whitestone, New York, and Newark, New Jersey. It would doubtless have pleased the aesthetic Stanford White to know that New York's graceful Bronx-Whitestone Bridge was named for his ancestors.

Stanford White's grandfather Richard Mansfield White was a successful New York shipping merchant in the clipper trade and repaid the city by founding the first Episcopal Sunday schools in both Brooklyn and Manhattan. Meanwhile, on his mother's side, Stanford White was descended from the plantation aristocracy of the Old South in Charleston, South Carolina.

Harry Thaw's father, by contrast, personified the nineteenth-century robber baron. William Thaw had started out as a teenager, on horseback, riding through the Ohio River valley making collections for the Bank of the United States, a job that required both ruthlessness and muscle. In 1877, a bloody strike on the Pennsylvania Railroad, in which scores of men were killed and which federal troops had to be called in to quell, had driven the railroad's stock down to a fraction of its value. Thereupon, William Thaw snapped up all the stock he could, using, it was alleged though never proven, "borrowed" money from his employer to make his purchases. The result was that William Thaw was able to leave his son Harry forty million dollars in Pennsylvania Railroad stocks and bonds. The enmity between Thaw and White began when White succeeded in putting the snobbish, upstart Thaw in his place — albeit playfully, as a kind of practical joke.

It all started in 1901 when young Thaw, moving to New York and intent on taking the city by storm, invited a number of his wealthy bachelor friends to a dinner in one of the private dining rooms at Sherry's. For entertainment, Thaw had asked an actress named Frances Belmont — no kin to August — from the cast of *Floradora* to round up some of the prettier girls from the chorus line and bring them to the party. Miss Belmont agreed, because the girls would be handsomely paid for their services.

The night before the party, however, Frances Belmont happened to walk into Sherry's main dining room on the arm of an escort, and there she spotted Thaw seated at a table with some of his society friends. She greeted him cheerfully, but Thaw snubbed her and refused to introduce her to the others at the table. Furious, Frances went backstage the next night and told the *Floradora* girls that the Thaw party was off. She and her chorus girls were not to be treated as mere playthings. Instead, as compensation, her friend Stanford White, who was a *real* gentleman, had invited the entire *Floradora* cast to his elegant digs — a private apartment at the top of the old Madison Square Garden, which he had designed — after the show. And so, while Thaw and his bachelors waited until the wee hours at Sherry's for the entertainment to arrive, the *Floradora* cast danced, sang, ate caviar, drank champagne, and got quite drunk at Stanford White's.

The next morning, *Town Topics* had the story: "Floradora beauties sing for their supper in White's studio, while Thaw's orchestra fiddles to an empty room at Sherry's." It made Harry Thaw look like a social-climbing fool, and Thaw would settle the score five years later with a pistol.

During the sensational murder trial, at which Harry Thaw's mother tried to bribe everyone connected with the prosecution (witnesses, the prosecutor, jurors, and even the trial judge himself) in order to obtain an acquittal for her son, the pay-'em-off psychology of the Great Splurge era was never more effectively displayed. In the end, Thaw was acquitted, though he was ordered remanded to a hospital for the criminally insane.

Harry Thaw himself, of course, may have been a victim of the Great Splurge philosophy of child rearing. His grandniece — or, technically, half grandniece, since William Thaw had five children by each of his two wives — was brought up during the tail end of the era, amid the same aura of careless unreality. She is Mrs. Virginia Thaw Wanamaker, a Southampton dowager, the widow of Rodman Wanamaker, who was the grandson of John Wanamaker, the Philadelphia dry-goods merchant. The elderly Mrs. Wanamaker confesses, "I was brought up to be almost helpless. As a young girl, I had no idea what things cost. One didn't know the value of money or where it came from. We took everything for granted. We didn't know how much the house cost, or what the cook was paid. My mother never knew how to cook, and it never occurred to her to go into the kitchen. She had a cook, a butler, a personal maid, a chauffeur — and we weren't the only people to live that way. Most of the people we knew did. It was automatic for children to grow up in this kind of atmosphere, without realizing it was very special. Young people all have worries today, and more sense of values."

Some people recall the Great Splurge era with a kind of fond and wistful nostalgia. One of these is John Preston, a Southampton bachelor who was born there in 1921 and whose grandfather's house was a copy of the Villa Medici. "We were very privileged characters," he says of his childhood. "We were brought up to think that we were a part of a certain way of life, and that way of life was splendid. I think that was excellent. My parents spoiled me, but I think it's awfully good when you're young to be spoiled a little. No one ever spoils you after a certain age."

Others disagree. In the 1920s, when the era began escalating to a kind of climax, children of the newly rich were not merely pampered by their parents. They were largely ignored by them. Children were raised by hired surrogates, and when special problems arose, appropriate outside experts were engaged to solve them. If you had enough money, the theory seemed to be, no dilemma or vicissitude was so great that it could not be corrected for a price. The sky was literally the limit. In Southampton, children were given automobiles to drive at age ten or eleven, the only restriction being that they were not to drive these vehicles beyond the village limits. As the numbers of these unlicensed drivers grew, the Southampton police indulgently looked the other way. "The only time you got into trouble," recalls one resident, "was in extreme cases — if your car hit someone, or a farmer's cow." Teenage drinking, during these Prohibition years, was not encouraged, but it was condoned. At the Canoe Place Inn, bootleg liquor was always available to customers of all ages, and so was illegal gambling. Boats dropped off their cases of liquor directly at the inn's dock, and since the inn had powerful Tammany Hall connections, raids were rare; when they occurred, the inn was tipped off well in advance. At the local drugstore, overprivileged children were allowed to go behind the counter and prepare their own ice cream concoctions, helping themselves to syrups, cherries, chopped walnuts, and whipped cream toppings. No wonder to people like John Preston it seemed like a magic kingdom — "Treasure Island," he says.

"It was as bad an upbringing as you could possibly get," says Mr. Craig K. J. Mitchell, a New Yorker in his late sixties, who likes to describe himself as a "survivor" of this sort of childhood. Indeed, Mitchell calls himself a survivor so often that one might suppose he was talking about being at Auschwitz instead of growing up the victim of benign child abuse. His father, Charles E. Mitchell, was president of New York's City Bank before its merger with First National, and his mother was the daughter of J. P. Rend, an Irishman who came to America, fought in the Civil War and rose to be a full colonel, and then went on to make a huge fortune in West Virginia mining. Thus the Mitchells are members of New York's "Irishtocracy," descendants of immigrants who left Ireland in the 1840s and 1850s following the Great Potato Famine and, by the turn of the century, had grown rich enough to "invade" Southampton in large numbers — families such as the Prestons, McDonnells, Murrays, Cuddihys, Jameses, O'Briens, and Cogswells.

"My mother's entire life was music," Craig Mitchell says today. "She was supposed to be one of the finest amateur pianists in the country, and much as I adored her she had very little time for her children, which was typical of the times. She played piano from four to five hours a day, and when she played she was not to be disturbed. My father, of course, as head of the bank, was all business. He had virtually *no* time for us, and so my sister had a governess, and I had a governess, and we were brought down to the guests at teatime to say hello — and then packed out of sight. I was rotten spoiled — a lot of us were — *rotten* spoiled! I grew up totally undisciplined."

The spoiling of Craig Mitchell was particularly intense because, as a child, he was considered sickly. He suffered from mastoid problems and then came down with scarlet fever. During his nearly two years of illness, he was showered with presents. He was given one new present every day and two on Sundays. Presently an entire room in the house had to be set aside for his collection of gifts and toys. Upon his recovery, his nurses and governesses were instructed that their young charge was to be given anything he asked for, and under no circumstances was he to be made aware of anything unpleasant that might possibly upset him. "I remember as a kid in the twenties people were talking about the Massey rape case in Hawaii," he recalls. "I remember hearing the subject come up at the family dinner table. I wasn't paying too much attention to the conversation, but I interrupted to ask some sort of question about the Massey case. There was a horrified silence, and the next morning I found myself packed off to see a psychiatrist to tell me all about the birds and the bees."

Craig Mitchell was raised in the family-built mansion at 934 Fifth Avenue that is now the French Consulate, and in weekend and summer estates in Tuxedo Park and Southampton. That, he recalls, was considered normal. "Typically, a family had three houses fully staffed, and those staffs were enormous," he says. "Mother had a housekeeper, and so she never dealt with the help at all. That was the housekeeper's job, to keep everybody happy, and to do all the hiring and firing."

Such efficiently run households, however, did not necessarily result in efficiently run children. "My family tried to put me through the New York day schools," Mitchell recalls. "I got thrown out of Buckley, I got thrown out of St. Bernard's — you name every school in New York, and I got thrown out for being incorrigible." To each of these dismissals, Mitchell's parents reacted with outraged indignation — not with their son but with the schools, which had obviously failed to understand their sensitive and highly bred child's special needs. To console him for the indignity he had suffered from expulsion, the boy was showered with more gifts. Being expelled, he decided, was not a bad thing at all.

Finally, when Mitchell was eleven, it was decided that the boy was ready for a boarding school, and the Fay School, in Southborough, Massachusetts, was selected. Fay at the time was a pre-preparatory school, a feeder school for Groton, St. Paul's, St. Mark's, and Hotchkiss. Naturally, it was unthinkable that an eleven-year-old boy, whom his "Mother Dear" still called a tiny tot, should make the journey from Manhattan to Southborough by train or any other form of public conveyance. So the tiny tot and Mother Dear set off for Massachusetts in the backseat of a chauffeur-driven Rolls-Royce, with the tot clutching a five-pound box of Louis Sherry chocolates that was his final bon voyage present. He was delivered at the school, and while the other boys who were to be his schoolmates watched "this ridiculous performance" from a discreet distance, Mother Dear, now in a flood of tears, embraced and kissed her darling good-bye again and again. Soon young Mitchell was weeping, too. But finally the disconsolate mother was helped back into her car and driven away.

The Rolls had no sooner rounded the corner and disappeared from sight than Mitchell was subjected to "the hog pile," the school's traditional welcome to new boys. The other boys jumped on him, knocked him down, and formed a sort of human pyramid on top of him. Needless to say, his Louis Sherry chocolates were snatched away and divided up among the others, and when his initiation rite was over, his brand-new clothes from Best's and De Pinna's were in shreds and he himself was covered with mud and bruises. "At Fay, and later at St. Paul's, I was taught discipline in a big way," he says. "I got knocked around — but *properly*." Both Fay and St. Paul's believed in peer discipline, but there was official discipline as well. At Fay, for example, there was fingernail inspection before every meal and room inspection every morning. Jackets and neckties had to be worn at all times, clothes were inspected for spots, shoes had to be polished, and a clean white handkerchief had to sprout from every breast pocket. For the slightest inattention — for so much as a whisper — in the classroom, the punishment was "the walk": a one-hour run, in silence, up hill and down dale, in the company of one of the more athletic masters. "When there is no discipline in the home," Craig Mitchell says, "it's got to come from the schools. If it hadn't been for the discipline of my schools, and the discipline I picked up in the army — tough discipline — I honestly don't think I'd have been able to get through life with the kind of upbringing I had."

By 1939, the Era of the Great Splurge was in its final death throes, after nearly a decade of terminal illness, and the end was not pretty to behold. The Great Depression had settled in, it began to seem, forever, and Roosevelt's New Deal taxation programs were claiming their intended victims. The great yachts had been sold, or put in dry dock, or left to molder and barnacle at their moorings. One by one, the lights in Newport had gone out, and the castles and châteaux — white elephants by now — were either sold, given away, or surrendered to the city for back taxes. Tuxedo Park, perhaps the most frivolous resort idea of them all, was even harder hit. The Tudor mansions, abandoned and vandalized, stood like shattered shipwrecks against the sky. Tennis courts sprouted dandelions, and tall weeds and wild sunflowers overbore the formal gardens. The once crystal lakes were green with the scum of algae. In Southampton, it was as though a vengeful Old Testament diety were seeking retribution against Sodom and Gomorrah: A polio epidemic swept the town with exceptional harshness, claiming some of the town's most social names as its victims. For an entire summer, Southampton was barricaded, and no one could go into the town or out of it. It became quarantined, an isolation ward, a place of pestilence and dread where the Era of the Great Splurge breathed its last, death-rattling gasp.

Of course there were a few people who were able to survive the Great Depression and the New Deal without seeming to have to trim their sails at all. Two of the most conspicuous of these were Mr. and Mrs. John Nicholas Brown of Providence and Newport, a couple who did not see fit to alter their fully staffed style of living for more than seventy years. Every evening of their married lives, the Browns dressed formally for dinner, even when they dined alone, though their son, John Carter Brown, suspects that this was principally because his father liked to make use of his large collection of dinner jackets in many styles, colors, and patterns.

The Browns of Rhode Island can almost be considered in a class by themselves. The very ordinariness of the name has served to give the Browns a certain protective anonymity and privacy, which the Browns have minded not at all. Next to Smiths and Joneses, Browns probably occupy more pages of American telephone directories than families of any other patronym. Then, too, there have been many Rhode Island Browns who have been given the first name John. Plain John Brown does not, it must be admitted, have the drumroll sound of a Leverett Saltonstall or a Godfrey Lowell Cabot, and this fact may have helped keep the aristocracy of the Rhode Island Browns a secret.

The Rhode Island Browns, it must be pointed out, should not be confused with Massachusetts Brahmins. They are better than that. The Brahmins of Boston have lost much of their social and political clout. The Browns of Rhode Island have not. The first Brown, Chad, arrived in Rhode Island by canoe from Massachusetts in 1638, one of a party of seven that was escaping the kind of rigid Puritanism in the Bay Colony that would lead to Brahminism. Just two years earlier, Roger Williams had arrived to found the city of Providence, the first American settlement dedicated to the precept of religious freedom. In Providence, the Brown and Williams families became allied through marriage.

Thus the late John Nicholas Brown was a direct descendant of Rhode Island's founder as well as of the industrialist-philanthropist who endowed Brown University in 1804. But Browns had been prominent in Rhode Island long before that, and by the early 1760s, four Brown brothers — Nicholas, Joseph, John, and Moses — were the most important and richest men in the colony. Moses Brown was a Quaker leader and abolitionist. Joseph Brown was an architect. Nicholas and John — the latter of whom characterized himself as "the cleverest boy in Providence" — were in whaling, shipbuilding, and, in a way the present-day Browns rather wish their ancestors had not been, in slavery. (They were involved in the famous triangle route of the slave trade: New England rum traded in Africa for slaves; slaves traded in the West Indies for sugarcane; sugar carried to New England to make more rum.) On the more positive side, the Browns built the first ships for the U.S. Navy, and one of these, the *Provi-*

dence, fired the navy's first shot in the Revolution. So displeased was the Crown with the activities of John Brown that a price was placed on his head. As an indication of the respect John Brown commanded in Providence, no one came forward to collect the reward.

From their whaling activities, and profits in whale oil and spermaceti, the Browns became the leading colonial candle makers, selling their candles in New York, Boston, Philadelphia, and West Indian ports. At the time the Revolution broke out, the Browns also owned an iron foundry, not a bad thing to have during wartime. With the help of a business ally named Samuel Slater, who had, incredibly, managed to smuggle out of England the designs for textile machinery by memorizing them — at a time when to try to get such plans to the colonies otherwise would have been suicidal — the Browns also came to own a textile mill, and they were involved in the China trade. Everything the Browns have touched has managed to turn to gold.

At the same time, the Browns have been notably philanthropic with an emphasis on education and the arts. The Browns gave the land on which Brown University now stands and for years resisted having it named after them (it was originally called Rhode Island College). Nicholas Brown II continued the family's support of the college and, each year, would personally make up any of the school's deficits out of his own pocket. John Nicholas Brown's father, John Carter Brown, was also generous to the college, contributing a library of books on the intellectual history of the New World. Because the Brown family businesses are among the oldest in America — the textile business lasted from Revolutionary times into the 1930s — the library is frequently consulted by business historians.

Browns have been proud to serve both education and God. One of John Nicholas Brown's more noteworthy gifts was the million-dollar Gothic chapel at St. George's School in Newport. Nor has public health been overlooked. Butler Hospital in Providence has had a Brown on its board of directors virtually throughout its existence. Part of the Brown family ethos has been a belief in doing *the right thing*. One of the more newsworthy events during the second attempted-murder trial of Claus von Bülow was the appearance, as a character witness for the defendant, of Mrs. John Nicholas Brown not long before her death. She was testifying on von Bülow's behalf, she explained with dignity, simply because she liked the man and didn't believe him capable of inflicting harm on anyone. Witnesses were impressed by the appearance of Providence's legendary *grande dame*.

"There are certain values that are passed along from generation to generation," says her son, J. Carter Brown today (who could, but does not choose to, style himself John Carter Brown II to distinguish himself from his grandfather*). "There's a strong sense of obligation in the family — that if you've been fortunate enough to have been given the wherewithal, you owe something back."

Along with these values goes a strict sense of priorities. The Brown family's relationship with Brown University is, understandably, a bit tricky, and as benefactors of the university, the family has tried to make it clear that they do not expect personal favors in return. In 1904, for example, when John Nicholas Brown was four years old, the college made him an honorary alumnus of that year's graduating class simply because his nanny happened to be walking him in his stroller during that year's commencement exercises and the small Brown heir was recognized. The family accepted this gesture in the good humor with which it was intended. But some fifty years later, when it came time for the little boy's son, J. Carter Brown, to be thinking about colleges, his parents were visited by President Henry Merritt Wriston of Brown University. Over tea, it was suggested to the senior Browns that their son would be most welcome at Brown, and, added the president, "You can be sure we'll do everything to make it easy for him." Without realizing it, the well-meaning President Wriston had stepped across the invisible aristocratic line dividing appropriate from inappropriate behavior. If there had ever been a question in the Browns' minds about where their son would be educated, it was decided at that moment, and young J. Carter Brown was sent, as his father had been, to Harvard, where he graduated summa cum laude in 1956.

John Nicholas Brown's wife was the former Anne Kinsolving of Baltimore, a descendant of a long line of southern clergymen and related to a constellation of aristocratic southern families including the Lees of Virginia. Her father was the Reverend Arthur B. Kinsolving of Baltimore, and her brother was the Reverend Arthur Lee Kinsolving, for years the rector of St. James Episcopal Church in New York, the city's most fashionable Anglican house of worship.

*He could also, quite properly, style himself John Carter Brown III.

As a result, Mrs. Brown was raised in a series of elegant, well-mannered rectories that were intended to compensate the rector and his family for the fact that his salary was inconsequential. Anne Kinsolving was "finished" at the Calvert School in Maryland, had no further formal education, and, in the tradition of the southern belle, was expected to do not much more than fox hunt in the Green Spring Valley and marry well. Considering this sheltered and genteel upbringing, then, it is surprising that Anne Kinsolving turned out to be something of a firebrand.

At age seventeen, for example, to help out a friend who worked for William Randolph Hearst's *Baltimore News,* she covered a local party and wrote it up for the society pages. Her editor, while pointing out that her story "contained enough scandal to bring on three libel suits," was nonetheless impressed with her lively style and hired her as a general-assignment reporter.

So popular did Anne Kinsolving's stories become that the *News* told her she could write about anything she chose. Always interested in music, she then asked to be made the paper's music critic. Even after her marriage to John Nicholas Brown she continued to write occasional pieces of music criticism, but marriage to a rich man allowed her time to indulge in another enthusiasm: military history. She started her extraordinary collection of tin soldiers that is now in a Providence museum, where, it might be noted, custodial funds have been provided by Claus and Martha Crawford von Bülow. Mrs. Brown's interest in military history sparked her family's interest — particularly that of her son Carter — in art history. Anne Kinsolving Brown, for example, could look at a portrait of a Revolutionary general and say, "That portrait could not have been painted as early as 1770. He's wearing a medal for the Battle of Bennington, and that battle didn't take place until 1777."

Today's most celebrated Brown is certainly John Nicholas and Anne Kinsolving Brown's son Carter, who, in 1969, at age thirty-four, made headlines in the art world when he was appointed director of the National Gallery of Art in Washington, becoming the youngest major museum director in the world. Since then, the still boyish-looking Carter Brown has mounted and toured exhibits that have broken attendance records all over the United States, including his "Treasures of Tutankhamen," "The Search for Alexander," and, most recently, the hugely popular "Treasure Houses of Britain: Five Hundred Years of Private Patronage and Art Collecting." At the time of Carter Brown's appointment to the National Gallery's top post, it was reported that, when he was twelve and first saw the National Gallery from the window of the family limousine, he announced, "Someday I'll be its director." Not so, said his mother, always a stickler for dates. "It was a year earlier, when Carter was eleven, and used to go sailing with John Walker, who was the museum's director then, at Fishers Island where the family spent summers." Carter Brown has a slightly different recollection. "I remember driving by the National Gallery, and admiring that beautiful pink stone building, and saying, 'Someday I'd like to work in a place like that.' "

Whichever way it happened, others have commented that Carter Brown was especially suited to put together "The Treasure Houses of Britain" since he himself grew up in houses filled with treasures and must have felt completely at home with — and like an aristocratic peer among — the proprietors of England's stately homes whom he visited in order to assemble his memorable show. The Brown mansions along Benefit Street in the College Hill section of Providence, where Browns have lived for generations, and still live, are architectural showplaces and family treasure houses, as is Harbour Court (English spelling, of course), the sprawling Newport estate overlooking the harbor that Carter Brown's grandmother built for his father. But the sad fact is that, by 1986, Harbour Court was for sale. "There are eight grandchildren who own it," Carter Brown explains, "along with spouses, and it's just too complicated trying to figure out who can use the house, and when, and for how long." The asking price: $4.5 million.

As befits a nautical family of whalers, shipbuilders, and China traders (not to mention seventeenth-century canoe paddlers), a love of the sea and sailing seems to have been passed along in the Browns' genes. The Browns are one of a very few American families — J. P. Morgan's was another — to have been granted a "private signal," a yachting burgee assigned to Brown vessels alone. Under this flag, Carter Brown's father skippered such famous yachts as the *Saraband,* and the *Bolero,* the largest boat allowed in the Bermuda Race. Carter Brown is also a sailor, though on a smaller scale, in a Rhode Island–built dinghy. He is, on the other hand, commodore of what may be the most exclusive, and smallest, yacht club in the world: the Little River Yacht Club, named after his weekend retreat in Virginia. The only members of the Little River Yacht Club are the immediate male members of his family. Wives are permitted to be honorary members.

When Carter Brown's grandfather John Carter Brown died in 1900, John Nicholas Brown was only three months old. His uncle, Harold Brown, was in London at the time, and he and Aunt Georgette immediately booked passage home to Providence for the funeral. But no sooner had the Harold Browns arrived than tragedy struck the family again. Harold Brown contracted typhoid fever and was dead within weeks of his brother. This was how the infant John Nicholas Brown, who inherited from both his father and his uncle, came to be labeled by the press "The World's Richest Baby," which was certainly an exaggeration, though not by much.

The distribution of the Brown fortune was decidedly unequal, but luckily this fact did not create the deep rift of jealousy and ill feeling among the Browns that similar situations have done among other moneyed families. One of Carter Brown's cousins — a first cousin once removed, in fact — is Mrs. John Jermain Slocum of Newport, a great-granddaughter of the first John Carter Brown. "The English system is by far the best," says Eileen Slocum emphatically. "Leave everything to the oldest son. That way, properties don't have to be broken up, and broken up again every time someone dies. John Nicholas Brown got ninety percent of the money. But Granny got the houses, the jewels, the portraits, the china, the silver, and so on. If you'll go to Harbour Court, you'll notice there are hardly any portraits. Whereas here" — and she gestures about her Newport mansion, whose walls are covered with portraits and punctuated by carved busts of Browns, along with cousins named Drexel and Sherman and Wilmerding, Peabody and Wetmore.

Since Anne Kinsolving Brown's death, Eileen Slocum, the wife of a retired foreign service officer, has become Newport's reigning *grande dame*. She is also a force in Rhode Island state politics as cochairman of the state's Republican party and a four-time delegate to the Republican National Convention. Known locally as a woman of extraordinary spunk and spirit, she once lay in wait in her darkened house in order to accost a burglar who had entered her property. When the burglar slipped inside through a French window, Mrs. Slocum cried, "Halt!" — and the burglar fled. Since that episode, she has acquired a brace of revolvers and has taken shooting lessons from her friend James Van Alen. "Jimmy taught me that the best way to shoot a man is to lie flat on your stomach," she says. "That way, if the man is armed, you present less of a target."

Mrs. Slocum, whose husband's diplomatic missions have taken the couple to posts in Moscow, Egypt, Iran, and Iraq, as well as Washington, is presently active in a Providence organization called Justice Assistance and in the movement for victims' rights. In this capacity, she became somewhat at odds with her cousin-in-law Anne Brown in that she supported the von Auersperg children in their grievances against their stepfather, Mr. von Bülow — a case that split Newport down the middle anyway. "All I said was that just before the first so-called Christmas coma, Sunny and Claus von Bülow came to my house for dinner, and Sunny seemed a happy, healthy, normal, charming girl," she says. "There were no signs of alcoholism, no sign of drugs. I have no idea why Anne decided to testify for him at the second trial, but if you ask me, that trial was *rigged!*

"Yes," says Eileen Slocum with her customary emphasis, "there is definitely such a thing as an aristocracy in America. It is based on breeding and behavior — *superior* behavior — and a willingness to work and to do what needs to be done. The word 'lady' and the word 'gentleman' meant a great deal to Mummy and Daddy. We were gentlefolk, and people who weren't were — well, you could tell who they were. Anyone who would strike a child, for example, or would strike an animal, would *not* be gentlefolk."

Among Eileen Slocum's other projects and enthusiasms is one that is more difficult to define — "keeping the putty in the stones of the family," as she puts it. This putty was perhaps most severely tested in the 1960s when the Slocums' daughter, Beryl, announced her engagement to Adam Clayton Powell III. Not only was Powell black — the son of the Harlem congressman and the nightclub entertainer Hazel Scott — but he was a Democrat, and his father had been indicted by a federal grand jury on charges of income tax evasion.

"We were opposed to it — vehemently," says Eileen Slocum forthrightly. "We did everything in our power to try to persuade Beryl not to do this thing. But when Beryl was at Radcliffe, she began associating with a number of very radical, left-wing types. Beryl and I don't see eye to eye on anything, and yet we're very much alike — stubborn, I suppose. To me, she's out of focus on what is important. I believe in achievement through work. Beryl's goals are different — that's all I really can say about it. She and Adam are separated now. And yet it's interesting — her son, Sherman Powell, my grandson, is now even more conservative than John and myself!"

If Eileen Slocum was keeping a stiff upper lip at the time of the marriage, it did not show. The Slocums gave their daughter and Powell a large and social wedding in Washington, as would befit a Brown heiress, and the parents of the bride were photographed wreathed in smiles. Was that difficult to do? "One does what has to be done," Eileen Slocum says. She and her daughter, and her daughter's dark-skinned children, are still close. "They're all coming for dinner at the house tonight," she says.

"We've always been a very united family," says Mrs. Slocum. "Our relationships are very close. Never for a moment is the dialogue broken. There must be continuity in a family, and when there is continuity in the things it treasures it is even better. I've said to my children, this house is your ancestral home. It is full of memories and it is full of meaning. After I'm gone, you must do everything in your power to keep this house in the family. This house is part of your family's heritage. If need be, I said to my daughter Marguerite the other day, sell off the front of the property, on Bellevue Avenue — that way the house wouldn't be taxed as Bellevue Avenue real estate — and use the side street for the entrance. But keep the house. Margie practically burst into tears, and said, 'But Mother, that would mean taking down all these beautiful trees!' I said to her, 'Perhaps you won't have to do it. But one does what has to be done.' "

The Era of the Great Splurge passed through and around families like the Browns of Rhode Island, leaving them untouched. Members of America's secret aristocracy are generally unaffected by social fads and phases. The flurry of pretentious château building that began in Newport in the 1880s and ended in 1929 came and went, and families like the Browns went on doing pretty much what they had always done. The face of Newport changed dramatically. ("When new people come, a place always changes," says Mrs. Slocum.) Large and comfortable beach houses built in the traditional New England shingle style were replaced with Florentine palazzi and Palladian castles, but behind these cosmetic changes the Browns remained secure in the secret that the real soul of Newport would always belong to them. After all, when one's family has lived in a place for ten or twelve generations, one gets accustomed to changes in the weather. It's the climate inside that counts.

The Browns were a part of the new milieu, of course. They went to the parties and the balls. But at the same time they were not a part of it. The competitiveness and social and fiscal Indian wrestling that characterized the era were of little concern to them. To them, it didn't matter which Mrs. Vanderbilt built the bigger mansion, which Mrs. Astor was entitled to be called *the* Mrs. Astor, or how Mrs. August Belmont, Jr., got along with her mother-in-law (badly). Let those people, families like the Browns seemed to say, get all the publicity, all the notoriety. We are a more private people, and we have our own concerns. We will be here long after they are gone.

And they are.

There is an easy, gentle style of life that old, aristocratic American families fall into that is special: formal and at the same time laissez-faire. Mrs. John Jermain Slocum, for example, smiles faintly when her butler refers to her husband's dinner jacket as his "tux coat." But she lets it pass. Her big stone house is on the "wrong," or inland, side of Bellevue Avenue and is all but invisible from the street (those trees). Across the street, on the side facing Rhode Island Sound, the bigger, newer, showier mansions seem to be fairly jostling each other for attention and to be saying, "Get a load of me!"

Breakfast at the Slocums', where the house guests are the Dillon Ripleys from Washington, along with a friend who has dropped by for coffee, is served in the small dining room rather than in the large dining room next door where twenty-four can be seated at one long table. The walls of the small dining room are lined, from floor to ceiling, with glass-enclosed cabinets containing what appear to be thousands of pieces of Lowestoft. But breakfast coffee is served in a chipped cup. In the center of the round table is a kind of lazy Susan, on which breakfast accompaniments are set out: several boxes of dry cereal, their tops sliced off at a diagonal for easy pouring; an opened two-quart carton of milk; a jar of honey; a jar of peanut butter; a jar of catsup. There are paper napkins. An electric coffee maker bubbles on an antique sideboard. A chest containing everyday silver — the good stuff is locked away — sits atop an antique German music box, a priceless family heirloom. In one corner of the room, an aluminum-and-plastic high chair sits waiting for a visiting grandchild. The morning papers — the *Providence Journal* and the *New York Times* — lie about while the Ripleys work the *Times* crossword in a unique way, taking turns. Mr. Ripley fills in one definition in blue ink, then hands it to his wife, who fills in the next in red. A maid in the kitchen answers the telephone, which rings constantly for Eileen Slocum in connection with one or another of her projects; this time it is a fund-raiser for Senator Bob Dole. "Tell them I'm in conference with my lawyer," she instructs the maid, adding, "That usually scares 'em off for a while." The butler, in shirt-sleeves, pads in and out.

Harbour Court, long considered the principal Brown house in Newport, is a more formal affair at first glance, built in the Norman style around an entrance courtyard. "Hey, get on in here out of the rain!" cries the cheery maid answering the door. "Great weather for ducks, huh? Sit in any room you like. God knows where Mr. Brown is! He said he was going for a walk. In this weather? He's crazy!"

Harbour Court is on the "wrong" side of Newport and not even on Bellevue Avenue. As its name implies, the house overlooks the old town harbor, rather than the Sound. Still, it is very grand, and for years magazines such as *Architectural Digest* and *House & Garden* have wanted to photograph the place. But the Browns have been unwilling to have this done, feeling that — at least until it is sold — it is a private family summer place and not for public consumption. One does notice the absence of family portraits. But this is more than compensated for by tables covered with family photographs in silver frames: Browns on horseback, Browns at the rudders of sail-boats, Browns as children in sailor suits, Browns as brides and grooms, Browns in evening dress, and Browns in swimsuits at family picnics on the beach: continuity.

Outside, from the edge of a broad harbor-facing terrace, a famous stretch of manicured lawn drops at a precipitous forty-five-degree angle toward the water. One would be frightened to walk down this steep lawn, much less try to mow it. This is accomplished by gar-deners who lash themselves and their machines together with ropes like mountain climbers to keep from plunging into Narragansett Bay.

The house is full of children — nieces, nephews, cousins. They come and go, in and out of the formal rooms, barefoot, in blue jeans and yellow slickers. Presently Carter Brown rushes in, all smiles and enthusiasm, wearing baggy trousers, a sport shirt, and worn-looking espadrilles. Though technically on vacation, he has spent much of the morning on transatlantic telephone calls between Newport and Athens, where he has been negotiating for a Byzantine exhibition at the National Gallery.

A teenage nephew, wandering through, smiles at his uncle's excitement but seems largely unimpressed. Here, after all, Carter Brown is only Uncle Carter, part of the family. There is a feeling, all at once, that while international success and celebrity may come along every generation or so and touch a member of the family, as it has done in the case of Carter Brown, this is all very nice — it is even to be expected — but it is not as important as continuity, family, and keeping the putty in the stones.

This is one of the secrets of our secret aristocracy: being able to live formally, without standing on formalities, to live pleasantly but not pompously, politely and not assertively, and never to bemoan the loss of an older, more rigid pecking order based on wealth alone.

Some families, whose wealth is newer, seem not yet to have learned this little trick. Stanley G. Mortimer, for example, is married to Kathleen Harriman, a granddaughter of E. H. Harriman, one of the great nineteenth-century robber barons who helped create the Great Splurge era. Several years ago, Mr. Mortimer was riding with his mother in her car in Tuxedo Park. They stopped at the drugstore in the village for something or other, and Mr. Mortimer stepped out of the car. His mother started to follow him, whereupon, on the sidewalk, she encountered her former butler, whom she had just retired from service. "Good morning, Mrs. Mortimer," said her ex-butler. Mrs. Mortimer sank back into the seat of her car in a state of shock. When her son returned to the car, he asked, "Mother, what happened? You seemed so shocked when Simpson said good morning." She replied, "Stanley, did you notice the way he addressed me? He called me Mrs. Mortimer instead of Madam."

As Heraclitus put it, there is nothing permanent except change.

26

The Family Place

On January 17, 1986, it was announced in the *New York Times* that the Jay collection of portraits, most of which had hung at Jay Farm in Bedford for two hundred years, would go under the hammer at Christie's, the New York auction house.

It wasn't that the Jay family needed the money, exactly, though more money is always a pleasant addition to any family. The problem, as with the Browns' Harbour Court, was multiple ownerships. Seven of the portraits — of Jay, Washington, John Adams, Jefferson, Madison, and others — belonged collectively, but in varying degrees, to seventeen people. These were the children and grandchildren of the late William Jay Iselin, the last descendant of John Jay to occupy the farm. The portraits represented an important part of the children's inheritance.

There were other considerations. Since William Jay Iselin's death in 1951, Jay Farm — renamed the John Jay Homestead — has become a New York State Historic Site. The portraits, along with other Jay-related antiques, books, papers, costumes, and uniforms, had been left on loan to the homestead, and the homestead lacked the curatorial staff to keep the paintings in shape. Furthermore, there was the insurance burden that William Jay Iselin's heirs had had to bear since the family farm had been opened to the public.

Meanwhile, the directors of the Jay Homestead were not pleased with the news that their Gilbert Stuarts, John Trumbulls, and Ezra Ameses were about to be taken down from their walls and sold. The January 25 sale, on the other hand, more than satisfied the heirs of William Jay Iselin, and the seven jointly owned portraits sold for a total of $1,600,000. The Stuart portrait of John Jay himself, commissioned while Jay was on his mission in London and which Christie's had estimated would sell for between $250,000 and $450,000, fetched double the highest estimate: $900,000. The Ames portrait of Thomas Jefferson was sold to investment banker Richard Jenrette. The Trumbull of John Adams was bought by the White House, which had lacked an Adams. The Stuart portrait of Stephen Van Rensselaer, who was lieutenant governor of New York when Jay was governor in 1795, was sold, appropriately, to a buyer from Albany.

One woman who certainly would not have approved of the sale of the portraits, and who the family was glad was no longer around to know about it, was William Jay Iselin's mother. As in the case of Eileen Slocum in the Brown family — and in so many other old families — the chores of keeping the putty firmly in the family stones and of reminding the family of its collective conscience fell upon the shoulders of a strong woman. In the Jay family, for many years, this was John Jay's great-great-granddaughter, Eleanor Jay Iselin. And Mrs. Iselin took up her tasks in her own distinctive fashion.

Eleanor Jay was the daughter of the Civil War colonel William Jay, and she was a woman whose life was devoted to preserving, and collecting, and enshrining, and never throwing away, anything that pertained to her Jay heritage. A family member who remembers her describes her as "the last of the great, aristocratic WASP *grandes dames* — every inch the cultivated lady, and yet every inch the sportswoman and outdoorswoman. She was elegant and dignified, but she was also a woman of the soil." Eleanor Jay Iselin's soil, not surprisingly, was that of Jay Farm, where even Old Fred, the horse that carried her father through the war, was buried under an entablature in the backyard.

America was invented and developed by white Anglo-Saxon Protestants, according to historian E. Digby Baltzell, "because they were outdoors people" — people happy on horseback, riding across open land, and on sailing vessels, plying their way across uncertain seas and up uncharted rivers. They were entrepreneurial adventurers who were attracted to the frontier, drawn to the wilderness, who could look into the virgin forests and see trees felled for lumber and houses, who could forge rivers and streams and see water harnessed for power, and who could cross a lake by canoe and see it one day spanned by a bridge for commerce. They were uncommonly fearless and, like Hannah Lawrence Schieffelin, could comfortably pass the night in an Indian encampment with a group of war-painted braves. The WASPs who came to America, according to Baltzell, seemed temperamentally suited to becoming pioneers, unsuited to urban life, and quickly set off toward the unexplored sunset in the West, even if it was no farther than to a trading post called Albany. This may explain why today, though most large American cities are dominated by other ethnic groups, most of provincial and rural America is still governed by WASPs. From New York City and elsewhere, the old WASP families have fled to the country, where they continued to enjoy their out-of-doors. Eleanor Jay was descended from people like this in all directions — her father's sister had married a Schieffelin — and, just as many of her male relatives were gentleman farmers, Eleanor Jay was a gentle*woman* farmer.

"My grandmother was of a generation that believed that when you married you moved back into the house where you were born, and where your parents and grandparents were born," says John Iselin. "I'm sure she would much rather have married someone named Jay — though the Iselins weren't *that* bad." Indeed they weren't, and the only thing wrong with the Iselins was that they weren't Jays. But there were practical things to be considered when Eleanor Jay married Arthur Iselin. Maintaining Jay Farm the way it needed to be maintained was already becoming a costly proposition, and the Iselins were very rich, with textile mills in South Carolina, Georgia, and New England. It was the familiar, pragmatic trade-off — old blood for new money. Certainly Eleanor Iselin and her husband had little in common other than her wish to keep up the farm and his willingness and ability to indulge that wish by means of the Iselin bank accounts. The Iselin marriage was not much more than a working business agreement, and as such, it was a peaceful and happy union in which both partners were able to do what they wanted. Still, there was no question in Eleanor Jay Iselin's mind as to which was the finer family name. When her son, William Jay Iselin, reached years of discretion, she repeatedly tried to persuade him to change his name to William Iselin Jay. This he politely declined to do.

Meanwhile, Eleanor Jay Iselin lived on the farm. Her husband lived at the Waldorf-Astoria in New York. Their paths crossed on occasional weekends. She was an avid and expert horsewoman. He was a yachtsman — his uncle, C. Oliver Iselin, had been four-time manager of the winning syndicates in the America's Cup races of 1893, 1895, 1899, and 1903 — and kept his yacht at Larchmont, on Long Island Sound. Every now and then his wife and children would join Arthur Iselin for a Sunday sail and picnic. On these outings, the children couldn't help but notice that their father was often accompanied by a lady friend. But everything was very civil and polite. If the lady friend sat in the bow of the yacht, Mrs. Iselin would seat herself in the stern.

From time to time, Arthur Iselin would complain that maintaining his wife's family homestead was costing him a fortune, to which she would counter that she was doing her best to make the farm a paying proposition, or at least one that was not losing as much as it might. She had turned it into a working farm. On it, she raised and sold Thoroughbred horses. She also maintained a herd of dairy cattle and sold the milk. But there were obvious large expenses. The barns were filled with old coaches and carriages and hung with ancient tack, and all this gear required an extra farmhand just to keep it saddle-soaped and polished. Eleanor Iselin's own saddle horse was a snappy Thoroughbred whom she whimsically named Socony — short for Standard Oil Company of New York — as a way of pointing out that she could get about without the aid of an internal combustion engine. She did, however, have an automobile. These were always Buicks, and she always had the wheels of these vehicles painted yellow. When one of her grandsons asked her why, she replied, "So it will be recognizable." The real reason, of course, was that the wheels of Jay horse-drawn carriages had always been painted yellow.*

At the farm, her most significant expenditure was to build a massive west wing onto the main farmhouse. The west wing contained what was called the ballroom, but it was never used for balls. (Unlike

*During World War I, her Buick was patriotically put up on blocks, and Mrs. Iselin rode everywhere on Socony, including to church, riding sidesaddle, or the so-called "Queen's seat." She was also a superb four-in-hand driver and had acquired four perfectly matched gray Thoroughbreds from Alfred Gwynne Vanderbilt. In 1917, to promote the Liberty Bond drive (as well as to publicize the family's patriotism and spunk), Eleanor Iselin drove her coach and four from Buffalo to New York City — a distance of nearly four hundred miles. Her feat made headlines across the country.

her cousin by marriage, Caroline Astor, Eleanor Iselin was not a ball-giving person.) Instead, it was designed as a room that could contain, and display, all the Jay family heirlooms and treasures. Here, in glass cases, were displayed John Jay's uniforms and the clothes he had worn when he was presented at the French court in Paris. More glass cases held medals, honors, decorations, ribbons, trophies, and citations won by various Jays. Still other cases displayed historic documents, presidential letters, old books, family records and Bibles, archives and family incunabula. And of course on the walls hung the portraits that had reduced John Jay Chapman to such feelings of inadequacy. To other Jay children and grandchildren who spent all or parts of their summers at the farm, the ballroom was an eerie and echoing space. One had to pass through it to get to the ping pong room. The children hurried through the room on tiptoes, speaking in whispers.

Eleanor Iselin had built the west wing to protect the family memorabilia from the possibility of fire. So it was built of solid stone, a family vault.

It had been hard enough on Eleanor Iselin to see the scale of Jay Farm gradually dwindle. Roughly a third of the farm's land had to be given up when New York City built its Cross River Reservoir on the property, and the new lake swallowed up the old family sawmill and gristmill. Other parcels were sold off to meet expenses. Still, by 1940, there were 370 acres left — a respectable piece. Jay Farm was still one of the largest working farms in Westchester County, and compared with the Rockefeller farm down the road in Pocantico Hills, which was a mere 200 acres, the Jay holdings were imposing. And they included something the Rockefellers would never have: all that family history that was collected in the ballroom. Those treasures were beyond monetary value, Eleanor Iselin used to say. They would enrich her family forever.

Eleanor Jay Iselin — whom the grandchildren, for reasons they don't quite remember, always called Mopsey — must have turned, ever so slightly, in her grave when the auctioneer's hammer fell on the last of the family portraits.

In 1986, too, the Livingstons held a family reunion at Clermont, now known as Clermont State Historic Site, high above the Hudson River. It was the second such family event. The first had been held five years earlier, but the latest gathering was intended as a somewhat special occasion. For it, family members from all over the United States had loaned whatever family portraits — mostly from the eighteenth and nineteenth centuries — they happened to own, and the exhibition that resulted was an imposing pantheon of Livingstons. While some four hundred contemporary Livingstons wandered through Clermont's spacious rooms and out onto the manicured lawns and gardens, sipping drinks from caterers' plastic glasses, three-hundred-year-old Livingstons gazed down on the assemblage from Clermont's storied walls.

During the course of the July weekend, the nearby Beekman Arms Hotel, as well as surrounding motels and guest houses, were fully booked with Livingstons and Livingston in-laws who passed their free time trying to figure out how they were all related to one another — which cousins were double cousins, or triple cousins, or fifth cousins once removed, and from which Livingston line each cousin descended. Several of the guests had never met each other before, though most knew that the others existed. To help keep matters straight, name tags were provided. A number of the names reverberated with the drumroll of early American history: Astor, Aldrich, Ripley, Roosevelt, Beekman. Others were less resplendent, and, it had to be admitted, a few were downright disreputable. But in this exercise in family nostalgia, all sins and shortcomings were forgiven, since the Livingstons were there at the family seat not so much to celebrate their accomplishments as to rejoice in the fact that they were all Livingstons, and still around.

The impresario of the event, as well as of the one in 1981, was Henry H. Livingston of Oak Hill. Since he is one of the last Livingstons to own a large piece of property on what were originally more than a million acres of Livingston landholdings, Henry Hopkins Livingston has been given the title of *present* lord of Livingston Manor. This honorific is treated as a little family joke. But in fact it is a joke at which no one is supposed to laugh. Henry Livingston admits that pulling off these quinquennial gatherings is no small task and requires months of planning and preparation. For the most part, though, the party came off without a hitch. The weekend got under way with a Saturday luncheon, climaxed with a formal dinner on Saturday night under a huge green-striped tent decked with pine boughs, and officially concluded with a Sunday luncheon the next day, after which most of the guests began heading home. For the few who remained,

Henry Livingston and his wife gave a small dinner party Sunday night at Oak Hill.

At the formal dinner, there were many toasts and a few speeches. Winthrop Aldrich put on a slide show, with commentary, on family homes and history, and Henry Livingston presented a series of awards to Livingstons who had helped assemble the portrait collection. In between the various festivities, a flotilla of chartered buses stood by to take the Livingstons on a tour through Livingston Country, visiting such Livingston family houses and estates as still remain. These, of course, are in varying states of repair — from the splendidly restored Clermont to the more down-at-the-heel Rokeby, which still bears some of the battle scars inflicted by the rambunctious Astor orphans.

Obviously, the weekend was not only a difficult one to orchestrate but also an expensive one to produce. As in 1981, the delicate matter of how it was to be paid for, and by whom, had to be addressed. While some Livingstons today are still quite rich, others are what can only be described as genteelly poor, and so no set attendance fee was charged. Instead, it was politely suggested that donations to offset costs would most certainly be appreciated, and each guest was asked to contribute according to his or her means.

A few weeks after it was over, Henry Livingston mailed out questionnaires to all who had attended. Should the Livingston party become a regular every-five-years event? Many responded enthusiastically that they were in favor of establishing it as a tradition. Others were less sanguine. Among these was Mrs. S. Dillon Ripley, the former Mary Livingston, of the Peter Robert Livingston line. "It seems to me," says Mrs. Ripley a little snappishly, "that these old families would be better off if they spent less time glorifying their families' past, and more time thinking about what they could do to help America's future."

There were a few other sour notes in the aftermath of the party. For one thing, several of the guests who showed up claiming to be Livingstons could not be found on the meticulously kept, and voluminous, Livingston genealogies that the family has labored to keep up to date for more than two centuries. New name tags had to be made for these people, and table-seating charts had to be hastily rearranged at the last minute to accommodate them. Who *were* they? Were they bogus Livingstons, gate-crashers, hoping that some of the

Livingston luster would rub off on them? But, if so, how had they gotten wind of the party? There had been no publicity, and the gathering had been designed as a private, by-invitation-only affair. The riddle of who these "extra" Livingstons might be was never solved, but in any event, the mystery guests were allowed to participate in the festivities unchallenged. They were behaving themselves, and they seemed to mean no harm.

Then there was the fact that no Jays attended the Livingston reunion, even though all American Jays descend from the memorable union of John Jay and Sarah Van Brugh Livingston in 1774. It is not that there is bad blood between the Jays and Livingstons, exactly, and it has nothing to do with the coolness and eventual political rivalry that developed between the onetime King's College classmates, friends, and former law partners John Jay and "Chancellor" Robert R. Livingston, and that culminated in Livingston's defeat by Jay in the race for New York's governorship in 1798. It is a little more complicated, and yet a little simpler, than that. Astonishing as it may seem, the fact is that, more than two hundred years later, the Livingstons continue to feel that John Jay elevated himself into the American aristocracy through his marriage, and that the Jays would have remained in relative obscurity if it hadn't been for their Livingston connections. In ways large and small, furthermore, the Livingstons have let the Jays know that they feel this way. For two hundred and *thirteen* years, to be precise.

"Yes, the Livingstons still take a rather superior attitude toward the Jays," says John Jay Iselin with a little smile. Iselin, a small, compactly built man in his early fifties, who has managed *not* to inherit the prominent Jay nose, has had a distinguished career in both book publishing and television broadcasting. "They tend to take the attitude that the Jays were nobodies until they started marrying Livingstons. I don't think you can give John Jay's wife *all* the credit for everything he did, even though she had very good connections. Why, even the Jays who stayed in Europe have done well for themselves. Peter Jay, who is a cousin from the French line, was British ambassador to the United States."

Does he, then, consider the Jays a more aristocratic family than the Livingstons? Iselin crinkles his nose slightly. "We don't like to dine out on that 'old family' business. In fact, one reason my father liked to pack us all off to Iselin relatives in South Carolina regularly was that he felt that entirely too much ancestor worship was going on at the farm. But we always knew we were from the top rung. It was a good-fellowship society — quite different from the swashbuckling, on-the-make Newport crowd. But I think you have to admit that the first John Jay was a remarkable man. Besides his more famous accomplishments, he also wrote the New York State Constitution, which was the model for the U.S. Constitution, and he was behind the Bill of Rights. The New York State Constitution set up the Board of Regents, an independent body appointed by the governor to supervise all forms of education. Even then he had the idea that a democracy had to be supported by a strong educational system. The New York State Board of Regents is now more than two hundred and ten years old, and still going strong! But I don't think you can say that one family is better than another."

Eleanor Jay Iselin's daughter, another Eleanor Jay Iselin — who is now Mrs. C. Wanny Wade, and who is John Jay Iselin's aunt — has a somewhat different view. Eleanor Wade is an outdoorswoman like her mother and runs a ranch thirty miles from the nearest town, in southwestern Montana, where she raises racehorses. "The family has always pulled its weight," she says. "We've pulled our weight, through good times and bad, and there were bad times for the family, too. My great-grandmother Jay had to drive a workhorse to church, but she drove it with head held high! We've always worked — worked like beavers — and we've always tried to make money for the family. My sister works in medicine, she's interested in genetics. My older brother Jay ran the family cotton mills. I work this ranch, my mother worked the farm, and after Mother died *I* worked the farm. Work is in the bloodline, just like the horses that I breed.

"My mother was an extraordinary person. She had no formal education whatsoever, and was raised entirely by governesses. But the family went regularly to Europe, and Mother learned everything about art — and history — and music — and language — from the *source,* on these travels. She knew more about European history than almost anyone I can think of, and of course she knew her American history inside and out. And literature — Edith Wharton was her close friend! And Harvard professors! I grew up surrounded by education and culture because of my mother, who never had a diploma in anything! And of course she taught us all to ride. A love of horses was in our bloodline, too, and I've been horse-crazy since before I learned to walk. And Mother drove four-in-hand better than any woman in America. She could drive a coach and four — with spirited horses — at a full canter, and make a ninety-degree turn without a single wheel going up on the curb!"

How did Eleanor Wade feel about the sale of the Jay portrait collection? "It was a terrible wrench," she says. "I'm just glad I was two thousand miles away when it happened. But it had to be done because of the multiple ownerships, as Johnny Jay tried to explain to the trustees of the homestead." She repeatedly refers to her nephew as Johnny Jay and not Johnny Iselin. "Well, Jays are always Jays," she says with a smile. "Mother was not all *that* fond of the Iselins. But my dad's business helped her keep the family place going. The family place . . . the family place. A great, huge part of my heart is still there. You know, it was very strange — a very strange feeling — to grow up there. Though no one talked about it very much, it was always clear that we were a part of American history. But it was as though we *belonged* to all that history. We didn't own the place — the place owned *us!* Going into the big room where the portraits hung, it seemed as though the past and the present positively *crashed together.* I swear there were voices in that room, even though the room was always absolutely still — whispers, whispers. Sometimes the feeling was absolutely overpowering — the feeling of the energy from the past flowing out from the walls of that room. We all felt it, the charge of energy, when we entered the ballroom. It was like — well, do you remember that moment in the movie *The Wizard of Oz* — when Dorothy arrives in Oz, and the movie suddenly goes from black-and-white to Technicolor? It was like that. Magical and wonderful, and awe-inspiring."

She smiles again and removes her glasses from her nose. It is time to make her weekly trek, thirty miles in each direction in a pickup, to purchase fresh provisions for the ranch. It is April, but the roads are still snow-covered, and from the mountains to the west fresh snow is blowing. "Guts," she says. "It takes guts to run a farm. But that's in the bloodline, too."

She pauses, considering what she has just said. "It's funny," she says. "I don't usually talk this way, about bloodlines and that sort of thing. One isn't supposed to talk about things like that. My mother felt that sort of talk was ill bred. But we were all brought up to feel that, secretly, we were richly endowed. Secretly, we knew we were the aristocracy, and we knew how to recognize each other — in terms of bloodline, breeding, background, tradition, and family — and not *necessarily* money. But it's not snobbishness. Snobbishness means climbing, trying to meet 'the right people,' and that sort of thing. We've never been that way — probably because we knew we didn't *have* to be! We knew that we were to use the same good manners whether we were talking to a duke or a doorman! I couldn't run a horse ranch, and deal with ranch hands and cowboys, if I were a snob. To them, I'm just a woman who works as hard as they do, and who can shovel manure out of a stable if it needs to be done — and believe me, I don't call it by such a polite word when I'm doing it! But still I have that feeling of what's bred in my bones, and I know others who have that feeling — who are members of these old American families. It's something you inherit, almost like a European title, and you can never really shake it off. The Livingstons have it too, I suppose, in their own way — that secret family pride, that feeling that if your name isn't Livingston you're not quite a *real* Livingston. You haven't inherited the proper title. But it's not snobbishness, and it's more like the opposite of snobbishness — though there's no real word for it."

But is there a word for it? And do they really *matter,* these old families? Is there a reason that, nowadays, no one snaps to attention when a Livingston — or a Pringle, or an Ortega — enters the room (except another Livingston, Pringle, or Ortega)? Most of their accomplishments, after all, are in the past, encapsulated in time, and so is most of their power, social, political, and economic. True, they are the families who invented America, who tamed the wilderness, irrigated the deserts, dammed the rivers, built the factories and mills, grew and harvested the wheat and corn, founded the colleges, museums, and hospitals, fought the wars, and prayed to a Christian Lord on Sunday. But are their jobs done now, and is their usefulness past? Are they nothing more than quaint anachronisms now, in danger of extinction? Though their names still decorate some old law firms — Cadwalader, Wickersham & Taft; Lord, Day & Lord — are they anything more than that, a kind of polite bit of ornamentation?

Perhaps so, because these families continue to teach the unenforceable standards that all upwardly mobile Americans, except the outlaws, strive to live by. It has often been said that America has an aristocracy of wealth. But these old families are a reminder that, in America, money alone won't do it. To money must be added a touch of — well, class.

"Class" is not a word America's old aristocracy likes to use much. It prefers, instead, to speak of breeding, but the concepts are the same. Breeding, of course, has a genetic ring to it, and most of the old families do feel that their good breeding is in their genes. But breeding can also be taught, and most Americans are eager to learn it, and there is a whole industry out there to teach it. Breeding was what Ivy Lee tried to teach his robber baron clients, taking his cues from the aristocratic Old Guard. Today's public relations men and women offer the same counsel. "Get involved with a charity," the P.R. man advises the ambitious newcomer to New York. "Hire a good decorator." "It is all right to mix your woods," counsels the decorator. "You don't want everything to look as though it came from the same store." "It is all right to mix your china patterns and silver settings," says the consultant at Tiffany's. "You don't want your table to look pretentious. There's nothing wrong with paper napkins." "Let me help you get rid of that Brooklyn accent," suggests the elocution coach. The quest for good breeding goes on at every social level, a kind of national yearning, visible in the syndicated columns of Dear Abby and Miss Manners. What is the *right* way of handling this thing and that? America wants to know.

Breeding is more, though, than just manners and morals. It is essentially a matter of achieving self-esteem, and self-esteem is a commodity the Old Guard has a wealth of. It comes with the name, like the Jay nose, passed from generation to generation. It serves as a kind of ballast, and even the most eccentric members of the old families had it, a feeling that their moorings were fast, that they could not go too far adrift, that they were anchored, rooted, in the past. With their self-esteem has gone a commitment to certain values and a belief in the great nouns: loyalty, honesty, dignity, duty, work, service, patriotism, courage, God, guts, and the golden rule.

These, of course, might be seen as old-fashioned values, and the Old Guard today are essentially old-fashioned people — not chic, or trendy, or with it. Their hairstyles don't change much, nor do their modes of dress, and they remain devoted to their antiques, portraits, and family silver. Their ancestors were for the most part outdoorsmen, men of the soil, suited to the wilderness, who headed eagerly toward the frontier, wherever it happened to be. The Old Guard today remain fond of outdoorsy pleasures: farming, gardening, riding, fishing, sailing, swimming, golf, and tennis. But values such as courage and dignity do not go in and out of fashion, even in a consumerist America of the 1980s, dedicated to making and spending big money. Self-esteem and the ability to rise to occasions will not go out of fashion, either. And if the old families themselves are not in a position to teach self-esteem, they are very much in a position to demonstrate how valuable a human resource this can be. They are in a position to set this example, and their descendants will doubtless be doing so for many years to come.

Good breeding — self-confidence, self-esteem, call it what you like — can show itself in the smallest ways, in the tiniest gestures.

Not long ago, Mr. and Mrs. S. Dillon Ripley were spending the weekend at Mr. and Mrs. John Jermain Slocums' house in Newport. It was late afternoon, and afternoon tea had segued, as it often does, into the cocktail hour. The Slocums' butler was new to the household and not fully trained, but he was young and eager to please, and he was able to clear away the tea things and serve the drinks without making too many mistakes. Then it was time for the hosts and their guests to repair upstairs and dress for dinner. Mary Moncrieffe Livingston Ripley rose first, carrying her empty cocktail glass, and moved toward the drinks cart. "May I fix you another drink, ma'am?" the butler said, a bit too loudly. "No, thank you," said Mrs. Ripley. "I'm just putting my glass back on the cart."

The right thing. A guest doesn't leave a hostess's sitting room with her glass left sitting on a coffee table. Just as, no matter how many people a hostess has on her staff, a house guest does not rise in the morning without making her own bed.

Mrs. Martha Ferguson Breasted is a woman of eighty whose Ferguson ancestors came to America from Scotland in the eighteenth century. Mrs. Breasted is the widow of Charles Breasted, the historian, and her mother, Isabella — one of New York's great beauties at the turn of the century — was a close friend of the Oyster Bay Roosevelts and was a bridesmaid at the wedding of Eleanor and Franklin Roosevelt in 1905. Mrs. Breasted spends most of her time at her house in Tucson, but her great love is her eighteenth-century farmhouse, which her ancestors built, in the horse-breeding country of northeastern Kentucky. Mrs. Breasted likes to spend a few months of each year at the farm. On a hill above the farmhouse, in the family cemetery, repose many of her Ferguson ancestors, under white headstones. In a separate corner of the cemetery, under black headstones, lie their slaves, who did not have last names and are simply identified as Ben, Mary, Emma, and so on. This bit of class differentiation amuses Martha Breasted today, and she has decided that her headstone, to atone for any past injustices, will be gray when she joins the little group.

Mrs. Breasted owns several parcels of farmland in the surrounding countryside — a hundred or so acres here, a couple of hundred there — where tobacco is grown. But some of her Boone County neighbors, in the hills and hollows surrounding her land, are poor Appalachian families whose menfolk, especially when they have been drinking, have a reputation for being rough customers. One night a while back, Martha Breasted was driving back to the farm in her battered pickup truck and, turning a corner, encountered a bit of unwelcome activity taking place on her land. A group of perhaps forty youths had built a bonfire and was having what was quite obviously a beer bash. The group had already grown quite rowdy.

Mrs. Breasted stopped her vehicle, fished an old-fashioned electric flashlight out of the glove compartment, got out of the cab, and headed across her field toward the partyers, limping slightly (a youthful bout with polio forces her to wear a leg brace). She approached the interlopers, a tall old lady, somewhat stooped, her tightly curled white hair tied back, characteristically, with a twisted length of woolen yarn, her flashlight her only means of self-defense.

As she approached the revelers and their bonfire, the young men suddenly grew still. Their silence was, at best, ambiguous, and Martha Breasted continued her approach.

One young man, who appeared to be some sort of leader of the group, stepped toward her. His fists were clenched. The two faced each other, Martha Breasted with her chin tilted upward just slightly. Mrs. Breasted was the first to speak. "May I *help* you?" she said.

Slowly, the young man lowered his eyes, then turned away from her toward the others. "C'mon guys," he said a little gruffly. "This lady doesn't want us here."

Silently, and with obvious reluctance, the young men began gathering up their empty beer cans and dousing their fire.

"This lady," he had called her.

Class.

A NOTE ON SOURCES AND ACKNOWLEDGMENTS

Two unusual sources were made available to me in the preparation of this book.

The first, and perhaps the more important, was the treasure trove of materials found in the New York apartment of Mrs. Margaret Trevor Pardee. For much the better part of a century, Margaret Pardee has collected anything of possible interest concerning her ancestors and relatives by marriage: the Schieffelins, Lawrences, Bownes, Jays, Trevors, Pardees, Lispenards, Roosevelts, Astors, Vanderbilts, and others to whom she is marvelously, almost Byzantinely, connected. This material includes genealogies, family histories, old diaries, sketches of personalities, family crests and mottoes, and much more that has never been previously published. Her collection also includes scrapbooks filled with family-connected newspaper and magazine stories and other documents. Unfortunately, most of these clippings were pasted in undated and without attribution to their specific newspaper or magazine sources. In some cases, I was able to arrive at approximate dates by guesswork — the scrapbook containing items from Mrs. Pardee's debutante year, for example — but in quoting, as I have done in the text, from some of these published accounts, it was impossible to ascertain exact dates or names of publications in which these stories appeared, particularly since in 1910 there were a great many more newspapers and magazines published than there are today. In the source notes that follow, therefore, I have been forced to be a little vague, and to attribute these sources to "Schieffelin-Trevor-Pardee family papers" or to "Pardee scrapbooks." This, however, does not diminish my gratitude to Mrs. Pardee for making her materials available to me for use in this book.

The second special source involved the lucky happenstance of my making the acquaintance of Mr. Scott Areman of Mount Vernon, New York. Mr. Areman, a talented young photographer, has spent many hours over the last several years photographing, and tape-recording interviews with, various members of old American families in and around New York with the idea of someday turning this material into a book. His book project may one day be realized, but in the meantime he was good enough to make his taped interviews available to me for first use here. Thus, in the following notes, the notation "interview with Scott Areman" indicates that this is material drawn from some forty-five hours of his taped conversations.

In addition to these two individuals, there are a number of other people who were generous with their time, memories, and family-related materials whom I would especially like to thank. For details relating to the Livingston family, I am indebted to Mr. and Mrs. Goodhue Livingston, Mr. Henry H. Livingston, and Mr. William W. Reese, all of New York, and to Mrs. James H. Livingston of Orlando, Florida, as well as to Mr. and Mrs. S. Dillon Ripley of Washington. For material pertaining to the Jays, I would like particularly to thank Mr. John Jay Iselin of New York and Mrs. Eleanor Jay Iselin Wade of Bozeman, Montana. For insights into the Brown clan of Rhode Island, I would like to thank Mrs. John Jermain Slocum of Newport and Mr. J. Carter Brown of Washington. The proud old Morris family of New York and New Jersey has an able spokesman in Mr. Benjamin P. Morris, Jr., whom I tracked down in McAllen, Texas. The late Mrs. Corinne Douglas Robinson Alsop Cole, in my hometown of Hartford, was helpful with Alsop-Roosevelt family tales. The genealogist Timothy Beard of Roxbury, Connecticut, applied his well-known expertise in helping me deal with the extraordinary intrafamily relationships that have evolved among our old American families. In San Francisco, the hidalgo pride — not to mention the extensive family papers — of Mr. George T. Brady, Jr., makes him one of the most knowledgeable men on the subject of the California land-grant aristocracy, including his own family, Carrillo-Ortegas.

I would also like to thank Miss Shannon Cunat of Cincinnati, who typed my manuscript from beginning to end and also saw it through many revisions. My Little, Brown editor, Fredrica Friedman, has a finicky eye, unerring taste, and a firm blue pencil, which were nothing but helpful. And I would also like to thank my friend and agent, Carl Brandt, who guided this project with his usual cool head, and his wife, Clare Brandt, whose own book on the Livingston family was a most valuable source for this one.

While all the above people were helpful to me in the preparation of this book, I alone must be held responsible for any sins of omission, errors, or shortcomings.

SOURCES

Part One: First Peers of the Realm

Chapter 2: A Royal Wedding

The Moot: G. Pellew, *John Jay,* pp. 19–20.

"It appeared to me that you have more vivacity": Quoted in L. Hobart, *Patriot's Lady,* p. 39.

Details of Jay-Livingston courtship and wedding: Ibid., p. 34 ff.

Virginia Gazette: Quoted in J. A. Osborne, *Williamsburg in Colonial Times,* p. 71.

"is involved in the horrible sin": Quoted in C. Brandt, *An American Aristocracy,* p. 163.

"That Englishman Dale": Henry H. Livingston, interview with author.

Chapter 3: Manor Lords

Henry H. Livingston quoted: Interview with author.

Mrs. Peter Van Brugh Livingston catches fire: Mrs. J. K. Van Rensselaer, *The Social Ladder,* p. 30.

Kiliaen Van Rensselaer's purchase: C. Amory, *Who Killed Society?,* p. 316.

Nicholas Van Rensselaer poisoned?: Henry H. Livingston, interview with author.

Chapter 4: Ancient Wealth

"an active and opulent merchant": Quoted in R. B. Morris, ed., *John Jay*, p. 29.
Vicissitudes of Jay's childhood and siblings: Ibid., p. 33.
"Considering the helpless": Quoted in ibid.
Dr. Stoope's school: G. Pellew, *John Jay*, p. 9.
College requirements: Ibid., p. 10.
"Not being of British descent": Ibid., p. 7.
Jay on slavery issue: Quoted in L. Hobart, *Patriot's Lady*, pp. 162–163.
Attitude of New York lawyers toward newcomers: Pellew, pp. 14–15.
College prank anecdote: Ibid., p. 13.
"eminent in the profession": Ibid., p. 14.
"Though vilified": Ibid., p. 46.
Spain's aid to colonists: J. Trager, *The People's Chronology*, p. 328.

Chapter 5: A Gentleman's War

William W. Reese quoted: Interview with author.
Henry H. Livingston quoted: Interview with author.
The lost needle tale: Mrs. J. K. Van Rensselaer, *The Social Ladder*, p. 24 ff.
The Nannie Brown story: Ibid., p. 22 ff.

Chapter 6: Coronation in New York

The Jays in Paris: E. Ellet, *The Queens of American Society*, p. 64 ff.
Sarah's letter to Mrs. Robert Morris: Quoted in ibid., p. 60.
Audience mistakes Sarah for queen: L. Hobart, *Patriot's Lady*, p. 125.
Sarah's "Dinner and Supper List": C. Amory, *Who Killed Society?*, p. 115.
Sarah's entertainments and menus: Hobart, p. 171.
de Moustier: Ibid.
"Mrs. Jay gives a dinner": Quoted in Ellet, p. 75.
Dr. Benjamin Rush: Quoted in L. De Pauw and C. Hunt, *Remember the Ladies*, p. 12.
de Chastellux: Quoted in ibid., p. 14.
Exchange of Sarah's and John Jay's letters: G. Pellew, *John Jay*, p. 279.
Love letters of the Jays: Ibid., p. 341.

Horace Walpole: Quoted in J. Trager, *The People's Chronology,* p. 344.
Guillotin: Quoted in ibid., p. 342.
John Jacob Astor: Quoted in C. Brandt, *An American Aristocracy,* p. 179.
George Washington inaugural festivities: J. and A. Durant, *Pictorial History of American Presidents,* pp. 16–21.
John Jay on the Cincinnati: Quoted in Hobart, p. 209.

Chapter 7: The Great Silverware Robbery

"John, the non-signer": Quoted in S. Alsop, *Stay of Execution,* pp. 89–90.
Peter Corne anecdote: Ibid., p. 90.
"an elegant draft dodge": Ibid., p. 55.
The Alsop silver story: Mrs. J. K. Van Rensselaer, *The Social Ladder,* pp. 27–29.
Mrs. Corinne D.R.A. Cole: Interview with author.

Chapter 8: From Camping Out with Indians . . . to Dinner at the Jays'

Schieffelin family history: Schieffelin-Trevor-Pardee family papers and genealogies, unpublished, courtesy of Mrs. Margaret Trevor Pardee, quoted with permission.
Hannah Lawrence's diaries: Ibid.
Hannah's poem: Ibid.
Mrs. Murray's diversionary tactic: Ibid.
Margaret Pardee quoted: Interview with author.

Chapter 9: Livingston Versus Livingston

New York–Massachusetts-Connecticut border disputes: C. Rand, "The Iron, the Charcoal, the Woods," *New Yorker* 39 (August 10, 1963): 31.
The Ancram Screechers: Ibid.
"dodging the line": Ibid.
"worse than northern savages": Quoted in C. Brandt, *An American Aristocracy,* p. 81.
"Our people are hoggish": Ibid.
The Indian-down-the-chimney story: As told to author by Henry H. Livingston in interview. (Brandt, p. 61, tells a different version that involves subduing, but not killing, the Indian.)
The Captain Kidd affair: Brandt, p. 41 ff.
The naming of Clermont dispute: Ibid., p. 76.

Chapter 10: Weak Blood

H. J. Eckenrode: Quoted in C. Amory, *Who Killed Society?*, p. 293.
"the weak strain": Ibid., p. 298.
"I am an aristocrat": Ibid., p. 300.
John of Roanoke on congressional salaries: Ibid., p. 303.
"I would not attempt": Ibid.
"is a man of splendid abilities": J. Bartlett, *Bartlett's Familiar Quotations,* p. 439.
"The surest way to prevent war": Ibid.
"The transmission of estates": Quoted in Amory, p. 294.
"a concealed voluptuary": Quoted in J. and A. Durant, *Pictorial History of American Presidents,* p. 33.
Jefferson's letter to his daughter: Quoted in Amory, p. 294.

Chapter 11: Morrises and More Morrises

"As New England": Quoted in C. Amory, *Who Killed Society?*, p. 318.
"An aristocrat!": Ibid.
Benjamin P. Morris, Jr., quoted: Interview with author.
Granny Morris and the Promoter: Ibid.
"Hell's bells, woman!": Ibid.

Chapter 12: Outsiders

"Big enough for two emperors": Quoted in J. and A. Durant, *Pictorial History of American Presidents,* p. 30.
Mrs. Douglas Cruger–John Van Buren anecdote: Mrs. J. K. Van Rensselaer, *The Social Ladder,* pp. 47–48.
Verse written after Mrs. Douglas's party: Quoted in ibid., p. 118.
"He dined here last night": Quoted in C. Amory, *Who Killed Society?*, p. 470.
"My son can afford it": Ibid.
"Really Mr. Astor is dreadful": Ibid.

Chapter 13: Endangered Species

"How New York has fallen off": Quoted in C. Amory, *Who Killed Society?*, p. 27.
"These leaders of gayety": E. Ellet, *The Queens of American Society,* pp. 456–458.
"The really excellent": Ibid., p. 458.
"We are all accustomed": Ibid., p. i.

"Died yesterday": Quoted in Amory, p. 27.
"love instead of lectures": J. Roosevelt, *My Parents,* p. 11.
James Roosevelt V funeral and will: Ibid., p. 5.
Laura Delano's eccentricities and quote: Ibid., p. 9.
"It will be too much Fun": Ibid., p. 15.
"dragging the whole country": Ibid., p. 16.
"Oh, dear me": Alice Longworth to author; similarly, all the Longworth quotes that follow in this chapter.

PART TWO: BRAHMINS, KNIGHTS OF THE CHIVALRY, AND CALIFORNIA GRANDEES

Chapter 14: Knowing One's Place

"Philadelphia was the first city": Mrs. George Brooke Roberts to author.
"In Boston": Miss Anna Ingersoll to author.
"When a Biddle is drunk": Popular Philadelphia saying.
"was larger than any others": Quoted in E. D. Baltzell, *Philadelphia Gentlemen,* p. 171.
"He had an English accent" and all subsequent J. Leland quotes: Mr. Leland to author.
"If a man's father": Mrs. St. J. Ravenel, *Charleston: The Place and the People,* p. 427.
"To be dropped": Ibid., p. 428.

Chapter 15: O Ancestors!

"A group of English immigrants": C. M. Andrews, *The Fathers of New England,* p. 19.
"Almost without exception": Quoted in C. Amory, *Who Killed Society?,* p. 40.
"Oh, no. We sent our servants": Ibid., p. 41.
"The Mayflower Society": Ibid., p. 43.
"Of the background": L. B. Wright, *The First Gentlemen of Virginia,* pp. 41–42.
"There was not a gentleman": Quoted in C. Amory, *Who Killed Society?,* p. 43.
"They have to be anonymous": Quoted in *New York Times,* March 26, 1985.
"We don't have the slightest interest": Ibid.

"I don't know very much about politics": Ibid.
"It was a very small dance group": Ibid.
"My mother keeps asking": Ibid.

Chapter 16: Beer and the Bourgeoisie

"The competitors were": Quoted in the *St. Louis Post-Dispatch,* May 15, 1977.
"What we all had in common": Ibid.
"Without a doubt": Quoted in *International Celebrity Register,* p. 115.
"I remember once": Quoted in *St. Louis Post-Dispatch,* May 15, 1977.
"For weeks afterward": Ibid.

Chapter 17: O Pioneers!

"Everyone knows": Gorham Knowles, interview with author.
"Each of these families knows": Quoted in K. Waller and B. P. Cullen, "California's Land Grant Aristocracy," *Town & Country* 139 (December 1985): 139–147, 227–232.
"Don José de la Guerra's house": Ibid.
Details of life at Rancho Los Dos Pueblos: W. A. Tompkins, *Santa Barbara's Royal Rancho,* p. 165 ff.
"Everybody is broke": Ibid., p. 182.
"The government does *nothing*" and subsequent Bernardo Yorba quotes in this chapter: Interview with author.
"We families are all mixed": Waller and Cullen, 142.
"Oh, about a thousand": Ibid., 230.
"If I'm not one, who is?": Mr. George T. Brady, Jr., interview with author. Similarly, other Brady quotes in this chapter.

Part Three: Heirs Apparent

Chapter 18: Secret Society

"Only recently": Mrs. J. K. Van Rensselaer, *The Social Ladder,* p. 32.
"That, sir": Quoted in C. Amory, *Who Killed Society?,* p. 83.
"He had the instinctive shrinking": Ibid.
"The first thing": Ibid., p. 84.
"If I have a hundred-thousand-dollar deal": Anonymous interview with author.
"Part of the fun": John Jay Iselin interview with author.

Chapter 19: Old Guard Versus New

"I think it's not only possible": Mrs. J. K. Van Rensselaer, *The Social Ladder,* p. 55.

"Mother told us": Mrs. Margaret Trevor Pardee, interview with author. Similarly, all other Pardee quotes in this chapter.

Chapter 20: The Gospel of Wealth

Mrs. Fish's landaulet accident: Pardee scrapbooks.

James Lee's stand on anti-Semitism and the "Cathedral of Cooperation": R. E. Hiebert, *Courtier to the Crowd,* p. 18.

McCosh influence on Ivy Lee: Ibid., pp. 21–22.

Carnegie's gospel of wealth: Quoted in ibid., p. 22.

Chapter 21: Comme Il Faut

Description of "Horseback Dinner": A. S. Crockett, *Peacocks on Parade,* p. 192.

Comments on the Bradley-Martin ball: Quoted in C. Amory, *Who Killed Society?,* p. 520.

Chapter 22: "To Serve . . ."

The *Fortune* articles: Quoted in L. T. Wertenbaker and M. Basserman, *The Hotchkiss School, A Portrait,* p. 133.

"It was the most natural thing": F. Ashburn, *Peabody of Groton: A Portrait,* p. 71.

"Groton School is perfectly incomprehensible": Quoted in Wertenbaker and Basserman, p. 135.

"He never seemed to enter": Ibid.

"If some Groton boys": Quoted in T. Morgan, *FDR,* p. 66.

"Don't let Papa worry": Quoted in ibid.

Henry Adams: Quoted in ibid., p. 60.

"In fact I've never understood" and other quotes in this paragraph: George Van Santvoord to author.

The new boys' rules: G. N. Stone, "What's Going On Here?", *Hotchkiss School Alumni Magazine* (Winter 1983): 9–10.

"What is it you want to know?": L. T. Wertenbaker and M. Basserman, *The Hotchkiss School: A Portrait,* p. 111.

"I am sure you have all heard": Van Santvoord quoted from author's memory.

Wilmarth S. Lewis quoted: Interview with author.

Chapter 23: The Bogus Versus the Real

Details of the Mabel Greer story: D. W. Peck, *The Greer Case.*

Chapter 24: Family Curses

"I happen to be a good Episcopalian": Mrs. Ijams quoted by Timothy Beard in interview with author.
"He was my grandfather's first cousin": John Jay Iselin, interview with author.
"very morbidly conscientious": R. B. Hovey, *John Jay Chapman,* p. 12.
"Certainly it is not respectable": quoted in ibid., p. 21.
"To play like that": Ibid., p. 20.
"The English stage": Ibid., p. 14.
"The next thing I remember": quoted in M.A.D. Howe, *John Jay Chapman and His Letters,* pp. 59–60.
"the great alienist": Ibid.
"I am perfectly well and happy": Ibid., pp. 60–61.
"Being an old agitator": Quoted in R. B. Hovey, *John Jay Chapman, An American Mind,* p. 287.
"sane, though imaginative": Ibid., p. 159.
Chapman's last words: Ibid., p. 347.
"Now may I have your attention!": Quoted in R. H. Boyle, *At the Top of Their Game,* p. 1.
"You have always said": Ibid., p. 2.
"They don't make any noise": Ibid., p. 3.
"You can abolish": Ibid.
"Close the blinds": Ibid., p. 4.
"Isn't it remarkable": Ibid., p. 5.
"Winty knits": Ibid.
The obscure Virginia statute: Ibid., p. 6.
The *New York Post* comment: Ibid., p. 7.
"Who's loony now?": Ibid., p. 7.
Ethel Barrymore quoted: Ibid.

Chapter 25: The Great Splurge

Town Topics: Quoted in M. M. Mooney, *Evelyn Nesbit and Stanford White,* p. 77.
"I was brought up to be": Mrs. Virginia Thaw Wanamaker, interview with Scott Areman.

"We were very privileged characters": Mr. John Preston, interview with Scott Areman.

"It was as bad an upbringing": Mr. Craig K. J. Mitchell, interview with Scott Areman. Similarly, all Mitchell quotes in this chapter.

"There are certain values": J. Carter Brown, interview with author.

President Wriston anecdote: Ibid.

"That portrait": Ibid.

"Not so": Ibid.

"I remember driving": Ibid.

"There are eight grandchildren": Ibid.

"The English system": Mrs. John Jermain Slocum, interview with author. Similarly, all other Slocum quotes in this chapter.

"Good morning, Mrs. Mortimer": Craig Mitchell, interview with Scott Areman.

Chapter 26: The Family Place

"The last of the great": John Jay Iselin, interview with author.

"My grandmother was": Ibid.

"It seems to me": Mary Livingston Ripley, interview with author.

"Yes, the Livingstons still take": John Jay Iselin, interview with author.

"We don't like to dine out": Ibid.

"The family has always pulled its weight": Eleanor Iselin Wade, interview with author.

The Mary-Ripley-at-Newport anecdote: Mrs. Ripley observed by author.

The Martha Breasted anecdote: Mrs. Breasted, interview with author.

BIBLIOGRAPHY

Adams, James Truslow. *The Adams Family*. Boston: Little, Brown, 1930.

Alsop, Stewart. *Stay of Execution: A Sort of Memoir*. Philadelphia: J. B. Lippincott, 1973.

Amory, Cleveland. *Who Killed Society?* New York: Harper & Row, 1960.

Andrews, Charles M. *The Fathers of New England*. New Haven: Yale University Press, 1919.

Ashburn, Frank D. *Peabody of Groton: A Portrait*. New York: Coward-McCann, 1944.

Baltzell, E. Digby. *Philadelphia Gentlemen*. Chicago: Free Press of Glencoe, 1958.

Boyle, Robert H. *At the Top of Their Game*. Tulsa, Okla.: Winchester Press, 1983.

Brandt, Clare. *An American Aristocracy: The Livingstons*. New York: Doubleday, 1986.

Bruce, William Cabell. *John Randolph of Roanoke, 1773–1833*. 2 vols. New York: Putnam's, 1923.

Crockett, Albert Stevens. *Peacocks on Parade: A Narrative of a Unique Period in American Social History and Its Most Colorful Figures*. New York: Sears, 1931.

De Pauw, Linda Grant, and Hunt, Conover. *Remember the Ladies:*

Women in America, 1750–1815. New York: Viking Press, 1976.
Durant, John and Alice. *Pictorial History of American Presidents*. New York: A. S. Barnes, 1955.
Ellet, Elizabeth. *The Queens of American Society*. Philadelphia: Porter & Coates, 1867.
Hiebert, Ray Eldon. *Courtier to the Crowd: The Story of Ivy Lee and the Development of Public Relations*. Ames: Iowa State University Press, 1966.
Hobart, Lois. *Patriot's Lady: The Life of Sarah Livingston Jay*. New York: Thomas Y. Crowell, 1960.
Hovey, Richard B. *John Jay Chapman, An American Mind*. New York: Columbia University Press, 1959.
Howe, M. A. DeWolfe. *John Jay Chapman and His Letters*. Boston: Houghton Mifflin, 1937.
International Celebrity Register. New York: Celebrity Register Ltd., 1959.
Kahn, E. J. III. "The Brahmin Mystique." *Boston Magazine* 75 (May 1983): 119–161.
Lundberg, Ferdinand. *America's 60 Families*. New York: Vanguard Press, 1937.
Mooney, Michael MacDonald. *Evelyn Nesbit and Stanford White*. New York: William Morrow, 1976.
Morgan, Ted. *FDR*. New York: Simon & Schuster, 1985.
Morris, Richard B., ed. *John Jay, The Making of a Revolutionary*. New York: Harper & Row, 1975.
Myers, Gustavus. *History of the Great American Fortunes*. New York: Modern Library, 1936.
Nelson, Edna Deu Pree. *The California Dons*. New York: Appleton-Century-Crofts, 1962.
Osborne, J. A. *Williamsburg in Colonial Times*. Richmond, Va.: Dietz Press, 1935.
Pearson, Edmund. "The Great Chowder Murder." *New Yorker* 11 (April 6, 1935): 53–57.
Peck, David W. *The Greer Case*. New York: Simon & Schuster, 1955.
Pellew, George. *John Jay*. Boston: Houghton Mifflin, 1890.
Rand, Christopher. "The Iron, the Charcoal, the Woods." *New Yorker* 39 (August 10, 1963): 31.
Ravenel, Mrs. St. Julien. *Charleston: The Place and the People*. New York: Macmillan, 1922.

Roosevelt, James. *My Parents.* Chicago: Playboy Press, 1976.
Stone, George Norton. "What's Going On Here?" *Hotchkiss School Alumni Magazine* (Winter 1983): 9–10.
Tompkins, Walker A. *Santa Barbara's Royal Rancho.* Berkeley, Calif.: Howell-North Press, 1960.
Townsend, Reginald T. *Mother of Clubs.* New York: Union Club, 1936.
Trager, James. *The People's Chronology.* New York: Holt, Rinehart & Winston, 1979.
Waller, Kim, and Cullen, Bernice Pons. "California's Land Grant Aristocracy." *Town & Country* 139 (December 1985): 139–232.
Wertenbaker, Lael Tucker, and Basserman, Maude. *The Hotchkiss School, A Portrait.* Lakeville, Conn.: Hotchkiss, 1966.
Wright, Louis B. *The First Gentlemen of Virginia.* San Marino, Calif.: Henry E. Huntington Library and Art Gallery, 1940.
Van Rensselaer, Mrs. John King. *The Social Ladder.* New York: Henry Holt, 1924.

INDEX